Iberian Empires and
the Roots of Globalization

HISPANIC ISSUES • VOLUME 44

Iberian Empires and the Roots of Globalization

*Ivonne del Valle, Anna More,
and Rachel Sarah O'Toole, editors*

Vanderbilt University Press
NASHVILLE

© 2019 by Vanderbilt University Press
Nashville, Tennessee 37235
All rights reserved
First printing 2019

This book is printed on acid-free paper.

A complete list of volumes in the Hispanic Issues series
follows the index.

LIBRARY OF CONGRESS CATALOGING-IN-PUBLICATION DATA

Names: Valle, Ivonne del, editor. | More, Anna Herron, editor.
| O'Toole, Rachel Sarah, editor.
Title: Iberian empires and the roots of globalization /
Ivonne del Valle, Anna More, and Rachel Sarah O'Toole, editors.
Description: Nashville : Vanderbilt University Press, [2020] | Series: Hispanic issues
; 44 | Includes bibliographical references and index. | Summary: "Interdisciplinary
essays that investigate the diverse networks and multiple
centers of early modern globalization that emerged in conjunction with
Iberian imperialism"— Provided by publisher.
Identifiers: LCCN 2019017929 (print) | LCCN 2019980680 (ebook) | ISBN 9780826522528
(hardcover) | ISBN 9780826522535 (paperback)
| ISBN 9780826522542 (ebook)
Subjects: LCSH: Globalization—History. | Imperialism—History. |
Spain—Colonies—History. | Portugal—Colonies—History.
| Spain—History. | Portugal—History.
Classification: LCC JV4011 .I34 2020 (print) | LCC JV4011 (ebook) |
DDC 909/.0971246—dc23
LC record available at https://lccn.loc.gov/2019017929
LC ebook record available at https://lccn.loc.gov/2019980680

HISPANIC ISSUES

Nicholas Spadaccini, *Editor-in-Chief*

Luis Martín-Estudillo, *Managing Editor*

Ana Forcinito, *Associate Managing Editor*

Megan Corbin, Nelsy Echávez-Solano, and William Viestenz, *Associate Editors*

Carolina Julia Añón Suárez, Collin Diver, Tim Frye, Heather Mawhiney, N. Ramos Flores, Javier Zapata Clavería, *Assistant Editors*

*Advisory Board/Editorial Board
Rolena Adorno (Yale University)
Román de la Campa (Unversity of Pennsylvania)
David Castillo (University at Buffalo)
Jaime Concha (University of California, San Diego)
Tom Conley (Harvard University)
William Egginton (Johns Hopkins University)
Brad Epps (University of Cambridge)
David W. Foster (Arizona State University)
Edward Friedman (Vanderbilt University)
Wlad Godzich (University of California, Santa Cruz)
Antonio Gómez L-Quiñones (Dartmouth College)
Hans Ulrich Gumbrecht (Stanford University)
*Carol A. Klee (University of Minnesota)
Germán Labrador Méndez (Princeton University)
Eukene Lacarra Lanz (Universidad del País Vasco)
Jorge Lozano (Universidad Complutense de Madrid)
Raúl Marrero-Fente (University of Minnesota)
Kelly McDonough (University of Texas at Austin)
Walter D. Mignolo (Duke University)
*Louise Mirrer (The New-York Historical Society)
Mabel Moraña (Washington University in St. Louis)
Alberto Moreiras (Texas A & M University)
Bradley Nelson (Concordia University, Montreal)
Michael Nerlich (Université Blaise Pascal)
*Francisco Ocampo (University of Minnesota)
Antonio Ramos-Gascón (University of Minnesota)
Jenaro Talens (Universitat de València)
Miguel Tamen (Universidade de Lisboa)
Teresa Vilarós (Texas A & M University)
Iris M. Zavala (Universitat Pompeu Fabra, Barcelona)
Santos Zunzunegui (Universidad del País Vasco)

CONTENTS

Acknowledgments — ix

Introduction: Iberian Empires and a Theory of Early Modern Globalization
IVONNE DEL VALLE, ANNA MORE, AND RACHEL SARAH O'TOOLE — 1

1. Precious Metals in the Americas at the Beginning of the Global Economy
   BERND HAUSBERGER — 23

2. A New Moses: Vasco de Quiroga's Hospitals and the Transformation of "Indians" from "Bárbaros" to "Pobres"
   IVONNE DEL VALLE — 47

3. Religion, Caste, and Race in the Spanish and Portuguese Empires: Local and Global Dimensions
   MARÍA ELENA MARTÍNEZ — 75

4. The Portuguese Inquisition and Colonial Expansion: The "Honor" of Being Tried by the Holy Office
   BRUNO FEITLER — 105

5. Jesuit Networks and the Transatlantic Slave Trade: Alonso de Sandoval's *Naturaleza, policía sagrada y profana* (1627)
   ANNA MORE — 131

6. Household Challenges: The Laws of Slaveholding and the Practices of Freedom in Colonial Peru
   RACHEL SARAH O'TOOLE — 159

7. The Reason of Freedom and the Freedom of Reason: The Neo-Scholastic Critique of African Slavery and Its Impact on the Construction of the Nineteenth-Century Republic in Spanish America
   MARÍA EUGENIA CHAVES — 183

8	Jesuits and Indigenous Subjects in the Global Culture of Letters: Production, Circulation, and Adaptation of Missionary Texts in the Seventeenth and Eighteenth Centuries	
	GUILLERMO WILDE	207
9	The Iridescent *Enconchado*	
	CHARLENE VILLASEÑOR BLACK	233
10	"Idolatrous Images" and "True Images": European Visual Culture and its Circulation in Early Modern China	
	ELISABETTA CORSI	271
11	*Barlaam and Josaphat* in Early Modern Spain and the Colonial Philippines: Spiritual Exercises of Freedom at the Center and Periphery	
	JODY BLANCO	303
	Afterword: Reimagining Colonial Latin America from a Global Perspective	
	RAÚL MARRERO-FENTE AND NICHOLAS SPADACCINI	*331*
	Contributors	*343*
	Index	*347*

◆   ACKNOWLEDGMENTS

This book has been a long time in the making and along the way we received the support and encouragement of many people and institutions we would like to thank. First, we recognize the patience and cooperation of our contributors, who edited their essays many times without complaining. We would like to express our deep appreciation as well to the Editorial Committee of Hispanic Issues, Vanderbilt University Press, and the anonymous readers who offered thoughtful comments and suggestions.

This volume had its origins in an international seminar held in Mexico City and funded by a Mellon-LASA Seminar grant. We would like to thank the Latin American Studies Association for its funding and the Museo Franz Mayer, especially the General Director, Héctor Rivero Borrell M., for the invitation to hold the seminar at this remarkable location. María Emma Mannarelli (Universidad Nacional de San Marcos, Perú) was a vibrant participant. We send a special thanks to curator María D. Sánchez Vega who secured the space for the seminar and provided the participants with a tour of the collection.

At the time this project started the three editors were faculty in the University of California system. We deeply appreciate the funding support we received from Anthony Cascardi, Dean of Humanities at UC Berkeley, the Humanities Commons and Dean Van Den Abbeele at UC, Irvine and from Dean David Schaberg at UCLA. We want to acknowledge as well the rewarding conversations with our colleagues in the UC system, especially John D. Blanco, Carolyn Dean, María Elena Díaz, Barbara Fuchs, Stella Nair, Patricia Seed, Kevin Terraciano, Charlene Villaseñor Black, and Charles Walker. Our thanks to all of them.

Shoshanna Lande (UCI) made critical edits, delivered sound advice, and executed speedy formatting. Sarah Gualtieri (University of Southern California) provided helpful feedback on María Elena Martínez's work.

Instituto Tepoztlán, a one-of-a-kind experience of a conference, has left its mark on the three of us. Our thanks to the Institute's Collective and our colleagues, who are faithful participants, for their rigor and passion toward our disciplines (History, Art History, Literary Criticism), and above all for their commitment to their subjects and areas of research. We also thank them for their camaraderie and friendship.

Last but not least, we want to say a few words about María Elena Martínez, to whom this volume is dedicated. We are forever indebted to her demanding scholarship, the brilliance of her mind, and the ways in which she opened new paths for research that were thorough and dedicated to liberating the subjects she approached from oftentimes constraining archives. Her ideas and friendship will accompany us always and we hope to be following faithfully in her steps. Hasta siempre, Patrona.

◆ INTRODUCTION

Iberian Empires and a Theory of Early Modern Globalization

Ivonne del Valle, Anna More, and Rachel Sarah O'Toole

How can one imagine the global scope of the early modern Iberian world? One of the most iconic depictions of early modern empires can be found among Theodor de Bry's illustrations of José de Acosta's *Historia natural y moral de las Indias* [Fig. 1].[1] In it, laborers cart loads of silver from the depths of the most famous mine in the Americas, Potosí. Interest in this image, and indeed in Acosta's work as a whole, reflected the overwhelming consciousness that American silver was the motor behind a complex new economy that dealt in large-scale extraction, commodity exchange, enormous sums of credit, and was global in reach. This version of a newly global world, ever expanding in its interconnections, was highly visible, even to contemporaries. Yet despite the visibility, anxiety or celebration of new forms of wealth, much of the mechanics of globalization has remained hidden. The story of how globalization came about through the labor and the skill of those depicted in the engraving is much more complex and difficult to tell. For this story, we will need to understand not only the structures that connected the globe to extract silver and convert it to financial credit, but also how the people of this newly globalized world constructed the specifics of these structures through their beliefs, social relations, and cultural practices.

III.
Wie die Indianer das Goldt auß den Bergen graben.

Je Indianer arbeiten auß dem Gebirge Potosi welchs wol für daß reichste Gebirg in gantz Indien mag gehalten werden/ daß Goldt herauß solcher gestalt/ wie man hie zu Land/ in den Bergwercken auch thut/ nemlich sie müssen es alle auß den Felsen herauß hawen/ vnnd theilen die Arbeiter in zwey Theil/ ein Theil arbeitet deß Tags vnd ruhet deß Nachts/ der ander Theil ruhet deß Tags vnd arbeitet deß Nachts/ wiewol sie eben so wenig Tag eine Zeit als die ander sehen/ sondern müssen sich stets mit Kertzen beheiffen/ dann sie wol 150. Klaffiern tieff vnter der Erden stecken/ doch müssen sie vnangesehen der grossen Höhe/ alle das Ertz auff ihren Rücken hinauff tragen. Darzu sie dann Leyter gebrauchen/ die gedoppelt nemlich zwo an einander gemacht seyn/ diese Leytern sind von gewundten Ochsenhäuten gemacht/ vnnd mit höltzern Staffeln durch zogen/ gehen also allzeit drey hinter einander hinauff/ vnd darneben drey auff der andern Seyten hinab/ vnnd weil sie sich allzeit mit beyden Händen halten müssen/ im hinauffgehen/ hat der förderst allezeit ein brennendt Liecht am Daumen gebunden/ weil auch wie gemelt/ der Weg hoch hinauffzusteigen ist/ haben sie vnterwegens Ruhebäncke/ darauff sie mit ihrer Last ruhen können.

Von

FIGURE 1. José de Acosta, *Neundter und Letzter Theil Americae*, Franckfurt am Mayn, 1601, Part 3, Plate 3, Courtesy of the John Carter Brown Library at Brown University.

In the mines of Potosí, indigenous laborers made decisions that shaped the practices of early modern Iberian colonization. Following Viceroy Francisco de Toledo's implementation of the colonial *mita* (a colonial labor quota based on a pre-Hispanic Andean practice), Andean men served indefinite terms as silver miners, while women and children processed ore in the mills that surrounded Potosí, the so-called "Rich Hill" (Cerro Rico). The silver mines pulled Andean people from their previous communities and agricultural economies into cycles of debt and death. Yet other indigenous men and women not only survived, but even prospered in these booming urban locations. Andean men became essential to producing silver for the global economy, as experienced muleteers, skilled smelters, and knowledgeable miners while indigenous women ran colonial market places and provided the colonial cities with domestic labor indispensable for a wage labor force (Stern 83; Mangan 158; Glave 42, 98; Bakewell 46, 163). Without seeing how indigenous people maintained their kinship networks and advocated to be paid for the labor that fueled global linkages and the profits for Iberian empires from silver mining, for example, it is impossible to understand the form that this newly globalized world took.

Local negotiations contributed to an extensive imperial network that transformed and linked regions to create early Iberian globalization. The changes wrought by long-distance trade, imperial governance, and new forms of finance and credit implicated even those most remote from administrative centers. Yet these changes often did not involve substitutions for old forms and practices, but rather the application of previous practices to new contexts. Andean deities (local *huacas*), sometimes manifested as Catholic saints, re-formed in the colonial or early modern era. These deities expressed the perspective of Andean laborers and intervened in the social and natural landscape of Iberian colonialism. On one hand, Catholic evangelizers punished Andeans for continuing their pre-conquest beliefs and practices, and associated Andean underground deities of death with Christian manifestations of the devil. Indeed, Andeans understood that the devil had arrived in the form of unreproductive currency and wage labor without sustainable relations. But rather than merely an exploitative system of colonial extraction, Andeans viewed the new globalized economy also as a manifestation of a paternalistic *tío*, or masculine deity, who negotiated with his clients (Platt 66). In the sixteenth and the seventeenth centuries, indigenous laborers negotiated with multiple underground deities, such as *supay*, who also manifested as the guardian mountain or the communicative *amaru*, or serpent. Through these figures, Andeans of the early modern period understood the silver mines as places of economic exploitation as well as locations of religious practice and called upon their deities to punish the excesses of colonialism. Underground, the uterus of the *tía pachamama* (or aunt mother earth) was the mine that produced for Andean people who, in turn, reciprocated through their offerings, including in the Catholic chapels dedicated to the Virgen de la Concepción throughout the city of Potosí (Salazar-Soler 173; Deustua 220–22; Platt 57).

By analyzing local and regional worldviews, scholars can understand how colonial Andeans shaped the economic and religious manifestations of Iberian colonialism. Outlining these beliefs, we can also observe the extent to which Andeans shared suppositions with Iberians, especially in regards to animistic beliefs about matter (Bentancor 351). While in distinct positions in the colonial order, some Spanish and Andeans began their encounter with a moral imperative to minimize the pillaging and exploitation that accompanied conquest and colonization. To understand the forms in which exploitation could take place one must understand the local manifestations of global institutions such as Christianity or finance capital. Without denying the coercive power of these institutions, we must also investigate interactions among these institutions at all levels of Iberian imperial networks to understand where they broke down, were diverted from intended ends or were resisted outright.

Early modern participants appear to have intuited these complexities, giving globalization and its consequences often deeply ironic twists even amid the dire conditions in which they were forced to live. Take for example Guaman Poma's words about the behavior of some *mitayos* (men who served as laborers in the *mita*). His long letter complaining to the King about corrupt tribute collectors, physically abusive rural priests, and unjust regional magistrates testifies to the economic, sexual, political, and social oppression of colonial rule. And yet there are moments in which one sees the active side of Andean colonial society. In his protests against the priests who abused the *mita* system, using Indians for all kinds of menial tasks, Guaman Poma introduces this note:

> Estos dos dichos yndios y el hornamento no se lleue y las dichas ymágenes ni ningún rrecaudo de un pueblo a otro pueblo, porque se pier de y se quiebra. Y en el camino con las hechuras de las ymágenes y hornamento andandan [*sic*] jugando los yndios. Y ancí lo tenga cada pueblo su rrecaudo de hornamento" (863)

> *These two aforementioned Indians and the vestments should not be taken away, nor are the images or any other supplies taken from one town to another because in this way they would get lost and broken. And along the way, the Indians play around with the crafted images and the vestments. And therefore each town should keep the vestments under its care.*[2]

What are we to make of Guaman Poma's protection of indigenous Andeans from the abuse of priests, but also of religious objects from the nonchalant attitude of their bearers? More importantly, why are the latter depicted cheerfully and carelessly traveling along the roads, breaking or losing supposedly sacred instruments while doing their *mita* service? Did they not know the value of those objects? Did they simply not care? Did they relate to material sacred objects in a distinct manner than what was dictated by Catholic missionaries? Did they consider themselves to be Christian? Andeans articulated irreverence for Catholic iconography, profound respect for Christian beliefs, and appropriated Catholic saints in their colonial religious practices, making possible a plethora of responses to these questions (Mills 259, 277). In this case, the two indigenous men in Guaman Poma's image appear somehow indifferent to and unimpressed by two of the main institutions in colonial Peru and the early modern world in general: Christianity and labor. While it is impossible to answer the above questions definitively, it is important to take documents like Guaman Poma's account not as confused interpretations but as accurate depictions of the multifaceted ways that imperial structures operated.

In *Iberian Empires and the Roots of Globalization,* men and women such as the Andean laborers and worshippers in the colonial mining city of Potosí provoke us to reflect on the global interplay of cultural and material forces that transformed the Americas, Europe, and Asia in the sixteenth and the seventeenth centuries. This volume collectively examines how economic forces and social hierarchies as well as how textual and visual discourses influenced the political intentions and administrative policies that structured early modern globalization. We argue that globalization did not emerge from Europe, but from the expansive early modern Iberian world. In order to decenter Europe in the story of globalization, we employ an interdisciplinary approach that reveals multiple centers as well as multiple actors. As specialists in Mexico (del Valle), Brazil (More), and the Andes (O'Toole), our geographical scope has forced us to take into account not only diverse regional forces, but clashing imperial agendas. Methodologically, as literary scholars (del Valle and More) and a historian (O'Toole), we insist on an integration of textual or representational evidence with material and economic circumstances. Our interest is to understand the specific mechanics of global networks that linked the multiple centers of early modern Iberian empires via the integration of economic and cultural forces. In other words, *Iberian Empires and the Roots of Globalization* moves beyond the argument among world historians that economic activities were social acts (Pomeranz and Topik xiv) to understand the interactions among economic, cultural and discursive practices. Most critically, we argue that crucial to an understanding of globalization is both the creation of networks—those of commerce and slavery, for example, or of art and religion—and their mutual and conflictive interactions. Indeed, global consciousness has always been rooted in local contexts, even when these become hidden behind universalizing structures and values. The essays that constitute this volume underline how multiple points of authority, flexible configurations of the state, and faith as a means of governmentality, defined early modern Iberian globalization.

Decentering Empire: Agents of Early Iberian Globalization

This volume seeks to counterbalance both Iberian imperial historiography and world systems approaches that remain centered on European processes to the detriment of local contexts. Iberian empires have been the subject of scholarship that has elucidated topics ranging from the Habsburg administrative model to the actions of remote missionaries.[3] We want to show how under the overarching sweep of empires, their bureaucrats, missionaries, infrastructures, and ideas worked in multiple locations. Beyond imperial structures, there were also lives and experiences that remained outside the administrative control that can be revealed with methods that work both against and along the grain of the colonial archive (Stoler 47, 51). To this record we bring a sensibility that comes from social history, especially post-colonial readings of the archive to look at who and what enacted global processes. Studies of both the contemporary dynamics of globalization and world systems as a grand narrative of capital accumulation tend toward binaries of center and periphery, universalism and particularism, and global and local. Furthermore, narratives of world history commonly explain processes of early modern globalization by putting forth all-encompassing structures that ignore how the specific agents, marked by age, gender, religion, or race negotiated structural impositions. In order to view the intricacies of structures through local agents that inhabited, enforced or resisted them, this volume approaches globalization as networks with multiple nodes or centers constituted by specific historical actors, whether or not these are clearly visible in the archive.

The rich historiography on Iberian imperialism tends to follow the administrative models imposed by metropolitan governance, even if the best historians nuance this centralization by acknowledging the flexibility of Habsburg governance. J.H. Elliott, for example, works to explain the differences between colonial societies and the metropolitan underlining a historiographical creation of periphery and center (Elliott xii). At the same time, the European metropole remains at the center for these scholars.[4] For Anthony Pagden, empire is defined by its ability or its intention to articulate "universal values," a decidedly western European concept (*The Burdens of Empire* 7).[5] Recent approaches to insert the Iberian empires into the predominately Anglo Atlantic world have also replicated the centrality of Europe.[6] In these scholarly narratives, particularly during the fifteenth, sixteenth, and seventeenth centuries, Europeans are the actors who made global events. The current shift to examining the logics and the mechanics of empires continues to center Europe and its institutions. In these global histories, European models predominate, while Africans, Asians, and indigenous peoples of the Americas react, but do not act as main protagonists, as their religious, social, and cultural logics are superseded by the teleological logic of conquest and colonization (Hart; Ferro). In this volume, we present the perspectives of Guaraní scribes and Michoacán inhabitants as well as Chinese Confucian scholars and Tagalog theologians. As actors, however, Africans and their descendants, enslaved and free, are marginal in this collection. Yet, we hope our approach of confronting the scholarly centralization of Europe with an interdisciplinary method will invite further exploration of visual, performative, and body manifestations of the African diaspora's theological and political articulation with early modern Iberian globalization.

Attention to agents does not detract from our emphasis on the power of empires or economics. We acknowledge that the study of empire requires an understanding of European institutions such as Spanish Crown law or the Catholic Inquisition, but we argue that their plans almost always produced very different results from what they were expecting. Thus, in the essays that follow, the authors focus on religiosity and culture, aspects not fully integrated into recent attempts to narrate the Iberian contribution to the making of the early modern world (Pagden, *Spanish Imperialism*). Furthermore, the essays engage with the material consequences of early modern global structures while accounting for the social, discursive, and cultural articulations of people who created these colonial Iberian worlds. We acknowledge that world systems approaches still provide a critical corrective to a liberal interpretation of global processes. In this vein, the scholars in this volume attend to the economic demands of private merchants and imperial governments as well as the inequities created by Iberian judicial exclusions of Africans and their descendants, or Crown labor impositions on indigenous communities of the Americas. At the same time, they also nuance material interpretations by using cultural, social, and literary methodologies to illuminate how colonial processes were often built through combinations of resistance and identification, ideology and brute violence. In other words, in this volume, economics is not treated as a principal motor of historical processes, relegating culture to a position of superstructure.

This volume defines Iberian empires as global institutions linked by various routes and forms of transmission in the diverse locales they reached. This perspective further challenges how scholars have understood the relation between the global and the local. Indeed, the chapters that follow underline the vision of the Iberian empires as "polycentric monarchies" where multiple centers negotiate with each other (Cardim, et al. 4, 5), moving beyond a focus on political and territorial control. By expanding our focus to include the Philippines, China, Goa, and Atlantic Africa as sites and influences of the Iberian early modern world, *Iberian Empires and the Roots of Globalization* creates space for inquiries into the non-European peoples who fashioned the economic regimes, religious beliefs, social structures, and moral codes of the European empires. The Iberian form of early modern globalization thus interrupts teleological narratives of unilateral orders by revealing shifting and multiple nodes of commercial and cultural power throughout the Atlantic and the Pacific. The dynamics of centralized accumulation and shifting arenas of extraction do not just characterize our current moment of globalization (Sassen) but began with early modern empires.

Empires, especially if they have an expansive reach, as Iberian empires of the sixteenth and seventeenth centuries did, can bring globalization about through the development of their multiple interests, linking regions in very diverse ways. If a particular place might have been a periphery from the perspective of commerce, for example, the same locale could have been pivotal in the protection of geopolitical interests (the case of Baja California in the eighteenth century for example). Silver, one of the drivers of early modern globalization, connected not only places, but also people who in most cases never met each other (an Angolan slave working in American gold or silver mines, the indigenous communities forced to work through the colonial *mita*, the Spanish Crown and German and Genoese bankers receiving the benefits, for example), but whose lives nonetheless were intertwined (in some cases forcibly), even if they were not fully aware of it. Empires connected sites of extraction (again as in the case of silver) to the places from which laborers (African slaves, indigenous people, and mestizos) were brought to work, to the areas where entire forests were cut down to provide wood for the constantly burning smelters. Banking sites that provided the funds allowing for the whole process to take place were also part of this network, as were the ports and routes from where silver departed and arrived, and the minting houses and artisans' workshops where it was transformed into the objects that gave elegance and luster to the royal courts and churches where it was displayed.

This complex network was anything but even and egalitarian. It was quite different to be one of the workers subjected to exhausting labor or to be the banker collecting profits, to be the Crown increasing its wealth and glory, or the Jesuit priest ministering to each of them. It was not the same for the places either. Entire regions were quickly devastated by environmental and social catastrophes while others became booming trading posts, banking centers, and elegant royal courts.[7] New or conquered cities often combined various elements, attempting to reproduce metropolitan forms but serving specific functions that responded to economic and imperial needs, especially defense (Cartagena or Luanda, for instance). This globalization produced striking differences among the geographies it connected: exorbitant inequality between points not immediately seen as connected since many layers of relationships and exchanges, and routes, separated them. Even when globalization brought about radical transformations, it did not homogenize the world, but rather created heterogeneity within a connected and complex system.

In this sense, *Iberian Empires and the Roots of Globalization* wishes to add nuance to attempts to write Iberian imperialism into world systems theories by focusing on the specific links, nodes, agents, and processes that produced the conditions for globalization. Walter Mignolo was one of the first to argue that imperial designs do not exhaust local possibilities and experiences (*Local Histories/Global Designs*), but his focus exclusively on cultural and epistemological structures ignores the economic aspects that have always accompanied imperial movement. A different perspective may be found in one of the most prominent theories of imperialism's impact on world systems: what Aníbal Quijano calls the "coloniality of power." But ultimately, terms like these, in their construction and use, mystify and disembody the complex material processes of colonization, lending a teleological aura to processes that took many unexpected turns and forms. Thus, Walter Mignolo's statement that "border thinking from the perspective of subalternity is a machine for intellectual decolonization," rests on the very binary he wishes to deconstruct and, in this sense, ends up reifying its terms (Mignolo 2000, 45). Furthermore, if historiography has emphasized the political models of Iberian expansion, often without acknowledging the consequences of these models when put in practice, even approaches that seek to provide political antidotes to imperialism often avoid analyzing the hard structures of coercion and violence that constrained many actors.

When understood as cultural production such as refracting images of Buddha and the Virgin, exchanged between Jesuit missionaries, indigenous inhabitants of colonial New Spain, and Confucian scholars in Qing China, globalization is hardly a "culmination" resulting in the domination of Europe and Europeans (Quijano 181, 183). On the contrary, in the case of Jesuits interacting with scholars in Qing China, globalization entailed a humbling of Christianity's universalizing expectations. Elaborating Iberian global history from the perspective of Guaraní scribes in Jesuit missions complicates the idea that all forms of labor, and more specifically the work of all colonial laborers, "were deliberately established and organized to produce commodities for the world market" (Quijano 183). Indeed, we suggest that laborers were organized in different ways in different places. In fact, just as Andean miners in Potosí may have imagined exchanges with a feminine earth deity as they extracted silver, enslaved men sold from the Bight of Benin to the northern Peruvian coast claimed their wages to remove their daughters and sons from slaveholding households. While economy and politics were not absent from fundamental structures, this volume details how particular local responses intervened in the original plans and practices of empire administrators to construct the actual processes of imperial globalization.

Ideas in Context: The Material Limits of Universalism

If globalizing structures were constructed in dialogue with local conditions, beliefs, and practices, these conditions also impacted and materialized the ideas that accompanied an early modern global world. In this sense, one of the questions this volume aims to answer is how the concept of globalization first became manifest in Iberian empires. How is it that parts of the globe which until recently had not only been separate, but completely unknown to one another, start to form a "world," a single entity whose parts, whether conscious of it or not, begin to feel the repercussions of historical events taking place thousands of miles apart? While the world has always been a globe (the word globalization comes, let us not forget, from the Latin, *globus*, globe, sphere), globalization describes the process by which this globe became a world, to the extent that its parts came to know themselves to be a world.[8] Awareness does not imply a conscious reflection of connectedness at all times; on the contrary, becoming a world might very well mean an unconscious given—the world is one and there is no further need to dwell on what is obvious. Whether taken for granted or all of a sudden present for reflection, an experience of the world started to become one in the fifteenth century with Portuguese and Spanish expansion into the Atlantic and the Indian oceans and the "discovery" of the Americas, events that brought new meanings to the previous engagements among Europe, Africa, and Asia. While these processes had origins in trade networks before the early modern period, it is only when the Americas entered the picture that historical events could become truly global.

Although becoming a "globe" suggests unity, the way that global connections played out was far from homogenous. Even when traceable through the institutions that upheld them (churches, missions, universities, books, laws, courts), culture, ideas, and religion created their own connections that challenge historiography.[9] There is ample historical evidence regarding the reception of some ideas, for instance, but in other cases it is hard to know how transmitted concepts traveled through time and space. Concepts aspiring to become universals in a world that initially did not even recognize them at all, but also legal systems (the possibility of an "international law," for example) and Christianity, created networks and hierarchies different than those of silver and other economic interests (Anghie; Scott; Schmitt). While they sometimes clashed openly, it was perhaps more common for religious and legal precepts to accommodate or adjust to economic interests, even if trying to moderate their most devastating effects. Art and science, for their part, could obliterate or renounce any pretense to a pure origin (Christianity, in contrast, had to present itself as the only true religion), but also flourished around or followed economic interests, be it the Silk Road or pearl fishing.

Globalization thus exhibits a contrast among truths and the practices that upheld them. The simultaneous circumstances of globalization presented in this volume allow us to look at particular manifestations (the transmission of art, for example) without compromising an overall definition of globalization as creating general networks and universalizing ideas. Yet by bringing together diverse media through which ideas were expressed and transmitted, we can also investigate distinct values within globalization. Some artistic manifestations, for instance, point to multiple sites of origin that are blended and transformed rather than ordered in taxonomies or hierarchies, as may be the case in European ideas of geography and race. It is true that globalization centralized accumulation and empowered some geographic locales. But even if one finds geographic centers, or agrees that Spain and Portugal were the first agents of globalization, were they unitary empires or several at the same time? How did the economy, Christianity, international law, and art interact among themselves in any of these various centers? Would we not flatten and distort all of the different components were we to try to give an overarching explanation of the whole? Were religion and culture leading the way, or was it the economy? And were art and ideas fully subordinated to either one of these two factors? And what would globalization look like from the perspective of the communities most affected, such as those working in the colonial *mita*? Would this latter perspective tell us something completely different from that of the centers of command or would it put forward a narrative that intersects in many points with what has been easiest to document?

One way to answer these questions is to approach the universalizing tendencies of globalization as a series of superimposed maps of networks and relationships based on the way in which ideas and reality interacted in specific locales. First, it would be possible to write a history of globalization that looked at the formation of centers and peripheries, as is common in both imperial historiographies and world systems approaches. In many instances it is the frontier-like nature of certain regions that allows for more openness and creativity, the experimental character of the responses to historical challenges such as the need to evangelize large populations under extreme circumstances. Second, one could also limit oneself to recounting the history of the *legal* or administrative connections among all the involved areas (as almost all of the chapters in this volume do). But another history would be that of the illegal or extralegal relationships that accompanied empire and that probably accounted for much of what occurred in it. In this respect, a revised picture would emerge from the way in which legal and illegal markets interacted, and how institutions confronted past practices, use, and habitus, or the other way around.

Finally, it is important to note, as these essays do, that Iberian empires could never have been "viewed" as a unified picture (cf. Heidegger). The multifaceted nature of globalization means its history looks different when seen from different places (Goa, Angola, Seville, Mexico City, the Philippines, or Rome), or when recounted from the perspective of a particular issue (such as the transmission of *enconchado* art or the theatrical rendition of the history of Buddha) or institution (the Inquisition, the *Casa de Contratación* in Seville). Likewise, globalization might appear as pious, bureaucratic, excessively violent, or immensely creative in an artistic sense, depending on the vantage point one occupies. Finally, as we know, the dialectic between the material substratum and that of ideas is not perfect. Ideas go beyond material realities and materiality demonstrates the limitations or blind spots of ideas that try to encompass it. Sometimes an idea might influence material processes, as was the case for Thomas More's *Utopia* for Vasco de Quiroga's hospitals in sixteenth-century New Spain, but the historical context in which these hospitals were founded modified the original idea. And this could happen to such a degree that the original idea might no longer be recognizable. Ideas therefore had consequences, but in turn materiality demonstrates and, to a great extent, continues to condition their capacity to be meaningful. Some of the articles in this volume emphasize one of the two sides of the equation (material reality/ideas), while others attempt to balance them. But all, to a greater or lesser degree, remain aware of the interlocking relationship among structures, institutions, and ideas.

Reframing Imperialism as Globalization: Historicism and Methodology

An investigation of the consequences of early modern globalization requires various methodologies that can capture these material forms of ideas, their relationship to practices in local sites, or as negotiated through institutional networks. Early modern studies, studies of Iberian empires, and Latin American colonial studies have all recently witnessed a shift in focus from a regional to a global framework.[10] This collection draws on this confluence by bringing together new work by scholars from Latin America, the United States, and Europe in the fields of history, art history, and literary studies to interrogate early Iberian empires as an initial form of cultural and economic globalization. By tracing how products, texts, and people bridged ideas and institutions, the essays collectively explore the construction of globalizing universals in tension with an imperial or world history perspective. The confluence of discussions on globalization, however, begs the question of whether globalization as a topic and approach to studying Spanish and Portuguese empires is inherently interdisciplinary and if so, why? What types of objects or social relations does globalization create or expose and how do these necessitate disciplinary dialogue? What types of methods should be used to bring to the fore and analyze globalizing ideologies and processes?

The essays in this volume suggest answers to these questions from distinct disciplinary and methodological practices. Rather than collapsing the distinction among disciplines, the authors of these essays delineate specific objects of study to focus on the interplay of institutions, social relations, mobility and contact constitutive of early modern globalization. Many of the objects studied or questions posed might otherwise have been invisible or subject to limited interpretations when viewed through national or regional frameworks. Charlene Villaseñor Black's essay, for instance, takes on the example of the *enconchados*. The *enconchado* technique, by which iridescent shell was embedded in art works, clearly resonates with Asian decorative techniques. Yet it has been impossible to trace the transmission routes through transpacific networks that resulted in the widespread use of the technique in New Spain. The *enconchados* also employed local materials and themes particular to New Spain. Given the opacity of transmission and influence, Villaseñor Black opts to investigate the surface effects of the *enconchados*, finding resonance in a general turn to iridescence during the period. While global networks structured by the transpacific imperial trade created the conditions for the emergence of *enconchados* as an artistic technique in New Spain, the archive is limited. Analysis from visual and material interpretation places *enconchados* in a web of global analogies and elucidates the regional nuances of a turn toward iridescence in the period.

In this way, objects produced under conditions of globalization force traditional disciplinary methods, such as literary, art historical or social history, to account for long-distance chains of transmission or for imported and recombined forms. John Blanco takes on this task by interpreting one of the most iconic theatrical works of early modern courtly theater, Calderón de la Barca's *La vida es sueño*, as a distant permutation of the life story of the Buddha. In this case, even if the exact route of transmission cannot be established, literary analysis can establish analogies among different versions of the *Buddasatra* narrative. Whereas this approach resonates with traditional philological studies, Blanco's essay asks what the passage through such diverse cultural contexts might mean for a work usually associated with the theorization of Spanish sovereignty. Guillermo Wilde interrogates a similar problem not to elucidate influence and transmission, and the consequences for ideas, but to approach the social history of indigenous subjects of the Jesuit missions in Paraguay. Printed books from the Jesuit Guaraní missions suggest the active participation of Guaranís. However, there is little evidence of how this participation took place or to what end. The circulation of works and the circulation of Jesuits created two dynamics: one focused on local relations in the missions and the other in the attempts to influence and control the missionary frontier from Europe. In this case, attention to the social production of knowledge on the Jesuit frontier contextualizes objects to elucidate the play between local relevance and central design in missionary practice.

Be it as it may, globalization, paradoxically, can exacerbate the local by making it more evident; oftentimes we can only see the way in which a universal—slavery, for example—is lived daily in a certain location. Again, we would like to acknowledge a limitation of this book: even though at the outset we hinted at how indigenous people working on the colonial *mita* gave us a glimpse of the impositions and negotiations that went on during early modern globalization, we recognize that a truly non-Western local vantage point is missing. Guillermo Wilde, Rachel Sarah O'Toole, and Elisabetta Corsi suggest how the world initiated with globalization might have looked to indigenous people in the Jesuit Paraguayan missions, enslaved African-descent people, or early modern Chinese people, respectively. But that is all they can give us, glimpses. We acknowledge that the global might look very different when accepted and constituted from a non-Western tradition. What did the Purépecha of Michoacán make of Vasco de Quiroga's hospitals? What did the hundreds of captives brought from Africa to the Americas make of the new worlds they encountered? How would they describe, in their own languages, with their own concepts, the processes in which they voluntarily or forcibly participated? These meanings unfortunately escape us, but the path to broadening and deepening how African Atlantic and indigenous peoples of the Americas shaped early modern globalization are growing.[11]

In other ways, individual disciplinary methodologies may well prove insufficient for capturing global structures. As Bernd Hausberger writes in his essay for this volume, the traditional methods of economic history cannot account for global flows of gold and silver, which were often contraband. The logic of precious metals, from extraction to finance, must be understood through social and political relations that shaped economic exchange and thus can only be approached in their full dimension by combining methods from various disciplinary traditions. In this sense, a global framework forces all the essays in this volume to read across disciplines or risk re-inscribing their objects in narratives that do not capture the complex networks through which Iberian imperialism took place. Readings of locally produced and circulated objects, such as the Jesuit missionary works in China, as studied by Elisabetta Corsi, or subjects whose lives are circumscribed to one geographical region, such as the African and Afro-descendants in Trujillo on the coast of Peru, as studied by Rachel Sarah O'Toole, register the local effects of conflicts and struggles that result from missionary diplomacy or the political economy of African enslavement. Whatever the disciplinary tradition of scholarship, studies of early globalization must read objects and subjects that combine traditions in specific political contexts.

This does not mean that disciplines have collapsed into one methodological and theoretical approach. Perhaps the strongest point of distinction among disciplines responsible for scholarship on Iberian imperialism has been the willingness to embrace theoretical models for understanding historical processes.[12] While to a certain extent, the essays collected in this volume continue to reproduce this fault line, they also represent a new movement of exchange between the more theoretically oriented disciplines of literature and art history and the more positivist legacy of historical empiricism.[13] It is worth asking whether this reflects a greater movement in the field, perhaps forged through interdisciplinary symposia such as the one that produced the essays in this volume, or whether the framework of globalization itself forces a dialectical movement between the historical archive and theoretical models.

One problem that has been shared among the disciplines of early modernity is that of the limits of historical documentation and the place of imagination in overcoming these limits. The glaring gaps in the archive of early globalization under Iberian empires cannot be ignored. The acknowledgment of the structured silences of the archive may lead to investigations of the conditions of the archive itself, such as occurs in Anna More's study of the Jesuit writings on the transatlantic slave trade or in Bruno Feitler's investigation of the global reach of the Portuguese Inquisition. And here, interdisciplinarity once again becomes important. As one of the contributors to this volume, María Elena Martínez, has argued in a recent article, rigorous imagination can come to the aid of historical accuracy. In her work on the experience of Mariano Aguilera with the legal, scientific, and religious institutions of colonial New Spain to determine his gender and allow him to marry the woman he chose, Martínez teaches us how to read gaps, silences, experiences that did not make it fully to the archive (the thoughts of Aguilera himself, his fiancé, the priests and doctors involved). In order to do so, Martínez suggests, we must devise interpretations with the scant elements the archive gives us. That is, we must dare to make suggestions, to open possibilities that, while remaining historically grounded, are also an exercise of the imagination. Literary studies, so used for this type of analysis, can help in the task, while historical method contributes to keeping the exercise of the imagination within the realm of what is not only possible, but also probable.

Theoretical paradigms prove fruitful for drawing out consequences, seeing patterns in comparisons and making links between the past and the present. This relationship, through comparison or genealogy, is inherent in the framework of globalization. As Ivonne del Valle argues in her reading of Vasco de Quiroga's plan for a missionary hospital in Michoacán, the paradigm previewed what Hannah Arendt later wrote about refugee populations after World War II. Without subordinating the meaning of archival documentation to theoretical paradigms, the comparison can tell us much about what has changed and what has not, about diverse genealogies and analogous processes at distinct historical points. These comparisons can also help us see the relevance of the past, not only as an origin, but also as an alternative, a warning, or a support for current political processes that might be at a standstill. By asking about globalization we have not approached the past from a point of neutrality, but rather from a political interest. The interest, however, does not imply a distorted interpretation of events in the past but rather readings that forces a dialogue between what was recorded and circumstances in the present that we urgently need to understand. Whatever the disciplinary training and methodological approach, authors in this volume share a will to dislodge both of these poles by engaging with historical interrogations in order to enrich an understanding of globalization that is often based solely on its present form.[14]

As one of the leading examples of an attempt to theorize from the archive, it seems fitting to end with a reflection on how theory can derive from the combination of archival work with a new framework such as globalization. María Elena Martínez's essay asks two questions of the Spanish and Portuguese imperial archive: whether racializing processes in one region of the Iberian empires were analogous to those of others; and whether the Spanish and Portuguese empires can be considered under one rubric. These two questions reach to the heart of the intention of inquiring into globalizing processes as constitutive and constituted by the earliest global imperial models of Spain and Portugal. Archival research offers nuances that adjust models but these adjustments must lead to a greater point about the structure and effects of globalizing processes. It becomes clear that while the design for Iberian imperialism often provided its own models, a priori assumptions and blind spots, the consequences of global processes could be more ambivalent. Subjects could link or delink, their movement empowered their actions, and paradigms that had one purpose originally might be employed for different ends. To understand the full extent of the structures, whether economic or juridical, that violently displaced people and kept actors subject to political and social hierarchies, we need to be able to see global processes in the past. Yet this same archive also provides a record of the unintended consequences of globalization that can implicitly help us rethink today's politics.

In the end, María Elena Martínez's essay in this volume provides a justification for the dialogue that this volume has intended to create among scholars who come from distinct disciplinary methods and traditions. Globalization under Spanish and Portuguese empires can be defined through a pretension of subordination and coordination of geographies and peoples previously separate. There was, indeed, much continuity between the two imperial models based in Catholic precepts and practices and whose own intertwined history created the conditions for the fool's errand of global subordination to one political theology. Whether we look closely at racial paradigms and their paradoxical use for understanding and coordinating populations in new political economies, or the economics of extraction and accumulation, early global processes became embedded in material and institutional consequences that still shape current globalization. The surprises in the archive, however, from objects that refract several traditions to subjects who fight to free themselves from the binds of globalization, also may inspire political intervention in our moment of renewed globalization.

NOTES

1. *Historia natural y moral de las Indias* was first published in Seville in 1590. Theodor de Bry's illustrations were included in various translations from the early seventeenth century.

2. Our translation. Please note that the grammar in the translation reflects the ungrammatical original text.
3. Among the scholars who argue that the Iberian empires were the first, powerful, early modern, global empires are Pedro Cardim, et al.; J. H. Elliot; Anthony Pagden, *The Burdens of Empire*; and Jorge Cañizares-Esguerra, *Puritan Conquistadors*.
4. Elliott explains that European emigrants to the Americas were united in their fears and expectations as they created empires "shaped by a home culture" (xii).
5. Anthony Pagden also defines empire according to a European model, that of Rome, suggesting that only Europe and Asia really experienced "a single society governed by a single body of law" (*The Burdens of Empire* 5).
6. Jorge Cañizares-Esguerra argues that the British Protestants and Spanish Catholics shared a similar Christian culture that shaped their colonial militancy against indigenous "demonic" practices (Cañizares-Esguerra 2006, 30).
7. For mining, see Nicholas A. Robins; Daviken Studnicki-Gizbert and David Schecter. For court life, see Byron E. Hamman.
8. The final suffix of the word, the *tion* of globalization, expresses its quality of constant movement. Globalization is a never-ending process, constantly changing, marching forward, pulling back from certain areas, taking hold in other ones, uneven. But since the fifteenth century, it has been ongoing.
9. See Daniel Nemser's work for the material underpinnings of colonial ideologies.
10. As examples of the "global turn" in early modern studies, one can cite the series of roundtables on the "Global Renaissance," held at the 2014 Renaissance Society of America meetings in Washington D.C., and new volumes such as Murherjee's edited volume that attempt to understand the structures of early modern globalization through networks. There are even more concerted attempts to delineate the specifics of oceanic regions, in critiques of the northern bias of Atlantic Studies as a model (Jorge Cañizares-Esguerra and Benjamin Breen) or "Transpacific" studies. Then again, there have been interesting attempts to outline the global nature of institutions such as the Society of Jesuits, such as Luke Clossey's work in *Salvation and Globalization in the Early Jesuit Missions*. Finally, there have been important steps toward drawing together Spanish and Portuguese empires into one frame, often implicitly global. On this last aspect of scholarship, see the seminal article by Sanjay Subrahmanyam.
11. By examining visual and artifact representations combined with textual descriptions of performances, Cécile Fromont has demonstrated how Kongo elite articulated double meanings, new religious languages, and a West African Christianity from local power objects, imported cloth, and Catholic crucifixes (Fromont 223, 252). Joanne Rappaport has argued that sixteenth-century Andean indigenous leaders who called themselves "mestizo" were not accommodating colonial structures, but combining their noble ancestry, astute literacy, and European dress to serve as intermediaries among their communities, colonial officials, and Spanish rural elites (Rappaport 154). In both cases, these scholars demonstrate how the Kongolese and Andean leaders claimed and created early modern Iberian globalization.

12. See for instance, Jorge Cañizares-Esguerra's critique of Mignolo (*How to Write the History of the New World* 67). Resistance to theory often means a more historicist stance, even within literary studies. See, for instance, Rolena Adorno.
13. For an excellent example that also gives a brief survey of new approaches to the archive, see María Elena Martínez's article, "Sex and the Colonial Archive."
14. For instance, *Globalization: The Reader* acknowledges the historical nature of globalization through periodization (Beynon and Dunkerley 10). But the majority of the reader focuses on the exceptional nature of post-fordist globalization, relegating the initial periods to a place of secondary importance.

WORKS CITED

Adorno, Rolena. *The Polemics of Possession in Spanish American Narrative*. New Haven: Yale University Press, 2007.

Anghie, Antony. *Imperialism, Sovereignty and the Making of International Law*. Cambridge, UK: Cambridge University Press, 2004.

Bakewell, Peter. *Miners of the Red Mountain: Indian Labor in Potosí, 1545–1650*. Albuquerque: University of New Mexico Press, 1984.

Bentancor, Orlando. *The Matter of Empire: Metaphysics and Mining in Colonial Peru*. Pittsburgh: Pittsburgh University Press, 2017.

Beynon, John, and David Dunkerley, eds. *Globalization: The Reader*. New York: Routledge, 2000.

Cañizares-Esguerra, Jorge. *How to Write the History of the New World: Histories, Epistemologies, and Identities in the Eighteenth-Century Atlantic World*. Stanford: Stanford University Press, 2001.

———. *Puritan Conquistadors: Iberianizing the Atlantic, 1550–1700*. Stanford: Stanford University Press, 2006.

Cañizares Esguerra, Jorge, and Benjamin Breen. "Hybrid Atlantics: Future Directions for the History of the Atlantic World." *History Compass* 11.8 (2013): 597–609.

Cardim, Pedro, Tamar Herzog, José Javier Ruiz Ibáñez, and Gaetano Sabatini. "Polycentric Monarchies: How Did Early Modern Spain and Portugal Achieve and Maintain a Global Hegemony?" *Polycentric Monarchies: How did Early Modern Spain and Portugal Achieve and Maintain a Global Hegemony?* Eds. Pedro Cardim, Tamar Herzog, José Javier Ruiz Ibáñez, Gaetano Sabatini. Eastbourne: Sussex Academic Press, 2012. 3–10.

Clossey, Luke. *Salvation and Globalization in the Early Jesuit Missions*. Cambridge, UK: Cambridge University Press, 2008.

Connor, Steve. "The Athropocene era of man's dominance began in 1610, claim scientists." *The Independent*. March 11, 2015. Web.

Elliott, J.H. *Empires of the Atlantic World: Britain and Spain in America, 1492–1830*. New Haven: Yale University Press, 2006.

Ferro, Marc. *Colonization: A Global History*. London: Routledge, 1997.
Fromont, Cécile. *The Art of Conversion: Christian Visual Culture in the Kingdom of Kongo*. Chapel Hill: The University of North Carolina Press, 2014.
Glave, Luis Miguel. *Trajinantes: Caminos indígenas en la sociedad colonial. Siglos XVI / XVII*. Lima: Instituto de Apoyo Agrario, 1989.
Hamman, Byron E. "The Mirrors of Las Meninas: Cochineal, Silver, and Clay." *The Art Bulletin* 92.1-2 (March-June 2010): 6-35.
Hart, Jonathan. *Empires and Colonies*. Cambridge, UK: Polity Press, 2008.
Heidegger, Martin. *The Question Concerning Technology and Other Essays*. Trans. William Lovitt. New York: Harper, 1977.
Mangan, Jane. *Trading Roles: Gender, Ethnicity, and the Urban Economy in Colonial Potosí*. Durham: Duke University Press, 2005.
Martínez, María Elena. "Sex and the Colonial Archive." *Hispanic American Historical Review* 96.3 (2016): 421-43.
Mignolo, Walter. *The Darker Side of Western Modernity. Global Futures, Decolonial Options*. Durham: Duke University Press, 2011.
_____. *Local Histories/Global Designs: Coloniality, Subaltern Knowledges, and Border Thinking*. Princeton: Princeton University Press, 2000.
Mills, Kenneth. *Idolatry and Its Enemies: Colonial Andean Religion and Extirpation, 1640-1750*. Princeton: Princeton University Press, 1997.
Mukherjee, Rila, ed. *Networks in the First Global Age, 1400-1800*. Delhi: Primus Books, 2011.
Nemser, Daniel. *Infrastructures of Race: Concentration and Biopolitics in Colonial Mexico*. Austin: University of Texas Press, 2017.
Pagden, Anthony. *Spanish Imperialism and the Political Imagination: Studies in European and Spanish-American Social and Political Theory, 1513-1830*. New Haven: Yale University Press, 1990.
_____. "Introduction: Anatomy of Empire from Rome to Washington." *The Burdens of Empire: 1539 to the Present*. New York: Cambridge University Press, 2015. 1-44.
Platt, Tristan. "Conciencia andina y conciencia proletaria: *Qhuyaruna* y *ayllu* en el norte de Potosí." *HISLA* 2 (1983): 47-73.
Poma de Ayala, Felipe Guaman. *Nueva Corónica y Buen Gobierno*. Tomo II. Mexico City: Fondo de Cultura Económica, 1993.
Pomeranz, Kenneth, and Steven Topik. *The World that Trade Created: Society, Culture, and the World Economy 1400 to the Present*. Armonk: M. E. Sharpe, 1999.
Quijano, Aníbal. "Coloniality of Power, Eurocentrism, and Social Classification." *Coloniality At Large: Latin America and the Postcolonial Debate*. Eds. Mabel Moraña, Enrique Dussel, and Carlos A. Jáuregui. Durham: Duke University Press, 2008. 181-224.
Rappaport, Joanne. *The Disappearing Mestizo: Configuring Differences in the Colonial New Kingdom of Granada*. Durham: Duke University Press, 2014.
Robins, Nicholas A. *Mercury, Mining, and Empire: The Human and Ecological Cost of Colonial Silver Mining in the Andes*. Bloomington: Indiana University Press, 2011.

Sassen, Saskia. *Expulsions: Brutality and Complexity in the Global Economy*. Kindle ed. Cambridge, MA: Harvard University Press, 2014.
Salazar-Soler, Carmen. *Supay Muqui, dios del socavón: Vida y mentalidades mineras*. Lima: Fondo Editorial del Congreso del Perú, 2006.
Schmitt, Carl. *The Nomos of the Earth in the International Law of the* Jus Publicum Europaeum. New York: Telos Press Publishing. 2006.
Scott, James Brown. *The Spanish Origin of International of Law: Francisco de Vitoria and His Law of Nations*. Oxford: Clarendon Press, 1934.
Stern, Steve J. "The Variety and Ambiguity of Native Andean Intervention in European Colonial Markets." *Ethnicity, Markets, and Migration in the Andes: At the Crossroads of History and Anthropology*. Eds. Brooke Larson, Olivia Harris, Enrique Tandeter. Durham: Duke University Press, 1995. 73–100.
Stoler, Ann. *Along the Archival Grain: Epistemic Anxieties and Colonial Common Sense*. Princeton: Princeton University Press, 2009.
Studnicki-Gizbert, Daviken, and David Schecter. "The Environmental Dynamics of a Colonial Fuel Rush: Silver Mining and Deforestation in New Spain, 1522–1810." *Environmental History* 15 (Jan 2010): 94–119.
Subrahmanyam, Sanjay. "Holding the World in Balance: The Connected Histories of the Iberian Overseas Empires, 1500–1640." *The American Historical Review* 112.5 (2007): 1359–85.

CHAPTER ONE

Precious Metals in the Americas at the Beginning of the Global Economy

Bernd Hausberger
Dexter Zavalza Hough-Snee, translator

Global History and Globalization

At a moment when debates about globalization are omnipresent, we need a new way of looking at history. Although there are dozens of proposed definitions, globalization tends to be understood as the growing interconnection and interdependence of (almost) all aspects of human societies at the planetary level.[1] In any case, its phenomena overwhelm both the concerns and the frameworks established, above all, by national histories, hegemonic since the nineteenth century. One can attribute the rise of "transcultural" and "transnational" perspectives, of "hybrid" histories and, last but not least, that of Global History to this situation. Following authors such as Patrick Manning or Jerry H. Bentley, I understand Global History as a historiographical current that studies the relations and connections at different levels and on different scales in fields such as the history of ideas, the history of science, the history of religion, economic history, or demographic history, and that transcend the borders between continents, countries, cultures, and civilizations. Globalization, in this sense, would be only one chapter of Global History, a chapter that starts when the aforementioned connections achieve a magnitude that allows us to speak of an (at least incipient) integration of the different parts of the earth, in an interdependent and "globalized" world.² But in what historical moment does this occur? There are authors that have placed the beginning of globalization at particular moments of the nineteenth or twentieth century. A. G. Hopkins, for his part, sustains that "modern globalization" emerged toward the end of the eighteenth century and for earlier periods he introduces the terms "archaic globalization" (until 1600) and "proto-globalization" (between 1600 and 1800) (4–6), while for C. A. Bayly archaic globalization ends circa 1750 and proto-globalization between 1850 and 1880 ("From Archaic Globalization" 56). One notices that in both chronologies Iberian expansion constitutes only the latest phase of archaic globalization.

In this essay, I wish first to argue that global or globalizing processes had already been at work for millennia, with numerous repercussions for our present, and that the history of globalization begins with the intensification of such processes during the "long" sixteenth century. Second, I will outline a proposition for reinterpreting the role of Latin America in this transition from a world of many connections to a globalized world. In order to do so, I will focus above all on the analysis of the flows of precious metals that spanned the globe since the sixteenth century. This may not seem a very novel proposal, especially after the already classic works by Earl J. Hamilton or Michel Morineau. Nonetheless, the question is not to define and quantify the flows of precious metals, but rather, and above all, to see how distinct parts of the globe are connected and transformed in a much more complex manner than what the quantification and the reconstruction of simple exchanges of metals and goods can describe.³ The production, flows, and monetization of precious metals formed a system that at all times and in all places produced a series of "forward" and "backward linkages," to use the terms of Hirschmann (*passim*, especially 77–80), forming a network of what at first glance appear inextricable causes and effects. In general terms, it is not a matter of merely defining the importance that these global interconnections had for the development of each implicated zone, but also interpreting the influence that each zone exerted on the configuration of the interconnection. This question is linked to the concern (highly popular among world historians) with the motor or dominant force behind the early world economy. The majority of world historians consider the importance of metals in the Americas for the role that they played in the Eurasian economic system, and yet the regions of origin of such metals are not of great interest.⁴ In the case of silver, these regions are located in Spanish America, first and foremost in the South American Andes and, in the eighteenth century, New Spain.⁵ In what follows, I would like to propose another vision that also permits a revalorization of the agency of Latin America in the development of early globalization. But let us proceed step by step.

The Beginnings of Globalization

In an illuminating polemic with Geoffrey Williamson and Kevin O'Rourke, Denis O. Flynn and Arturo Giráldez have highlighted the historicity of globalization.[6] They describe the relationship between modern globalization and its antecedents by appealing to the concept of "path dependence": the dependence of any historical phenomenon upon the historical trajectory in which it is constructed.[7] The two authors recognize that any conjecture about the beginning of globalization obviously depends on how we define our concepts and how we hierarchize the forces at play. They signal that "globalization" is derived from "globe," a spatial term, and from there sustain that globalization began when the expeditions under the patronage of the Iberian monarchies resulted in the irreversible connection of the large land masses of the globe. Turning to the work of historians such as Serge Gruzinski, they decidedly oppose—and I along with them—an exclusively economic definition of globalization because it does not fully express the complexity of the globalizing process. The linking of cultures, continents, countries and actors was not established exclusively by economic forces. More than anything, what distinguished the development of the sixteenth century from previous events was that, for the first time, connections were established across the entire globe and this with a consciousness of their scope. These ties were accompanied by a profound cosmographic transformation that, from its origins in the West, did not take long to affect other parts of the earth. The new consciousness of the configuration of the globe would serve as a framework for the economic, political, scientific, and cultural processes and activities to come, within which people, goods, and knowledge moved and became interconnected.

The early advance of globalization produced a new spatial political order because it gave way to the emergence of great empires: the domains of the Ming in China, the Mogul in India, the Safavid Dynasty in Persia, and the Ottomans in southwest Asia, southeast Europe and north Africa; and the maritime empires of the Portuguese and Spanish and, later, the British, Dutch, and French (those that James D. Tracy has characterized as "merchant empires," because they primarily sought to control, protect, and promote long-distance commercial routes for their own benefit) (Tracy, *The Rise of Merchant Empires*). This history did not end with the arrival of modernity and the nation-state between the eighteenth and twentieth centuries, but opened the path to current globalization. As Bayly has argued in his *Birth of the Modern World*, the order of nation states themselves was an essential part and product of the integration of space by progressively denser networks and connections. As such, empires continued to mark world history at least until the middle of the twentieth century, and the work of Krishan Kumar, among others, has put into doubt whether their history has effectively ended. In any case, the imperial order is important for understanding the flows of precious metals that originated in America beginning in the sixteenth century and it is these that I will now discuss in greater detail.

The Role of Precious Metals in the Americas

In historiographic debates about the genesis of globalization, it is clear that Latin America is rarely conceded a central role and, from Immanuel Wallerstein to Andre Gunder Frank, Latin America is considered, among other things, peripheral, marginal, exploited, dependent and lacking protagonism. That a renowned historian such as Patrick O'Brian wrote his programmatic introductory text in the first number of the *Journal of Global History*, edited by the University of Cambridge in 2006, and only mentioned Latin America on a pair of occasions, while references to Asia, Africa and the North Atlantic abound, serves to illustrate this point.

On the contrary, the precious metals first exported from America beginning in the initial decades of the sixteenth century never tend to be forgotten. One must emphasize that in 1492 when Christopher Columbus first landed in the Americas, gold and silver already functioned as methods of payment in broad economic spheres of the space of an early "world system," as Janet Abu-Lughod has claimed (3–42), a system that extended from Europe in the north to the eastern coasts of Africa and on to China and Japan, yet whose center, nevertheless, was formed by the Indian Ocean. Among other things, the silver produced primarily in central Europe served to cover the West's commercial deficit with Asia. There the demand for metals was high. In China, the use of paper money fell into disuse after 1430 (von Glahn 79–80); until 1600, the fiscal revenue of the peasants was converted into taxes charged in silver monies and the economy had in large measure been monetized. In India taxes were also paid in silver coinage, the rupee, whose raw materials were almost exclusively imported, and the same occurred in Safavid Iran (Matthee). The supposed Asian inclination to store precious metals, above all in periods of crisis, had possibly reinforced their economies' thirst for precious metals.[8] Metals from the Americas emerged within this growing world of monetization. As a general tendency, silver, abundant in the West since the conquest of America and scarce—and as such, more expensive—in China, flowed from America and Europe to Asia. It was this difference in value that sustained this flow until gold and silver were among the first products to achieve a convergence of prices between China and Europe in the mid-seventeenth century (although only temporarily) (Flynn and Giráldez, "Born Again" 377–79, 383).

Although metals of different origins always entered into global circuits, between the sixteenth and eighteenth centuries the primacy of mining production in the Americas became undeniable.[9] With all of this, one must take into account that the raw production of metals is perhaps in no part of the world as well documented as it is in Spanish America. We owe this above all to the centralizing and bureaucratic efforts of the Crown that, like Sisyphus, struggled for three centuries to control the flows of precious metals. It is necessary to mention the pioneering works of John J. TePaske and Herbert S. Klein, which have made this invaluable information available to researchers (without being able to discuss here the methodological difficulties that fiscal sources pose).[10] There possibly are also mining zones in other parts of the globe whose production has not been adequately considered. Accordingly, if Harry Cross has estimated that 68.5 percent of global silver production came from Spanish America in the sixteenth century, 84.4 percent in the seventeenth century, and 89.5 percent in the eighteenth century, these figures amount only to an approximation (403).

Upon verifying the role of Latin American mining, it is necessary to examine more closely the consequences of the enormous rise in the supply of gold and silver. These can be summarized in four points. Firstly, the increase in the mass of precious metals available not only expanded the system of transcontinental connections, but also gave it a global dimension—in the strictest sense of the word—by encompassing all of the continents (with the exception of Australia). Secondly, it had a strong impact on international monetary systems, with short term consequences (highly debated, certainly) such as inflation and the devaluation of money, while nonetheless it facilitated the monetization of growing segments of economic activity at the level of commerce, salaries, and fiscal extraction in many parts of the world. Although other forms of payment (cacao beans, kauri shells, copper coins, and many other forms of barter) persisted, they were subordinate to the convertibility of metal (Vollmer; Yang). This made way for a reconceptualization of exchange value that was subjected to an abstract arithmetic, materialized, among other things, in the difference between the intrinsic value of the form of payment and its nominal value, which at the same time favored the expansion of the use of bills of exchange.[11] Thirdly, mining prosperity lent a unique dynamic to Spanish colonization of the New World, which thereafter experienced what was probably the most radical transformation in all of its history. The foundations of an extremely durable political, economic and social order were established. Finally, control over the global distribution of American metals evolved into an instrument for diverse groups, institutions and states in Western Europe to increase their importance as global actors. That the globe began to be covered by a network of European strongholds was of transcendental importance. Thus a communicative advantage (in the broadest sense of the word) was established that would be the base for later colonial and imperialist expansion, when industrialization and the development of capitalism would give Europeans a clear military superiority.

All of this should justify speaking of globalization already in the sixteenth and seventeenth centuries. But it is still necessary to bolster this argument. It is true that gold and silver were produced in modest amounts compared to the quantities generated during the nineteenth and twentieth centuries, with different technologies and production techniques in various parts of the world, and that the bonds that these precious metals established never homogenized economic, political, and social systems nor ways of life, except in limited spheres. The heterogeneity of the consequences of early global connections has been used to minimize the importance of these processes.[12] This seems reductionist and unsustainable, for it was characteristic of the early globalization between the sixteenth and eighteenth centuries that irreversibly connected large parts of the globe, that it leveled some differences as much as it created new ones.[13] But although early global relations and connections did not abolish differences, they did lastingly transform many parts of the world, in accordance with new transregional roles and divisions of labor. As I will demonstrate later, nowhere was this transformation as definitive as in Latin America. We therefore emphasize the importance of the connections over the homogeneity of the related entities.

Silver circuits were expansive or global, even more so if one takes into account their close relationship with other circuits. Due to the limitations of this essay, I can only mention the technological transfers that emerged around mines, from Europe to the Americas, within the Americas, and from the Americas to Europe and, although without lasting success, from the Americas to Japan (Hausberger, "El universalismo"). Mining production also gave origin to an extended supply network of mercury for mines in the Americas that has been analyzed by Mervyn Lang, among others. From the moment amalgamation technologies were introduced in Spanish American mines between 1560 and 1570, mercury became an indispensable material for silver production. From then on, mercury was transported to American mines from Almadén in Spain, from Huancavelica in Peru, and from Idrija in present-day Slovenia. The Crown administered this circuit as a monopoly and sought out, in vain, additional sources of provision in China (Lang 137–46). The distribution of mercury was probably the most efficient means of control that the Crown employed to regulate mining production, as they attempted to calculate production amounts from the quantity of mercury distributed to mine owners, with which they established certain controls over tax evasion. The provisioning of mercury, lastly, permits a view of the systemic dynamic of these interconnections, as problems with production in Almadén or Huancavelica regularly had severe repercussions on silver production, and these in turn influenced imperial politics in Spain.[14]

Above all, the flows of silver went hand in hand with mercantile circuits, improving interregional commerce and funding the West's trade deficit with Asia. Even in Madagascar, from the sixteenth century onward the prices of slaves were calculated in *pesos* primarily minted in Mexico (Bechtloff). In the whole of Asia, Spanish monies became the dominant means of payment for long-distance commerce (Barendse 214–31; Atwell 469–70). In the eighteenth century, thanks to the royal policy of maintaining (relatively) constant stores of silver, the Mexican peso became reliable legal tender and gained repute as a marker of quality, becoming the monetary standard not only in diverse parts of Asia, but also in the young United States until well into the nineteenth century (Marichal; Irigoin).

Supplied with a common method of payment, trade achieved the compatible practices that enabled its long-distance operation. Yet trade connected geographies that were in other aspects very dissimilar. As a consequence, the effects of silver circuits were necessarily uneven. The persistence or emergence of such discrepancies is significantly owed to the fact that the insertion of silver into different economies and societies was profoundly affected by extra-economic factors such as imperial competition. Not only did European powers participate in imperial competition, but the Ottoman Empire, Safavid Iran, the Mogul Empire of India, and the Ming and Manchu Empires of China, among others, were also immersed in specific economic and political circumstances each with their own cultural baggage and institutional framework. Even so, all of these spaces were linked by a series of apparatuses (legal and illegal, formal and informal), of which metals from the Americas were the lubricant.

Latin American Agency at the Onset of Globalization

It is worth repeating that the connection of the so-called New World with the Old World and "the invention of America," to take up the phrase coined by Edmundo O'Gorman, was established on multiple levels, as much political as cultural and religious. Nevertheless, the motivations behind this process were, first and foremost, material, and the continent's form of economic insertion into global relations demonstrated great durability. Latin America established itself as an importer of European, Asian and African goods (if we consider slaves merchandise) and an exporter of precious metals, that, in a period in which the nominal value of a coin was equivalent to the intrinsic value of its metal content, were monetary substances, that is, raw material and money at the same time.[15] In order to explain the role of America in early globalization, I focus, therefore, on the flows of precious metals. Traditional historiography has always seen Europe as the center of universal history. But with the rise of Global History the debate has become multifaceted. André Gunder Frank was one of the first to "reorient" this vision by placing China in the center of what he has called an "Asian era" in which Europeans played merely a secondary role. He maintains that in the sixteenth century it was the thriving Chinese economy that sustained the profitability of the so-called European expansion, since with its products it attracted Europeans and with its insatiable demand for silver, ensured the buying power of growing American exports at an astonishing rate. Since then, a lively comparative debate has emerged around China, India, and the West, a debate whose most notable exponent has probably been Kenneth Pomeranz. But, once again, it appears that Latin America is not considered worthy of greater interest. And it is precisely the study of silver flows that lends itself to remedy this lack of attention.

It is not my intent to place the origin of globalization in Latin America. By understanding globalizing ties as a system of interconnections, I rather seek to reconsider the hierarchization of global regions and to reevaluate terms such as "center" and "periphery." These tend to express power differentials that are insufficient for explaining development, to begin with, because no power ever prevails completely. Latin American mining has been interpreted as an exploitative colonialist practice realized by Europe or as a consequence of Asian demand. Now, neither China nor Europe ever considered giving up the importation of American silver and, at the same time, America never thought of halting mining because silver was needed in China and Europe while America needed goods from the Old World. It would be arbitrary, in my opinion, to state which region depended upon the other in this historical moment.

Who, then, propelled global silver flows? Obviously, the mass exportation of precious metals from America benefited the Spanish Crown and the merchants assembled under the Consulado de Sevilla (to whom the Crown had conceded the monopoly on commerce with the Indies) as well as the economy and administration of the Chinese Empire. It is also true that upon receiving the earliest news of American mineral wealth, even the German banker-merchants of Augsburg sent their business agents to the New World and although their activity was short-lived, their participation carried out an important function by transferring

Central European mining technologies to the Americas.[16] What enabled the circulation of precious metals was not the will of the king of Spain or the emperor of China, nor that of the bankers of Genoa, Augsburg or Amsterdam. These monarchs could only promote—but not manage—mineral production, and the Chinese could aspire to control such management of mineral production to an even lesser degree. From the perspective of the actors, the situation is very clear. First of all, I want to highlight that at least in economic terms, it does not make sense to consider the Spanish colonizers who settled in the Americas as Europeans, but rather one must understand that very rapidly, and without regard to their origin or their persistent ties to the Iberian Peninsula, these colonizers formed a new American elite who profoundly transformed the Americas. They settled there, they worked there, and, soon after, they were born there. They also acquired their wealth there and invested it in land, mines, workshop manufacturing (*obrajes*), commercial enterprises and other businesses such as the purchase of public service positions and political distinctions—such as titles of military orders (*caballería*)—which served to consolidate their social position. And a significant percentage of their income was destined for consumption.[17] Spanish members of colonial society did not enter into the new circuits of global exchange with their metals because someone obliged them to do so or entrusted them with such investment. They did so because it corresponded with their interests in accumulating wealth and elevating their social status and although the Spanish Crown intended to control the rules of the game from Madrid, the colonists always maintained sufficient autonomy to manipulate the situation to their favor. Through the mining industry and export economy directed toward global markets, the American merchant elite amassed enormous wealth and ensured their interests in consumption, status, and power. Obviously, they never acted in favor of the indigenous population, African slaves, or the lower classes in general. Inequality and exploitation did not emerge so much between the Old World and the New World as between new American elites and the American lower classes and social groups (as it was the case among European elites and subaltern classes).

How can the formation of this order be explained? The conquistadors' occupation of new territories—from its beginning a fundamentally private enterprise (Kamen 95-97) (imperfectly regulated by the Crown)—had not resolved the exploitation that would benefit them in the long run. The desire of the conquistadors to fill their purses with gold and take it to Europe only became a reality for a select few. It is sufficient to examine the example of Hernando Pizarro, who in 1534 returned to Spain bringing 150,069 gold *pesos* and 5,048 silver *marcos* for the king and 708,580 gold *pesos* and 49,008 silver *marcos* for private individuals (Varón Gabai and Jacobs

664). But the vast quantities of metals amassed by the pre-Hispanic cultures and, in this case, stolen by Pizarro, were exhausted all too quickly.

What other benefit could be derived from the New World? One must remember that in 1492 Columbus's journey had the objective of finding a direct route to the opulence of the Orient.[18] Even if Columbus's enterprise united forces of a diverse nature, his economic motivation was primarily mercantile: his travels sought to establish access to the treasured goods of the Orient. These dreams soon vanished, as Columbus never arrived to India or China, but rather to a world unknown to Europe. These new lands delighted and challenged the Western cosmovision. But they did not offer the conditions to establish commercial relations such as those that the Italians sustained in the Eastern Mediterranean or those that the Portuguese would organize with considerable violence in South and Southeast Asia after Vasco de Gama arrived to India in 1498. The conditions in the Americas were too different. In Asia, above all along the maritime routes between the coasts of the Indian Ocean and the western Pacific, there was an almost millenary tradition of intensive, long-distance trade whose final western extension was commercial exchange with Europe. The goods traded among these routes were produced by an active manufacturing infrastructure such as the porcelain and silk workshops in China, the Indian cotton industry, and the sugar plantations of Egypt.[19] Additionally, in all of Eurasia, even in large coastal regions of Africa, commerce was to a high degree monetized on gold and silver. As a result, Asian products were known and demanded in Europe and Europeans, whose industry scarcely generated products exportable to wealthy Asia, were able to finance their purchases with precious metals that they extracted from the mines or acquired in North Africa.

Those of the autochthonous societies of the Spanish Indies lived under different circumstances. There was no maritime commercial network comparable to that which existed in the Indian Ocean. The production capacity was not sufficient to undertake transatlantic exportation. And most importantly, as a consequence of the millenary isolation of the Euro-Asian-African continental mass, products from the Americas were not known to the Old World and, as a result, had neither preexisting demand nor established prices among Old-World consumers. In the Americas, silver and gold currencies were also unknown, with which the possibilities of selling European products to the Americans were reduced to barter. Certainly, it was only a question of decades until tobacco and cocoa began to be valued outside of America. But until that moment arrived, it was impossible for navigators and explorers to become immediately rich through trade with the Americas and, as a consequence, they became conquistadors. In order to understand these difficulties, it is worth taking into account the limited timespan that these historical actors had for their personal projects. Francisco

Pizarro, for example, was already nearly sixty years old in 1532 when he confronted the Inca in Cajamarca; his time was running out.

The economic problem that the Spaniards confronted after taking power in the American territories could only be resolved within the cultural parameters and mentalities of the conquistadors. The option of becoming lords in the style of the Aztecs, who adorned themselves with quetzal feathers and turquoise stones and drank *pulque* as consumptive demonstrations of status, was, it seems, never considered and it is important that *pulque*, once stripped of its sacred significance, became a means of getting drunk among the lower classes.[20] The desires for wealth and elevated social status that the conquistadors wished to achieve corresponded to Western concepts. They hoped to be lords in the European sense. It was important to them to wear Italian or Asian cloth, drink wine, season their food with spices from the Orient, use glass objects, celebrate mass in churches adorned with oil paintings and arm themselves with steel and firearms. For the conquistadors, this meant that their security as much as their status depended on the quantity of goods brought from the Old World. As a consequence, from the beginning post-conquest America developed a decisive demand for imported products.[21] Spanish transpacific expansion and the establishment of the regular trade route between Manila and Acapulco in the 1570s can be seen as a continuation of the original project of Columbus; but it also served—aside from the geo-strategic considerations of the Crown—to give the residents of New Spain access to coveted products of the Orient. Their prominence in inventories of goods that, for example, Paulina Machuca has analyzed for the province of Colima in New Spain, well demonstrates how those that had the means to do so "apostaron por una cultura material del prestigio y el lujo" (114) (opted for a material culture of prestige and luxury). In order to purchase these products, one needed a means of payment; in other words, in order to be able to import, it was essential to export. It occurred that, despite the revitalization of feudal values in the context of the conquest, commerce continued to be of crucial importance. The internal New Spanish economy was, in this way, an economy built on exportation.

Because indigenous societies in the Americas did not provide sufficient exportable products, the Spanish were forced to organize a production of goods destined for external markets. Before the construction of trains and steamboats in the second half of the nineteenth century, high transportation costs limited the range of saleable products across long distances to those of high value and reduced weight.[22] A fortuitous event provided the solution. Already among the inhabitants of the Antilles islands, the Spanish had found considerable quantities of gold, not in the form of currency, but as artisanal objects. The Spaniards quickly located the gold-bearing sands from which the Native Americans extracted the yellow metal. On a much larger scale, this experience would be repeated in Mexico and in Peru. The Spaniards confiscated the gold accumulated over the centuries by indigenous people and exploited the gold-holding sandbanks. Fray Bartolomé de las Casas had already signaled that Columbus permitted the enslavement of the natives of Hispaniola in order to search for gold to pay for "los mantenimientos y otras mercaderías traídas de Castilla" (440) (supplies and other merchandise brought from Castile). They soon discovered the first silver mines and, in 1545, the deposits of the Cerro Rico of Potosí in the Andes and those of Zacatecas in New Spain, to mention only the most important ones. From then on, silver would become the most important export commodity of Spanish America.[23] One must highlight that mining was nearly completely organized by private initiatives. In this way, Spanish America became both producer and exporter of currency in order to purchase merchandise in external markets. This "currency," in countless diverse forms and coinages, was distributed around the world from America.

Obviously, the mass arrival of precious metals also went quite well for the royal treasury, which was perpetually in need of money. From the onset of Spanish control in America, the crown monitored navigation and commerce, created and defended monopolies, gave privileges and charged taxes. But faced with these measures the Spanish Empire's internal subjects (as well as its external competitors) reacted by seeking out forms of cooperation and resistance, of which the most important was contraband. Even still, silver from the Americas afforded resources for the financing of Madrid's imperial politics. But a greater quantity of private silver always flowed to Europe and the Philippines than that possessed by the Crown: of nearly 500 million *pesos fuertes* that arrived to Spain between 1503 and 1660, only 26.2 percent was from the royal treasury (Hamilton 34). Throughout the centuries, this rate diminished constantly: between 1503 and 1540 it was still 52.5 percent (Hamilton 34), between 1717 and 1738, 14 percent, and between 1747 and 1778, 9 percent (García-Baquero 231). Of the silver exported to the Philippines between 1591 and 1640, according to TePaske (444–45) 59.6 percent was privately held. It can be assumed that due to smuggling, private control of American metals was even greater than the stated rates. It was the Spanish-American demand for European and Asian products that unleashed and, above all, maintained these flows, and not necessarily the monarchs nor Chinese demand. These latter, nevertheless, ensured the establishment of a stable system of intercontinental exchange that, by absorbing great quantities of silver, prevented the devaluation of the price of metals and kept markets in the Americas from losing their purchasing power.

Mining Economy and the Globalization of America

In this last section, I want to outline how the mining industry affected the internal economic organization in the Americas. Silver mining was a complex enterprise. Silver was not found in a virgin state, but rather in underground veins linked to minerals that had to be brought to the surface in order to be refined. For this, workers, technologies, energy, supplies, a certain transportation infrastructure, capital and investments were needed. Given the size of this task, the organization of silver flows implied a deep restructuring of conquered spaces.

Mining had to be organized as an activity added onto the activities practiced in a world that had its own economic life, with different priorities than those of the Spaniards that were settling in the New World. To the extent required, the cooperation of the indigenous workers could only be achieved through extraeconomic forces. This implied a great challenge that differed according to the situation confronted, eliciting one type of strategy among Mesoamerican or Inca cultures on the one hand, and another among the hunter-gatherers of Northern Mexico on the other.[24] In the first context, the Spanish had to resolve two key problems: organizing the export economy and, at the same time, preventing the dissolution of indigenous economic systems whose production served the subsistence of the majority of the population; with its surpluses, as well, indigenous economic structures provisioned urban centers until growing businesses and, above all, the demographic catastrophe provoked change and Spanish land-ownership emerged, whose most famous form would be the *hacienda* (ranch). Before this occurred (in New Spain during the second half of the sixteenth century), a considerable part of the agrarian surplus and the indigenous labor force were designated for tribute and services to the *encomenderos* (Spanish conquerors rewarded with indigenous workers) (González Casasnovas 4–29). Afterwards, new forms of forced labor were introduced: in Mexico, the *repartimiento* (literally, "distribution"), and in the Andes, the *mita* (labor draft). These were controlled by the royal administration in order to guarantee the regular flow of labor to mining activity and to avoid the overexploitation of the communities of origin, affected ever more greatly by epidemics (it goes without saying that abuses abounded as well) (Cole).

Indigenous peoples were, in this way, the bases of colonial exploitation: with their economy they sustained the reproduction of labor that the Spaniards could use and provided urban mining consumption with agricultural products. In the case of Potosí, Enrique Tandeter has spoken of mining "subvention" by the indigenous economy. As such it was the indigenous subsistence production that covered the costs of the provisioning and partial maintenance of mining labor, costs that would have otherwise had to have been covered by salary increases or by shifting the buying price and diet of slaves. The fact that there was no shortage of indigenous laborers who settled into the colonial reorganization does not contradict such an interpretation. It owed in part to the fact that the Spanish needed allies and intermediaries within indigenous societies, most importantly the *caciques* and *kurakas* (indigenous nobles), and, in part, to indigenous strategies of adaptation and everyday resistance. As such, there was no lack of indigenous laborers who went to the mines voluntarily, seduced by the promise of income or to escape the growing pressures to which they were exposed in their communities (for example, by the threat of being recruited as forced laborers for the mines).

Voluntary relocation was a key phenomenon for the development of the mines in the north of New Spain, where the situation was radically different due to the lack of indigenous societies whose agrarian surplus and labor force could be exploited. As a remedy, the Spanish allowed an influx of migrants to relocate from the center of the country to the northern mines, where salaried work became dominant (Bakewell; del Río). In these regions, due to the lack of indigenous settlements, from the beginning the Spaniards organized agricultural and livestock production in order to support mining. One variant was the missionary regime that the Jesuits established in the northwest, where mission communities served to mirror the Mesoamerican communities and furnished the mines with farming products and labor (Hausberger, "Comunidad indígena").

It therefore seems reductionist to explain the colonial economy as a typical economy of the *ancien régime*, as fundamentally agrarian, subjected to the cycles of good and bad harvests and characterized by personal consumption and bartering, slow technological development, the strictness of highly-regulated markets, reduced labor freedoms, and the limited demographic dynamic.[25] According to this reasoning, mining would form only an enclave within an archaic agrarian world, without greater repercussions for the majority of the population. Such an interpretation does not fully capture the peculiarity of the Spanish American colonial economy; it rather seems to imply that it was not peculiar at all.

Carlos Sempat Assadourian's model of the "colonial economic system" (especially 22–55, 112–15, and 277–93) offers a broader and more flexible vision for taking into account all of the assorted forms that the colonial economy could take in space and time. Assadourian maintains that the colonial economy revolved around mining and its sweeping effects. As a result of sustained demand for foodstuffs, textiles, leather, coal, wood, salt, work animals, forage, etc., mining stimulated the internal development of the most diverse activities and it was, in this way, the motor of economic growth. Within the framework of this dynamic, for example, Andean space was organized into different production zones, in which each specialized in a few products demanded by the mines and was dynamically connected to others by mercantilization. Additionally, the height of mining stimulated European immigration, the forced immigration of Africans, and internal migration, especially of indigenous laborers from the countryside to new urban population centers. In this way, mining fostered urban growth and strengthened demand and consumption. Cities became the second pole of growth as, in quantitative terms, the urban market exceeded that of the mines. The argument of Assadourian that I have until now summarized, is reinforced by the fact that in Spanish America urban development only achieved considerable dimensions in zones supported—directly or indirectly—by the export economy. This is shown in the emergence of mining cities such as Potosí or Zacatecas, of administrative centers such as México or Lima, and of ports such as Veracruz, masterfully analyzed by Antonio García de León, on the one hand, and the long blockage of Buenos Aires before the leather boom, on the other. As such, elites located in the cities, in one way or another, depended upon the stimulus and dynamic pull of external sectors.

The ultimate aim of the colonial economic system was to channel silver production (or that of any other saleable product) to ports of export. This did not function as a simple exchange of imported products and metals. In short, in the mines a greater quantity of internally produced goods was consumed than imported goods. Following the argument of Assadourian, the importance of the sale of provisions to the mines was that by being paid for in metallic currency, such transactions gave way to internal circulation and the partial monetization of the economy. In chains of transactions, silver flowed from hand to hand until finally arriving to the strongboxes of the *Real Hacienda* and, above all, to the purses of the large merchants who then transferred this silver to exterior circuits. In this manner, the export sector was integrated into a complex system of internal exchanges that Assadourian has termed "the internal colonial market" ("el mercado interno colonial") (*passim*, especially 255–99). In this way, colonial society was subjected to the interests of the mining-merchant economy independently of the fact that the agrarian sector employed the majority of the population.

Obviously—and Assadourian has never proposed the opposite—the internal colonial market did not indicate the broader workings of a capitalist market. As such, it does not make much sense to identify pre-capitalist elements, such as forms of forced labor, widespread subsistence production, and non-monetary exchanges, to invalidate the model, as the colonial economy can only be understood as a whole within the colonial context (as, for the same reason, it is likewise untenable to consider the colonial economy as the roots of capitalism based on the presence of salaried workers and an agricultural market destined for the mining economy, as John Tutino has recently suggested). Referring to the "internal *colonial* market" describes how space was organized around mining through a regional specialization of production, without equating modes of production to labor relations. That is, forms of "natural" economy coexisted, as Ruggiero Romano (*Moneda*) has termed them, such as those that were based upon slave labor and others that widely turned to voluntary salaried labor. But these elements not only continued to work side by side, but also to interact complexly. Even within the largest mines a combination of different forms of labor existed (salaried free labor, slave labor, *mitayos*, for example). Those that performed salaried work, in many cases did so to complement agricultural production in their communities of origin; for them, a small income was sufficient, as they did not have to support themselves with their salaries. The subsistence economy did not operate in a separate sphere isolated from the merchant economy, but instead achieved a political, social, and economic function, above all to lower the costs of products destined to market, as the aforementioned study of Tandeter has shown.

I would like to conclude with one final observation: as the merchant elite's objective was to finance importation, they were interested in accumulating silver at the lowest possible cost and as quickly as possible. The Crown harbored the same priority in regard to the metals collected by its fiscal apparatus, that is, to quickly acquire silver for its primordially European political projects. There was little interest in keeping silver in the region to accelerate internal production. This is why large investments were not made outside of the most immediate production processes: the road system remained poorly developed, the mule remaining the most important form of transportation, salaries were low (albeit high for the few specialized laborers), and forms of coercion and manipulation of salaries were common. The priority assigned to lowering costs also explains the preservation of indigenous communities, whose own lands were allocated for their subsistence. All of this enabled lower production costs in American territories and assured the wellbeing of the merchant elite, although in the long term it hindered the invigoration of the economy's development. We are still a far ways from the forms of liberal capitalism and Fordism that seek to convert the very workers into consumers. Imports were not destined for mass consumption due to relatively expensive transportation costs but they guaranteed wide profit margins thanks to protectionist and monopolistic trade policies. On the other hand, perhaps we are very close to contemporary globalization, where transnational enterprises wager more all the time on the lowering of their (local) production costs in favor of their global sales, to the detriment of the consumptive power of internal markets.

Conclusion

In summary, I believe that it would be an error to understand globalizing processes as inherently limited to the nineteenth or twentieth centuries, especially in Latin America. This would mean diminishing the historicity of globalization which would mean losing sight of how the continent and its inhabitants, indigenous as well as those of European and African origin, were transformed by their insertion into a multitude of global relations after the conquest. Mining production was a key factor for this transformation and the establishment of a properly "colonial economic system" ("sistema económico colonial") (Assadourian). This establishes clear analogies with the "pre-modern world economy" ("economía mundial premoderna") that I outlined at the beginning of this essay, within whose range varied parts of different economic, political, and social forms of production were connected through commerce (and, I must repeat, by multiple other political, cultural, religious, etc. ties). That is, Asian manufacturing systems, miners in the Americas, and European merchants were firmly related, just as different Spanish American agricultural and manufacturing production zones were connected with mining centers and urban centers. It would be equally erroneous to place Latin America on the periphery of world history as mainstream research prefers to render the region, when, in many aspects, such as in supplying the globe with precious metals, the New World performed a key role during the onset of globalization.

NOTES

1. Compare this interpretation with Jones 4.
2. I've posed this question in greater detail in my article "Acercamientos a la historia global." The book edited by Margarete Grandner, Dietmar Rothermund and Wolfgang Schwentker also offers a broad discussion of this theme.
3. Here I continue the line of research presented, among others, in two volumes edited by Flynn and Giráldez, *Metals and Monies*, and by Flynn, Giráldez and von Glahn, *Global Connections and Monetary History*.
4. See, for example, the renowned book by Bayly, *The Birth of the Modern World*.
5. The height of New Spanish silver production in the eighteenth century was, according to Herbert S. Klein, "the big shift" in mining history.
6. See O'Rourke and Williamson, "When Did Globalization Begin?"; Flynn and Giráldez, "Path Dependence, Time Lags and the Birth of Globalisation"; O'Rourke and Williamson, "Once More: When Did Globalization Begin?"; Flynn and Giráldez, "Born Again: Globalization's Sixteenth Century Origins."

7. Regarding this concept, see the article by Boas, for example.
8. This has been the key argument of Kindleberger.
9. Blanchard (3–55) offers a highly useful, although a bit outdated summary of the global silver mining situation. Also see the work by Renate Pieper, "Las repercusiones."
10. See my book on the subject, *La Nueva España y sus metales preciosos* 13–20.
11. This is not the place to discuss the scope of the consequences and imbalances that this process brought with it. Regarding its origins in Spain, see Vilches.
12. Bayly's definition of Iberian expansion as "archaic" again serves as example.
13. Although one also observes a dialectic between homogenization and differentiation in the current phase of globalization, we are in the presence of a manifest process that, although not linear, demonstrates an accelerated assimilation of mature cultural and ethnic differences, not to mention production systems and financial systems.
14. The dependence of Spanish politics upon American silver is well summarized in the book by Stanley Stein and Barbara Stein, especially 40–56.
15. According to Hamilton, for example, in 1594, 95.6 percent of Spanish American exports were precious metals (33).
16. I would like to thank Renate Pieper for bringing this point to my attention. See, for example, her article "Innovaciones" 357.
17. All of this has been reconstructed in numerous case studies that are largely regional in scope. By way of illustration, in the case of New Spain I would like to mention José F. de la Peña's book and José Rojas Galván's recent article about Guadalajara. For the territory of the Audiencia of Charcas (including Potosí), see Ana María Presta's work.
18. On the subject, see the letters that geographer Paolo Toscanelli addressed to Columbus and that Las Casas later reproduced (64–67).
19. Janet Abu-Lughod and the series *East Asian Maritime History*, coordinated by Angela Schottenhammer, provide considerable information on the subject.
20. See Corcuera de Mancera and de Taylor's books on the subject (30–72).
21. Renate Pieper's 1984 article "Die Exportstruktur" provides one of the few studies of early imports to Spanish America. According to the author, in 1524 the 110-ton ship *La Trinidad* transported the following cargo to Santo Domingo: 7,560 liters of olive oil, 3,850 liters of wine, 276 kg of soap, 257 kg of wax, 36 meters of Rouen, 278 meters of velvet, 20 meters of *veinticuatreño* handkerchiefs, 159 shirts, 128 pairs of leather shoes, 8,072 iron nails, 600 horseshoes, and 45 reams of paper.
22. See the groundbreaking article by Russell R. Menard.
23. According to Hamilton, between 1521 and 1530, silver constituted three percent of precious metals exported to America, a level that would rise to 97 percent by the 1570s (40).
24. I have attempted to summarize each situation in my article "Comunidad indígena y minería en la época colonial."
25. Above all, see the two books by Ruggiero Romano, *Moneda* and *Mecanismo y elementos*.

WORKS CITED

Abu-Lughod, Janet L. *Before European Hegemony: The World System A. D. 1250–1350*. New York: Oxford University Press, 1989.
Assadourian, Carlos Sempat. *El sistema de la economía colonial: Mercado interno, regiones y espacio económico*. Lima: Instituto de Estudios Peruanos, 1982.
Atwell, William S. "Another Look at Silver Imports into China, ca. 1635–1644." *Journal of World History* 16 (2005): 467–89.
Bakewell, Peter. *Silver Mining and Society in Colonial Mexico. Zacatecas, 1546–1700*. Cambridge, UK: Cambridge University Press, 1971.
Barendse, R. J. *The Arabian Seas: The Indian Ocean World of the Seventeenth Century*. New York: M. E. Sharp, 2002.
Bayly, Christopher A. "From Archaic Globalization to International Networks, circa 1600–2000." *Globalization in World History*. Ed. A. G. Hopkins. New York: Norton, 2002. 45–72.
_____. *The Birth of the Modern World, 1780–1914: Global Connections and Comparisons*. Oxford: Blackwell Publishers, 2004.
Bechtloff, Dagmar. "Comercio, plata y prestigio social en el Madagascar precolonial: Introducción, divulgación y utilización de la moneda considerando especialmente el papel del peso mexicano." *Contribuciones desde Coatepec* 1 (2001): 72–88.
Bentley, Jerry H. "Cross-Cultural Interaction and Periodization in World History." *The American Historical Review* 101 (1996): 749–70.
Blanchard, Ian. *Russia's "Age of Silver": Precious-metal Production and Economic Growth in the Eighteenth Century*. London: Routledge, 1989.
Boas, Taylor C. "Conceptualizing Continuity and Change: The Composite-Standard Model of Path Dependence." *Journal of Theoretical Politics* 19 (2007): 33–54.
Cole, Jeffrey A. *The Potosi Mita, 1573–1700: Compulsory Indian Labor in the Andes*. Stanford: Stanford University Press, 1985.
Cross, Harry E. "South American Bullion Production and Export, 1550–1750." *Precious Metals in the Later Medieval and Early Modern World*. Ed. J. F. Richards. Durham: Carolina Academic Press, 1983. 397–423.
Corcuera de Mancera, Sonia. *El fraile, el indio y el pulque: Evangelización y embriaguez en la Nueva España (1523–1548)*. Mexico City: Fondo de Cultura Económica, 2010.
del Río, Ignacio. "Sobre la aparición y desarrollo del trabajo libre asalariado en el norte de Nueva España (siglos XVI y XVII)." *El trabajo y los trabajadores en la historia de México*. Eds. Elsa Cecilia Frost, Michael C. Meyer and Josefina Zoraida Velázquez. Mexico City: El Colegio de México, 1979. 92–111.
Flynn, Dennis O., and Arturo Giráldez. "Path Dependence, Time Lags and the Birth of Globalisation: A Critique of O'Rourke and Williamson." *European Review of Economic History* 8 (2004): 81–108.
_____. "Born Again: Globalization's Sixteenth Century Origins (Asian/Global Versus European Dynamics)." *Pacific Economic Review* 13 (2008): 359–87.

———, eds. *Metals and Monies in an Emerging Global Economy*. Aldershot: Variorum Publishing, 1997.

Flynn, Dennis O., Arturo Giráldez, and Richard von Glahn, eds. *Global Connections and Monetary History: 1470–1800*. Burlington: Ashgate, 2003.

Frank, André Gunder. *ReOrient: Global Economy in the Asian Age*. Berkeley: University of California Press, 1998.

García de León, Antonio. *Tierra adentro, mar en fuera: El puerto de Veracruz y su litoral a Sotavento, 1519–1821*. Mexico City: Fondo de Cultura Económica, 2011.

García-Baquero González, Antonio. *La carrera de Indias: Suma de la contratación y océano de negocios*. Sevilla: Algaido/Expo92, 1992.

González Casasnovas, Ignacio. *Las dudas de la corona: La política de repartimientos para la minería de Potosí (1680–1732)*. Madrid: Consejo Superior de Investigaciones Científicas, 2000.

Grandner, Margarete, Dietmar Rothermund, and Wolfgang Schwentker, eds. *Globalisierung und Globalgeschichte*. Viena: Mandelbaum, 2005.

Gruzinski, Serge. *Les quatre parties du monde: Histoire d'une mondialisation*. Paris: Editions de La Martinière, 2004.

Hamilton, Earl J. *American Treasure and the Price Revolution in Spain 1500–1650*. Cambridge, Mass: Harvard University Press, 1934.

Hausberger, Bernd. "Comunidad indígena y minería en la época colonial: El Alto Perú y el noroeste de México en comparación." *Ibero-Amerikanisches Archiv* 23 (1997): 263–312.

———. *La Nueva España y sus metales preciosos: La industria minera colonial a través de los "libros de cargo y data" de la Real Hacienda, 1761–1767*. Frankfurt a. M.: Vervuert, 1997.

———. "El universalismo científico del barón Ignaz von Born y transferencia de tecnología minera entre Hispanoamérica y Alemania a finales del siglo XVIII." *Historia Mexicana* 59 (2009): 605–68.

———. "Acercamientos a la historia global." *Entre Espacios. Movimientos, actores y representaciones de la globalización*. Eds. Carlos Alba et al. Berlin: edition tranvía/Verlag Walter Frey, 2013. 83–98.

Hirschmann, Albert O. "A Generalized Linkage Approach to Development with Special Reference to Staples." *Economic Development and Cultural Change* 25, Supl.: *Essays on Economic Development and Cultural Change in Honor of Bert F. Hoselitz*. Ed. Manning Nash. Chicago: University of Chicago Press, 1977. 68–98.

Hopkins, A.G., ed. *Globalization in World History*. New York: Norton, 2002.

Irigoin, Alejandra. "The End of a Silver Era: The Consequences of the Breakdown of the Spanish Peso Standard in China and the United States, 1780s–1850s." *Journal of World History* 20 (2009): 207–43.

Jones, Andrew. *Globalization: Key Thinkers*. Cambridge, UK: Polity, 2010.

Kamen, Henry. *Empire: How Spain Became a World Power, 1492–1763*. New York: Harper Collins, 2004.

Kindleberger, Charles P. *Spenders and Hoarders: The World Distribution of Spanish American Silver, 1550–1750*. Singapore: Institute of South East Asian Studies, 1989.

Klein, Herbert S. "The Great Shift: The Rise of Mexico and the Decline of Peru in the

Spanish American Colonial Empire, 1680–1809." *Revista de Historia Económica* 13 (1995): 35–61.
Kumar, Krishan. "Nation-states as Empires, Empires as Nation-states: Two Principles, One Practice?" *Theory and Society* 39 (2010): 119–43.
Lang, Mervyn F. *El monopolio estatal del mercurio en el México colonial (1550–1710).* Mexico City: Fondo de Cultura Económica, 1977.
Las Casas, Bartolomé de. *Historia de las Indias.* Vol. 1. Ed. André Saint-Lu. Caracas: Biblioteca Ayacucho, 1986.
Machuca, Paulina. "De porcelanas chinas y otros menesteres, Cultura material de orígen asiático en Colima, siglos XVI–XVII." *Relaciones* 131 (2012): 77–134.
Manning, Patrick. "The Problem of Interactions in World History." *The American Historical Review* 101 (1996): 771–82.
Marichal, Carlos. "The Spanish-American Silver Peso: Export Commodity and Global Money of the Ancien Regime, 1550–1800." *From Silver to Cocaine: Latin American Commodity Chains and the Building of the World Economy, 1500–2000.* Eds. Steven Topik, Carlos Marichal and Zephyr Frank. Durham: Duke University Press, 2006. 25–52.
Matthee, Rudi. "Mint Consolidation and the Worsening of the Late Safavid Coinage: The Mint of Huwayza." *JESHO* 44/4 (2001): 505–39.
Menard, Russell R. "Transport Costs and Long-range Trade, 1300–1800: Was There a European 'Transport Revolution' in the Early Modern Era?" *The Political Economy of Merchant Empires: State Power and World Trade, 1350–1750.* Ed. James D. Tracy. Cambridge, UK: Cambridge University Press, 1991. 228–76.
Morineau, Michel. *Incroyables gazettes et fabuleux métaux: Les retours des trésors américains d'après les gazettes hollandaises (XVIe–XVIIIe siècles).* Paris: Editions de la Maison des Sciences de l'Homme, 1985.
O'Brien, Patrick. "Historiographical Traditions and Modern Imperatives for the Restoration of Global History." *Journal of Global History* 1 (2006): 3–39.
O'Gorman, Edmundo. *La invención de América: El universalismo de la cultura de Occidente.* Mexico City: Fondo de Cultura Económica, 1958.
O'Rourke, Kevin, and Jeffrey G. Williamson. "When Did Globalization Begin?" *European Review of Economic History* 6 (2002): 23–50.
———. "Once More: When Did Globalization Begin?" *European Review of Economic History* 8 (2004): 109–77.
Osterhammel, Jürgen. *Die Verwandlung der Welt: Eine Geschichte des 19. Jahrhunderts.* München: C. H. Beck, 2009.
Peña, José F. de la. *Oligarquía y propiedad en la Nueva España.* Mexico City: Fondo de Cultura Económica, 1983.
Pieper, Renate. "Die Exportstruktur des spanischen Amerikahandels." *Scripta mercaturae* 18 (1984): 61–95.
———. "Innovaciones tecnológicas y problemas del medio ambiente en la minería novohispana." *IX Congreso Internacional de Historia de América, AHILA, Actas.* Sevilla: AHILA, 1992: 353–68.

———. "Las repercusiones de los metales preciosos americanos en Europa, siglos XVI y XVIII." *Oro y plata en los inicios de la economía global: De las minas a la moneda.* Eds. Bernd Hausberger and Antonio Ibarra. Mexico City: El Colegio de México, 2014. 273–98.

Pomeranz, Kenneth. *The Great Divergence: China, Europe, and the Making of the Modern World Economy.* Princeton: Princeton University Press, 2000.

Presta, Ana María. *Encomienda, familia y negocios en Charcas colonial (Bolivia): Los encomenderos de La Plata, 1550–1600.* Lima: Instituto de Estudios Peruanos, 2000.

Rojas Galván, José. "Las élites políticas y militares y su correlación con la conformación regional de la Nueva Galicia (México), 1530–1792." *HiSTOReLo: Revista de Historia Regional y Local* 4 (2012): 110–43.

Romano, Ruggiero. *Moneda, seudomonedas y circulación monetaria en la economía de México.* Mexico City: Fondo de Cultura Económica, 1998.

———. *Mecanismo y elementos del sistema económico colonial americano, Siglos XVI–XVIII.* Mexico City: Fondo de Cultura Económica, 2004.

Kangying, Li. *The Ming Maritime Trade Policy in Transition, 1368 to 1567.* East Asian Maritime History 8. Ed. Angela Schottenhammer. Wiesbaden: Harrassowitz, 2010.

Stein, Stanley J., and Barbara H. Stein. *Silver, Trade, and War: Spain and America in the Making of Early Modern Europe.* Baltimore: John Hopkins University Press, 2000.

Tandeter, Enrique. "Forced and Free Labour in Late Colonial Potosí." *Past & Present* 93 (1982): 98–136.

Taylor, William B. *Drinking, Homicide, and Rebellion in Colonial Mexican Villages.* Stanford: Stanford University Press, 1979.

TePaske, John J. "New World Silver, Castile and the Far East." *Precious Metals in the Later Medieval and Early Modern World.* Ed. J. F. Richards. Durham: Carolina Academic Press, 1982. 425–45.

TePaske, John J., and Herbert S. Klein. *The Royal Treasuries of the Spanish Empire in America.* 3 vols. Durham: Duke University Press, 1982.

———. *Ingresos y egresos de la Real Hacienda de Nueva España.* 2 vols. Mexico City: Instituto Nacional de Antropología e Historia, 1986–1988.

Tracy, James D., ed. *The Rise of Merchant Empires: Long Distance Trade in the Early Modern World 1350–1750.* Cambridge, UK: Cambridge University Press, 1990.

———., ed. *The Political Economy of Merchant Empires: State Power and World Trade, 1350–1750.* Cambridge, UK: Cambridge University Press, 1991.

Tutino, John. *Making a New World: Founding Capitalism in the Bajío and Spanish North America.* Durham: Duke University Press, 2011.

Varón Gabai, Rafael, and Auke Pieter Jacobs. "Peruvian Wealth and Spanish Investments: The Pizarro Family during the Sixteenth Century." *The Hispanic American Historical Review* 67 (1987): 657–95.

Vilches, Elvira. *New World Gold: Cultural Anxiety and Monetary Disorder in Early Modern Spain.* Chicago: University of Chicago Press, 2010.

Vollmer, Günter. "Über den Wechselkurs von Cacaobohnen und den Preis der Schokolade: Ein mexikanisches Problem." *Dinero y negocios en la historia de América*

Latina / Geld und Geschäft in der Geschichte Lateinamerikas. Eds. Nikolaus Böttcher and Bernd Hausberger. Frankfurt a. M.: Vervuert, 2000. 59–84.

von Glahn, Richard. "Myth and Reality of China's Seventeenth-Century Crisis." *Journal of Economic History* 56/2 (1996): 429–54.

Yang, Bin. "The Rise and Fall of Cowrie Shells: The Asian Story." *Journal of World History* 22 (2011): 1–25.

CHAPTER TWO

A New Moses

Vasco de Quiroga's Hospitals and the Transformation of "Indians" from "Bárbaros" to "Pobres"[1]

Ivonne del Valle

> One thus gets an impression that civilization is something which was imposed on a resisting majority by a minority which understood how to obtain possession of the means to power and coercion.
> SIGMUND FREUD, *The Future of an Illusion* (7)

In response to a recently-issued royal order that authorized, once again, the enslavement of "Indians" captured in "just war," Vasco de Quiroga, lawyer-oídor of the Second Audiencia of Mexico, writes in 1535 his *Información en derecho* [Report of law], a document that demonstrates the fragility of the binary civilization/barbarism that presumably differentiated Spaniards from indigenous people.[2] In spite of his certainty as to the superiority of Spanish culture and customs, in the many passages in which the excesses of the conquest are manifest, Quiroga suggests that the colonizing project was a new and extended (both spatially and as to its extractive power) system of exploitation that far surpassed any that might have existed among the indigenous groups. Unwittingly, his text recreates the dilemma of Spanish colonization that wavered between apparently incompatible projects: on the one hand, reducing the indigenous population to a mere instrument of labor (slaves); while on the other, constructing them as subjects shaped by erroneous cultures and beliefs requiring elimination and replacement.[3]

Quiroga's ambivalence in *Información*, and the indirect dialogue he maintains with other humanists and jurists of the first half of the sixteenth century, takes us to the very heart of the contradiction, and a decisive one it is: how the Christian West understood itself as a civilizing project. This core self-understanding consisted of the myth of a *civilization* born with monotheism and the abandonment of paganism and idolatry, elements of a rejected—perhaps even already forgotten—past but which, at the moment of the encounter with societies that followed different models of civilization, becomes reactivated and *globalized* in the form of a presumed "natural law" applicable to all human groups. Indeed, if conquest is what first allowed for the creation of very real global economic networks—those of production and labor (silver, slavery, etc.), but also legal and administrative (international law, the Inquisition, etc.)—the forced entrance of millions of people into monotheism shaped a universal idea of what civilization ought to be. There is no economic and cultural globalization without first, violence, and second, the forced displacement of polytheism and what it implied. That is, alongside substantial material developments—such as the staggering death toll of the conquest, or the destruction of indigenous cities and the erection of Spanish ones—the expansion of Christianity brought about other abstract, but equally dramatic, transformations.

In the context of the dual failure of Spanish colonization—that of the continuation of indigenous customs so alien to so-called natural law, and the unstoppable violence of extraction—the founding of "hospitals" that partially followed Thomas More's utopian designs arises as a potential solution for Quiroga. Of these, Quiroga founded two, both named Santa Fé—one in central Mexico, and another one (Santa Fé de la Laguna) close to Pátzcuaro, Michoacán.[4] There, the indigenous population could be protected from the abuse that had driven him to write *Información*, while at the same time they could be civilized and transformed into a labor force.

Nevertheless, Quiroga's solution—the hospitals—are not presented as such. There is a disconnect between *Información*, the founding of hospitals, and *Ordenanzas* (1555–1565) [*Ordinances*], the document he would leave as his legacy for the correct management of the hospitals.[5] Writing these two texts as if they were unrelated permitted Quiroga to avoid the economic function the hospitals would have, which he foregrounds in *Información* by exposing a problem but not offering a solution: the need to exploit the native population in a more humane way.

Another trait that further complicates the reading of his work is the way Quiroga's writing maintains the tension between a natural law of divine origin, such as that put forward by thinkers like Ginés de Sepúlveda (all order comes from God), and a secularized natural law similar to that posited by Francisco de Vitoria (although order comes from God, there is a positive law that determines the relations between kingdoms and persons). The *Ordenanzas* that he writes so that the residents of the hospital might become transformed (civilized) and come to govern themselves and the institution make Quiroga a patriarch of sorts of a new and different people, the "poor," who were defined by the rules he bequeathed to them. The current-day omnipresence of the name and image of the man who was also the first bishop of Michoacán (and particularly in the P'urhépecha region of the state) confirm his Moses-like, foundational role: there was one Michoacán before Quiroga, and another that arose afterwards and whose continuity and legacy are suggested in the urban configuration and the nomenclature of several of the state's villages and cities.

Through an analysis of *Información* and *Ordenanzas*, texts written by Quiroga in response to the extreme exploitation of the "Indians," I aim to show two things in this essay: on the one hand, the function that the colonies and their inhabitants served in early globalization; and, on the other, the paradoxes inherent in the civilizing and economic processes that were drawing far-flung portions of the world together. Although Quiroga's work is limited in scope and is circumscribed to New Spain, and more particularly to the region of Michoacán, his ideas have global implications in at least two senses. First, because in many of its variants, Spanish colonization was based on a civilizing mission—on the necessity of transforming the indigenous communities' customs in the spheres of religion, civic life, and everyday existence. That is to say, beginning with the Spanish colonization of the Americas, a certain idea of civilization is affirmed as the only, *universal* option, as an ideal of how to live in society.[6] Secondly, Quiroga's texts demonstrate that for the "Indians," this new civilization also represented their consignment to a particular *labor and economic category*. If in the twentieth century, Immanuel Wallerstein assures us that the economic world system in which we still find ourselves came into being in the sixteenth century, when various territories were articulated, not through unitary political or cultural systems, but rather through the division of labor, then Quiroga in the sixteenth century shows us how, in the case of the "Indians," culture and division of labor are inseparably intertwined—indeed, they are coextensive (Wallerstein 23). The Indian hospitals created by him to resolve the problems laid out in *Información* implied at one and the same time a cultural transformation (from "Indians" to merely "the poor") and a division of labor (they would be the laborers who would sustain the Spanish colonial world). In this fashion, Quiroga offers a commentary on Freud's insight as expressed in the epigraph to the present essay: in the colonies, to civilize and to exploit were essentially the same thing. Of course, the blame for this confluence cannot fairly be laid at Quiroga's doorstep. Rather, it's a matter of considering, with Fernando Gómez, how narrow was the space for maneuver afforded to projects that attempted to protect "Indians," given the imperative conditions of the new, colonial order.[7]

Nueva Galicia and Michoacán in the Sixteenth Century

Información is an early sixteenth-century text that offers solutions to the grave situation of the "Indians" in New Spain, who, as Quiroga states again and again, were in danger of disappearing altogether if their treatment continued as it had been for the last decade. In this already unacceptable situation, new legislation encouraged the propagation of slaveholding practices that, according to the lawyer, threatened the native population with further, irremediable harm: "Ha de ser el fin y el cabo, y destruición también de toda esta tierra, como lo fue en las Islas e Tierra Firme, si Dios no lo remedia" (77–78) (It must prove the final end, and the destruction too of this whole land, just as it did in the Islands and on Tierra Firme, if God does not provide a remedy). In order to save the "Indians" from disappearing "en breve" [in short order], as he feared, and as the new royal orders made inevitable, Quiroga proposes measures that, while not dispensing with exploitation, would moderate it (Gómez; Bentancor).

Información has two main components: a central one consisting of a mixture of juridical argument and historical investigation that attempts to demonstrate the inexistence of slavery among the different indigenous groups, and to reveal the illegality of the Spanish practice of capturing and enslaving "Indians." The second component is Quiroga's proposal: the creation of a mixed system of civic life adequate to the predispositions of each group (the Spanish order, the order for the indigenous people) that would protect the "Indians," civilize them, and put them to work. I shall examine, in this section, what, according to Quiroga, were the consequences of the Spanish practices of conquest, and in the following section, the manner in which the hospital becomes a solution.

The legal argument against the enslavement of "Indians" is built on a demonstration of the inadequacy of this type of labor extraction for people who had not known it previously and for whom, for that very reason, it was onerous in the extreme: "Esta manera y género de esclavitud que nosotros tenemos, que pierden la libertad e ingenuidad, ciudad y familia, que es la máxima civil disminución . . . para ser verdaderos esclavos entre nosotros, que son reputados nada . . . yo entre éstos no la veo" (127) (This manner and type of slavery that we have, where they lose their liberty, innocence, city, and family, which is the greatest possible civic diminution . . . in order to be true slaves among us, who are held to be nothing . . . among these people, I simply do not see it). Quite to the contrary, in Quiroga's view, what the indigenous people had were innocuous forms of service that deprived them of neither liberty nor rights. Indigenous people who before and after the arrival of the Spaniards performed services for other indigenous persons (that is, those who, according to the Spaniards, were slaves) "retienen todo: libertad, familia y ciudad o lugar, y que no mudan estado ni condición, y que no pierden cosas de él . . . que es señal e indicio grande que no son verdaderos esclavos, porque si lo fuesen, tendrían las condiciones dellos" (127) (retain everything: liberty, family and city and place, and suffer no change in state nor condition, and that lose no aspect of it . . . which is an important sign and indicator that they were not truly slaves, for if they had been such, they would have experienced the corresponding conditions).

Indeed, in the indigenous languages there was no word to designate that zone of absolute subjugation and insignificance (to be "reputados nada" [held as nothing]) to which the Spanish theory and practice of slavery ultimately led: a person bereft of his/her very personhood. Thus, the early modern Spanish system of slavery could find no justification in the indigenous past, nor could it consider itself a continuation of indigenous practices. While among indigenous groups so-called "slavery" was nothing but a form of perpetual rental of labor power that allowed the individual to retain all of his or her rights, the Spanish system implied an absolute emptying—of rights, needs, and of personal, family, and civic relationships—that therefore meant an absolute transformation: entry into a zone of annihilation as subjects (they were considered nothing, without hometown, friends, kin) that required their compliance with whatever might be demanded of them, even if it meant their physical destruction (128). In dealing with such slaves, one could "sacar sangre y raer hasta lo vivo" [squeeze the blood from them and scrape them to the bone]" and suffer no consequences, Quiroga denounces (85).

If Quiroga's point against the enslavement of indigenous people is a comparative analysis of each group's historical characteristics and cultural practices, the second argument is legal in nature: it lays bare the stratagems of the conquistadors, who drew on every resource at their disposal to facilitate invocation of the notion of "just war," which would thus enable them to freely enslave "Indians" captured in the course of same. According to Quiroga, whether by falsifying or by inciting wars against indigenous groups, the Spaniards had found that "just war" provided the means to obtain easy riches:

> Y esto es lo que quieren y buscan los españoles, porque resistan o huyan de miedo y no vengan de paz [los indios]; porque si no resistiesen y luego viniesen, paréceles que se les pierde su derecho, trabajo e interese y que decaen de su intento que es poblar, no la tierra, sino las minas de estos tales (119)
>
> *And this is what the Spaniards desire and seek, that they (the "Indians") should resist, or flee in fear, or come other than in peace; for if they shall fail to resist, and shall come forward, it seems to them (the Spaniards) that they lose their right, work, and interest,*

and that they fail in their attempt which is to populate not the land, but rather the mines with them.

On this last point, the historical record supports the preoccupation of Quiroga who, before marching to Michoacán as the first bishop of that province, had witnessed from Mexico City the effects of Nuño de Guzmán's conquest of New Galicia and Michoacán. It was none other than Quiroga who, in his position as judge of the Second Audiencia, sentenced Nuño de Guzmán to prison for his treatment of the indigenous people. As Quiroga says, referring to the problem of the unjustified and wholesale enslavement carried out in western Mexico:

> han hecho y hacen esclavos hasta las mujeres con hijos de teta de tres o cuatro meses a los pechos de las madres, y herrados todos con el yerro que dicen del Rey, casi tan grande como los carrillos de los niños y los traen a vender a esta ciudad, *en los ojos de esta Audiencia*, como hatos de ovejas, a mi ver y creer, por lo que dello sé, inocentísimos . . . la cual crueldad por mandado de esta Audiencia fuimos *ayer* a ver un oidor e yo con escribano; y vimos todo esto y más, que algunos estaban enfermos y enfermas, casi que para expirar. Escriben de allá que se asuela la tierra (182, emphasis added)

> *they have enslaved and continue to enslave even women with nursing babies of three and four months of age at their mothers' breasts, and have branded everyone with the iron brand which they call of the King, almost as large as a child's cheeks, and they bring them to this city for sale under the very noses of this Audiencia, like flocks of sheep, as I see and believe it, based on what I know, utterly innocent . . . which cruelty I went yesterday with a judge, in the company of a notary, to witness, by order of this Audiencia; and we saw all of this and more, that some were ill, male and female, and almost at death's door. They write from there that they are laying waste to the land.*

As the passage indicates, what was occurring in Michoacán and Nueva Galicia could be read in the physical condition, and in the very faces of the "flocks" of indigenous people presented ironically and constantly before the Audiencia, the very site that presumably was to guarantee the legality of the conquest. As Quiroga insists, though, the deeds of a handful of men could thwart not only any aspiration to legality, but the very viability of the whole undertaking:

> Esto digo, porque al cabo por estas inadvertencias y malicias e inhumanidades, esto de esta tierra temo se ha de acabar todo, que no nos ha de quedar sino el cargo que no tiene descargo, ni restitución ante Dios (83)

I say this because, in the end, by reason of these blunders and evils and inhumanities, I fear that our entire venture in this land will come to an end, with nothing remaining to us but a debt for which there is no possible penance or restitution before God.

In the face of this, there was nothing to do but intervene:

Y si la verdad se ha de decir, necesario es que así se diga; que untar el casco y quebrar el ojo, o colorar y disimular lo malo y callar la verdad, yo no sé si es de prudentes y discretos, pero cierto sé que no es de mi condición (83)

And if the truth be said, it must be said in this way: for to beat about the bush or turn a blind eye, to gild evil or cover it with a fig leaf—I do not know if such is the way of prudence or discretion, but I can say for certain that it is not my custom.

Indeed, the actions of Nuño de Guzmán and his band damaged western Mexico so deeply and for so long that the consequences of his slaving expeditions were still felt as late as the mid-seventeenth century, according to chronicles complaining about a desolate, unpopulated area.⁸ The very early "Relación de ceremonias y ritos y población y gobernación de los indios de la provincia de Mechoacán" [Account of Indian ceremonies, rites, population and government in the province of Michoacán], quite succinct on the whole, goes on at length in describing Nuño de Guzmán's imprisonment of the *cazonci* (or *irecha*, in P'urhépecha), the local chief, as if to say that the arbitrariness and violence visited upon Tangoaxan II and his circle accounted for the exodus of a population stunned by the violence they had just witnessed.⁹ This text and many other similar ones coincide with Quiroga's reading of the region's condition whose inhabitants were fleeing en masse in the face of the conquest. According to the "Relación," the first exoduses took place when, at the orders of Nuño de Guzmán, the *cazonci* has his people called and they begin to be captured. The indigenous perception of the conquest is well conveyed by the text, which states: "empezaron a tomar los españoles los ocho mil hombres que habían traído, y a repartirlos entre sí, quien más podía, sin contarlos" ("Relación" 26) (the Spaniards began to take the eight thousand men that had been brought (there) and to divide them up amongst themselves, every man for himself, taking as many as he could, without counting them). The second mass dispersion took place when, after several days of public torture, Tangoaxan II finally dies. Then, the text relates, "echó a huir la gente por su muerte de miedo" ("Relación" 28) (the people began to flee when he died, frightened).

In this, as in many other cases, the actions of the Spanish soldiers produced not the effects sought by the intellectual apologists for the enterprise—the civilizing and evangelizing of the natives—, but rather the very opposite: the abandonment of the old indigenous order, with no possibility of its replacement by a new one. This is the paradox faced by Quiroga: having to recognize that the conquest meant not the end of (a presumptive) barbarism but rather its extension and transformation into what would in fact constitute new forms of barbarism. In this sense, and in view of the fact that a similar contradictory situation occurred in numerous territories during the sixteenth century (throughout the Americas as well as southwest Africa undergoing military conquest by the Spanish and the Portuguese), we can fairly say that wholesale chaos and the creation of vast populations dispossessed of *all rights* (they were reduced to "nothing") marked one of the earliest forms of globalization (and perhaps one of the most recent as well).

Approaching Sepúlveda's view of natural law, and despite recognizing elsewhere that the indigenous people had governing authorities and institutions, Quiroga says that the indigenous people's way of life justified the necessity of instructing them in Christian civilization:

> Pues que basta vivir en notoria ofensa de Dios su Criador, y en culto de muchos y diversos dioses, y *contra ley natural* y en tiranía de sí mismos, como gente bárbara y cruel, y en ignorancia de las cosas y del buen vivir político, y sin ley ni rey como son estos naturales, que además y allende de su infidelidad, eran entre sí mismos crueles, bárbaros y feroces, y aún son bárbaras naciones y sus principales tiranos contra los menos y maceoales que poco pueden y tienen opresos, sin tener entre sí policía alguna que fuese libre y buena como debe tener todo hombre razonablemente humano (93, emphasis added)

> *For it is enough to live in manifest offense against God their Creator, and in worship of many and varying gods, and counter to natural law and in tyranny over themselves, as barbarous and cruel people, and in ignorance of the things that conform to good political order, and without law nor king as these natives are, who, besides and beyond their being infidels, they were among one another cruel, barbarous, and fierce, and they remain barbarous nations and their principals, tyrants over the most wretched of them and the commoners (maceoales) who have little power and whom they maintain in oppression, and without having among them any free and just police such as any reasonably humane man should possess.*

If polytheism and the tyranny of their institutions over the many in favor of a few "principal tyrants" demonstrated that indigenous religion and government were entirely barbarous, the indigenous civilization could not change unless they were given "otro mejor estado, orden y manera que al presente tienen" (141) (another and better state, order, and way than those which they have at present). Nevertheless, as I have already pointed out, Quiroga indirectly recognizes that the conduct of the Spaniards prevented the attainment of the minimal conditions for the existence of civilization, that is, indigenous settlement in a town or at least their concentration in a single place. If civic order (*policía*) was only possible among persons who inhabited the same delimited space, and was unattainable for those who "estovieren derramados por los campos, que son casi todos, salvo éstos desta comarca en derredor de México" (85) (were scattered across the countryside, which was almost everyone, save those in this district around Mexico), this situation would not change unless the Spanish tactics that provoked indigenous flight were altered.[10]

In spite of the fact that he considered them still "barbarians," the gaps Quiroga constructs in the historical record allow him to forget, or put aside, the fact that in the region of Michoacán and Nueva Galicia, the indigenous people had generally lived settled lives, gathered in defined villages, and that the Spaniards had obliged them to abandon those settlements haphazardly. This was the heart of the dilemma: from the conquest forward, the options were the barbarism of settled populations who supposedly violated all of the principles of natural law, on the one hand, and the barbarism of groups forced to abandon *all* civic existence on account of the violence used to deliver them into the new and genuine "civilization," on the other.[11]

In the sixteenth and seventeenth centuries, the exodus of various indigenous groups from their territories furnishes an initial response to the uncertainty over the methods and goals of the establishment of Christian-Western civilization in the territory of the Americas. Sigmund Freud, in his ambivalent defense of civilization in which, as the epigraph shows, he also recognized a potentially coercive system of exploitation, concedes that those "discontented" with it might perhaps ask themselves if its achievements were worth defending (7).[12] In the cases presented here, the answer is eloquent. If the abandonment of all that was known and familiar was necessary, perhaps the conquest amounted to the replacement of one system of exploitation by another that proved far worse. As Quiroga allowed, even though Moctezuma had not been but a tyrant, the new order brought with it "tantos Motezumas que mantener" (102) (so many Moctezumas to be supported) that the burden was intolerable; and if previously native peoples had been "en una tiranía ... opresos" (123) (oppressed ... under a tyranny), after the arrival of the Spaniards "están en ciento" (123) (they suffer under a hundred). This, then, was the situation that had to be ameliorated.

Hospitals: The Transformation of Barbarism into Poverty

Quiroga's research into the inexistence of slavery among indigenous groups notwithstanding, his interest was neither ethnographic nor historical. Unlike Bernardino de Sahagún, whose lengthy inquiry into the history, knowledge, and customs of the Nahuas had led him to conclude that conquest and colonization had put an end to the grandeur of pre-Hispanic culture and devastated its inhabitants—to whom "ninguna apariencia les quedó de lo que eran antes" (Sahagún 8) (nothing remained of what they had once been)—for Quiroga this contrast between before and after passed without notice, or was cast aside. Although he had documented the relatively benign nature of their system, wrongly termed "slavery" by the Spaniards, Quiroga considered every indigenous institution to be tyrannical. The barbarism of their prior institutions required no explanation, nor did it demand to be understood in all its particulars; there was no need to take into account the impact that war and the slaving expeditions might have wrought either on the native population, or on their culture more broadly. What was necessary, quite apart from any ethnographic investigation, was to protect the indigenous people from the effects of Spanish violence and from themselves, once the Spaniards had overthrown the barbaric order of the old indigenous lords. To that end, Quiroga founded hospitals, and in order to secure the continuity of his legacy, he later writes *Ordenanzas*, a series of regulations for the administration of these institutions dedicated to the "hospitalidad y remedio" (hospitality and remedy) of these poor and needy "Indians" (*Ordenanzas* 268; see also Verástique 131).

Oddly, the *Ordenanzas* were directed not toward other Spaniards—whether civil authorities, or religious—but rather to the indigenous people themselves, by which means Quiroga intended to ensure that the order and administration of what on another occasion he would call the "Republic of the hospital" should fall to none other than their own residents (*Ordenanzas* 279). I know of no other similar document in the entire colonial corpus. It is not merely a matter of Quiroga having written the text with the indigenous population's welfare in mind, but, beyond that, his taking it upon himself to bequeath to them a new dispensation, "new tablets" which would guarantee them self-sufficiency and self-rule. *Ordenanzas* may be seen, from this perspective, as a new law and Quiroga as a sort of new Moses who (thus) vouchsafed the civilization and protection of the indigenous people. Later I shall take up the implications of reading Quiroga as a modern Moses, whose tablets placed the indigenous people "out of danger," while at the same time freeing them from their traditional "idleness." That is to say: the new law civilized them and transformed them into productive beings (*Ordenanzas* 269).

The "republic of the hospital" represents the ideal remedy for the numerous problems documented in *Información*: it safeguarded the native population from the dangers of slave raiding and it restored to them the potential for a congregation—for building, within what might be thought of as an island, not a city, but an institution that might serve as an indispensable center for *a particular form* of civilization. In the hospital, they would be safe, too, from themselves: from the possible contamination of the example of the Spaniards, and from the gradual change of aspects of their character worth preserving, "fuera del peligro de las tres bestias que todo en este mundo lo destruyen, y corrompen, que son *soberbia, codicia y ambición*, de que os habeis, y os desamos mucho guardar y apartar, quitándoos lo malo, y dexándoos lo bueno de vuestras costumbres, manera y condición" (*Ordenanzas* 269, emphasis in original) (away from the danger posed by those three beasts that destroy and corrupt everything in this world, namely, *pride, greed, and ambition*, from which you ought to be, and which we desire that you be, protected and separated, taking from you all the evil, and leaving you all the good in your customs, ways, and condition).

This republic offered protection against the evils that, according to Quiroga, plagued the Spaniards, who had caused the very crisis in which he was intervening "la codicia desenfrenada o soberbia grande nuestra" (120) (our unrestrained greed or overweening arrogance) while at the same the hospital turned them into "Indians" who were *useful* to those afflicted with those ills.[13] As Gómez has pointed out, Quiroga's work represents a sort of protocapitalism that sought to convert the "Indians" into simple workers (Gómez 121–23). The combined logic of *Información* and *Ordenanzas* is, as Gómez has noted, an economic one.[14] This logic allowed the "Indians" to be brought back, getting them down from the "monte" [hills] and taking their place in the colonial system of production by means of a complex series of operations (a complexity which Quiroga fails to recognize) in which the new civilizing order understood them as a particular group solely according to their place in the economic system, and not through their history or their culture.

Given that neither the excesses of the recent history revealed by Quiroga in his *Información*, nor the desire to continue practicing their pre-contact culture appear to affect or modify the viability of the "hospital republic," there are grounds to speculate that, as the lawyer saw them, not only the native people's long- and short-term historical memory, but also even their capacity to feel aggrieved, must have been weak. Unlike Sahagún, Quiroga believes that somehow the indigenous people will remain unaffected by the situation. As if there were something in their makeup that rendered unnecessary any consideration of their possible reticence, fear, or simple rejection of the protection offered them, the "Indians" would enter the hospital free of the present and of the past. There, they would conserve from their pre-contact culture only their social position—the fact of belonging to the lower, tribute-paying classes. For this reason, it is no accident that Quiroga refers to them by the Nahuatl world *macehual* ("pobre gente maceoal" [poor maceoal people]), by which one named the common people, the peasants, defined in the Nahua world in contradistinction to the lords, the *pilli* (97). The "Indians" of the hospital were nothing more than the exploited of the old order—the barbarian order, because of its tyrannical nature, an order in which they had lived under the oppression of lords like Moctezuma.

In this way, he who the day before had been a barbarian on account of his culture, or on account of having abandoned urban environs and its civic order in the face of the slaving expeditions, entered the hospital and was transformed simply into a poor man. This transformation of barbarism (a specific indigenous civilization or culture, or its absence—living in the hills) into an economic category (poverty), took place without major stumbling blocks. The "Indians" had entered the hospital as *macehuales*, and would continue to exist there in the same category—although henceforth always in Spanish, as "indios pobres, y huérfanos, pupilos, y viudas, y miserables personas" (*Ordenanzas* 268) (poor Indians, orphans, wards, widows, and wretched persons). Economic determinism is so powerful that, on occasion, "Indians" even cease to be such, becoming simply "the poor" or "poor men" who carry out the occupations of carpenter, bricklayer, etc. (*Ordenanzas* 281).

The historical investigation Quiroga carries out in the *Información*, so as to determine whether slavery existed among the various ethnic groups of the region, is swept aside by the order and operation of the hospital. Their entire history is reduced to the existence of tyrants and subjects, these latter oppressed by the former. Body painting, the only recognizable cultural feature that appears in those pages, is imagined by Quiroga not as an obstacle to the civilization and Christianization of the indigenous population, or even as a mere irksome remnant of something that has come to an end, but rather as a deficiency of hygiene, a stain that the application of soap and water could dispel: "Ni os imbixeis, ni pinteis, ni os ensucieis los rostros, manos, ni brazos en manera alguna como lo solíades hacer" (*Ordenanzas* 283) (Do not daub, nor paint, nor soil your faces, your hands, nor arms in any way, as you used to do). Except in cases of illness, the cleanliness of face and body must replace the grime of colors and figures that appear here bereft of importance or meaning.

But if the "Indians" would continue to be "poor Indians" or "poor men," it was because Quiroga understood the "hospital-republic" as a civilizing order that was at the same time a form of exploitation, though one preferable to the model of slavery. As a means of enrichment, this latter system was not only immoral, but also unprofitable and, in the long run, unsustainable: if it was seriously thought that "por esta vía de esclavos . . . han de sustentar en esta tierra los españoles" (183) (by means of these slaves . . . the Spaniards in these lands are to be supported), says Quiroga ". . . muy triste, miserable, sangrienta, frágil y perecedera sustentación es ésta y todo se asolaría y perecería" (183) (it will be a terribly sad, wretched, bloody, frail, and fleeting form of sustenance, and everything will be destroyed and will perish). For that reason, it was necessary to see to it that the natives lay aside their inclination to idleness—to civilize them, if through less despotic means than those available through the barbarism of their ancient culture, and thus achieve the continued sustenance, through their labor, of the totality of the Spanish population:

> Y de aqueste grand contentamiento y poco mantenimiento y de la mucha seguridad y fertilidad de la tierra, les nace tanta ociosidad y flojedad y descuido, lo cual conviene que se les quite con alguna buena orden de república y policía, porque aunque dejados así como agora están, para su miseria y buen contentamiento sean bastantes, *para nuestro fausto y soberbia*, cierto no lo son (223, emphasis added)
>
> *Out of their utter contentment and scant effort, and out of the great security and fertility of the land, arise their great idleness, weakness and neglect, which it would be good to root out of them by means of some well-ordered republic and police; for, though it is true that if allowed to remain in their present condition they are adequate to maintain their own contented misery, they clearly cannot support* our luxury and pride.

The dilemma for those implementing the new order was even greater with respect to the old indigenous tyrants: the Spaniards had to find ways of extracting from the *macehuales* double or even triple the work, a situation the *macehuales* were neither accustomed to nor inclined to tolerate. Thus, though Quiroga could dispense with studying and understanding their culture, there was still a quality in the "Indians" that had to be taken into account. If the boundless greed of the Spaniards is the text's very raison d'être, the "Indians's" character, "so very strange and different," demanded a particular response to the problem of labor and civilization (160).[15] This character, which had to do with their obedience, patience, docility, and humility, was so powerful that it overwhelmed the ethno-historical distinctions that had been so important to the indigenous people before the coming of the Spaniards. For Quiroga, to speak of a Nahua, a Tarasco (P'urhépecha), or a Chichimeca was all one and the same; even these last, he remarks, "no son menos dóciles que estos otros" (209) (are no less docile than the others).

This quality, of course, is none other than that belonging to those whom Sepúlveda considered to be "esclavos por naturaleza" [slaves by nature], those who, quite apart from whether under the tyranny of a single indigenous ruler, or a hundred Spaniards, could do no other thing than serve.[16] Anthony Pagden has already pointed to the similarity between Quiroga's ideas and Sepúlveda's—a likeness that, in the case of Quiroga (as Bernardino Verástique has remarked, though without making explicit the link to Sepúlveda), demonstrates that humanism is not necessarily humanitarian (Pagden 26–27, Verástique 111). However, the similarity to Sepúlveda is important not on account of the greater or lesser humanitarianism of Quiroga's proposals, but rather due to the way in which the premises underlying his notions of the "hospital republic" overspill the boundaries of colonial thought. Quiroga's project presents the "Indians" strictly as people who had previously been exploited, who were being exploited at that moment, and who would go on being exploited in the future, although in less brutal fashion, by those Spaniards whose pride and luxury had to be supported—though without consequently forcing the native population to renounce wholesale a certain idleness, rest, family, possessions, and self-care. This trajectory erases the colonial fissure. Without regard to who made up the minority that imposed order on the majority composed of poor *macehuales*, their destiny, determined by a makeup so different from that of the Spaniards, condemned them to serve.

In spite of this destiny, or precisely because of it, the hospital became necessary. To a certain extent, Quiroga's recourse to the notion of "hospital" is not strange. Since the Middle Ages and throughout the sixteenth to eighteenth centuries, hospitals in Europe were something very different from the institutions this concept names now: they encompassed multiple meanings and functions. Associated in the Christian world with spiritual affairs, they were originally created to alleviate poverty, not health (Ramos 187). In Spain they were also associated with the *Reconquista* and the destruction of war, which was also the context in which viceroy Francisco de Toledo created them in Peru. Under this name, also, were places dedicated to temporarily housing pilgrims and homeless people about to die, the sick, and destitute soldiers. Others provided a home for orphans who there learned to read and count, while others served as temporary correctional facilities.[17]

What is remarkably new in Quiroga's vision of hospitals is, first of all, the dramatic transformation they were meant to accomplish among the indigenous residents. Whereas in Europe orphans, poor people, soldiers, and others would enter hospitals and leave them in an improved condition (knowing how to read, fed, cured, etc.) but still being what they originally were, the P'urhépechas did not have this option. Secondly, there is their all-encompassing nature: for the indigenous people residing in them, hospitals were a place for life itself: primarily a workplace, but one in which all of life was regulated—schedules of work and rest, time for Christian instruction, education in letters and in mechanical arts, relations within the family and between families, relations between countryside and hospital.

For the indigenous population, or for the poor, the hospital was, as I said before, the equivalent of the *urbs*: from its functioning would emerge the norms, the order to be internalized. To that end, Quiroga writes *Ordenanzas*, addressing himself directly to those very persons who had to comply with them, no less than see to their compliance: "reglas del Hospital y *de vosotros mesmos*" (*Ordenanzas* 265, emphasis added) (rules of the Hospital and *for yourselves*) indicates the lawyer from the very beginning to those who had before them the tablets for an alternate civilization, but who would be in contact with the civilization that emerged from the city and whose extravagance they would have to support.

If in some respects this hospital might resemble the long European medieval tradition in which Josefina Muriel inscribed it—along with all the other hospitals of New Spain, whether for the native population or otherwise, at its core the institution is something else.[18] In this case, and given the specific circumstances in which Quiroga founds them (war, slavery), it is pertinent to recall Émile Benveniste's cautioning us on the ambiguity running through the series of words derived from the term "hospital" and the idea of hospitality. The Latin *hospes*, "an ancient compound" whose literal meaning was "guest-master," gives rise to words in various Indo-European languages which come to designate identity, simply: from referring to a lord, these words began to convey the idea of oneself (Benveniste 72–74). According to Benveniste, this change implied a weakening of the word, by which a person ("the master") was transformed into a general, abstract notion ("oneself") (74). However, given that the unexpected example provided by Benveniste refers to a Hittite text in which there is a reference to "oneself" in connection with slaves who were to be captured, I suspect that the case is more nearly the opposite one ("If a slave flees, and if he goes to an enemy country, the one who brings him back *he is the one* who takes him"): that is, a situation in which oneself, identity, is defined in relation to a group none of whose members were considered a being unto himself, a "oneself," someone who could exist for himself. The exact language matters because Benveniste presents the shift from master-lord to oneself as puzzling—he mentions "the singularity of the problem" that this implies—and he wonders "under what conditions can a word denoting 'master' end up by signifying identity" (73). The answer, connected with the strange passage about slaves, can also be found in another, parallel development.

In Roman law, according to Benveniste—that is, ancient Roman law—the *hostes* was the non-Roman who had the same rights as the Romans; the term implied a relationship of equality and reciprocity, a relationship of equality in difference or in spite of difference (77). This sense, nevertheless, disappears with the rise of nations, at which point the only element that persists is the distinction "between what is inside and outside the *civitas*" (78). Benveniste recalls, too, the close relationship between *hostes*, guest, and *hostis*, foe, enemy. Both words are united by the notion of the stranger—he who could be enemy or guest; and if, at one point, the terms had pointed to a certain ambivalence, later on the favorable stranger came to be called *hospes*, guest, while the negative was *hostis*, foe (74–75). We can think of the definition of oneself, of the being for itself, as taking shape in relation to that enemy, the slave hunted, captured, unable to be for himself. And here it is important to keep in mind that, as Quiroga had pointed out, in the Spanish system the slave lost precisely every characteristic of personhood, of humanity, being transformed into nothingness.

The historical-etymological ambiguity of the concept of "hospital"—which, in Quiroga's text, is *the* place where civilization, hospitality, and order are possible—reemerges in all its complexity in Quiroga's *Información* and *Ordenanzas*. The hospital appears, then, as a dividing line, a spatial marker that separated guest from enemy, although with one difference with respect to what Benveniste indicates. The hospital separates the place where the "pobres maceoales" [poor *macehuales*] would live—and who, thenceforth, would be seen as "guests," that is, as strangers in their own lands—from the space in which they could continue to be seen as enemies—and where outside of the hospital and its order, outside of its care and protection, they could be hunted and exploited without restraint. Nevertheless, what this notion of "hospital" fails to take into account is the possibility of equality in difference. The hospital reminds us, then, that this poverty either created or discovered in the "Indians" by Quiroga, and perhaps even, and by extension, all poverty that is colonial in origin, implies a certain excess beyond simple economic determinism: that which oscillates between reference, on the one hand, to a condition of strangerhood *necessarily* beyond the reach of the laws of equity and reciprocity (and therefore requiring protection); and, on the other, pointing to the threat represented by any and all enemies.[19] Such is the *hospitality* offered by Quiroga to the barbarians who were also "the poor" (*macehuales*), or to the poor who had once been barbarians.

New Tablets, New Order

Anthony Pagden, as I have already noted, understood the ideas of Quiroga, for whom every political right or right of possession (*dominium*) depended on men living in "civil communities" (in contrast to primitive or tyrannical societies), as kindred to those of Sepúlveda (27). According to Sepúlveda, and unlike other organic intellectuals of the Spanish Empire, natural law coincided with Divine law: God was the foundation and principle of humanity and of civilization, that is, of what it meant to be a man living as one should, and not simply as a potential man, as was the case of the indigenous population—"hombrecillos en los que apenas se puede encontrar restos de humanidad" (35) (little men in whom one can barely find traces of humanity). Since *naturally* all imperfection must be subordinate to what is perfect, for Sepúlveda any doubt with regard to the conquest was entirely superfluous: the Spanish Crown had the right to conquer the indigenous people and force them to realize their potential for attaining humanity.[20] To accomplish this, waging wars was necessary and entirely justifiable. Sepúlveda recalls how St. Augustine had recognized that correcting imperfection occurred against the will, perhaps, of the individuals who underwent such processes, which could even be painful ("a pesar del sufrimiento" [in spite of all suffering]), but this made the process no less necessary: for their own benefit and salvation, inferior beings must suffer the dominion of "los hombres buenos, excelentes por su virtud, inteligencia y prudencia" (23) [good men, excellent on account of their virtue, intelligence, and prudence].[21]

In order to explain the divine and natural quality of Spain's jurisdiction and dominion over the Indies, Sepúlveda has recourse to what, in his argument, is the point of origin of what we might call Western-Christian civilization: Moses, to whom he refers as "el mejor intérprete de la voluntad divina" (41) (the foremost interpreter of the Divine will), the creator of the order that must rule over the Jewish people and distinguish it from all others. In pointing out, however, that the Mosaic law was "una ley no sólo divina sino también natural y aplicable a todos los hombres" (40) (a law not only Divine, but also natural, and, as such, applicable to all men), Sepúlveda extends this ancient, particular, and theological nucleus into an imperative for all humankind. Monotheism is the impulse that obliges all men, universally, to cease to live "como las bestias" [like beasts], an option he associates with polytheism and human sacrifice, "crimes" that made men like "los puercos [que] siempre tienen su vista dirigida a la tierra" (Sepúlveda 38) (swine, that always have their gaze directed downward at the earth). But if sacrifice is rejected, the new order founded by Moses brings with it no renunciation of killing; quite the contrary, killing continues to be a practice that is present at the very birth of a new form of civilization, just as it is seen in the destruction by Israel, under God's command, of all the peoples living in the promised land who remained "pecadores" [sinners]. The new order put an end to sacrifice in favor of an emphatically non-ritual killing.

More than the tablets, nevertheless, Sepúlveda emphasized the legacy of Moses in Deuteronomy, the text that represents the restatement and amplification of the law, once the people reached the promised land, and in the face of the dual peril of apostasy and the accompanying return to slavery. In this sense, it is interesting not only that Quiroga (like Moses, the Egyptian vis-à-vis the Jewish people, and Utopus, the benevolent colonizer who founds Thomas More's Utopia) is a foreigner in relation to the people he leads, and that his *Ordenanzas*, included in his will, are at one and the same time new tablets and a new Deuteronomy. The ordinances are a series of commands written from the hospital to ensure that its order should continue even, in Quiroga's own words, "después de mis días" (*Ordenanzas* 276) (after my days are done). But if Moses had chosen to address the people of Israel once more at the moment when they were to take possession of the promised land ("Behold, I have set the land before you: go in and possess the land which the Lord sware unto your fathers," Deut. 1.8), a land of riches and promise after having prevailed against more powerful groups ("After he had slain Sihon the king of the Amorites ... and Og the king of Bashan," Deut. 1.4) and there he chooses sages, rulers for them ("Take your wise men ... and I will make them rulers over you," Deut. 1.13); Quiroga's admonition to the indigenous population ushers in a very different sort of order.

The hospital, the place of refuge of the *macehuales*, is the necessary counterpart to the order established by the *other* people who had reached their promised land and a life of riches and abundance; it was a place of protection and reformation for the "Indians" invited to forswear polytheism. In this way, it supposedly softened, in *Christian* fashion, the old Mosaic law, by saving them from the death that in ancient times would have been the destiny of all who lived outside of the natural-Divine law. Where Moses had commanded that idolaters be put to death, Quiroga creates hospitals for their protection. There they would learn useful trades—"carpinteros, albañiles, herreros" (*Ordenanzas* 265) (carpenters, masons, ironworkers). There, to avoid the excesses of the chosen people in their drive to gain command of the new territories, these poor persons would work six hours daily while learning letters, Christian doctrine, and farming. *Sin capitanes, ni hombres sabios* [Without captains, nor wise men], however, they would have the right to select, from among the mothers and fathers of the families who were the backbone of the hospital, their representatives before the Rector and the Directors (*Ordenanzas* 279). Doubtless, as I have already pointed out, there is in Quiroga's text a desire to endow this "republic" with a certain degree of autonomy. Its affairs were to be decided internally, avoiding at all costs recourse to the colonial legal system in order to prevent "[que] pagueis derechos y después os echen en la cárcel" (*Ordenanzas* 282) (your having to pay fees and afterwards being thrown in jail). The world beyond the hospital walls, the lawyer recognized indirectly, was simply too hostile. At the same time, and in order to avoid contamination from the outside—the world of arrogance, greed, and ambition—the "Indians" would be held in a kind of monastic poverty, visible in every aspect of the life of the hospital, including attire (*Ordenanzas* 277; Gómez 76–81). In this way, barbarism would be corrected, and the poor, to whom a basic, if rudimentary, culture was guaranteed (minimal letters, Christian doctrine, mechanical trades, agriculture), would continue to be poor, as seemed to befit their natural makeup and inclinations.

In spite the overlap of Quiroga's ideas with Sepúlveda's that Pagden remarks on, Gómez is quite right in situating at least one central aspect of Quiroga nearer to Vitoria than to Sepúlveda: Quiroga's thought cannot be considered theological, even if the latter is his foundation (129). More interestingly, Christianity makes its appearance in the hospital as but one civilizing element among others; the hospital's core is undoubtedly the regulation of labor. For this reason, and given that in the hospitals, the heart of the matter was work more than Christianization, Quiroga represents a sort of secularized Christianity that displaced itself on the ground by an economic logic. He is then a sort of civic Moses, one that funds hospitals-republics in order to create a new group of people—the "Indians" as forever poor agricultural and artisanal workers who must carry within themselves, in their very being, their humble place in society. In "[R]eglas del Hospital y de vosotros mesmos" (*Ordenanzas* 265) (rules of the Hospital and for yourselves), he had instructed the "Indians" in a sentence that resembles that of Moses directing the Jews who, like the indigenous population, had recently been delivered from slavery, to pay heed to God's commandments: "Circumcise therefore the foreskin of your heart" (Deut. 10.16). And just as among God's commandments to his people there is the injunction to "keep the sabbath" (Deut. 5.12), Quiroga limits the Indians' working hours to six, perhaps in order to remind them, like Moses did to the Jews, that they were no longer slaves (*Ordenanzas* 267). Yet Quiroga's new people, no longer enslaved and protected, would never be equal to those who could potentially enslave them. It is perhaps because of this paradoxical combination of autonomy and total subordination that, as Krippner's work shows, Quiroga's body of thought lent itself well to revival by the Partido Revolucionario Institucional (PRI) during the period after the Mexican Revolution.[22]

In conclusion, we would do well to reflect on what the colonial period has to say to us about later processes by which other vast populations were, and are, deprived of the totality of their rights. We may recall, for instance, Hannah Arendt's exasperation over the way in which the processes of denationalization forced on a great many population groups by European nations in the first half of the twentieth century produced, at one and the same time, barbarians and people whose most basic rights were denied. Arendt, who demystified the problem of human rights by pointing out its being mainly a political problem, a question about sovereignty and statehood—people needed a state that could defend them—recognized that this anomaly was similar to the colonial situation, an injection of "colonial methods into European affairs" (271). That is, just as the colonies were made possible by not recognizing American political entities as rightful states, the creation within Europe of people without rights (and barbarians) owed to their first being rendered stateless.

For Arendt, the struggle for human rights had revealed the unexpected rise in the very heart of Europe of human groups (those recently denationalized by internal European conflicts) that had none (whatsoever). The most to which these groups could aspire, since national sovereignty and self-determination were beyond the bounds of the possible, was (to) a "humane method of assimilation," and Arendt points out ironically how the "internment camps" had become "the only practical substitute for a nonexistent homeland" (272, 284). These camps would thus be, in the twentieth century, the European equivalent of Quiroga's hospital, the place for the confinement of the stranger to whom the same rights as a citizen were not accorded, the stranger to whom, according to Arendt, citizenship was systematically denied.

The "calamity" of this new situation had to do, in Arendt's view, with the fact that these human groups (Jews, Armenians, Slovaks, and others) had lost their rights but *not* due to a lack of civilization, as had happened before: "if a tribal or other 'backward' community did not enjoy human rights, it was obviously because as a whole it had not yet reached a stage of civilization, the stage of national and popular sovereignty, but was oppressed by foreign or native despots"; rather, the situation that obtained was entirely the reverse (291). At the time when Arendt was writing, there were no longer, she points out, any uncivilized places; the world was truly "one world" (297). In spite of not following the argument through to its ultimate consequences, Arendt nevertheless suggests that at that precise moment, when there was no longer any place left to colonize, to civilize, the civilized world turned against itself and artificially generated new forms of barbarism and of defenselessness.[23] Barred from participating in the creation and distribution of the most prized objects of civilization—art, education, philosophy, technology—these groups without rights were transformed irremediably into barbarians, whose situation, even in the midst of civilization, reverted to the primitive state of nature. What was worse, on being excluded from participating in the (attractive) universe that surrounded them, these new barbarians grew to resent the culture that they had always received fully made, becoming a danger, a mass whose growing numbers, according to Arendt, made them a "deadly danger" that threatened "our political life, our human artifice, the world that is the result of our common and co-ordinated effort" (300–2). It is impossible for me to know if it was this threat that truly worried Arendt, or if she simply raises it as a rhetorical device to avoid writing (once more) about the immorality and injustice of a system that selectively strips naked certain human groups and dispossesses them of all rights. Perhaps it was more effective simply to appeal to the fear of the resentful masses rather than to political sensibility or to a sense of justice.

In any case, what really matters is that, in spite of the fact that for Arendt the situation of those Europeans was worse than that of slaves in earlier eras—who, since there were those who desired to exploit them, at least occupied a place in society through their labor—she nonetheless recognizes a colonial origin for the civilization-barbarism dialectic (297). Historically, it had (always) been the barbarian who had no rights by virtue of not having reached the level of development that would have freed him from being at the mercy of those who *could* hunt him down and enslave him. In this sense, we can doubtless say of Quiroga in sixteenth-century New Spain, and unlike the creators of the European "internment camps," that he attempted to create a basic and alternative culture, a potential situation of hospitality toward those "poor" who had been unable to defend their sovereignty and their nationhood, to resist as "oneselves" in the face of a more powerful group. The globalization and temporal expansion of this problem leads us to wonder, nevertheless, if this is all that we can aspire to: a dialectic of colonization and hospitality, exploitation and poverty, prolonged to infinity. But we are also drawn to reflect on what it might mean that this system of thought that breaks certain civilizations down, transforming them into mere poverty and then, later (as notes Arendt), converts poverty into barbarism, has a very particular point of origin: the violence of the vast economic project launched in the colonies of the "New World" centuries before the present.

NOTES

1. I would like to express my thanks to my colleagues from the 2014 Instituto Tepoztlán (in particular to Pamela Voekel and Josefina Saldaña) for their feedback on a first version of this essay, and to Adam Warren, who generously offered his bibliographical knowledge on hospitals—a future essay on Vasco de Quiroga will do justice to this complex history. My appreciation also goes to the Early Modern Sodality group at UC Berkeley. I hope this version at least partially engages their thoughtful comments and suggestions. Last, but not least, my thanks to my co-editors, Rachel Sarah O'Toole and Anna More, for their edits and comments.
2. Vasco de Quiroga (ca. 1470–1565), canon law lawyer, arrived in New Spain in 1531, after having held several bureaucratic positions in the recently conquered north of

Africa (judge, mediator, legal representative of the Spanish Crown). In New Spain he served first as a lawyer (*oídor*) of the Segunda Audiencia, and was appointed bishop of Michoacán in 1538. He died in Michoacán, after spending several years in Spain where he participated in the famous debates between Bartolomé de las Casas and Ginés de Sepúlveda regarding the rights of the Spanish Crown over the indigenous populations. Quiroga's opinions were closer to the latter's. See Serrano 29–30. *Información en derecho* is fighting against a law allowing the re-establishment of slavery (dated February 20, 1534). This court order repealed another one from August 2, 1530 forbidding Indian enslavement. See Quiroga, *Información*, notes 2, 9, pp. 65, 67.

3. Racial thinking is another element that should be taken into consideration. Colonial texts are split between those that attributed the natives' character (their supposed mental, physical, and social traits) to culture and education, and those (the majority) that, without mentioning the concept of race, indicated that the "Indians's" "nature" was inherent and/or due to climatic and geographical factors. Notwithstanding this difference, even in the writings of the clearest representatives of the first position (José de Acosta's, for example), there are always tensions that bring them close to the position of the second group. Quiroga's ideas on the disposition and nature of the Indians developed in this article could be considered an example of racial thinking. Nevertheless I prefer not to engage in this debate. For a comprehensive history of the complex, shifting, and prolonged formation of racial thinking in Spain and its relationship to religion and blood from the Middle Ages to the eighteenth century, María Elena Martinez's book is essential.

4. Even though the information about what happened to these hospitals in the following centuries is still imprecise, the influence of Quiroga in the region of Lake Pátzcuaro in particular, and Michoacán in general, is undeniable. It is debatable, though, whether this influence should be credited to the local memory of the indigenous populations, grateful for what "Tata Vasco" (as Quiroga is referred to, locally) did for them in the sixteenth century, or if it is the product of Creole and mestizo elites who, since the eighteenth century, have promoted the image of Quiroga. For this, and for the history of the hospitals, see Krippner; Martínez; Verástique; and Muriel. To differentiate quotes coming from *Información en derecho* and those of *Ordenanzas*, I'll indicate in parentheses the title of the latter. Quotes from *Información* are indicated with page number only.

5. This disconnect is not exclusive to Quiroga, as other early modern/colonial theorists proceed in the same way. Francisco de Vitoria, considered the father of international law, lecturing around the same time Quiroga writes, addressed what was happening in the Indies in two lessons: "On the Indies" and "On War," as if the real issue were not—as is evident in both texts—the question of the war being waged in the Indies. This permits Vitoria to speak of war and the Indies in the abstract as if the war were merely a possibility and not an ongoing reality.

6. In the sixteenth century, the notion of "police" comprised the elements of what we call "civilization." Police depended on "natural law" (that which supposedly

was natural and common to all human beings). I understand police the way it was understood by colonial writers, both as government and discipline, the functioning of which is recognized in two different, but related orders: on the one hand, the order provided by institutions—some form of state, religion, urbanization, education, etc.; and, on the other, a people's behavior—their following of the laws, their level or education, their religious and civic conduct, their family structure. It should be remembered that even though Spanish colonization vouched for an important and dramatic civilizing shift for the indigenous populations, this did not mean that the transformation was complete or that it took shape the way their promoters expected it to.

7. Even though the native population and the Franciscan order accused Quiroga of oppressing indigenous people, there is no doubt that he wanted to defend the indigenous people from the unbridled exploitation of slave hunters and *encomenderos* (Verástique; Serrano). Many historians have recognized the ambivalent nature of Quiroga's project (Serrano, for example), but the great majority of the books dedicated to this topic stress the positive effects Quiroga had in the region, and/or the contrast between what Quiroga achieved in the sixteenth century and the growing vulnerability of the native people in the following centuries (Muriel 109–10). Fernando Gómez's work is, in this sense, unique. While recognizing the improvements Quiroga wanted to implement, he explains them both in the context of his time and in what they might mean for twentieth-century readers. By doing this, he foregrounds the limits the new colonial order imposed on Quiroga's project and the fact that Quiroga subscribed to this order without reservations. My own work connects Gómez's conclusions with a local history (Michoacán, Mexico) that was (and is), nevertheless, repeated in many other spaces: that of the multiple populations violently displaced from their own history and territories and transformed into "nothing" or into poverty in need of protection.

8. Yáñez and Verástique study the effects of Nuño de Guzmán in what is now western Mexico. Verástique claims that the rapid and sharp decline in the population of Michoacán can be credited to the "cruelty" of this conqueror and his men (76, 83–84). For her part, Yáñez documents how Guzmán's excessive violence drove even some of the allied "Indians" that marched with him to this conquest to suicide (63–64). Fray Antonio Tello and Domingo Lázaro de Arregui, writing in the seventeenth century, provide a portrait of a forsaken area almost a century after Nuño de Guzmán's conquering raids.

9. See Espejel's excellent work for information about its author and the circumstances in which this text was written during the first half of the sixteenth century.

10. See as well Cabeza de Vaca's narration of the devastation caused by Spaniards in Nueva Galicia (208, for example). See also Guamán Poma's account of the indigenous people fleeing to the *punas*, the high deserts of Perú, to avoid the injustices of the colonial order (445).

11. When Quiroga considered the indigenous people "fleeing" to the mountains as an impediment to civilization, he did not take into account—he could not have

known this—that this massive displacement gave rise, in turn, to processes that went in the opposite direction, such as the creation of new population centers comprised of several ethnic and cultural groups. I don't know of any work that investigates the regrouping and recomposition of social life in sixteenth-century Michoacán, but many indigenous groups that now inhabit Western Mexico are the result of the coming together of multiple peoples, who, forced to escape from their villages, gathered in inaccessible mountainous areas where they joined already existing towns and together created new societies. See Weigand.

12. In the case of the colonial experience, it is necessary to adjust Freud's notion of *exploitation*. This is what I'll do in the next pages, especially in the section discussing the origin of the word "hospital."

13. This is one of the most persistent complaints of the lawyer, who constantly insists on the unrestrained greed of the Spanish.

14. According to Gómez, this economic determinism, that necessarily de-emphasized the ethnic, indigenous, element in these populations, was accompanied by a utopian project (155). For him, the ambiguous pairing of economic interests with utopia is representative of the repressive culture of Spanish Indian Law. As he indicates, "colonial reformation, in order to have any chance to make any difference must of necessity internalize most of the normative or prescriptive protocols, textual and *otherwise*, proper to the tentacular hegemony of Spanish Indian Law" (71, emphasis added). That is, in the context of the colonies, utopia—the influence of Thomas More on Quiroga—continues to be *colonial*. My discussion of the hospital as an alternative order to that of the city is a variant of what according to Gómez constitutes the utopic-repressive and legalistic nucleus in Quiroga's work. I leave for another place an analysis of the complexity of this mixed Republic, the fact, for example, that even when it can be rightly considered, as Gómez indicates, proto-capitalist, it contains elements that are semi-communist as well. In this other essay, I'll also address the influence of More's *Utopia*, a text that was central for Quiroga's hospitals.

15. The necessity of creating a police system adequate for the natives' disposition is a recurrent theme in Quiroga. See for example, *Información* 160, 163, 204–5, 218, 223–24.

16. Bentancor analyzes how Quiroga sees the natives as "wax," matter open to a superior "form." Nevertheless, as I suggest, Quiroga seems to concede that the matter the "Indians" are made of has within itself a tendency to take a certain form—that of serving.

17. This passage comes from Ramos's very interesting analysis of hospitals in mid-sixteenth- to eighteenth-century colonial Perú (see especially 187–92), and from Carmona García's book on the origins, history, and flexible character of hospitals in Seville (see for example 48–52). Tellingly, for my later discussion of Moses and Deuteronomy, Carmona García associates European hospitals with Jewish houses for pilgrims and foreigners (20, 22). My thanks to Adam Warren for directing me to these texts.

18. Without emphasizing it, Muriel acknowledges the difference between most hospi-

tals for the native population—places of temporary refuge for sick and homeless people—and those founded by Quiroga. The latter functioned more as alternative "republics" created to fulfill needs brought about by a state of war (slavery, the many orphans). See for example Muriel 56–58.
19. I'm thinking about the immense economic consequences for populations that during several generations lived (and still live) under formal or informal colonial rule.
20. For Quiroga's case, see Bentancor.
21. According to Serrano Gassent, Quiroga indirectly participated in the debate between Sepúlveda and Las Casas. He wrote a treatise (now lost) that Sepúlveda considered favorable to his position. In this document Quiroga is said to have advocated for wars to pacify as opposed to exterminating wars (Serrano Gassent 15–16).
22. Krippner analyzes different moments in which the image of Vasco de Quiroga has been revived for different projects. One of these projects, perhaps the strongest one in fact, occurred during Mexico's post-Revolutionary period, under the PNR (Partido Nacional Revolucionario) which was going to become the PRI (Partido Revolucionario Institucional), especially during the presidency of Lázaro Cárdenas (1936–1940), himself from Michoacán. Krippner does not explain it in such terms, but it is easy to see how the mix of protection and tutelage offered by Quiroga to the indigenous communities would be attractive for Mexico's postrevolutionary *indigenismo*, which even if in different ways, did not, like Quiroga, consider the indigenous communities as equals.
23. These consequences could refer either to Arendt's vouching for the desirability of and/or need to achieve a single, civilized world or, more interestingly, to her understated way of demystifying natural law. If, at the moment when one of its most important premises had finally been achieved—the creation of a single world, as Sepúlveda and Vitoria and other promoters had stated it ought to—there appeared mechanisms to radically upend things by depriving people of their rights as inhabitants of a single, civilized world, then natural law had been nothing but a colossal ruse.

WORKS CITED

Arendt, Hannah. *The Origins of Totalitarianism*. New York: Harcourt, Barce and Company, 1951.
Arregui, Domingo Lázaro de. *Descripción de la Nueva Galicia*. Guadalajara: Unidad Editorial del Gobierno del Estado de Jalisco, 1980.
Bentancor, Orlando. "La disposición de la materia en *La Información en Derecho* de Vasco de Quiroga." *Estudios transatlánticos postcoloniales. II. Mito, archivo, disciplina: Cartografías culturales*. Eds. Ileana Rodríguez and Josebe Martínez. Barcelona: Anthropos, 2011. 171–207.

Benveniste, Émile. *Indo-European Language and Society*. London: Faber and Faber Limited, 1973.

Carmona García, Juan Ignacio. *El sistema de hospitalidad pública en la Sevilla del antiguo régimen*. Seville: Diputación Provincial de Sevilla, 1979.

Deuteronomy, The Fifth Book of Moses Called. *The Bible. Authorized King James Version with Apocrypha*. Oxford: Oxford University Press, 1998. 216–62.

Espejel Carbajal, Claudia. *La justicia y el fuego: Dos claves para leer la Relación de Michoacán*. Zamora: El Colegio de Michoacán, 2008.

Freud, Sigmund. *The Future of an Illusion*. Ed. James Strachey. New York: W. W. Norton & Company, 1961.

Gómez, Fernando. *Good Places and Non-Places in Colonial Mexico: The Figure of Vasco de Quiroga (1470–1565)*. Lanham: University Press of America, 2001.

Krippner Martínez, James. "Invoking 'Tata Vasco': Vasco de Quiroga, Eighteenth-Twentieth Centuries." *The Americas* 56:3 (2000): 1–28.

Martínez, María Elena. *Genealogical Fictions: Limpieza de Sangre, Religion and Gender in Colonial Mexico*. Stanford: Stanford University Press, 2008.

More, Thomas. *Utopia*. Hollywood, Fla: Simon and Brown, 2011.

Muriel, Josefina. *Hospitales de la Nueva España, Tomo 1: Fundaciones del Siglo XVI*. Mexico City: Instituto de Historia, 1956.

Núñez Cabeza de Vaca, Álvar. *Naufragios*. Madrid: Cátedra, 2001.

Pagden, Anthony. *Spanish Imperialism and the Political Imagination: Studies in European and Spanish-American Social and Political Theory, 1513–1830*. New Haven: Yale University Press, 1990.

Paredes Martínez, Carlos, and Marta Terán, coords. *Autoridad y gobierno indígena en Michoacán*. Vol. 1. Zamora: El Colegio de Michoacán, Centro de Investigaciones y Estudios Superiores en Antropología Social, 2003.

Poma de Ayala, Felipe Guamán. *Nueva corónica y buen gobierno*. Vol. II. Ed. Franklin Pease. Mexico City: Fondo de Cultura Económica, 1993.

Quiroga, Vasco de. "Información en derecho." *La utopía en América*. Ed. Paz Serrano Gassent. Madrid: Historia 16, 1992. 65–262.

———. "Ordenanzas." *La utopía en América*. Ed. Paz Serrano Gassent. Madrid: Historia 16, 1992. 265–86.

Ramos, Gabriela. "Indian Hospitals and Government in Colonial Andes." *Medical History* 57:2 (2013): 186–205.

"Relación de las cerimonias y rictos y población y gobernación de los indios de la Provincia de Mechoacan." *Crónicas de Michoacán*. Ed. Federico Gómez de Orozco. Mexico: Universidad Nacional Autónoma de México, 1954. 1–30.

Sahagún, fray Bernandino de. *Historia general de las cosas de Nueva España*. Vol. 1. Mexico City: Editorial Pedro Robredo, 1938.

Serrano Gassent, Paz. "Introducción." *La utopía en América*. Ed. Paz Serrano Gassent. Madrid: Historia 16, 1992. 7–51.

Tello, Antonio. *Crónica Miscelánea de la Sancta Provincia de Xalisco*. Book II. Vol. 1–3. Guadalajara: Gobierno del Estado de Jalisco, Universidad de Guadalajara, Instituto Cultural Cabañas, 1968, 1973, 1984.

Verástique, Bernardino. *Michoacán and Eden: Vasco de Quiroga and the Evangelization of Western Mexico*. Austin: University of Texas Press, 2000.

Vitoria, Francisco de. *Relecciones de Indios y del Derecho de la Guerra*. Madrid: Espasa Calpe, 1928.

Yáñez Rosales, Rosa H. *Rostro, palabra y memoria indígenas: El occidente de México, 1524–1826*. Guadalajara: Instituto Nacional Indigenista, Centro de Investigaciones y Estudios Superiores en Antropología Social, 2001.

Wallerstein, Immanuel. *World Systems Analysis: An Introduction*. Durham: Duke University Press, 2004.

Weigand, Philp C. *Ensayos sobre el Gran Nayar: Entre coras, huicholes y tepehuanos*. Mexico City: Centro de Estudios Mexicanos y Centroamericanos, Instituto Nacional Indigenista, El Colegio de Michoacán, 1992.

◆ CHAPTER THREE

Religion, Caste, and Race in the Spanish and Portuguese Empires
Local and Global Dimensions[1]

María Elena Martínez

Studying the Spanish and Portuguese empires together can expand understandings of early modern colonialism and globalization. But even though various scholars have acknowledged the importance of this joint approach, scholarship that applies it is relatively rare.[2] Particularly scarce are analyses that focus on cultural domains as opposed to economic or political ones. This dearth is puzzling given the similarities and intersections in the cultural institutions, ideological concepts, and practices that the Spanish and Portuguese used, both in the metropolitan and colonial contexts, to establish socio-religious and racial hierarchies and to police sexual and conjugal arrangements. The similarities included the establishment and use of their own Inquisitions to monitor religious beliefs and activities, the creation and deployment of notions of race (*raza*), caste (*casta*), and purity of blood (*limpieza de sangre*) and the implementation of requirements of genealogical purity for accessing a number of secular and religious institutions, professions, and offices.

To be sure, the religious and racializing projects of the first two global empires of the early modern world were not identical, and their usage of concepts such as *raza*, *casta*, and *limpieza de sangre* (*limpeza de sangue* in Portuguese) could vary. There were also differences within each empire by region, not to mention by period, and local responses to colonial rule also varied. The way that the Portuguese defined "impure blood" in Portuguese Asia versus Brazil, for example, was not the same and the deployment of the concept of *limpieza de sangre* within Spanish America was not uniform either across space or time. These and other internal imperial differences mean that careful attention must be paid to what parts of those empires are compared and more broadly to the period and regions that are considered.

Despite these and other challenges of a comparative approach, identifying general parallels and distinctions between the two empires can aid in clarifying certain historical problems, opening new lines of investigation, or simply raising new questions. In order to generate new historical insights and paths of inquiry for the study of the emergence and global scope of early modern racial discourses, this essay thus collapses Spanish and Portuguese analytical fields (separated because of the continued importance of the nation-state in determining areas of research) and analyzes sixteenth- and seventeenth-century concepts of religion, caste, and race in each empire. It also explores the nature and connections of the two imperial projects, networks of knowledge production and diffusion, and the role of indigenous and other local actors in shaping colonial relations and notions of human difference and hierarchy.

Religion

Scholarship has tended to distinguish the two empires by emphasizing the maritime and commercial character of the Portuguese one versus the more territorial and tribute-based nature of its Spanish counterpart (with Brazil and parts of Africa recognized as exceptions), but acknowledged that they had much in common, particularly in their justifications for expansion. Seeing their spiritual and temporal goals as working in complete harmony, both crowns defended their territorial appropriations and colonial projects in Africa, Asia, and the Americas on the basis of having a providential mandate to spread their civilizations and the Christian faith (Boxer, *Race* 1–3).[3] To accomplish their goals, the two relied heavily on religious orders, secular clergy, and inquisition officials. Iberian missionaries began to descend on parts of Africa, including the Congo, in the latter part of the fifteenth century, and into Portuguese India, Spanish America, and Brazil in the first half of the fifteen hundreds.

In these different contexts Iberians faced the same challenge of converting native populations to Christianity and turning their beliefs in deities into monotheism. Not normally viewed side by side, early conversion projects in India and parts of the Americas followed a similar course. For example, in 1510 the Portuguese began a systematic conquest campaign of destroying idols in Goa (part of the *Estado da Índia*, or the Portuguese territories in Asia; Russell-Wood 20–21), and in subsequent decades the Spaniards did the same in New Spain and Peru. In both India and central Mexico Franciscan friars initiated the first phase of conversion, but by the 1540s other orders (Dominicans, Jesuits, and Augustinians) had a prominent presence (with the Jesuits leading the missionary effort in Goa as of 1542). While members of religious orders were conducting mass conversions in the *Estado da Índia*, their counterparts in New Spain and other parts of the Americas were doing the same, and as part of a broader colonization project, Iberians in all those places gave political and economic incentives to indigenous government or spiritual leaders to attempt to co-opt them.

The logic behind these incentives was straightforward: if traditional leaders cooperated with colonial authorities and converted, the rest of the population would follow suit. Thus, in Goa members of the high castes who accepted baptism were allowed to ride on horses, wear boots, and have retinues of slaves (Mendonça 39–40). In the Americas the Spanish gave the descendants of pre-Hispanic rulers and nobles similar privileges, and also allowed them to hold offices in local government and for a time continue to receive tribute from commoners in their jurisdictions. Perhaps nowhere did these strategies of political and spiritual conquest have the exact desired results. In Goa and New Spain, for example, the realization that the conversion campaigns were failing, which occurred roughly at the same time, the 1540s, gave way to a more militant phase of uprooting traditional beliefs and practices and punishing converts who continued to hold rituals to honor their old deities.[4]

The general climate of religious militancy in these different Iberian colonial regions led, in the second half of the sixteenth century, to the establishment of several overseas inquisitorial tribunals. This metropolitan institution would become a critical weapon in the policing not just of the spiritual but also cultural and sexual practices of colonial populations. Portugal was first. In 1560, it established a tribunal in Goa that had jurisdiction in its territories in Asia and East Africa. Spain established Holy Office tribunals in Lima in 1570, in Mexico City in 1571, and in Cartagena in 1610, with the one in the capital of New Spain enjoying jurisdiction over that entire viceroyalty, which included the Philippines.[5] With the extension of these four tribunals to parts of Asia, Africa and the Americas, the Iberian Inquisitions, which at times collaborated to extradite subjects, spread its presence and developed networks of informants in four continents.[6] By the end of the sixteenth century, Portugal and Spain had centralized the Holy Office's authority in Lisbon and Madrid, respectively.

That the official arrival of the Holy Office in Goa, Peru, and New Spain, occurred roughly in the same decade, or from 1560 to 1571, was largely due to the movement of Portuguese New Christians (Jewish converts to Christianity, called *cristãos novos* in Portuguese, and *conversos* or *cristianos nuevos* in Spanish) to Castile and throughout each empire. This migration of *conversos*, many of whom were merchants, was not new, but it had increased in the 1560s and especially in the 1580s because of the "union" of the two crowns.[7] The union exacerbated concerns among ecclesiastical authorities about the influence that this population would have, given its suspected attachment to Judaism, on the rest of the European population and on the natives of overseas regions. The decision to transplant the Inquisition to parts of Asia and the Americas, then, had as much to do with colonial conversion campaigns as with what was happening in the Iberian Peninsula. In particular, the transplantation was related to the Iberian creation of a New Christian Diaspora, which as various scholars have demonstrated, did not respect imperial territorial boundaries, Iberian and otherwise.[8]

The Spanish Carvajal family serves to illustrate the point. In 1579, Luis de Carvajal, a New Christian, received a royal contract from Philip II granting him the governorship of the New Kingdom of León, in New Spain. He and part of his family therefore went to Mexico, but some of his relatives went to Italy and other parts of Europe (including Salonika which was part of the Ottoman Empire). In New Spain, members of the family were accused and convicted of "judaizing" (practicing Judaism) and some, including Luis de Carvajal "the younger" (nephew to Carvajal the governor), were executed in the last years of the century.[9] If the arrival of Castilian New Christians in Spanish America concerned some ecclesiastical and secular authorities, they worried even more about the growing presence of Portuguese *cristãos novos* because of the widespread assumption that they had remained even more loyal to Judaism than Spanish *conversos* and would therefore aggressively seek to preserve and spread their secret religion.

The New Christians were of course not the only early targets of the Iberian overseas Inquisitions. In Spanish America the Holy Office also persecuted Protestants (whose presence was forbidden but nonetheless increased in the last decades of the sixteenth century) and the rest of the Christian population, including Spaniards and blacks, who were constantly charged with committing religious or moral transgressions. The indigenous people were technically removed from the jurisdiction of the Inquisition in 1575, but unofficially continued to be tried within the Holy Office and by a parallel institution that was headed by local bishops.[10] Even before the tribunals were set up in Goa, Mexico City, and Lima, inquisition officials (or bishops acting as inquisitors) together with members of the regular and secular clergies monitored the religious practices of the native populations of Portuguese India, Spanish America, and Brazil to ensure their conversion.[11]

In the process of trying to eradicate "idolatry"—a term deployed by theologians, writers and colonial officials against Jews, *conversos*, and indigenous peoples everywhere—these officials devoted themselves to gathering information not just about the religious, but also marital, domestic, and sexual practices of the people that fell into their jurisdictions, which in India and East Africa included Hindu and Muslim converts to Christianity.[12] In Mozambique, for example, the Goa-based inquisition tried to eradicate the Muslim local practice of showing stained linen as evidence of sexual consummation among newlyweds. It also tried to prevent Islamic rituals pertaining, among other things, to baptism and a girl's first menstruation. In Africa and Brazil, inquisition and church officials persecuted a category of cross-dressers that in Central Africa were called *jinbandaa* and that Europeans treated as "sodomites" (Sweet 54).[13] In Spanish America, inquisitors and church officials tried to eliminate polygamy among the surviving native nobility and although the crime of sodomy technically fell under secular tribunals, they worked with government authorities to identify and punish indigenous "sodomites." And so forth.

The Holy Office's targeting of practices that did not technically fall under the category of "heresy" (publicly challenging main Christian tenets, such as the Holy Trinity) was not unique to the colonial context. In Spain and Portugal, the Inquisition tried to eradicate (though the emphasis varied by region and period) a host of practices among Jewish and Muslim converts to Christianity identified as contrary to Christian principles and morality, or as signs of loyalty to Judaism or Islam. These practices included not eating pork or pork products, changing into clean clothes on Saturday, preparing meat according to Judaic law, circumcising boys, using Arabic names for children, and the purportedly local Muslim patriarchal institution of "double marriages."[14]

As of about the middle of the sixteenth century, the Iberian Inquisitions also tried Old Christians, *cristianos viejos* or people theoretically of "pure" Christian ancestry. In Castile the Holy Office was busiest in rural areas, where Christian instruction was minimal and where it discovered that the ground was particularly fertile for sexual and marital offences (including bigamy and bestiality), blasphemy, and solicitation (sexual abuse on the part of priests) (Kamen 255–59). In Aragón, the Inquisition also prosecuted sodomy. It became the only inquisitorial tribunal to have jurisdiction over that crime in 1524, the year that the pope decreed that in the rest of Spain and in Spanish America it could only be tried by secular tribunals. For some scholars, the decision to allow the Aragonese Inquisition to handle cases of sodomy, sanctioned by the Spanish Crown, was related to the existence of significant populations of *moriscos* (Muslim converts to Christianity) in the region and the association that Christian Spaniards made between Muslims and the practice.[15] Linking religious infidelity and heterodoxy with "sexual deviance," some ecclesiastical and secular authorities not only connected sodomy with Islamic practices, but also, in colonial situations, with idolatry.[16]

The sixteenth-century campaigns by the two Iberian Inquisitions to police the socio-religious and sexual practices of *conversos* and *moriscos* (and indeed, of Old Christians) within and outside Iberia's borders, of the native peoples in the Americas, and of Muslim and Hindu converts to Christianity in Goa and East Africa, serves not just to highlight the extensive territorial reach of the Holy Office. The campaigns also raise questions about how the treatment of certain Spanish and Portuguese populations shaped the policing and discursive construction of native peoples in different colonial contexts and vice-versa. That in early Spanish descriptions of the Americas the sexual and marital practices of indigenous people (such as polygamy) were compared with those of the "Moors" is but one example of the slippage that occurred in the rhetorical "othering" of certain populations in metropolitan and colonial spaces or what Jonathan Burton and Ania Loomba refer to as "discursive scrambling," or the transfer of notions of difference from one region or people to another in order to help establish the terms of their assimilation or exclusion (Burton and Loomba 20).[17] Such scrambling was a messy—not automatic, not uniform—but critical early phase of the construction of ethnographic knowledge and of the tortuous history of modern racial discourses.

The sixteenth-century Iberian inquisitorial and Christianizing campaigns make evident the continuous movement of religious officials to different parts of the globe, producing and circulating reports, texts, and images that helped to create transregional and transimperial ethnographic knowledge. Many of the Franciscan friars who first went to Mexico had been active in the conversion and education of *moriscos* in southern Spain, for example, and a good number of Jesuits who went to do missionary work in Asia had first been based in New Spain (Mills and Taylor 47; Brading 102–27). These religious wrote letters, accounts, and histories that were translated, printed, and diffused, resulting in a wide information-sharing network. The governing policies of the Jesuits, an order that was more directly accountable to the papacy than to Spanish or Portuguese monarchs and which included a relatively high number of missionaries that were not from Iberia but other parts of Europe, referred explicitly to the importance of correspondence among its members wherever they were based. Letters by Jesuit missionaries sent from different regions to Rome were translated and printed and had wide readership, which implies that the order played a prominent role in the production and circulation of ethnographic knowledge in the early modern world.[18]

How did the networks of information created by Jesuits and other missionaries as well as inquisitors and priests shape the invention of *indios* (Indians) in different parts of the Spanish and Portuguese empires and beyond? In the sixteenth-century Iberian world, this category was highly unstable and in Castile alone could refer to people with origins in America, Asia, and even Africa. What meanings did the term have in different geographic and cultural contexts, how did these meanings change over time, and why? Scholars have begun to examine these questions and to explore the complex cultural links between different Iberian imperial spaces, but there is much more work to be done in order to reveal the nature and implications of those connections.[19]

Such work is especially crucial to advancing current understandings of the early modern Iberian Christianity—its global conversion projects, methods, and institutions—as a critical early site of orientalist knowledge production, or what Edward Said referred to as the discursive construction of the "occident" and "orient," Europe and its others (*Orientalism* and *Culture*).[20] Comparing developments in sixteenth-century New Spain and Goa offers a particularly fruitful line of investigation for analyzing this historical phenomenon because of the aforementioned simultaneity and similarity of certain imperial designs, methods, and practices in the two regions. In particular, during the 1530s and 1540s both places underwent processes of imperial reorganization that included the religious orders stepping up efforts to stabilize colonial rule.[21] These were decades in which the Franciscans and Dominicans in Mexico and Jesuits in Portuguese India undertook aggressive campaigns not just to eradicate traditional religious beliefs but to radically alter the cultural and linguistic traditions of subject populations and their spatial organization. Indeed, efforts to eradicate "idolatry"; to destroy native temples and replace them with churches; to set up convents; to establish schools, *doctrinas* (classes on the main tenets of Christianity) and "hospitals-towns" for native populations and colleges for members of the local elite; to nucleate and reorganize towns and villages (*reducciones*); and to spread Christian religious images and translate catechisms into local languages, occurred virtually simultaneously in central New Spain and Goa and knowledge of these projects circulated across the two empires.[22]

During this period members of the religious orders that were based in those regions began to generate histories, descriptions, and representations of the Americas and the *Estado da Índia* that helped to produce early modern orientalist discourses. Of course, in neither the Portuguese empire nor the Spanish one was the construction of orientalist discourses a monopoly of religious and inquisition officials. At the same time that friars, priests, and inquisitors studied all sorts of religious and social practices among the people that fell within their jurisdictions—whether in the mission, the confessional, the community in their charge, the inquisition cell—secular officials also collected ethnographic information about local populations and generated reports, censuses, *relaciones geográficas*, histories, treatises, and so forth. Together these agents of the church and state helped to produce discourses of "caste."

Caste

To speak of caste in the early modern Iberian empires is to step on shaky terrain, in part because in early modern Portuguese and Spanish, the term *casta* had multiple meanings (including "species," "breed," and "lineage") and tended to be applied differently in Portuguese Asia and Spanish America (Pitt-Rivers 231–54, esp. 234–35). When the Portuguese arrived in India at the end of the fifteenth century, they first applied the term to the Hindu socio-religious distinctions they saw, or thought they saw.[23] They identified four main endogamous "castes": the Brahmins or priestly caste; the Kshatriyas (Charodos) or warrior caste; the Vaysias (Vanis) or merchants and peasants; and the Sudras or menial class. At first, the Portuguese tried to abolish these distinctions among the Hindus who converted to Christianity, but found it too difficult and therefore kept them, creating five Christian castes out of the four. They essentially took the last two from the first system and created a separate category for landless peasants and workers; thus, they put all people who labored with their hands in one caste. This new version of "caste" retained the privileged status of those that had Brahmin ancestry (among other ways, by making them eligible for the priesthood) and, following previous traditions, preserved endogamy among the five (Christian) castes, which did not intermarry.

In the Americas, *casta*, whether used by the Portuguese in Brazil or Spain in its territories, retained its multiple connotations. Spaniards sometimes used it, for example, to distinguish between different indigenous lineage groups, such as Mayan *castas*.[24] Furthermore, in areas with significant slave populations, such as Peru and Brazil, slave owners tended to classify their slaves by African "castes" or what they classified as main African ethno-linguistic groups (O'Toole). But the "classic" use of the term *casta*, that which emerged in the main seats of the Spanish empire, referred to the three main colonial categories—Spaniards, Indians, and blacks—and in particular to the people who were in between. In other words, *españoles* (Spaniards), *indios* (Indians), *negros* (blacks), as well as *mestizos, mulatos* and *zambos* (people of indigenous and African descent) were all considered principal lineage groups, and thus *castas*, but the term was more often than not reserved for the last three and other "mixes." These classifications appeared gradually in parish records and censuses as well as in chronicles, reports, and geographies written by religious and secular officials during the second half of the sixteenth century (Martínez, "Interrogating" 196–217, *Genealogical Fictions* 142–70).

For example, in 1574, Juan López de Velasco, cosmographer-chronicler of Castile's "Indies" from 1571–1590, completed his *Geografía y descripción universal de las indias* (Geography and Universal Description of the Indies), in which he described the population of the land as consisting of its native inhabitants as well as *españoles* [Spaniards born in Spain], *criollos* [Creoles or "Spaniards born in the Indies"], and *mestizos, negros, mulatos, y zambaigos*.[25] These were the main categories of Spanish America's *sistema de castas*, the system of classification that in theory was based on proportions of indigenous, Spanish, and black blood.[26] Contrary to how caste operated in Portuguese India, then, in the Americas *casta* did not translate into a system of marriage prohibitions or endogamy; nor was it used to mainly refer to social distinctions among the native population. That caste generally meant something different in Portuguese Asia and Iberian America had to do with a complicated set of factors, including the particularities of colonial projects pursued in different regions, local demographic and social traditions, and indigenous responses to Iberian rule (a point discussed below). However, drawing a stark distinction between the meaning of *casta* in the *Estado da Índia* and the Spanish "Indies" (*"las Indias"*) is untenable because, as stated earlier, in certain parts of Spanish and Portuguese America Europeans distinguished indigenous or African groups by *casta* and regarded ethnolinguistic differences among them as ascribed statuses. Furthermore, although a Spanish-style *sistema de castas* may not have appeared in the *Estado da Índia*, at least not formally or to the same degree as in the Americas, similar classifications and orderings appeared in sixteenth- and seventeenth-century descriptions of the population of India under Portuguese rule.

For example, in 1580, six years after López de Velasco finished his *Geografía y descripción universal de las indias*, Alessando Valignano, an Italian Jesuit Priest who arrived in Portuguese India in 1574 was appointed Visitor of Missions there.[27] Valignano divided the population of the region into five categories: the *Reinól* (European-born Portuguese); the Portuguese who were born in India; the *castiços* (children of a European father and Eurasian mother, or more generally someone who was three-fourths European and one-fourth Asian); the *mestiços* (half European, half Indian); and the indigenous or "pure" Indians.[28] The categories and logic of the descriptions that López de Velasco produced in the 1570s of Spanish America's population and Valignano's of Goa's in 1580 were similar in various respects. The two writers distinguished between Europeans born in the metropole and those in overseas territories but put both at the top of the colonial social and spiritual pyramid. Both placed "pure Indians" at the bottom (or nearly at the bottom in the case of López de Velasco, who reserved that place for *castas* of African ancestry). And both ordered the middle categories according to proportions of blood from Europeans and the local population (as well as from blacks in the case of Velasco). Predictably, the more Spanish or Portuguese blood, the higher in the ranking. Thus, López de Velasco noted that *criollos* had different skin color and stature than their parents, that their *ánimo* or spirit was different too, and that they were less virtuous than their progenitors. But he described the *castas* (particularly those of African descent) as the worst segments of the population, lowest in the virtue and spirit scales (López de Velasco 20–22).

For his part, Valignano believed that people with dark skin (his terms were "*gente morena*" and "*de color negra*") fell short in their capacity to understand Christianity and spiritual matters more generally, and he suggested that they belonged to the Aristotelian category of humans whose underdeveloped rationality made them more apt to serve. Skeptical about the progress of the conversions campaigns in Goa, he instructed the other missionaries to explain to Hindu converts to Christianity that their adoption of the new faith did not imply "mudar casta y modo de vivir dexando la casta de los gentiles y haziendoze de la casta de los christianos" (cited in Barreto Xavier, *A Invenção* 145) (moving from the caste of gentiles to that of Christians).[29] While emphasizing that conversion should be conceived as an internal, spiritual process and not as vehicle to obtain temporal favors, Valignano seemed to be defining the term *casta* as an ascribed status—as something that did not change with the adoption of another religion—, and therefore as something that maintained a boundary between "new" and "old" Christians. Regardless of what social "caste" they belonged to locally, then, in the eyes of the Visitor of Missions all indigenous converts in Goa had originated in the "caste of gentiles" and this would continue to mark them as different from the Portuguese.

It could be argued, then, that in both Portuguese Asia and Spanish America, there were at least two discourses of caste, with one prevailing in one region and the other in the other region. One type, ostensibly based on preexisting ethnolinguistic or social distinctions, recognized different indigenous *castas* (Mayan *castas*, former Hindu-castes, African lineages, etc.); the other collapsed all local indigenous populations into one category (*indios*) and ordered it below the population of European and mixed descent (with the important caveat that the descendants of indigenous nobilities or high castes were officially recognized as more or less socially equal to Europeans). Versions of each system surfaced around the same time in parts of the Iberian colonies, from Goa, to central New Spain, to the Yucatán Peninsula, to Peru, to Brazil. Furthermore, in various parts of both empires the rise of a population of mixed descent provided the main impetus not just for the elaboration of classifications based on descent, but also for the establishment of mechanisms of exclusion based on the notion of "pure blood."

Blood and Race

A development of paramount importance in early modern Iberia was the emergence of a discourse of *limpieza de sangre* that linked blood and faith, ancestry and the capacity to fully convert to Christianity. According to this discourse, which began to surface in the latter half of the fifteenth century and led to the establishment of the statutes or purity of blood (requirements of "Old Christian" ancestry) by a host of religious and secular institutions, the *conversos* and *moriscos* were impure because they had proven to be unstable Christians, untrustworthy converts who carried the faith of their ancestors in their "blood." The notion that some populations were not able to fully convert to Christianity because of their ancestry as well as the association of the process of conversion to whitening that started to become prominent in the late sixteenth century were not unique to Iberians but prevalent in other early modern European countries, including England. What set Iberia apart was the early penetration of the idea of blood-purity into different cultural domains as well as the extent of its institutionalization through the statutes of *limpieza de sangre* (Martínez, Nirenberg, and Hering Torres 2).[30] In both Spain and Portugal, supporters of the statutes first justified them on the basis of the need to protect the Catholic faith from potentially subversive New Christians—from back-sliding converts—and in both places the blood purity requirements reinforced the idea (the genealogical fiction) that a person's religious ancestry shaped his or her religious and spiritual tendencies.[31]

When Iberians began to expand to other continents they seemed to be more optimistic about the conversion potential of the peoples they encountered; after all, one of their objectives for expansion was to spread their faith. Thus, as they were arriving and settling in parts of Asia and the Americas they were experimenting with the creation of native clergies in parts of West Africa and the islands of Cape Verde and São Tomé, and the pope was issuing decrees allowing the ordination of "Ethiopians, Indians, and Africans" (Boxer, *Race* 16, 33).³² But such experiments were always accompanied by some ambivalence, for missionaries and priests tended to infantilize the native peoples they sought to convert in different parts of the globe. In Goa, for example, the Franciscans and Jesuits viewed the Hindus like children, lacking real knowledge of God, and members of the regular and secular clergies in the Americas generally depicted the indigenous populations there in similar terms. Whether in Asia or the Atlantic world, the European infantilization of colonial populations was normally rooted in claims about inadequate rational capacities. As evidenced by the Spanish juridical debates about the humanity status of the native people of the Americas during the first half of the sixteenth century, reason was treated as both a marker of civility and precondition for Christianization and thus performed crucial ideological work for colonial domination and dispossession.³³ It was no coincidence that discourses of rationality and depictions of "Indians" as childlike were particularly prominent during times when native lands, political authority, and control over other economic resources were being transferred to Iberian hands, as occurred in mid-sixteenth century New Spain and Goa.

By and large Iberia's theologians and jurists did not claim that colonial subjects lacked rationality—doing so would have been tantamount to recognizing the futility of the conversion project—but they depicted them as in need of spiritual and secular guidance in order to fully develop it and become self-governing Christians, in other words, as requiring colonial mentorship. If the church accepted some members of indigenous nobilities or high castes as priests it was generally due to a shortage of secular clergy or to efforts to secure the loyalties of those sectors. Native priests, however, could normally not gain access to the top offices of the church and, in keeping with a colonial paternalistic logic, were usually placed under the tutelage of Iberian missionaries. If the secular clergy was not very open to them, the religious orders were even more exclusive. In Goa, for example, the Jesuits admitted very few converts into their institutions, though they were more open to it in China and Japan (Boxer, *Race* 65–66). In other words, local and contingent factors such as the lack of applicants of European descent for religious vocations or the church's need for cultural-linguistic intermediaries in their evangelization projects made it possible in some places for people of indigenous or mixed ancestry to become priests or friars; but in general, they could not reach the top ecclesiastical echelons and were officially excluded from various religious orders, including the Jesuits and Franciscans.

Signs that these exclusions and hierarchies would surface started to appear in the 1540s when the more militant phase of conversion began in the *Estado da Índia* and Spanish America, and growing skepticism about the loyalty of indigenous leaders to Christianity among ecclesiastical authorities called into question any efforts to create native clergies. Decades later when López de Velasco and Valignano were describing and classifying the populations of New Spain and Goa, respectively, there were ongoing discussions in both the Portuguese and Spanish empires about the eligibility of colonial subjects for the religious and secular administrations. Crucially, such discussions increasingly introduced matters of *casta*, *raza*, and *sangre*, thus incorporating and adapting the terms, suppositions, and meanings of the discourse of *limpieza de sangre* to colonial contexts. For example, in the 1570s and 1580s some of New Spain's cathedral chapters were trying to make certain priests ineligible for ecclesiastical posts and benefices on the basis that that they were of the "*raza de mestizos*" and not "pure Old Christian Spaniards" (Martínez, *Genealogical Fictions* 28). Furthermore, some religious orders that were based in the region were starting to curtail membership by extending the purity of blood requirement to "recent converts" from the land.[34]

In those same decades, the Jesuits who had gone to India and other parts of Asia were also establishing similar membership criteria and casting people of "mixed blood" in increasingly negative terms.[35] Thus, in his description of Goa, Valignano stated that he doubted that anyone in India was suitable to enter into his order, including the *Reinól* because they were undereducated or being trained primarily as soldiers. But he reserved the most damning words for *castiços* and *mestiços*, and in general he stressed that those people with more native ancestry than European blood were the least qualified (Boxer, *Race* 62–63). The *mestiços* were therefore worse than the *castiços* and the "basest" of all were the *indios*. As Valignano's arguments for keeping people of mixed ancestry and especially "pure Indians" out of the Society of Jesus and other historical sources indicate, then, in the last decades of the sixteenth century *casta* classifications and hierarchies were surfacing in different parts of the Iberian empires in close relationship with the deployment of discourses about lineage or "blood" as a reliable indicator of whether a person was a good, bad, or suspect Christian, or simply a "neophyte" (a Christian in the making).

In this context, a number of Portuguese and Spanish colonial institutions came to treat certain *castas* as bad *razas* (as in "*raza de mestizos*" in the earlier Mexican cathedral chapter example) and to regard their caste statuses as a legitimate basis for exclusion.[36] That the religious orders were among the first institutions to establish these exclusions was partly due to their early role in spreading the faith to different parts of the Iberian empires, which made them have to consider the issue of who in the colonies was eligible to join their ranks. But the question of membership eligibility and restrictions on access to offices and honors was by no means confined to religious institutions (nor was the preoccupation with purity and caste exclusive to Iberian missionaries, as the Valignano example demonstrates). In the course of establishing Portuguese and Spanish rule in parts of Africa, Asia, and the Americas, similar questions arose about the qualifications of people of mixed ancestry to exercise professions such as that of alderman, soldier, and scrivener and to enter certain colleges, military orders, guilds, universities, and so forth. The responses to these questions varied somewhat by region and time. But in general, Iberians tended to limit the access that indigenous and people of mixed ancestry in conquered regions had to certain professions and to the secular and ecclesiastical administrations. These limitations, based on the Iberian discourse of *limpieza de sangre*, were one of the main pillars of the regimes of classification and exclusion that Spain and Portugal created in different parts of the globe.

Such regimes help to unveil the duplicitous nature of early modern empires, their propensity to claim to rule the territories they incorporated by force under a principle of equal subjecthood while actually governing them through what Partha Chatterjee calls the logic of "colonial difference."[37] Though to varying degrees, the Iberian, French, and English empires all espoused the idea that people living in the lands they conquered—Europeans and natives—were equal in their relationship of subjecthood to the crown (Pagden 260). More often than not, this principle was rhetorical rather than real, for another characteristic that these empires shared was the sustained production of colonial social, cultural, and political distinctions based on caste and race, *casta* and *raza*. In Spanish America, for example, indigenous people who converted to Christianity were incorporated into the Crown of Castile as vassals and thus potentially "Spanish," but tributary, labor, and segregation laws (among other things) perpetuated differences between them and the rest of the population. Like other empires, the Iberian ones were thus characterized by their ability to combine and recombine incorporation and difference, to sustain rule through the balancing of policies that promoted assimilation and distinction.[38]

Particularly (though not exclusively) in the Catholic empires, the political fiction of equal subjecthood was accompanied by the fantasy of Christian unity, that is, by the religious precept that all those who converted to Christianity were redeemed by baptism and thus equal members of the church. Thus, from 1562 on through the second half of the eighteenth century, the Portuguese issued laws affirming the principle of equality between the Portuguese and Asian converts to Christianity (Figueira 88; Mendonça 21–22). The church and Spanish legislation made similar proclamations about subjects in Spanish America.[39] However, despite the iteration of principles of equal subjecthood and religious status for their Asian and American territories, Spain and Portugal allowed their overseas institutions to adapt one of the principal Iberian mechanisms of exclusion and social differentiation to colonial contexts: statutes of purity of blood.

The adaptation of these statutes signals the deployment of discourses of lineage and blood—of *casta* and *raza*—to create internal hierarchies in their different Spanish and Portuguese colonial territories and within the Iberian Peninsula as well as the connected histories of the two empires during the sixteenth and seventeenth centuries. It also raises questions about how exactly the discourse of *limpieza de sangre* functioned in different parts of these empires, about its relationship to indigenous notions of lineage, blood, and kinship, and about the responses of native and other populations to Iberian purity concepts. It was one thing for the Spanish and Portuguese to attempt to impose their notions of blood-purity in different parts of the globe; quite another was the fate that those notions—and their implication for such things as marriage, intimacy, and social relations—would have in different contexts.

In Goa, for example, the Portuguese policy of encouraging marriages between Portuguese soldiers and Indian women of high caste (and preferably of light skin), which was introduced by Afonso de Albuquerque during his tenure as Viceroy of the *Estado da Índia* (1509–1515), turned out to be controversial. Although some marriages took place, Indians of Brahmin and Kshatriya origins saw the Portuguese soldiers as inferior and thus damaging to their lineages. Indeed, as Ângela Barreto Xavier has written, Goan elites not only tended to be reticent about creating marriage ties with the Portuguese but to deploy their own notions of blood purity against them ("O lustre" 73). In New Spain and Peru, by contrast, marriages between the daughters of the surviving Nahua and Inca nobilities and Spanish men took place, which though not large in number were highly important in socio-political terms, and in neither place was there a strong rejection of "mixing" with Spaniards, at least not one that was recorded and preserved in writing. It is true that some native writers, most notably the Andean Guaman Poma de Ayala, disapproved of the "mixture" they saw occurring around them and argued for an orderly and hierarchical society that maintained the purity of Spaniards and Indians.[40] But in general the Goan elite's response to Iberian blood-purity concepts and to the idea of "mixing" seems to have differed from that of the descendants of indigenous rulers and nobles in central Mexico and Peru.[41]

The reasons for these different responses are difficult to isolate, but it is probable that they were related to the particular legal status and social condition of the indigenous nobilities of New Spain and Peru after the conquest, native concepts of blood, lineage, and purity, and the political alliances that some community leaders built with Spaniards after the fall of Tenochtitlán and Cuzco.

Among the Nahuas of central Mexico, for example, there was a strong tradition of governing elites cementing political pacts and creating military coalitions by marrying their women to rulers of strategic neighboring communities or conquered groups, especially if such marriages allowed them to claim Toltec descent (Calnek 43–62).[42] Mesoamerica's Late Post-Classic period (1200–1521) might have been characterized by an acute preoccupation among ruling elites of different polities with creating noble dynasties and basing political legitimacy on Toltec pedigree, but the obsession with nobility and descent did not result in rigid notions of blood purity, at least not ones that would prevent kinship ties being forged—through a transfer of women—across social statuses or cultural groups. These long-standing political and genealogical practices influenced the social relations that the surviving Nahua rulers and nobles established with the Spanish, who like the Portuguese had their own traditions of trying to consolidate political control after military victories by marrying their soldiers and colonists to the women of conquered ruling groups. These traditions had begun during the "Reconquista," or Christian crusade to recover Iberian regions under Muslim rule, and were revived in parts of Africa, Asia, and the Americas but with different regional results.

Local traditions, local developments, and local actors (indigenous and otherwise) mattered in the construction of discourses of caste and race and they ultimately help to explain why Iberian discourses of blood purity and nobility would acquire distinct valences in different colonial regions. Although the Spanish and Portuguese tried to impose similar strategies of colonization and conversion in the various parts of their empires, their efforts to convert, to co-opt, and to control faced different cultural responses and forms of resistance and in most cases they had to accommodate, at least temporarily, traditional notions of political authority, land, kinship, and spirituality, among other things. In other words, policies of accommodation were not only the *modus operandi* of Jesuits in parts of China and Japan, where colonial authority was relatively weak or missing altogether, but also the common approach of Iberian empires in India, the Americas, and Africa. Less a function of brilliant strategies of colonial expansion, it was an approach driven by the resilience and responses of the cultures that Iberians encountered in different parts of the world.[43]

Conclusion

This overview of religion, caste, and race in the early modern Spanish and Portuguese empires highlights a series of historical and analytical issues related to Iberian colonization. First, that the two empires were global rather than just

Atlantic productions has several methodological and conceptual implications.[44] It suggests the need among scholars of colonial Latin America to widen the analytical geographic frame and pay great attention to how developments in Africa and Asia, both prior to and after 1492, influenced religious, cultural, and political practices and policies in the Americas. This more global approach should also be attentive to the overlapping or connected histories of the two empires, which was particularly strong during the union of the two crowns (1580–1640). Although more formal than real (and arguably it helped to strengthen distinctions between them), the union led, among other things, to greater movement of people from one empire to another, a more militant effort to police the socio-religious and sexual activities of different populations in Iberia and its overseas territories, and an easier circulation of ethnographic descriptions, texts, manuscripts, images, and idolatry treatises between Castile's and Portugal's imperial spaces and beyond. Understanding how institutions and agents of Iberian expansion generated and circulated information about religion and caste and created networks within, between, and outside the two empires is crucial to unraveling not just how early modern racial knowledge was constructed, but the extent to which racial discourses were cosmopolitan, and not national, enterprises.

Focusing on both empires and their connected histories in the sixteenth and seventeenth centuries also helps to illuminate Iberia's precocious contribution to orientalist discourses. The European depiction of the Orient as an exotic place of wonders, monsters, and human and social oddities had a deeper trajectory and many of the discriminatory features and tropes of colonialism had medieval antecedents (especially in religious discourses), but the early modern expansion of Portugal and Spain to Asia and the Americas and their invention of *"las Indias"* and *"indios"* earned the Iberian empires a special place in the history of orientalism.[45] As with the orientalism of the nineteenth and twentieth centuries that Edward Said and other scholars have studied, during this "Iberian phase," religion, caste, and sexuality were interconnected sites in the production of racial knowledge and reproduction of colonial rule. As Iberian (or Iberian-commissioned) missionaries and inquisition officials fanned out to different parts of Africa, Asia, and America to convert native populations and keep European colonists in line, these agents of imperial expansion also tended to target the social norms, domestic arrangements, and sexual practices of native populations. What sexual practices were targeted in particular contexts; how their persecution generated discourses, for example, about sodomy or polygamy that were mapped on to certain populations; how this knowledge shaped understandings of "caste" and "race"; and how those understandings circulated on transcolonial and transimperial scales—these are among questions that are central to the study of race and European imperialism over the longue durée. Another, the investigation of which requires bridging economic and cultural analytic approaches, is how the political economy of particular regions was related to, or worked through culture, and more generally how it might have shaped local and global racial discourses.

A running theme in the essay has been the role of religious orders and religion in early modern Iberian colonization projects. Though with varying militancy, idolatry eradication campaigns and evangelization projects in parts of the Americas, Asia, and Africa continued into the eighteenth century (in the Spanish borderlands, for example) and involved instruction on spiritual matters but also on a host of living, marital, and sexual practices. The broad pedagogical labor on the part of friars and priests—which, at least in sixteenth-century central New Spain and Goa resorted to similar institutional and ideological instruments—exposes the role of religion not just as an impulse for imperial expansion, not just as a simple justification for political domination and economic exploitation, but as kind of incubator of Iberian colonial and racial ideologies.[46] Christianity was a crucial framework through which colonized subjects were ideologically, politically, and culturally incorporated, excluded, and ranked and "Christian" "gentile" and "pagan" as well as *raza* and *casta* were main categories through which these processes took place. Deployed within the discourse of *limpieza de sangre* with religious valences, the latter two concepts generated protoethnographic projects and knowledge that in the course of time helped to constitute colonial notions of race and shape marital practices, political imaginaries, and sexual desires.

Notions of blood-purity and caste, conversion discourses that linked Christianization and whitening, and classification schemes involving *casta* or "mixed" categories were not unique to Iberia but part of a broader European Christian culture. Spain and Portugal stood out, however, in terms of the early and extensive institutionalization that the concept of *limpieza de sangre* and related ideas of *casta* and *raza* achieved in the Iberian Peninsula and its colonial territories. The deployment of these concepts occurred in the face of an imperial rhetoric of equal subjecthood and spiritual status for all loyal Christian vassals living in the territories of the crown, and together with colonial economic regimes and social relations worked to produce and reproduce colonial difference. Stated differently, the political and religious fictions of empire favored inclusion, while colonial policies and practices tended to promote hierarchies and exclusion.

This discussion of the early modern Spanish and Portuguese empires has also emphasized that, in analyzing the imperial and global dimensions of Iberian racial discourses, it is crucial not to lose sight of on-the-ground interactions and in particular of the role that local traditions, people, and developments played in shaping colonial policies, cultural practices, and social relations. Iberians might have transplanted their institutions (such as the Inquisition), mechanisms of social differentiation and exclusion (such as concepts and statutes of purity of blood), and cultural practices (such as campaigns of idolatry extirpation) to their colonial territories, but as numerous studies of the past three decades have demonstrated, often they had to adapt them to those contexts, to negotiate with local actors, and to contend with challenges to their methods, demands, and ideologies by different native peoples.[47] Moreover, the existence of imperial discourses of inclusion based on loyalty to king and faith alongside the extension of notions of *limpieza de sangre* and *casta*, and *raza* not only created profound political ambiguities but also spaces of resistance and native appropriations of categories such as "Christian," "purity of blood," and "vassal." To ignore these points is to flatten indigenous societies, collapse native people under the category of "colonized," and render them insignificant to historical processes. In short, it is to revive old imperial histories when the objective should be to interrogate the complex relationship between empire and local contingencies and how at times different actors in colonial situations could shape, challenge, or reinforce the former. Studying empire from the vantage point of the local can help re-think the global.

Finally, this discussion of the early modern Iberian empires serves to underscore the importance of studying the influence of Spanish and Portuguese colonial projects on other empires. As the founders of the first (and in parts of Africa and Asia some of the most enduring) colonial regimes of the modern world, the Iberians did not just interact with one another, but set a tone, albeit to different degrees, for other expansionist states. To provide one obvious example, when the British used the word "caste" in India, they borrowed it from the Portuguese (Pitt-Rivers 236). A growing number of works on the Iberian Atlantic are demonstrating, furthermore, that the imaginations of sixteenth-century British imperial agents were strongly influenced by the natural histories, chronicles, medical and legal treatises, and other writings produced by the Spanish and Portuguese (Cañizares-Esguerra and Breen 597). Further research on the circulation of information regarding the terms as well as practices that were part of the religious and *casta* discourses of the first "globe-encircling empires" of the modern world will thus help to reveal the extent to which they produced ethnographic knowledge that served as models (to follow or reject) for other empires and their own systems of racial classification and colonial domination.

NOTES

1. Research for this essay was partly made possible by a 2012–2013 Fulbright Scholars Fellowship. I am grateful for the comments I received from participants at various venues where the paper was presented, including the symposium "Spain and Por-

tugal: One Kingdom, Two Empires?" (Stanford University, November 11, 2011), the workshop "The Colonial Roots of Globalization" (Mexico City, March 24–27, 2013), and the seminar "Race, Across Time and Space" (McNeil Center for Early American Studies, Mellon Sawyer Seminar, University of Pennsylvania, October 4, 2013).

2. Exceptions include Sanjay Subrahmanyam, who emphasizes the need for more studies that focus on the cultural dimensions of the two empires together.

3. Both crowns claimed their right to conquer and colonize lands in part on the papal bulls that starting in 1415–1416 granted Portugal and later Spain different parts of Africa, the Atlantic islands, and the Americas.

4. One of the most brutal anti-idolatry campaigns took place among the Maya of Yucatán in the 1560s. Led by the Franciscan Diego de Landa, they resulted in the torture of more than 4500 Mayas, of whom at least 150 died (Clendinnen, esp. 72–111).

5. Scholarship on the establishment of inquisitorial tribunals in the Americas and Asia includes Roth 208–26; Boxer, *The Church* 84–93; Chuchiak; and Meyuhas Ginio.

6. See Soyer, "An Example" and "Nowhere to Run."

7. The Union of the Spanish and Portuguese Crowns (1580–1640) was more formal than real, beset with problems, and did not result in subjecthood to two kings. When the imperial marriage took place, for example, Spain's King Philip II declared that Castile's and Portugal's administrations would be kept separate and that in Spain's territories the Portuguese remained foreigners unless they were naturalized. Therefore, to participate in commerce in Spanish America, Portuguese subjects had to obtain licenses. In part because *cristãos novos* were its main lenders, the Spanish Crown readily granted Portuguese merchants of Jewish ancestry such licenses. Whether with permits or not, in the last decades of the sixteenth century members of New Christian entrepreneurial families dispersed to various parts of both empires and began to play a prominent role in commerce in cities such as Mexico and Peru. As their population increased, so did Spanish regulations and inquisitorial persecution to restrict their commercial and religious activities. See Cross; Hordes; and Silverblatt, "New Christians."

8. See, for, example, Graizbord; and Bodian. The relatively large scholarship on New Christians and Jews in the Americas includes Uchmany, *La vida entre el judaísmo*, and "The Participation"; Alberro; and Feitler, "Jews and New Christians." For the Philippines, refer to Uchmany, "Criptojudíos."

9. Carvajal "the younger" wrote his memoirs before his death in 1596. See Liebman; and for more on the Carvajal family, see Toro; and Martin Cohen.

10. For New Spain, refer to Greenleaf; and Moreno de los Arcos. For the Andes, see Mills; and Ramos and Urbano.

11. Although Portugal did not establish an inquisitorial tribunal in Brazil (or in West and Central Africa for that matter), it relied on non-inquisitorial institutions and personnel—the bishops and archbishops for example, and more generally the secular clergy as well as the Jesuits—on the other side of the Atlantic to police orthodoxy. Furthermore, the Lisbon-based Inquisition periodically sent agents to Brazil to conduct investigations (Wadsworth 19–27; and Feitler, *Inquisition*).

12. On the concept of idolatry in early modern Europe and its shifting meanings due to colonialism and internal continental developments such as the Reformation, see MacCormack; Johnson; and Tzoref-Ashkenazi.
13. More generally on Portuguese treatment of same-sex relations among African slaves in Brazil and what appear to be third-gender categories in Central Africa, see Sweet 50–58.
14. Practices that were popularly associated with Judaism and Islam along with beliefs or speech that were considered blasphemous or heretical were read publicly during the announcement of "Edicts of Grace," periods that the Inquisition gave to people to confess or denounce others whom they suspected of heresy. See Starr-LeBeau 53–89; and Roth 76–83.
15. See, for example, Haliczer 302. Also refer to Monter 276–302.
16. On the quite prevalent representation of native people as "sodomites" in sixteenth- and seventeenth-century texts by Spanish conquistadors, chroniclers, royal historiographers, and members of the clergy, and how they associated sodomitic practices with anthropophagy, human sacrifices, idolatry, and diabolism, among other things, see Garza Carvajal 133–54; and Olivier Durand 47–63. And on how idolatry and sodomy were described and discursively linked through metaphors of disease, infection, and conspiracy in seventeenth-century Mexico, see Gruzinski 200–1.
17. Spain's policies toward *moriscos* influenced how other European countries depicted and treated other populations. For the example of England and the Irish, see Fuchs 33–52.
18. See Giard 74–78. And on eighteenth-century Jesuit writings and global networks of knowledge, see del Valle 46–63. I thank Larissa Brewer-García for reminding me of the importance of the Jesuit Order's tight relationship to Rome and the international character of its members.
19. Recent works on *"indio"* and other *casta* categories include van Deusen; Baber; Rappaport; and O'Toole.
20. Said's work, based mainly (though not exclusively) on analyses of British and French writings on Middle Eastern cultures in the nineteenth and twentieth centuries, inspired studies of orientalism in different fields. The literature (and scholarship criticizing it) is too vast to cite here, but for a discussion of how India could figure in German thought, see Tzoref-Ashkenazi. On how European representations of the Americas and India both stemmed from and transformed European epistemological traditions as well produced new discourses of the body, subjectivity, and race, see Seth. And for one of the first works to think through the intellectual and discursive implications of early modern European colonial expansion (including the invention of America or the "Indias"), see O'Gorman, which was first published in Spanish in 1948 as *La Invención De América: investigación acerca de la estructura histórica del Nuevo Mundo y del sentido de su devenir*.
21. See Ruiz Medrano, esp. 13–134; and Barreto Xavier, *A Invenção* 31 and 37–80.
22. Barreto Xavier rightly calls attention to the need to study this "institutional simultaneity" in Mexico and India further in order to better understand not just the role of religious orders in consolidating Iberian imperial rule, but also the relationship

of the two empires and their influences on each other (*A Invenção* 109, 451). And on the activities of the Jesuits in different Goan villages in the sixteenth century, including their establishment of schools, hospital-towns, *doctrinas*, and churches, and efforts to change local rituals, ceremonies, and family life, see Barreto Xavier, *A Invenção* 145–269. "Hospital-towns," modeled after Thomas More's Utopia, congregated native people in order to teach them Christianity, crafts, and the basics of self-government. In central Mexico the first, called Santa Fe, was established by Bishop Vasco de Quiroga in the 1530s.

23. There is some scholarly disagreement on whether using the term "caste" to describe the hierarchical social system that existed in India prior to European colonization is appropriate given that it was introduced by the Portuguese. Barreto Xavier believes that Goans who claimed to have Brahmin and Kshatriya stock provided their particular version of the caste system to the Portuguese (*A Invenção* 274). Mendonça points out that even the word "Hindu" was invented by the Portuguese, for it does not appear in sixteenth-century Indo-Portuguese historiography. "*Goan*" and "*Canarim*" do, on the other hand, both designating inhabitants of Goa (41).

24. In colonial Yucatán, pre-Hispanic ruling dynasties became less provincial (more local due to the political fragmentation that colonialism encouraged) but survived and continued to play an important role in town government, in large part because of the strong link between political legitimacy and lineage among the Maya since at least the Classic period. It does not appear that the word *casta* was used much by the colonial Maya to describe their social distinctions, but rather was a term that was mainly applied to them by Spaniards and creoles well into the nineteenth century. On the survival of Mayan lineages in colonial times, see Farriss 231–55. And for more on colonialism, conversion, and language among the Maya, see Hanks; and Restall.

25. See López de Velasco 20–22. The work was sent to the Council of the Indies, which prohibited the circulation of the few copies that were made because its information on geography and hydraulics were considered state secrets (Portuondo 172).

26. Although the categories alluded mainly to descent or bloodlines, scholarship of the past three decades has demonstrated that in practice classifications were often also based on factors such as behavior, phenotype, language, social status, and religious standing. For New Spain, early works include Seed, "Social Dimensions"; McCaa; Cope; and Boyer.

27. After his years in India, Valignano went to work in the Jesuit Missions of China and Japan, where he promoted a policy of accommodation or adjusting to local socio-political traditions to facilitate conversion. See Brockey; and Hoey.

28. Boxer, *Race* 62–63. As Boxer notes, the meanings of the categories were not stable. In the seventeenth century, for example, the term *castiço* was used to refer to Portuguese born in India, without any Asian blood (so that it was similar to *criollo* in Spanish America) and *mestiço* came to refer to anyone with a European ancestor (to anyone who was "mixed"; 63, n. 18) In Portuguese, *reinól* refers to someone "born in the kingdom" or *reino*.

29. For Valiagno's references to color and rationality, see 147 and fn. 428.
30. On the prevalence of links between religious conversion and genealogical or quasi-biological notions of difference in early modern England and other parts of Europe, see Burton and Loomba 16–17.
31. The literature on the *limpieza de sangre* statutes is too vast to cite here, but for what remains one of the best introductions to the topic, see Sicroff. Scholarship on the use of the concept of purity of blood in Portugal and Brazil includes Tucci Carneiro.
32. On the Portuguese incursion into Africa see the classic article by Viotti da Costa. Also refer to Thornton.
33. See, for example, Seed, "'Are these not men'?"
34. On the adaptation of the concept of *limpieza de sangre* in New Spain, see chapter six of Martínez, *Genealogical Fictions*, which includes a section on the Franciscan Order's establishment of the blood-purity requirement in central Mexico. In Peru too, the issue of *limpieza de sangre* surfaced relatively soon in the religious orders. On the role that it played in the politics and admission requirements of Jesuit colleges at the end of the sixteenth century, when the order extended the blood exclusion to "recent converts," see Coello de la Rosa. And on how only a few *mestizos* would ascend the ecclesiastical and secular administrative ranks in Santa Fe de Bogotá (though some were ordained as priests), see Zambrano.
35. The implementation of a statute of purity within the Jesuit Order was resisted until 1593 and included debates about how it might compromise colonial missionary enterprises. See Domínguez Ortiz; and Thomas Cohen, "Nation, Lineage," and "Racial and ethnic."
36. On the introduction of Portuguese concepts and requirements of blood purity in Goa and likening of the converted population to New Christians, see Barreto Xavier, *A Invenção* 395–97.
37. With the term "colonial difference" Partha Chatterjee extended Michel Foucault's notion of "governmentality" (the classifications and organized practices that governments establish to produce, and rule over, citizens) to colonial situations (16–18).
38. Frederick Cooper discusses this aspect of empires (*Colonialism*, 27; and "Provincializing France," 354).
39. On Spanish legislation and debates about the political and religious status of native people in the Americas, see chapters four and eight of Martínez, *Genealogical Fictions*.
40. Guaman Poma's arguments for preserving the purity of Spaniards and indigenous Andeans in his chronicle to the king are discussed in Silverblatt, *Modern* 128–30.
41. For more on indigenous notions of nobility and uses of lineage in Mexico and Peru, see Martínez, "Indigenous Genealogies." On notions of "mixing" (*mestizaje*) not taking root in Goa as they did in Spanish and Portuguese America because of the ideal of purity in India, see Barreto Xavier, "O lustre" 97–98. When analyzing the different trajectories and consequences of Iberian rule in American versus other contexts, one factor that cannot be ignored is the demographic one. As historian José C. Moya has pointed out, the high number of Iberians who migrated to the

Americas over the centuries made a tremendous difference in terms of language and religion, as opposed, say, to the case of the Portuguese or British in India and other colonial situations (6–8).

42. For a detailed discussion of Mexica rulers' dynastic unions with women of Toltec descent, see Gillespie, esp. 21, 25–56. Also refer to Socolow 16–31.
43. See Cañizares-Esguerra and Seeman's book, which includes a number of articles on the importance of local conditions in shaping Atlantic and global history.
44. Although some historians argue that it was not until the nineteenth century that globalization actually occurred, an increasing number of new works are demonstrating strong connections among the ocean worlds of the Atlantic, India, and the Pacific. See, for example, Lane, who charts the intricate trading networks through which South American emeralds circulated.
45. Burton and Loomba stress this point (10).
46. This is one of the main arguments I make for New Spain in *Genealogical Fictions*.
47. The literature on the Inquisition, for example, has shown that it was an institution that adapted to local and historical changes. A discussion of this literature is provided in Böttcher. For New Spain, scholarship on indigenous responses to Spanish rule includes the pioneering work by Farriss.

WORKS CITED

Alberro, Solange. "Crypto-Jews and the Mexican Holy Office in the Seventeenth Century." *The Jews and the Expansion of Europe to the West 1450–1800*, Ed. Bernardini and Norman Fiering. New York and Oxford: Berghahn Books, 2001. 172–85.

Baber, Jovita. "Categories, Self-Representation and the Construction of the *Indios*." *Journal of Spanish Cultural Studies* 10:1 (2009): 27–41. Web.

Barreto Xavier, Ângela. *A Invenção de Goa: Poder Imperial e Conversões Culturais nos Séculos XVI E XVII*. Lisbon: Imprensa de Ciências Sociais, 2008.

———. "'O lustre do seu sangue': Bramanismo e tópicas de distinção no contexto português." *Tempo* 30 (Brazil) (Jan. 2011): 71–99.

Bodian, Miriam. "'Men of the Nation': The Shaping of *Converso* Identity in Early Modern Europe." *Past and Present* 143 (May 1994): 49–76.

Böttcher, Nikolaus. "Inquisición y limpieza de sangre en Nueva España." *El peso de la sangre: Limpios, mestizos y nobles en el mundo hispánico*. Ed. Nikolaus Böttcher, Bernd Hausberger, and Max S. Hering Torres. Mexico City: El Colegio de México, 2011. 187–218.

Boxer, Charles R. *Race Relations in the Portuguese Colonial Empire, 1415–1825*. London: Oxford University Press, 1963.

———. *The Church Militant and Iberian Expansion, 1440–1770*. Baltimore and London: The Johns Hopkins University Press, 1978.

Boyer, Richard. *Caste and Identity in Colonial Mexico: A Proposal and an Example.* Storrs, Providence, and Amherst: Latin American Studies Consortium of New England, 1997.
Brading, D. A. *The First America: The Spanish Monarchy, Creole Patriots, and the Liberal State, 1492–1867.* Cambridge, UK: Cambridge University Press, 1991.
Brockey, Liam Matthew. *Journey to the East: The Jesuit Mission to China, 1579–1724.* Cambridge, Mass: Belknap Press of Harvard University Press, 2008.
Burton, Jonathan, and Ania Loomba. *Race in Early Modern England: A Documentary Companion.* Basingstoke: Palgrave Macmillan, 2007.
Calnek, Edward. "Patterns of Empire Formation in the Valley of Mexico, Late Postclassic Period, 1200–1521." *The Inca and Aztec States, 1400–1800: Anthropology and History.* Ed. George A. Collier, Renato Rosaldo, and John D. Wirth. New York: Academic Press, 1982. 43–62.
Cañizares-Esguerra, Jorge, and Benjamin Breen. "Hybrid Atlantics: Future Directions for the History of the Atlantic." *History Compass* 11:8 (2013): 597–609.
Cañizares-Esguerra, Jorge, and Erik R. Seeman. *The Atlantic in Global History, 1500–2000.* Upper Saddle River, NJ: Pearson Prentice Hall, 2007.
Chatterjee, Partha. *The Nation and Its Fragments: Colonial and Postcolonial Histories.* Princeton: Princeton University Press, 1993.
Chuchiak, John F. *The Inquisition in New Spain, 1536–1820: A Documentary History.* Baltimore: Johns Hopkins University Press, 2012.
Clendinnen, Inga. *Ambivalent Conquests: Maya and Spaniard in Yucatan, 1517–1570.* Cambridge, UK: Cambridge University Press, 1991.
Coello de la Rosa, Alexandre. "Pureza, Prestigio y Letras en Lima Colonial: El conflicto entre el Colegio de San Martín y el Colegio Real de San Felipe y San Marcos (1590–1615)." *El peso de la sangre: Limpios, mestizos y nobles en el mundo hispánico.* Ed. Nikolaus Böttcher, Bernd Hausberger, and Max S. Hering Torres. Mexico City: El Colegio de México, 2011. 137–68.
Cohen, Martin A. *The Martyr: Luis de Carvajal, a Secret Jew in Sixteenth-Century Mexico.* Albuquerque: University of New Mexico Press, 2001.
Cohen, Thomas M. "Nation, Lineage, and Jesuit Unity in Antonio Possevino's Memorial to Everard Mercurian (1576)." *A Companhia de Jesus na Península Ibérica nos séculos XVI e XVII: Espiritualidade e cultura.* Porto: Editora Universidade do Porto, 2004. 543–61.
———. "Racial and ethnic minorities in the Society of Jesus." *The Cambridge companion to the Jesuits.* Ed. Thomas Worcester. Cambridge, UK: Cambridge University Press, 2008. 199–216.
Cooper, Frederick. *Colonialism in Question: Theory, Knowledge, History.* Berkeley: University of California Press, 2005.
———. "Provincializing France." *Imperial Formations.* Ed. Ann L. Stoler, Carole Granahan, and Peter C. Perdue. Santa Fe: School for Advanced Research Press, 2007. 341–78.
Cope, Douglas R. *The Limits of Racial Domination: Plebeian Society in Colonial Mexico City, 1660–1720.* Madison: The University of Wisconsin Press, 1994.

Cross, Harry E. "Commerce and Orthodoxy: A Spanish Response to Portuguese Commercial Penetration in the Viceroyalty of Peru, 1580–1640." *The Americas* 35:2 (1978): 151–67.
del Valle, Ivonne. *Escribiendo desde los márgenes: Colonialismo y jesuitas en el siglo XVIII*. Mexico City: Siglo XXI, 2009.
Domínguez Ortiz, Antonio. *Los judeoconversos en la España moderna*. Madrid: Editorial MAPFRE, S.A., 1992.
Farriss, Nancy M. *Maya Society Under Colonial Rule: The Collective Enterprise of Survival*. Princeton: Princeton University Press, 1984.
Feitler, Bruno. *Inquisition, juifs et nouveaux-chrétiens au Brésil: Le nordeste XVIIe et XVIIIe siècle's*. Leuven: Leuven University Press, 2003.
_____. "Jews and New Christians in Dutch Brazil, 1630–1654." *Atlantic Diasporas: Jews, Conversos, and Crypto-Jews in the Age of Mercantilism, 1500–1800*. Ed. Richard Kagan and Philip D. Morgan. Baltimore: John Hopkins University Press, 2009. 123–51.
Figueira, Dorothy. "Civilization and the Problem of Race: Portuguese and Italian Travel Narratives to India." *Imperialisms: Historical and Literary Investigations, 1500–1900*. Ed. Elizabeth Sauer and Balachandra Rajan. New York: Palgrave Macmillan, 2004. 75–92.
Fuchs, Barbara. "Learning from Spain: The Case of the Irish Moriscos." *Imperialisms: Historical and Literary Investigations, 1500–1900*. Ed. Elizabeth Sauer and Balachandra Rajan. New York: Palgrave Macmillan, 2004. 33–52.
Garza Carvajal, Federico. *Butterflies Will Burn: Prosecuting Sodomites in Early Modern Spain and Mexico*. Austin: University of Texas Press, 2003.
Giard, Luce. "Scientific Activity in the Old Society." *Los jesuitas y la ciencia: Los límites de la razón*. Ed. José Luis Bermeo. Mexico City: Artes de México, 2007. 74–78.
Gillespie, Susan D. *The Aztec Kings: the Construction of Rulership in Mexica History*. Tucson: University of Arizona Press, 1989.
Graizbord, David L. *Souls in Dispute: Converso Identities in Iberia and the Jewish Diaspora, 1580–1700*. Philadelphia: University of Pennsylvania Press, 2004.
Greenleaf, Richard. "The Inquisition and the Indians of New Spain: A Study in Jurisdictional Confusion." *The Americas* 22:2 (1965): 138–66.
Gruzinski, Serge. "The Ashes of Desire: Homosexuality in Mid-Seventeenth-Century New Spain." *Infamous Desire: Male Homosexuality in Colonial Latin America*. Ed. Pete Sigal. Chicago: University of Chicago Press, 2003. 197–214.
Haliczer, Stephen. *Inquisition and Society in the Kingdom of Valencia, 1478–1834*. Berkeley: University of California Press, 1990.
Hanks, William F. *Converting Words: Maya in the Age of the Cross*. Berkeley: University of California Press, 2009.
Hoey, Jack B. III. "Alessandro Valignano and the Restructuring of the Jesuit Mission in Japan, 1579–1582." *Eleutheria* 1:1, Article 4 (Fall 2010): 23–42. Web.
Hordes, Stanley M. "The Inquisition as Economic and Political Agent: The Campaign of the Mexican Holy Office against the Crypto-Jews in the Mid-Seventeenth Century." *The Americas* 39:1 (1982): 23–38.
Johnson, Carina. "Idolatrous Cultures and the Practice of Religion." *The Journal of the History of Ideas* 67:4 (2006): 597–621.

Kamen, Henry. *The Spanish Inquisition: a Historical Revision*. New Haven and London: Yale University Press, 1998.
Lane, Kris E. *Colour of Paradise: The Emerald in the Age of Gunpowder Empires*. New Haven: Yale University Press, 2010.
Liebman, Seymour B., ed. *The Enlightened: The Writings of Luis de Carvajal, el Mozo*. Trans. Seymour B. Leibman. Coral Gables: University of Miami Press, 1967.
López de Velasco, Juan. *Geografía y descripción universal de las indias*. Biblioteca de Autores Españoles. Vol. 248. Ed. don Marcos Jiménez de la Espada. Madrid: Ediciones Atlas, 1971.
Martínez, María Elena. "Interrogating Blood Lines: 'Purity of Blood,' the Inquisition, and *Casta* Categories in Early Colonial Mexico." *Religion in New Spain*. Ed. Susan Schroeder and Stafford Poole. Albuquerque: University of New Mexico Press, 2007. 196–217.
_____. *Genealogical Fictions: Limpieza de Sangre, Religion, and Gender in Colonial Mexico*. Stanford: Stanford University Press, 2008.
_____. "Indigenous Genealogies: Lineage, History, and the Colonial Pact in Central Mexico and Peru." *Indigenous Intellectuals: Knowledge, Power, and Colonial Culture*. Eds. Yanna Yannakakis and Gabriela Ramos. Durham: Duke University Press, 2014. 173–201.
Martínez, María Elena, David Nirenberg, and Max S. Hering Torres, eds. *Race and Blood in the Iberian World*. Zürich: Lit, 2012.
McCaa, Robert. "*Calidad, Clase*, and Marriage in Colonial Mexico: The Case of Parral, 1788–90." *Hispanic American Historical Review* 64:3 (1984): 477–501.
MacCormack, Sabine. "Gods, Demons, and Idols in the Andes." *Journal of the History of Ideas* 67:4 (2006): 623–47.
Mendonça, Délio de. *Conversions and Citizenry: Goa under Portugal, 1510–1610*. New Delhi: Concept Publishing Company, 2002.
Meyuhas Ginio, Alisa. "The Inquisition and the New Christians: The Case of the Portuguese Inquisition of Goa." *The Medieval History Journal* 2:1 (1999): 1–18.
Mills, Kenneth R. *Idolatry and its Enemies: Colonial Andean Religion and Extirpation, 1640–1750*. Princeton: Princeton University Press, 1997.
Mills, Kenneth, and William B. Taylor. "Orders Given to 'the Twelve.'" *Colonial Spanish America: A Documentary History*. Eds. Kenneth Mills, and William B. Taylor. Wilmington: Scholarly Resources Inc., 1998. 46–51.
Monter, William. *Frontiers of Heresy: The Spanish Inquisition from the Basque Lands to Sicily*. Cambridge, UK: Cambridge University Press, 1990.
Moreno de los Arcos, Roberto. "New Spain's Inquisition for Indians from the Sixteenth to the Nineteenth Century." *Cultural Encounters: The Impact of the Inquisition in Spain and the New World*. Ed. Mary Elizabeth Perry and Anne J. Cruz. Berkeley and Los Angeles: University of California Press, 1991. 23–32.
Moya, José C. "Introduction: Latin America—The Limitation and Meaning of a Historical Category." *The Oxford Handbook of Latin American History*. Ed. Jose C. Moya. New York: Oxford University Press, 2011. 1–24.

O'Gorman, Edmundo. *The Invention of America: An Inquiry into the Historical Nature of the New World and the Meaning of Its History.* Westport, Conn: Greenwood Press, 1972.

O'Toole, Rachel. "From the Rivers of Guinea to the Valleys of Peru: Becoming a Bran Diaspora within Spanish Slavery." *Social Text* 92, 25:3 (Fall 2007): 19–36.

Olivier Durand, Guilhem. "Conquistadores y misioneros frente al pecado nefando." *Historias* 28 (Mexico City) (1992): 47–63.

Pagden, Anthony. "Afterword: From Empire to Federation." *Imperialisms: Historical and Literary Investigations, 1500–1900.* Ed. Elizabeth Sauer and Balachandra Rajan. New York: Palgrave Macmillan, 2004. 255–71.

Pitt-Rivers, Julian. "On the Word 'Caste.'" *The Translation of Culture: Essays to E. E. Evans-Pritchard.* Ed. T. O. Beidelman. London: Tavistock Publications, 1971. 231–54.

Portuondo, María M. *Secret Science: Spanish Cosmography and the New World.* Chicago: University of Chicago Press, 2009.

Ramos, Gabriela and Henrique Urbano. *Catolicismo y extirpación de idolatrías: Siglos XVI–XVIII.* Cusco: Centro de estudios regionales andinos Bartolomé de Las Casas, 1993.

Rappaport, Joanne. "'Así lo paresçe por su aspeto': Physiognomy and the Construction of Difference in Colonial Bogotá." *Hispanic American Historical Review* 91:4 (Nov. 2011): 601–31.

Restall, Matthew. *The Maya World: Yucatec Culture and Society, 1550–1850.* Stanford: Stanford University Press, 1997.

Roth, Cecil. *The Spanish Inquisition.* New York and London: W. W. Norton and Company, 1996.

Ruiz Medrano, Ethelia. *Reshaping New Spain: Government and Private Interests in the Colonial Bureaucracy, 1531–1550.* Boulder: University Press of Colorado, 2006.

Russell-Wood, A. J. R. *The Portuguese Empire, 1415–1808: A World on the Move.* Baltimore: Johns Hopkins University Press, 1998.

Said, Edward W. *Culture and Imperialism.* New York: Vintage Books, 1993.

———. *Orientalism.* New York: Vintage Books, 1994.

Seed, Patricia. "Social Dimensions of Race: Mexico City, 1753." *Hispanic American Historical Review* 62:4 (1982): 568–606.

———. "'Are these not men'? The Indians' Humanity and Capacity for Spanish Civilization." *Journal of Latin American Studies* 25:3 (1993): 629–52.

Seth, Vanita. *Europe's Indians: Producing Racial Difference, 1500–1900.* Durham: Duke University Press, 2010.

Sicroff, Albert A. *Los Estatutos de limpieza de sangre: Controversias entre los siglos XV y XVII.* Trans. Mauro Armiño. Madrid: Tauros Ediciones, S.A., 1985.

Silverblatt, Irene. "New Christians and New World Fears in Seventeenth-Century Peru." *From the Margins: Historical Anthropology and its Futures.* Ed. Brian Keith Axel. Durham: Duke University Press, 2002. 95–121.

———. *Modern Inquisitions: Peru and the Colonial Origins of the Civilized World.* Durham and London: Duke University Press, 2004.

Socolow, Susan. *The Women of Colonial Latin America*. Cambridge, UK: Cambridge University Press, 2000.
Soyer, François. "An Example of Collaboration Between the Spanish and Portuguese Inquisitions: The Persecution of the Converso Diego Ramos and his Family (1680–1683)." *Cadernos de Estudos Sefarditas* 6 (2006): 317–40.
———. "Nowhere to Run: The Extradition of Conversos between the Spanish and Portuguese Inquisitions during the Sixteenth and Seventeenth Centuries." *The Conversos and Moriscos in Late Medieval Spain and Beyond. Volume Two: The Morisco Issue*. Ed. Kevin Ingram. Leiden: Brill, 2012. 251–78.
Starr-LeBeau, Gretchen D. *In the Shadow of the Virgin: Inquisitors, Friars, and Conversos in Guadalupe, Spain*. Princeton: Princeton University Press, 2003.
Subrahmanyam, Sanjay. "Holding the World in Balance: The Connected Histories of the Iberian Overseas Empires, 1500–1640." *American Historical Review* 112:5 (2007): 1359–85.
Sweet, James. *Recreating Africa: Religion, Culture, and Kinship in the African-Portuguese World, 1441–1770*. Chapel Hill: University of North Carolina Press, 2004.
Thornton, John. *Africa and Africans in the Making of the Atlantic World, 1400–1800*. Cambridge, UK: Cambridge University Press, 1998.
Toro, Alfonso. *La familia Carvajal: Estudio histórico sobre los judíos y la Inquisición de la Nueva España en el siglo 16, basado en documentos originales y en su mayor parte inéditos, que se conservan en el Archivo General de la ciudad de México*. Mexico City: Ed. Patria, 1944.
Tucci Carneiro, Maria Luiza. *Preconceito Racial: Portugal e Brasil-Colônia*. São Paolo: Editora Brasiliense, 1988.
Tzoref-Ashkenazi, Chen. "India and the Identity of Europe: The Case of Friedrich Schlegel." *Journal of the History of Ideas* 67:4 (2006): 713–34.
Uchmany, Eva Alexandra. "Criptojudíos y cristianos nuevos en las Filipinas durante el siglo XVI." *The Sepharadi and Oriental Jewish Heritage Studies*. Ed. Issachar Ben-Ami. Jerusalem: The Magnes Press, 1982. 85–103.
———. *La vida entre el judaísmo y el cristianismo en la Nueva España, 1580–1606*. Mexico City: Archivo General de la Nación and Fondo de Cultura Económica, 1992.
———. "The Participation of New Christians and Crypto-Jews in the Conquest, Colonization, and Trade of Spanish America, 1521–1660." *The Jews and the Expansion of Europe to the West 1450–1800*. Ed. Paolo Bernardini and Norman Fiering. New York and Oxford: Berghahn Books, 2001. 186–202.
van Deusen, Nancy E. "Seeing *Indios* in Sixteenth-Century Castile." *The William and Mary Quarterly* 69:2 (Apr. 2012): 205–34.
Viotti da Costa, Emilia. "The Portuguese-African Slave Trade: A Lesson in Colonialism." *Latin American Perspectives* 12:1 (1985): 41–61.
Wachtel, Nathan. *The Faith of Remembrance: Marrano Labyrinths*. Trans. Nikki Halpern. Philadelphia: University of Pennsylvania Press, 2013.
Wadsworth, James E. *Agents of Orthodoxy: Honor, Status, and the Inquisition in Colonial Pernambuco, Brazil*. Lanham, Md.: Rowman and Littlefield Publishers, 2007.

Zambrano, Marta. "Ilegitimidad, cruce de sangres y desigualdad: Dilemas del porvenir en Santa Fe colonial." *El peso de la sangre: Limpios, mestizos y nobles en el mundo hispánico*. Ed. Nikolaus Böttcher, Bernd Hausberger, and Max S. Hering Torres. Mexico City: El Colegio de México, 2011. 263–65.

CHAPTER FOUR

The Portuguese Inquisition and Colonial Expansion

The "Honor" of Being Tried by the Holy Office

Bruno Feitler
Payton Phillips Quintanilla, translator

The Holy Office was founded in Portugal between 1536 and 1547 as a result of the petition of King João III. Following the model of the Spanish Tribunal, the objective of the Inquisition in Portugal was to battle Jewish heresy that continued more than a quarter of a century after the forced conversion of the kingdom's Jews in 1497.[1] At the same time that the Inquisition's activities began, the Portuguese consolidated their presence in Asia and the *de facto* occupation of Brazil began.[2]

Although a direct relation cannot be made between the consolidation of colonial Portuguese expansion and the establishment of the Inquisition, it is evident that the tribunal's judges had to adapt their methods of religious and social regulation to the new circumstances of the overseas conquests. The structure of the Portuguese Holy Office was firmly established in 1565 with three metropolitan tribunals (Lisbon, Coimbra, and Évora), and a single tribunal outside of Europe in Goa, capital of the *Estado da Índia*, which covered the Portuguese territories in Asia. In spite of the efforts of Philip III and Philip IV, a tribunal was never established in Brazil, in contrast to Spanish America where three tribunals were created (Lima, México, and Cartagena de Indias). Rather, the Portuguese territories in America, along with the rest of their Atlantic possessions, including the western and northern African territories, remained under the jurisdiction of the inquisitorial tribunal in Lisbon, to which the accused of these regions were taken and where they were tried. In order to function locally, and according to different moments and contexts, the inquisitors of Lisbon had the support of the episcopal structure, the religious orders, and, from the end of the seventeenth century, their own network of commissioners (Feitler, *Nas malhas da consciência*, 127–48).

How did this institution—which was created to address, above all else, the question of Jewish converts—adapt to the new imperial Portuguese situation and its massive contact with cultures viewed as radically different and described as idolaters, as opposed to Muslims and Jews who, because of their familiarity, were called "infidels"? What we seek here is not to write a history of the behavior of the local populations in the face of Catholic imperialism, but to understand the logic of how the inquisitorial institution functioned when confronted with these populations. In this way we can understand how, in spite of the coercive force of the tribunal of the Holy Office, it also adapted to different contexts of Portuguese domination, which in turn can give us the key to think in a new way about the globalization that arose from the Iberian empires.

In Brazil, an ordinance signed in 1579 by the King and Inquisitor General, Dom Henrique, gave the Bishop of Bahia, Antonio Barreiros (who was to be supported by the Jesuits), jurisdiction to try cases of heresy that arose among the "newly converted"—that is to say, Christianized Amerindians—, while recommending special moderation "in order not to intimidate the others" (Rosa Pereira 56–57). This was meant to avoid interference with the catechism and conversion of the Amerindians, who would surely resist converting if they found themselves being handled with inquisitorial rigor. The 1579 ordinance, according to Giuseppe Marcocci, also ratified the continuing roles of bishops and Jesuits in protecting Amerindians from colonists, who could use the Inquisition as a weapon in their own interests against native peoples ("A fé de um império" 88). We will see that, in spite of the fact that the King and Inquisitor General's regulations appeared to have been forgotten (as they do not appear nor are debated in the historical documentation), the number of native Brazilians tried by the Portuguese tribunal was minimal. Therefore, the situation in Brazil was similar to that which prevailed in Hispanic America: after the foundation of the local tribunals in 1560, the Amerindians in Spanish territories no longer found themselves under inquisitorial jurisdiction (Tavares 81–100).

In contrast to the Amerindians of the New World, persons of African and Asian origin within Portuguese territories were never exempt from inquisitorial jurisdiction. Furthermore, Africans, as well as Asians, soon had to face the Holy Office as the tribunal's prisoners. Few investigations have focused on the question of the Inquisition's different treatment of native Amerindians, Africans, and Asians, including the institution's reasoning.

This historiographic gap—which holds as much for the Portuguese world as for the Spanish—does not seem to be related, as one might imagine it might be, to a nationalist vision of the history of the Inquisition. Rather, the gap is a result of a certain tendency to naturalize the exemption or inclusion of different populations from inquisitorial jurisdiction. Solange Alberro, in her important and systematic work on the Inquisition in New Spain, is one of the few scholars who have delved deeply into this problem, and she suggests a political solution. For Alberro, the different ways in which African neophytes and Mexican Amerindians were treated (the first being tried by the Inquisition, the second being exempted) was a direct result of the fact that the Amerindians represented a majority of the population. From a Spanish colonial perspective, excessive pressure exerted on them could produce rebellions, which was supposed to not be the case with the African slaves whose numbers were infinitely smaller in New Spain and who, in addition, had been "inevitably uprooted and [. . .] scattered through the entire territory" (Alberro 26–27). As we will see, this demographic question, the cause of grave security problems to European domination, also influenced the cases of Portuguese possessions in North Africa and in Asia, but did not result in an exemption for converted North Africans, Indians, Chinese, and Javanese from inquisitorial jurisdiction. That is to say, I believe that it is necessary to seek other explanations beyond this question of the different methods of control over the native or transplanted populations.

Although the difference in treatment has not been addressed in the historiography on the Portuguese Inquisition, Giuseppe Marcocci has recently made an effort to arrive at a unified vision of the institution's policies. Marcocci affirms that the Portuguese Inquisition had a "unitary vision, on a global scale, with the objective of monitoring orthodoxy in imperial Portuguese spaces" ("A fé de um império" 74). In other words, the Inquisition was founded with a global institutional policy throughout Portuguese overseas territories, or, as indicated by Marcocci, its existence allows one to discuss "inquisitorial colonialism" ("A fé de um império" 100).[3] There is no doubt that the Portuguese tribunal—as with the Spanish—had as its final intention the Catholicization and Westernization (in the sense that Serge Gruzinski uses the term), or perhaps more precisely, the total Iberianization of the populations under its authority. Nonetheless, although this vision applies to the Portuguese territories in South Asia, the Inquisition had to adapt its forms of action to different local situations.[4] Furthermore, the rigor of these actions had to be adapted to the image that European Christian (or more precisely, Iberian) society had of those local populations. It is this intersection of inquisitorial jurisdiction and the Iberian social and missionary imaginary of the *ancien régime* that we will study here. The goal is to show how the Inquisition came to operate, not in a totalizing manner—it did not address all of the populations living in the lands under Iberian domination in the same way—, but instead by making distinctions not only between Christians and non-Christians (with exceptions that we will study) but also among Christians of European, Amerindian, African, or Asian origin. This distinction reproduced the prejudices present in Portuguese society against persons of ethnic origins different from their own, and against persons recently converted. What we intend to present here is a more refined study of how the Inquisition treated the "natives" of various localities—not by making comparisons, but through an attempt at a "common history" of inquisitorial action in those territories. This will also permit us to understand the limits of local adaptations in the face of the overall normalizing and coercive mission of the institution.

Iberians in the Face of "Others"

Although we call attention to the temporal coincidence between the consolidation of colonial expansion and the foundation of inquisitorial tribunals in Portugal, in light of the older expeditions and conquests of North and West African territories, and also with respect to Islam and Judaism, Europeans had much earlier experience with culturally diverse populations. This experience served as a model for the form in which the Portuguese (and also the Spanish) related to black Africans, Amerindians, and Indians (Xavier, "Conversos"; Marcocci, "A fé de um império"). One must also acknowledge that the 1540s, when the Portuguese tribunals began functioning, was a period of great change in the ideological references of this developing empire.

In reaction to the Protestant threat, the conciliatory and relativistic thought that impregnated the monarchy's elite before 1550 was tossed aside, and an intolerant discourse based in the ideals of the Tridentine reformations rapidly gained more currency. During the decades of the 1550s and 1560s, "the true Catholic faith" was in this way more clearly delineated, circumscribing the manner in which faithful Iberian Catholic Christians should see, understand, and relate to those who were not of their ethnicity or faith. Simultaneously, the ideology of blood purity, like the old Aristotelian and Biblical cosmovision of difference among peoples, helped to develop the concept of the capacities, strengths, and weaknesses of non-Europeans that would become normative.[5]

There exist, then, beyond the experience of contact, two principal points of reference for the construction of the image of the people who the Iberians encountered in the Indies (Western and Eastern), and likewise of the ways in which the Inquisitions reacted when faced with the deviant behavior of the recently converted: the Judeo-Islamic referent and the philosophical-theological Aristotelian-Thomist referent, to which Charles R. Boxer has called attention (*A Igreja e a expansão ibérica* 32). These referents formed the image of a stable and hierarchical society in which some races were naturally inferior to the rest, in spite of the affirmations of theologians (above all, those of Bartolomé de las Casas) who called the differentiation among those whom God had made equal and the contradiction of the universal message of conversion close to heretical thought.[6] The work of María Elena Martínez is, for example, an account of the construction of such hierarchies as they stemmed from imperial expansion, based in readings of authors such as Pedro Mártir de Anglería (1520), or the Jesuits José de Acosta (1577), and Alessandro Valignano (end of the sixteenth century) (25-41). In his work, Francisco Bethencourt also recently showed how the creation of hierarchies among continents and populations served as one of the principal strategies of the Europeans to legitimate their alleged supremacy (*Racisms* 65-82). It is important to underscore that this image changed not only in this new global context, but also in the context of the formulation of the ideals of the Tridentine Church, with a rapid evolution beginning in the 1530s and 1540s toward a doctrine ever more rigid in relation to the margin of possibilities of the religious experience and, above all, the Catholic experience. This mutation also signifies that, from the most strictly political point of view, the Inquisition was transformed into an important pillar of an exclusive, confessional Catholicism—an important element of Portuguese self-identification in the Early Modern Age. In other words, following the argument of Carina Johnson, during the sixteenth century (and more precisely, according to Marcocci, in the 1540s and 1550s, at least for Portugal), the form in which Catholics perceived those persons culturally and religiously different from themselves took a new, stricter and, one can say, more exclusivist form.[7] It is in this changing context that the Portuguese confronted different people and established the inquisitorial jurisdiction. Finally, it is very important to note that the categorizations of local populations constructed by Europeans had the objective of ordering "races," or "castes," or "nations" hierarchically, a subject that has been exhaustively studied for the Spanish world, but less for the Portuguese. It seems to us that, following the affirmation by Tamar Herzog, this compartmentalization and classification was in reality a discourse on civilization (not nationality, as has been habitually supposed), and what interests us here is not a reflection of the success of the segregationist policy of the Iberians but, to the contrary, a reaction to its (partial) failure. As a result of the fluidity of different racial identifications, and above all with the emergence of what scholars have understood as a *mestizo* world, it was far from unusual—at least in Iberian America—that *mestizos* and Amerindians changed their identities within the span of a lifetime.[8] In Brazil, although the general condition of social hierarchies and the place of *mestizos* were distinct from those of the Spanish Americas, there, too, many direct descendants of Amerindians could "disappear" as such by being identified as *mestizos* (Celestino 85–106).

To understand how expansion determined inquisitorial action, we are going to look here more specifically at how the Portuguese saw the natives in terms of their potential (although sometimes difficult to isolate from others also considered "civilizing"), not so much for conversion, but for understanding and assimilating the complex combination of dogmas of Roman Catholicism, the greatest corollary to which would be admission to the sacrament of the order, the priesthood. As opposed to tracing how the inquisitors made direct (and specific) analogies between customs or local rites, and heresies (although without a doubt these interpretations contributed to the more general image that they had of these cultures), it seems to me that this is the best way to understand why the Inquisition took such different paths regarding different populations. Objectively, these sacramental criteria of cultural "cataloging," if we can call it that, impacted the form in which these populations could integrate into the social structures of the dominant culture. In effect, it does not seem out of place to think that access to the priesthood was only possible among those populations that were considered perfectly capable of assimilating everything that the Church of Rome not only taught and believed, but that were seen as sufficiently reliable and responsible as to be capable of administering the sacraments—the central nucleus of Catholic life over which much of the Tridentine reforms were based. The criteria used to identify, it seems to me, those who would have the great "honor"—because of the possibility of their deviant conduct, and in spite of being indigenous—to be detained and tried by the tribunals of the Inquisition. Upon passing from one continent to the other, the chronologies of Portuguese imperial expansion and the Inquisition crossed, and these intersections explain why Africans and Asians, and not the Amerindians, remained under the jurisdiction of the Holy Office. Critical to this policy were, on the one hand, the historical period in which natives entered into the clergy, and on the other hand, the crystallization of the elements of hierarchy and how Europeans defined the capacities of different peoples.

Africa

Given the fact that Muslims and Jews had almost always lived alongside Christians in the Iberian kingdoms, the first "exotic" population—if we can classify them in this way —Christian Iberians encountered was that of black sub-Saharans (Saunders; Marcocci, *A Consciência de um império*). Perhaps because this relationship was in itself very old and produced through the complex filter of slavery, the image that Iberians had of black Africans was slowly configured, and this resulted in sometimes contradictory characterizations.

Although the relationship between the Portuguese and black Africans has almost always been defined by the slavery of the latter, during the fifteenth century, according to the observations of Boxer, those who arrived in Portugal were not exclusively captives, but also free people, as well as people who were later freed. Some of the free and freed received religious education and became ordained priests, possibly with the intention of being sent to Senegal, Congo, and São Tomé as catechists, priests, interpreters, or emissaries of the Portuguese king (Boxer, *A Igreja*).

The earliest examples of the incorporation of priests found by Boxer date to 1444 and 1445, but the best-known case is that of the son of King Afonso I of Congo, consecrated Bishop of Utica on May 3, 1518 by Pope Leo X (Jordão [1171–1600]). In addition to his son, King Afonso sent various nephews and cousins to Portugal so that, after an adequate religious education, they could also be ordained priests and eventually consecrated bishops. The number of these candidates for the priesthood (or, to receive the sacrament of the order) must have been significant because on June 12, 1518—certainly to dissipate doubts in relation to these ordinations—the Pope emitted a brief through which the royal chaplain in Lisbon was authorized to ordain "Ethiopians, Indians, and Africans" who had reached the moral and educational standards necessary for the priesthood (Brásio 308–13). Again, in the words of Boxer, "the path seemed to be open for the formation on two continents of a qualified native clergy" (Boxer, *A Igreja*, 15–16). Of course, the ever greater connection made between slavery and skin color, the exponential growth in slave trafficking, and the gradual application of the purity of blood statutes in Portugal between the end of sixteenth century and the middle of the seventeenth century meant that racial prejudice against persons of African descent grew and prompted heated debates over the abilities of those priests (Boxer 17).[9] Nonetheless, the ordination of blacks was essential and never questioned in the Portuguese strongholds and territories of West Africa, while it was prohibited in Portugal and Brazil, at least theoretically, as is indicated in the episcopal constitutions that prohibited men of pagan, heretic, Jewish, Moorish, black, or mulatto origin to receive ordination, even if it was for the first tonsure (that is to say, minor orders).[10]

The contradiction between the liberating promise of conversion, which was the foundation of the enslavement of the black Africans, and the reality of the slave condition was perhaps, according to Marcocci, "the most critical point for the imperial consciousness" of Portugal (*A Consciência de um império* 53). In effect, the papal bull *Dum Diversitas* of 1452 legitimated the perpetual slavery of blacks, even after baptism, but did not impede the emergence, at least from the middle of the sixteenth century, of voices opposing the inexorability of the slave condition in the face of baptism.

Although the Inquisition tried people of African descent for a series of crimes, the effective action of the tribunal in territories to the south of the Sahara rarely had as a direct goal the persecution of black heretics, but rather the ongoing repression of crypto-Judaism. This goal was reflected in the (weak) figures of inquisitorial activity in Guinea, Cabo Verde, São Tomé, and Angola, places where the establishment of permanent inquisitorial tribunals were never planned (Horta 387–418; F. da Silva 157–73). Nonetheless, from the decade of 1550, enslaved West African Wolofs, and also Africans of other origins, were accused and tried by the Holy Office in Lisbon for practicing Islam, sodomy, and blasphemy, as well as for practicing witchcraft and making pacts with the devil, as animistic religious and cultural practices were characterized (Saunders 210–16). This early entry of Africans and their descendants into the inquisitorial jails is a clear signal that if there were doubts about the Holy Office's jurisdiction (and it is not known that there were), these doubts quickly dissipated.

Therefore, in places of greater inquisitorial presence, such as in Portugal and later in Brazil, but also in Spanish America, the cases of imprisoned Africans and their descendants were frequent, principally for "witchcraft" (Calainho). To prosecute these crimes, the Portuguese Inquisition formulated even at the end of the seventeenth century a specific edict, sent to different parts of Brazil but also to Cabo Verde, Azores, and Madeira, urging that people who utilized amulets of syncretic origin, known as *mandinga* pouches be denounced, while the Mexican Inquisition emitted edicts against African-descent ventriloquist ("who speak from the chest") women (ANTT, IL, Book 20, Folios 3v, 4v, 5v–7v; Alberro 74–75).[11] Nonetheless, it is necessary to account for the small number of trials against Africans and their descendants in general when compared to the total number of trials. Since the inquisitors could not ignore the frequent denunciations against Africans, there could have been many causes for these low numbers. The limited inquisitorial structure in Africa and the high cost of trying prisoners who had no property (which could cover the cost of the legal procedures), the already fixed prejudice against blacks (in spite of their being considered worthy of the priesthood in cases of necessity), and the reticence of the Portuguese tribunals to try cases of witchcraft (seen increasingly as superstition rather than as pacts with the devil): all of this can explain the relatively small effort of the inquisitors in relation to the accused of African origin (Novinsky 35; Paiva 331–47).

India

The reaction of Vasco da Gama upon arriving in Calicut in 1498 is well known: when the people of the land asked him what he was doing there, he said that he was searching for Christians and spices (Velho 51). What is more, in accordance with relations of the same expedition, he thought to have before him Christians (Barros 303-4). This corresponded not only with King Manuel's objectives for the Indian expedition (which included, among others, to establish an alliance with Prester John against the Muslims), but also undoubtedly the belief that the apostle Saint Thomas had Christianized the local population, whose avatars would be those known as the Christians of Saint Thomas (Aubin 305-21). This capacity for the comprehension and assimilation of Catholic dogmas by the locals, even if in a far-off past, seems to be one of the explanations for the initial acceptance of (or even the propensity to) ordain Indians as priests.

After a series of battles, the Portuguese presence in India stabilized, first in Baçaim and then in Goa in 1510, and a little later in Malaca (1511) and Ormuz (1515). In spite of the presence of a secular clergy and of Franciscans in these territories, the diocese of Goa was not established until 1534, and the real missionary impulse began only with the arrival of the Jesuits in 1542 (Mendonça 107-9). As we have seen, the brief dispatched by Leo X in 1518 already foresaw the possibility of ordaining priests of Indian origin. In effect, in spite of the resistance on the part of the ecclesiastic hierarchy, which maintained a constant suspicion of the converted Hindus and viewed them, according to Ines Županov, as second-class Christians, the ordination of local priests was common in India. Županov also reminds us how the Indian provincial councils (specifically, the third, of 1585, and the fifth, of 1606) created barriers, although never total, to the elevation of Indians to the priesthood. First, the converted could only be ordained fifteen years after baptism, and after having reached at least thirty years of age. Second, the conciliar decrees assimilated the local hierarchies: only the members of the Brahman and Prabhu castes, or of other "noble" castes, could be admitted into the priesthood (Županov). Nonetheless, the formation of a native clergy was rapidly institutionalized with the creation in 1541 of a seminary in Goa with this specific end. In spite of being subordinated and defined as inferior to the clergy of European origin, at least from the middle of the seventeenth century, as highlighted by Boxer, "this native clergy was not only already numerous, but was also firmly established" in the same manner, though to a lesser degree, as the black clergymen in West Africa (*A Igreja* 25-28).

The great difference between the positions achieved by Indian and African clergy, pointing toward a certain flexibility of the application of racial prejudices, is also worth mentioning. While black Africans, in light of the total lack of priests, were elevated to important positions in the hierarchy of the local Church as members of the episcopal canonry (as was the case in the bishopric of Cabo Verde), this did not happen in India, where the natives of Hindu or Muslim origin were excluded from any ecclesiastic honor afforded to the Portuguese (Carlos Melo; Boxer, *Relações raciais*; Xavier, "Conversos and Novamente Convertidos," 282–83). This difference was due to variations not only in place, but also in time. Given the chronic lack of qualified candidates to occupy inquisitorial positions (that is to say, Old Christian men born in the Kingdom and with studies in law), it is interesting to see how, beginning in 1645, Christians of Indian origin, not Portuguese born in India, were named as assistants, and from the end of the seventeenth century, as notaries of the Inquisition of Goa, a position of great responsibility (Monteiro 16–20). This naming to posts that implied the priestly status of the candidate shows how—at least at that moment—the "native Christians" (*cristãos da terra*) had already managed to attain positions of greater honor, including inside the Inquisition, which was always seen as a bastion of Catholic purity and Portuguese blood. Of course, the named were always Brahmans, the caste accepted by the Portuguese as the most noble of the local social hierarchy (Baião, vol. I, 179–82). The local converted populations were in this way clearly inserted into Christianity, although they may have been excluded rapidly from Portuguese "citizenship" or from a complete integration into Portuguese society. Still, if in the first years of the Portuguese presence in India the local converts (as was the case of the converted Jews in Portugal) could occupy diverse positions within the *res publica*, then very quickly—and in contradiction with inclusive legislation—segregationist decisions were published, excluding the Christians of Indian origin from the most important positions in the civil government, the military, and the Church (Xavier, "Conversos and Novamente Convertidos," 282–83). But, as we also saw, in the case of an extreme necessity, these rules were flexible to a certain degree.

What was the role of the Inquisition in the control of the religious behavior of these persons? Registers of religious control existed even before the foundation of the tribunal of Goa. The Indian apostates had to pass through a ceremony of public penitence—organized possibly (the documentation does not make it clear) by Jesuits—for the edification of all, before being accepted again into the Christian community (Mendonça 298). But in general, in the first years of the Portuguese presence, the control of the recently converted does not appear to have been very strict, as it would increasingly be after the foundation of the local tribunal of the Inquisition in 1560.

As with the foundation of the Spanish and Portuguese tribunals, the creation of a repressive religious organism in the Portuguese territories of the East was motivated by the presence and apparent religious liberty of New Christians, as the descendants of Jews converted by force in Portugal in 1497 were called. In the Indian case, however, it was also motivated by the scandal caused locally by the apostasy of the "native Christians" whether of Hindu or Muslim origin (Marcocci and Paiva 109). From the first intent to establish a tribunal (to be composed only of the Bishop of Goa and his Vicar General), in 1554, the Inquisitor General Dom Henrique ordered that:

> those who commit crimes of heresy after having recently converted to the faith from the sect of Mohammed or as gentiles, confessing after imprisonment, should not be immediately reconciled nor abjure, but should rather be placed where they can be instructed in the matters of faith and well taught in things pertaining to their salvation and other important [things] to prevent their falling into similar errors. And after this they should be reconciled and abjure as legally mandated (cited in Cunha, *A Inquisição no Estado da Índia*, 294).[12]

In this way, these initial instructions already foresaw a differentiated treatment, but not a total exemption from inquisitorial jurisdiction as would be the case of the Amerindians a little more than twenty years later, of the neophytes occasionally imprisoned by the Inquisition, in view of their weak Christian identities. The death of the Bishop of Goa, Juan de Albuquerque, and that of the Vicar General, who set sail from Lisbon with said orders, delayed the establishment of the tribunal, which finally came to pass in 1561 with the arrival to India of the first inquisitors carrying similar orders to those of 1554 (A. Cunha 295–301).

In spite of the inclusion of the "native Christians" in inquisitorial jurisdiction, Dom Henrique anticipated a certain gentle treatment of them, similar to that utilized in North Africa with the so-called renegades, or Christians who, locally enslaved, converted to Islam. As Marcocci reminds us, this policy suggests (as in the North African case) a frontier Inquisition, a fact that gave rise to various other peculiarities, but, in particular, the types of crimes addressed and the way that the institution operated ("A fé de um império" 85). This tender re-entry into to the Church was often publicized by edicts of grace, valid during six months, in favor of those who had abandoned Catholicism in "lands of infidels."[13] The integration of the realities of North Africa and Asia emerge nominally in the correspondence of the inquisitors, including from the quill of the Inquisitor General. In one letter sent to Goa, probably in 1586, Cardinal Archduke Alberto informed local inquisitors of the progress of the publication of a special bull so that the "newly converted" (the Indian neophytes) could be reconciled to the Church more than once, against the precepts of canon law that dictated the accused be handed over (or "relaxed") to the secular arm (to be burned at the stake) in the case of a second lapse (Baião vol. 1, 267). The Archduke wrote:

> [that I] ordered that this be investigated and it was found that there were several Briefs conceded by the Apostolic Holy See in favor of newly converted Moriscos [men of Muslim heritage] from the kingdoms of Valencia, Aragón, and Catalunya and I have ordered a request made to the Pope so that he concede that the same [privilege] be granted to the *Estado da Índia* (Baião vol. 1, 267).

The brief was finally granted in 1599 after deliberations in the Roman Congregation of the Holy Office, and had to be reconfirmed every five years. Although it specifically mentioned "the neophytes and descendants of gentiles and infidels," the brief appears to have been employed in a broad manner, including, at least in one case, to defend a mestizo, who could employ the ruling to enjoy inquisitorial leniency (Marcocci, "A fé de um império," 87–88).[14]

Another specific characteristic of the Goa tribunal, given its nature as a border tribunal, was the act of detaining and trying not only baptized persons, but also infidels. Very rare in the metropolis, but common in India, these trials against non-Christians were one of the most unique characteristics of the Indian tribunal. The proceeding had as an objective, above all else, to punish Hindus and Muslims who tried to impede the conversion to Catholicism of their co-religionists, or to bring them back to their religion of origin. These lawsuits also had the objective of prohibiting Hindu rituals and cults in lands under Portuguese dominion. The inquisitors took this so seriously that they had to be restrained in moments by the General Counsel of the Holy Office in Lisbon. For example, in a letter from 1601, ministers of the Counsel recommended that the inquisitors proceed only against the "native Christians" who heard Brahman preaching, and not against the gentiles, unless they sought to convert Christians to their religion. In another letter, it is recommended to the inquisitor Antonio de Barros that he not interfere in the business of the *pagodas* (images of the gods of India or of their temples, here probably used to designate mosques) of Ormuz nor proceed against those who use them, since the worshippers were not baptized Christians (Baião vol. 1, 318).[15] Nonetheless, at least from the end of the seventeenth century, detention and lawsuits against non-baptized persons were habitual. In this manner, in the auto-da-fé celebrated in the courtroom of the Inquisition of Goa on October 16, 1695, fourteen infidels heard their sentences for "holding a gentile banquet dedicated to the memory of their deceased" or "for attending a sacrifice and offer made at a pagoda [temple]," in all cases "within our territory" (Inquisition of Goa).

This custom subsequently gave rise to another, very unique practice that consisted of an absolution of the accused (often condemned to lashings and exile) in exchange for conversion to Catholicism. Conversion (and absolution) meant avoiding not only the trial, but also above all the shameful autos-da-fé and the punishments that ranged from heavy fines to exile, whippings to forced labor. There are various examples of these types of cases, like that of the Hindu Antecamotim, detained "for taking Christians to the mainland to turn them into gentiles," and who was absolved in a sentence dated August 10, 1575 (BNL, Codex 203, Folio 105). There were also more dramatic episodes, like one in which one hundred individuals were detained on July 22, 1685:

> for having been found on the island of Goa celebrating a marriage with gentile rites and ceremonies, and various other crimes, and having asked for Holy Baptism in the course of their cases, were ordered to be instructed in Christian doctrine and baptized with their families in the College of Saint Paul the Elder in this city on different days between January and November of 1686 (BNL, Codex 203, Folio 105; ANTT, Conselho Geral, Bundle 31, Document 28).

Another extreme case, which might be considered exceptional (but not unique), is that of Amet, a Muslim from Baçaim, detained for sodomy, and who was also absolved *ab instancia* on January 27, 1612 by becoming Christian (BNL, Codex 203, Folio 152).

Another instance that demonstrates a catechistic preoccupation of the inquisitors was the exile to Portugal, and also to Brazil, of persons tried for practicing Islam or paganism; in other words, inquisitors exiled some to places where the interaction with Islam and Hinduism would be much less than in South Asia, and as a result lessen the possibility of relapse from outside influences. This appears to have been the reasoning behind the sentence published against the Gujarat slave, Domingos Fernandes, who abjured for practicing Islam in the auto-da-fé of September 22, 1586, and was "sent to be sold in the kingdom [Portugal]" (BNL, Codex 203, Folio 174). This was also the case of the "native Christian," Antonio Lourenço, native of Rachol in the outskirts of Goa, also arrested for the offense of practicing Islam and condemned to exile in Portugal in the auto-da-fé of December 10, 1623 (BNL, Codex 203, Folio 243v). Much later, in the auto of April 21, 1697, Deugo, a Brahman, already imprisoned once for building "temples" (*pagodas*) in Portuguese lands and sent to the house of catechumens after saying he wanted to convert, was imprisoned yet again, this time with the punishment of whippings and an exile of ten years to Brazil (BNL, Codex 201, Folio 46). The local population, both of Hindu and

Muslim origins, converted or not, were in the same way clearly inserted into the inquisitorial jurisdiction.

America

We return now to our point of departure: the integration of America and its populations into the Christian world. Even with the pre-existing negative associations attributed to Asians and Africans in European culture, nothing compared to the doubts that arose once confronted with the diversity of the New World and the attempts to define the Americans' nature as different from that of Europeans. If we follow the hierarchy articulated by José de Acosta, the Amerindians of Brazil—semi-nomadic peoples who lacked writing and were accused of cannibalism and a lack of religion—were without a doubt in the lowest substratum on the scale of civilizations (Bethencourt, *Racisms*, 78–82). Or, as it was synthesized and made canonical by the Jesuit Gandavo in 1570, who lexicalized a characterization made by Americo Vespucci, the Amerindians did not know how to pronounce the letters F, L, or R, "because they have no faith, nor law, nor king" (*por que assim não têm fé, nem lei, nem rei*) (Cunha, "Imagens de índios do Brasil," 97–98).

Contrary to what occurred in New Spain, where in 1536 during an initial wave of optimism a college was founded with the project of educating the sons of the indigenous and *mestizo* elite in the priesthood (Santa Cruz de Tlatelolco) and where the possibility of an indigenous clergy was repeatedly debated, in Brazil the creation of a college for the natives was never proposed.[16] Still, on the eve of the expulsion of the Jesuits from Brazil in 1759, the provincial João Honorato (1754–1758) wrote to Lisbon to give account of the impossibility of separating the temporal from the spiritual governance of the villages with the purpose of "civilizing the Indians," mixing into his argumentation the incapacity of the Amerindians "for political commerce" and their inability to "produce any disciple capable of the ecclesiastic position" (Honorato). Upon evoking the recent (and unsuccessful) attempt made by the first bishop of São Paulo, Bernardo Rodrigues Nogueira (1745–1748), to educate in his own palace an Amerindian "in the local customs [*políticas*]," Honorato not only mentioned previous half-hearted attempts, but also offered a very useful comparison with Africans and their descendants, indicating that not only in São Tomé and Angola, but also in Brazil itself—at least in the mid-eighteenth century—there was a black lower clergy:

> there has been an attempt [. . .] to civilize the Indians administratively, through communication with secular administrators, who by profession are dedicated to political affairs. This goal has been frustrated by the natural and invincible incapac-

ity of the same Indians for political commerce. With how much hard work did the first Jesuit missionaries build villages in Brazil to civilize these Indians through the liberal arts that they normally taught? [. . .] [But they did not] produce a single disciple capable of the ecclesiastical vocation. There are black canons in São Tomé, regular priests in Angola and a few in Bahia, where they were able to be trained in Philosophy, but there is no Indian in all of Brazil who has reached a similar level in a given time (Honorato).[17]

In other words, he claims a total incapacity of the Amerindians to reach the necessary understanding either for self-governance or for the priesthood. The implementation of the Directorate of Indians (in 1755 for Maranhão and Grão Para, and in 1758 for Brazil) suffered from a similar problem: although it opened up the possibility that Amerindians might occupy some posts of the Republic, in the end they were restricted by white lay "directors" because they were considered "rustic and incapable of governing themselves" by law (Moisés 115–32).

The 1579 decision of King Henrique (still acting as Inquisitor General) to exempt the Amerindians of Brazil from the jurisdiction of the Holy Office for heretical crimes, thereby leaving the matter to the local bishop—contrary to the case of Spanish America—does not ever seem to be mentioned, at least not in the known documentation. Just as the possibility of ordaining converted Amerindians or their direct descendants was not debated in Portugal or Brazil, neither was the question of their trial by the Inquisition debated. For as strange as it seems, possibly this unanimity on the (in)capacity of the Amerindians meant that, in cases of denunciations against them (including in the era of the Marquis of Pombal and of his policy of annulation of ethnic differences), the representatives of the Holy Office followed the most common legal procedures and ignored the fact that the accused might not be under the Inquisition's jurisdiction.[18]

Still, mild variations in procedures continued to arise, pointing consistently toward an image of Amerindians as incapable of understanding the mysteries of Christianity. First, it is necessary to note that the first great intervention of the Inquisition in Brazil—the Visitation to the city of Salvador and its surroundings between 1591 and 1593—gave rise to many trials against *mestizos* (those known as *mamelucos*, children of white Portuguese men and of Amerindian women) and some Portuguese for pagan practices, in what became known as the *Santidade de Jaguaripe*. This was, in reality, a syncretic cult led by Amerindians who had fled the Jesuit missions, and which was exploited, in this case, by a member of the local elite. By 1585 the movement had already been disbanded by the civil authorities, and the Amerindians were re-enslaved and sent to the missionary towns. In spite of the fact that Amerindians were also denounced, the Visitor ignored them completely, concentrating above all on dietary deviance (not observing fasts and perhaps even cannibalism) and the motivations of the *mamelucos* for having adopted scarifications and other indigenous practices (Vainfas). The possibility that the inquisitorial emissary would try Amerindians does not seem to have even been considered.

Second, it is important to note that the two apparently unique cases of Amerindians that were effectively tried by the Inquisition in the seventeenth century—and which are known thanks to the research of Maria Leônia Chaves de Resende—were without a doubt seen as extremely serious, either because of the scandal that they could provoke, or because of the gravity of what was reported. These did not have to do with blasphemy, nor with the practice of pagan rituals, but in one case of a pact with the devil and in the other an interesting report of generalized bigamy (portrayed as a contagion) that the inquisitors could not ignore (Resende 349). Of course, it should also be noted that the cases of the eighteenth century, a little more numerous, also refer to bigamy and the suspicion of pacts with the devil. It is symptomatic in any case that, although Maria Leônia Chaves de Resende had preliminarily enumerated thirty-three denunciations implicating Amerindians in the seventeenth century, not one of those resulted in a formal trial (Resende 349–74). We will see, nonetheless, from the only two examples of trials conducted against Amerindians in Brazil in the seventeenth century, that this was not due simply to a lack of jurisdiction on the part of the inquisitors, but to the inquisitors' image of Amerindians as extremely brutish (*rústicos*).

Brizida was a freed Amerindian woman (*índia da terra*) born in Recife to parents who, like her, were probably enslaved and also baptized. As a consequence of the Dutch invasion of Pernambuco, in May of 1636 she was in Bahia, accompanying the captain João Lopes Barbalho. At Easter of that same year she had confessed two times with a Benedictine monk who, according to Brizida, absolved her of a pact with the devil. The mention of this double absolution is an important indication of the common belief that the Amerindians, including those who lived in the cities, should not be treated with the same rigor as someone of European or African origin, whom the friars, without a doubt, would not have absolved, not having the power to absolve cases of demoniacal pact. Still, probably due to the knowledge that one of her partners in the crime (the captive *mulata*, Argueda) was already imprisoned by order of the Bishop of Bahia, Brizida presented herself to the prelate to confess her errors. It is important to mention that Pedro da Silva e Sampaio, before being named as Bishop of Bahia in 1633, had been an inquisitor in the tribunal of Lisbon, and that his role in the Portuguese colony partially occupied by the Dutch was very important (Lipiner 34–35; Feitler, *Nas malhas da consciência*, 201–6). So, it is not surprising that the confession (or rather, the judicial interrogation) of Brizida clearly indicates that it was a proceeding planned for the Inquisition. From this, it is possible to infer that the events related by Brizida were considered very serious, and were even classified as a classic witches' Sabbath ("Treslado da confissam").[19]

What drove the Bishop to send Brizida's formal confession to his ex-colleagues of the Inquisition rather than resolving it himself? Without a doubt, one factor was the gravity of the confession, which directly implicated two other persons; another was possibly that Brizida did not live in the more sheltered and isolated environment of a mission (a village administrated by priests), but in an urban zone, a fact that diminished her indigenous identity; and a third that upon investigating the knowledge that Brizida had of Catholicism, she responded that she was baptized "as a girl" (and not as an adult), that every year she confessed during Lent, and, above all, that she received communion. At that time, communion was not permitted for all Amerindians, but only to those who had a basic comprehension of the dogmas of the Church. On her knees, she knew how to cross and bless herself, and of the prayers she knew only the Our Father and the Ave Maria. Yet this limited knowledge of the prayers was doubtlessly acceptable as basic knowledge for an Amerindian.

In the letter that he wrote on December 2, 1639 to the inquisitors in Lisbon (he also mentions having written directly to the Inquisitor General), calling attention to this and another case of concern (that of a very poor bigamist native of Azores), Bishop Pedro da Silva characterized Brizida not as an Indian woman, but as "a daughter of Indians," distancing her in this way, although only slightly, from her origins and approximating her to the European ideals of civilization. Nevertheless, because she was Amerindian, "she should be treated with mercy." The difficulties of travel due to the war and Brizida's poverty ("she owns nothing more than the shirt she is wearing and a cotton cloth with which she ties it"), led the Bishop to ask for authorization to reconcile her to the Church himself, as because of his previous experience as inquisitor he knew "what kind of penance she would deserve." Surprisingly, the inquisitors decided that as an exception, the Bishop could undertake her reconciliation—without a doubt because of the great confidence that they had in their former colleague—advice the General Counsel followed (Pedro da Silva).

The case of Brizida is exceptional above all else for having arrived at a final sentence elaborated by delegation, in the name of the Inquisition, although we do not know what finally happened to her. Pedro da Silva would not have written to the inquisitors if he were going to try her based on his "ordinary" jurisdiction as Bishop, rather than the jurisdiction that Cardinal Henrique had bestowed upon his antecessor in 1579 in the cases of heresy among Amerindians. Another case, a little later, but which also implied grave disruption to the proper order of Tridentine Christian society, came to the attention of the inquisitors.

At the end of the seventeenth century, the Inquisition once again confronted a case implicating Amerindians that could not be ignored, even if in the end, because of the impossibility of attaining testimonies, the case was closed without a sentence. On October 1, 1696, friar Antonio Gonçalo, a Carmelite of the mission of the mouth of Rio Real in Bahia, wrote to the inquisitorial commissioner in Salvador relating cases of bigamy of four Amerindians, three of whom had been married following the Catholic rites in villages of the bishopric of Pernambuco under his administration.[20] Friar Antonio learned from other Amerindians, who "commonly wander these roads," that the denounced had married again, a fact which he reported to clear his own conscience. The missionary hoped in this way to fulfill his obligation as a priest and a good Catholic, and asked that the commissioner act "to the best of his knowledge in accordance with the Regulations received from the Holy Office," and that they inform him of what to do in similar cases, since he was the spiritual administrator of those Amerindians (Gonçalo). The commissioner sent the letter to the Tribunal of Lisbon, in which the prosecutor, believing to have sufficient material to begin legal procedures, required that the inquisitors open an investigation in the village of Rio Real, and in those of Camarão and Carecé in Pernambuco, in order to prove the two marriages of the denounced and the survival of the first spouses. The inquisitors complied with the petition and reports were made, but they did not find Amerindians who knew the denounced and the case was closed (ANTT, IL, Book 266, Folios 217–229v).

Would these mission Amerindians have been arrested and sent to Portugal if their simultaneous marriages had been proven? The inquisitors made no special reference to the fact that the denounced were Amerindians or to the decree of 1579 that legally exempted them from inquisitorial rules. In short, as noted by Resende, "the long arm of the Inquisition did not exempt Indians and mestizos from its reach since it ended up adopting the same procedures in practice that it deployed against other colonists" (352). Nonetheless, it is important to note that while the Inquisition did not reject denunciations against Amerindians (how could they?), the opening of processes, as in the case of the bigamists of Rio Real, and even further, trials that reached sentences, were very rare occurrences, a fact almost always based on the "ignorance, great rusticity, and lack of instruction" of the Amerindians (cited in Resende 367). This included cases of bigamy. According to Resende, of the seven cases of bigamy that reached final sentences from the Inquisition, six were taken as "extraordinary cases of absolution," and only one defendant, the freed Custódio da Silva, was effectively condemned and heard his sentence in a public auto-da-fé in Lisbon on September 26, 1745, even though he did not speak Portuguese.[21]

Since the delegation of powers bestowed upon the Bishop of Brazil by Cardinal Henrique did not seem to have been put into practice, the Amerindians in the end were not effectively, or better said, legally excluded from inquisitorial jurisdiction. Still, the denunciations made against them that managed to attract the attention of the inquisitors and which, for their gravity, resulted in trials were very rare. Thanks to the prejudices that the Portuguese had with respect to the capacity of the Amerindians, in the great majority of the cases that came to be denounced to the Holy Office, the Inquisition was not added to the many tragedies that poured down upon them.

Conclusion

This chapter has examined three continents and surveyed the different reactions of Portuguese society regarding their incapacity to accept others as members of the same Catholic world. This rejection was an essential element of their identity and the Inquisition naturally reflected, as we see, in a type of reverse mirror, the mental universe and the prejudices of the societies that created them, respecting more or less the cultural hierarchies that were settled by the mid-sixteenth century. While at one point the Inquisition could be seen as a tribunal with virtually unrestricted jurisdiction over all Christians, with the establishment of the hierarchies described by Acosta or later by Valignano the institution became specialized, practically renouncing the vast world of indigenous America, considered as insufficiently reasonable to have a perfect understanding of the mysteries of Catholicism, to administer the sacraments, and, in the end, to have the honor of being judged by the Holy Office.

Nonetheless, the tribunals also learned to adapt to the conditions that they found, as much from the institutional as from the local points of view. In terms of their actions, if we pause on the fascinating case of the Tribunal of Goa, the inquisitors in some way exceeded their repressive function to take on a missionary character with respect to the "gentiles" or the "Moors" who dared insert themselves into the process of conversion and assimilation of the natives of the land. In relation to the institutional configuration, the Inquisition delegated broader powers to local inquisitors and commissioners in Asia, and adopted an attitude of leniency toward the *moriscos* and later, although in a different way, to the Indians and other Asian peoples, while the Amerindians passed practically unharmed by inquisitorial repression.

The Inquisition without a doubt played an important role in the religious and cultural configuration of the different parts of the Portuguese empire, but with contrasting results. The immensity of the territories, the limited means of action, but also the *mentalité* of the society meant that the Holy Office did not have a single project for all these overseas spaces and that the institution used instruments and means adapted for eminently specific ends, on a case-by-case basis.

NOTES

1. For a general context of the foundations of the Iberian inquisitorial tribunals, see Prosperi, Lavenia, and Tedeschi.
2. On Portuguese colonization during these years, see Russell Wood. On the foundation of the Inquisition, see Bethencourt, *The Inquisition*.
3. To synthesize Marcocci, this "inquisitorial colonialism" unfolded, on the one hand, through the intimate relationship that existed between missionaries and the Inquisition, and on the other hand, through the authority that the inquisitors of Goa had to judge not only Christians, but also infidels. For a recent re-visitation of these assertions, see Marcocci and Paiva 125–26.
4. For Gruzinski, "globalization" is above all the acceleration of the process of the circulation and mixing of persons, goods, and ideas beginning at the end of the sixteenth century, while "Westernization" implies not a unidirectional process (it is not established out of whole cloth), but the imposition of parameters that change the manner in which the dominated live and think. Gruzinski, *Las cuatro partes del mundo*.
5. The classic text on the reactions of lettered men to the discovery of the Americas is Anthony Pagden's *The Fall of Natural Man*. On the censorship of "relativism," see the analysis of Hans Böhm's *Omnium gentium mores leges et ritus* (1520) in Pirillo; and Marcocci, "L'ordine cristiano."
6. On the fusion of Biblical and Aristotelian categories in the formation of medieval and *ancien régime* societies see Phillips; and Hespanha. For an Iberian theological current critical of the distinction among Christians, see Pastore.
7. Johnson and Marcocci each draw on previous findings, but the depth of their respective analyses complicates and, at the same time, shines new light on the subject. In regards to Portuguese theologians' condemnation of Ethiopian Christianity and the censorship of a conciliatory vision, as presented in Damião de Góis's *Fides, Religio Moresque, Aethiopium* (1534), see chapters 4–5 in Marcocci, *A Consciência de um império*.
8. See Herzog's text and extensive bibliography.
9. For a detailed chronology of the institutionalization of the statutes of blood purity in Portugal, see Olival; and Figueirôa-Rego and Olival.
10. The episcopal constitutions used in Portuguese Africa were those of Lisbon or

Bahia, meaning that they were guided by the same general rules, but local necessities meant that this (and many other clauses) were tossed aside (hence the use of "theoretically" in the text). This was not exactly a problem for the Law of the Old Regime. See, for example, Vide (book I, title LIII, paragraph 224, n. 2 and 4); Rodrigo Cunha (book I, title XXI, paragraph 1); and Sousa (book I, title 3, constitution IV). For other older constitutions promulgated in the second half of the sixteenth century that are more generic, such as those of Évora, which did not admit "captive slaves, nor bigamists, nor others forbidden law," see João de Melo. Title VII, chapter 1. See also, "Introduction" in Vide.

11. For more on the mandinga pouches, see Souza.
12. The Edict of the Inquisitor General was intended to create and regulate the tribunal of the Holy Office in Goa, but was not put into effect. See Ana Cannas da Cunha 294.
13. The Inquisitor General would have promulgated these decrees. See, for example, the letter from Inquisitor General Jorge de Almeida, March 8, 1585, in Baião, vol. I, 304–6.
14. More than a way for Rome to obtain access to funds, these quinquennial briefs were a very practical way to cancel a decision that was not meant to be permanent. For another example, also in relation to the Inquisition, see Floriano, Castro, and Craesbeeck, fl. 94v–123.
15. For the different meanings of *pagoda*, see Dalgado 129–37.
16. See, for example, book III, treaty VIII, section II in Peña Montenegro, 356–57.
17. I am immensely grateful to Evergton Sales Souza for letting me know of the existence of this document.
18. On the politics of the Marquis de Pombal in relation to the Amerindians, see Domingues.
19. For a more detailed description and an analysis of the (mixed) origins of these Sabbaths, see Mott. Note that in the case studied by Mott, the "witches" do not appear to have been judged by the inquisitors.
20. For the friar's Carmelite identity, see Franco.
21. Another two trials may have been completed if the prisoners had not died en route to Lisbon or in the inquisitorial jail. See Resende.

WORKS CITED

Alberro, Solange. *Inquisición y sociedad en México, 1571–1700*. Mexico City: Fondo de Cultura Económica, 1996.

Almeida, Maria Regina Celestino de. "Índios mestiços e selvagens civilizados de Debret reflexões sobre relações interétnicas e mestiçagens." *Varia Historia* 25:41 (2009): 85–106.

Arquivo Nacional da Torre do Tombo (ANTT). Conselho Geral do Santo Ofício. Book 840, Bundle 31, Document 28. Lisbon, Portugal.

———. Inquisição de Lisboa (IL). Book 20, Folios 3v, 4v, 5v–7v. Lisbon, Portugal.
———. Inquisição de Lisboa (IL). Book 266, Folios 217–229v. Lisbon, Portugal.
———. Inquisição de Lisboa (IL). Pc. 2703. Lisbon, Portugal.
Aubin, Jean. "Vasco da Gama, 1502." *Le latin et l'astrolabe: Études inédites sur le règne de D. Manuel, 1495–1521*. Vol. 3: Édition posthume préparée d'après les papiers laissés par l'auteur. Ed. M. da C. Flores, L. F. F. R. Thomas, and F. Aubin. Paris: Centre Culturel Calouste Gulbenkian, 2006. 305–21.
Baião, António. *A Inquisição de Goa: Tentativa de Historia da sua origem, estabelecimento, evolução e extinção*. 2 vols. Lisbon: Academia das Ciências, 1930–1945.
Barros, João de. *Dos feitos, que os Portugueses fizeram no Descobrimento, e conquista dos Mares, e Terras do Oriente*. Decada Primeira. Lisbon: Na Regia Officina Typografica, 1777.
Bethencourt, Francisco. *The Inquisition: A Global History, 1478–1834*. Cambridge, UK: Cambridge University Press, 2009.
———. *Racisms: From the Crusades to the Twentieth Century*. Princeton: Princeton University Press, 2013.
Biblioteca Nacional de Portugal (BNL). Codices 201 and 203. Lisbon, Portugal.
Boxer, Charles R. *Relações raciais no império colonial português, 1415–1825*. Porto: Afrontamento, 1988.
———. *A Igreja e a expansão ibérica*. Lisbon: Edições 70, 1989.
Brásio, António. *História e Missiologia*. Luanda: Instituto de Investigação Científica de Angola, 1979.
Calainho, Daniela. *Metrópole das mandingas: Religiosidade negra e Inquisição portuguesa no Antigo Regime*. Rio de Janeiro: Garamond, 2008.
Collectorio das bulas e breves apostolicos, cartas, alvarás e provisões reaes que contem a instituição & progresso do Sancto officio em Portugal. Vários indultos & Privilégios que os Summos Pontífices e Reys destes Reynos lhe concederão. Impresso per mandado do Illustrissimo & Rmo Senhor Bispo Dom Francisco de Castro. Inquisidor Geral do Conselho de Estdo de Sua Magestade. Em Lisboa nos Estaos: Lourenço Craesbeeck Impressor Del Rey, 1634.
Cunha, Ana Cannas da. *A Inquisição no Estado da Índia: Origens (1539–1560)*. Lisbon: Arquivos Nacionais/Torre do Tombo, 1995. 294–301.
Cunha, Manuela Carneiro da. "Imagens de índios do Brasil: O século XVI." *Estudos Avançados* 4:10 (1990): 91–110.
Cunha, Rodrigo da. *Constituiçoens synodaes do Arcebispado de Lisboa: Novamente feitas no synodo diocesano que celebrou na Sé Metropolitana de Lisboa . . . D. Rodrigo da Cunha em os 30 dias de Mayo do anno de 1640*. Lisbon: Na Officina de Paulo Craesbeeck, 1656.
Dalgado, Sebastião Rodolfo. *Glossário luso-asiático* [facsimile reproduction of the 1919 and 1921 original editions]. Volume 2. New Delhi: Asian Educational Services, 1998.
Domingues, Ângela. *When the Amerindians Were Vassals: Power Equations in Northern Brazil (1750–1800)*. New Delhi: Transbooks, 2007.
Feitler, Bruno. *Nas malhas da consciência: Igreja e Inquisição no Brasil, Nordeste 1640–1750*. São Paulo: Phoebus/Alameda, 2007.

———. "A delegação de poderes inquisitoriais: O exemplo de Goa através da documentação da Biblioteca Nacional do Rio de Janeiro." *Tempo* 24 (2008): 127–48.
Figueirôa-Rego, João, and Fernanda Olival. "Cor da pele, distinções e cargos: Portugal e espaços atlânticos portugueses (séculos XVI a XVIII)." *Tempo* 30 (2011): 115–45.
Franco de Oliveira, João. Relation of the Archbishop João Franco de Oliveira, from 15 December 1696. Relationes Doecesium, 712 (Salvatoris in Brasilia). Archivio Segreto Vaticano, Congregazione del Concilio, Vatican City.
Gonçalo, Antonio. Letter to the inquisitorial commissioner in Salvador. 1 October 1696. Book 266, Folio 218. Inquisição de Lisboa. Arquivo Nacional da Torre do Tombo (ANTT), Lisbon, Portugal.
Gruzinski, Serge. *Las cuatro partes del mundo: Histoira de una mundialización*. Mexico City: Fondo de Cultura Económica, 2010.
Herzog, Tamar. "Can You Tell a Spaniard When You See One?: 'Us' and 'Them' in the Early Modern Iberian Atlantic." *Polycentric Monarchies: How did Early Modern Spain and Portugal Achieve and Maintain a Global Hegemony?* Eds. Pedro Cardim, Tamar Herzog, José Javier Ruiz Ibáñez, and Gaetano Sabatini. Brighton: Sussex Academic Press, 2012. 147–61.
Hespanha, António M. *Imbecillitas: As bem-aventuranças da inferioridade nas sociedades de Antigo Regime*. São Paulo: Anna Blume, 2010.
Honorato, João. Box 14, Document 1230. Conselho Ultramarino. Arquivo Histórico Ultramarino, Bahia, Portugal.
Horta, José Augusto Nunes da Silva. "A Inquisição em Angola e Congo: O inquérito de 1596–1598 e o papel mediador das justiças locais." *Arqueologia do Estado*. Lisbon: História Critica, 1988. 387–418.
Inquisition of Goa. Auto-da-fé list of 16 October 1695. Book 840, Bundle 31, Document 6. Conselho Geral do Santo Ofício. Arquivo Nacional da Torre do Tombo (ANTT), Lisbon, Portugal.
Johnson, Carina L. "Idolatrous Cultures and the Practice of Religion." *Journal of the History of Ideas*, 67:4 (2006): 597–622.
Jordão, Levy Maria, coord. *Bullarium patronatus Portugalliae regum in ecclesiis Africae, Aslae atque Oceaniae: Bullas, breves epistolas, decreta atque sanctae sedis ab Alexandro III ad hoc usquetempus amplectens* [1171–1600]). Olisipone: Ex Typographia Nationali, 1878.
Lipiner, Elias. *Izaque de Castro: O mancebo que veio preso do Brasil*. Recife: Massangana, 1992.
Marcocci, Giuseppe. "A fé de um império: A inquisição no mundo português de quinhentos." *Revista de História* 164 (2011): 65–100.
———. "L'ordine cristiano e il mondo: Francisco de Támara traduttore di Hans Böhm." *Per Adriano Prosperi: L'Europa divisa e i nuovi mondi*. Vol. 2. Orgs. Massimo Donatini, Giuseppe Marcocci, and Stefania Pastore. Pisa: Edizioni della Normalle, 2011. 79–92.
———. *A Consciência de um império: Portugal e o seu mundo (sécs. XV–XVII)*. Coimbra: Imprensa da Universidade de Coimbra, 2012.

Marcocci, Giuseppe, and José Pedro Paiva. *História da Inquisição portuguesa, 1536–1821*. Lisbon: Esfera dos Livros, 2013.

Martínez, María Elena. "The Language, Genealogy, and Classification of 'Race' in Colonial Mexico." *Race and Classification: The Case of Mexican America*. Eds. Ilona Katzew and Susan Deans-Smith. Stanford: Stanford University Press, 2009. 25–41.

Melo, Carlos Mercês de. *The Recruitment and Formation of the Native Clergy in India, 16th–19th Century*. Lisbon: Agência Geral do Ultramar, 1955.

Melo, João de. *Constituições do Arcebispado dEvora novamente feitas por mandado do illustrissimo e reverendissimo señor dom Ioam de Mello, arcebispo do dito arcebispado &c*. Évora: Em casa de André de Burgos, 1565.

Mendonça, Délio de. *Conversion and Citizenry: Goa under Portugal, 1510–1610*. New Delhi: Concept Publishing Company, 2002.

Moisés, Leila Perrone. "Índios livres e índios escravos: os princípios da legislação indigenista do período colonial." *História dos índios no Brasil*. Ed. Manuela Carneiro da Cunha. São Paulo: Companhia das Letras, 1992.

Monteiro, Frey Pedro. "Catalogo dos notarios que tem havido nesta Inquisiçam [. . .]," and "Ajudantes da mesma Inquisiçam [. . .]." *Collecçam dos documentos e memorias da Academia Real da Historia Portugueza* [. . .]. Lisboa Occidental: Na Officina de Pascoal da Sylva, 1724.

Mott, Luiz. "Um congresso de diabos e feiticeiras no Piauí colonial." *Formas de crer: Ensaios de história religiosa do mundo luso-brasileiro, séculos XIV–XXI*. Eds. Lígia Bellini, Evergton Sales Souza, and Gabriela dos Reis Sampaio. Salvador: Corrupio/EdUFBa, 2006. pp. 129–60.

Novinsky, Anita. *Inquisição: Prisioneiros do Brasil (séculos XVI–XIX)*. São Paulo: Expressão e Cultura, 2002.

Olival, Fernanda. "Rigor e interesses: Os estatutos de limpeza de sangue em Portugal." *Cadernos de Estudos Sefarditas* 4 (2004): 151–82.

Pagden, Anthony. *The Fall of Natural Man: The American Indian and the Origins of Comparative Ethnology*. Cambridge: Cambridge University Press, 1982.

Paiva, José Pedro. *Bruxaria e superstição num país sem "caça às bruxas" (1600–1774)*. Lisbon: Editorial Notícias, 1997.

Pastore, Stefania. *Una herejía española: Conversos, alumbrados e Inquisición (1449–1559)*. Madrid: Marcial Pons, 2010.

Peña Montenegro, Alonso de la. *Itinerario para Párrocos de Indios* [. . .]. Madrid: En la Oficina de Pedro Marin, 1771 [1668].

Phillips, Seymour. "The Outer World of the European Middle Ages." *Implicit Understandings: Observing, Reporting, and Reflecting on the Encounters Between Europeans and Other Peoples in the Early Modern Era*. Ed. Stuart B. Schwartz. Cambridge, UK: Cambridge University Press, 1994. 23–63.

Pirillo, Diego. "Relativismo culturale e 'armonia del mondo': L'enciclopedia etnograica di Johannes Boemus." *Per Adriano Prosperi: L'Europa divisa e i nuovi mondi*. Vol. 2. Orgs. Massimo Donatini, Giuseppe Marcocci, and Stefania Pastore. Pisa: Edizioni della Normalle, 2011. 67–78.

Prosperi, Adriano, Vincenzo Lavenia, and John Tedeschi, eds. *Dizionario Storico dell'Inquisizione*. Vols. 1–4. Pisa: Edizione della Normale, 2010.
Resende, Maria Leônia Chaves de. "Cartografia gentílica: Os índios e a Inquisição na América Portuguesa (século XVIII)." *Travessias inquisitoriais das Minas Gerais aos cárceres do Santo Ofício: Diálogos e trânsitos religiosos no império luso-brasileiro (sécs. XVI–XVIII)*. Eds. J. F. Furtado and M. L. Chaves de Resende. Belo Horizonte: Fino Traço, 2013. 349–374.
Rosa Pereira, Isaías da. *Documentos para a História da Inquisição em Portugal (séc. XVI)*. Lisbon: Cáritas Portuguesa, 1987.
Russell Wood, A. J. R. *The Portuguese Empire, 1415–1825: A World on the Move*. Baltimore: Johns Hopkins University Press, 1992.
Saunders, A. C. de C. M. *História social dos escravos e libertos negros em Portugal (1441–1555)*. Lisbon: Imprensa Nacional/ Casa da Moeda, 1994.
Sousa, João de. *Constituições synodaes do bispado do Porto* [. . .]. Porto: Joseph Ferreyra, 1690.
Souza, Laura de Mello e. *The Devil and the Land of the Holy Cross: Witchcraft, Slavery, and Popular Religion in Colonial Brazil*. Trans. Diane Grosklaus Whitty. Austin: University of Texas Press, 2004.
Silva, Filipa Ribeiro da. "A Inquisição na Guiné, nas ilhas de Cabo Verde e São Tomé e Príncipe." *Revista Lusófona da Ciência das Religiões* 3 (2004): 157–73.
Silva, Pedro da. Letter to the Holy Office in Lisbon. 2 December 1639. Book 151, Folio 370. Inquisição de Lisboa. Arquivo Nacional da Torre do Tombo (ANTT), Lisbon, Portugal.
Tavares, David. "Legally Indian: Inquisitorial Readings of Indigenous Identity in New Spain." *Imperial Subjects: Race and Identity in Colonial Latin America*. Eds. Andrew B. Fischer and Matthew D. O'Hara. Durham: Duke University Press, 2009. 81–100.
"Treslado da confissam que fez Brizida India do gentio do Brasil ante o Illmo Snor d. Pedro da Silva Bispo do Brasil &c." Book 226, Folios 313–17. Conselho Geral do Santo Ofício. Arquivo Nacional da Torre do Tombo (ANTT), Lisbon, Portugal.
Vainfas, Ronaldo. *A Heresia dos índios: Catolicismo e rebeldia no Brasil colonial*. São Paulo: Companhia das Letras, 1995.
Velho, Álvaro. *Roteiro da viagem que em descobrimento da India pelo Cabo da Boa Esperança fez dom Vasco da Gama em 1497: Segundo um manuscripto coetâneo existentena Bibliotheca publica portuense*. Ed. D. Kopke and A. da Costa Paiva. Porto: Typographia Commercial Portuense, 1836.
Vide, Sebastião Monteiro da. *Constituições primeiras do arcebispado da Bahia (1707)*. São Paulo: EdUSP, 2010.
Xavier, Ângela Barreto. *A Invenção de Goa: Poder imperial e conversões culturais nos séculos XVI e XVII*. Lisbon: ICS, 2008.
_____. "'O lustre do seu sangue': Bramanismo e tópicas de distinção no contexto português." *Tempo* 30 (2011): 71–100.
_____. "Conversos and Novamente Convertidos: Law, Religion, and Identity in the Portuguese Kingdom and Empire." *Journal of Early Modern History* 15 (2011): 255–87.

Županov, Ines. "História da Expansão Portuguesa: O Império Oriental, 1458–1665, A Religião e as Religiões." Trans. Margarida Vale de Gato. Web. October 6, 2016. www.ineszupanov.com/publications/HIST%D3RIA%20DA%20EXPANS%C3O%20 PORTUGUESA%202001.pdf.

◆ CHAPTER FIVE

Jesuit Networks and the Transatlantic Slave Trade

Alonso de Sandoval's *Naturaleza, policía sagrada y profana* (1627)[1]

Anna More

The precarity of life imposes an obligation on us.

JUDITH BUTLER, *Frames of War* (2)

Ao todo, os testemunhos conhecidos sobre os tumbeiros portugueses, brasílicos e brasileiros (durante o Império) não devem passar de três dezenas. Muitos provêm de estrangeiros, mas nenhum deles dos padres que mais viajaram no percurso, os jesuítas portugueses. Por quê? Porque existiam, certamente, instruções da ordem no sentido de evitar tais narrativas (In total, the known firsthand accounts of the Portuguese, Brazilian and Brazilian-Angolan slave ships [during the Empire] do not number more than three dozen. Many come from foreigners, but none of them from the priests who most traveled the journey: the Portuguese Jesuits. Why? Because there surely existed in the Order instructions to avoid such narratives).

LUIZ FELIPE DE ALENCASTRO, *O Trato dos Viventes* (83)

Perceiving the effects of globalization, whether past or present, has always been subject to a paradox. Current transportation and communication systems have given production chains, markets and finance capital a global reach. Integration into a common market, however, has not had an overall positive effect on world populations. Finance capitalism has destabilized many communities, increasing inequality and contributing to what has been called "precarity" as a normal social condition.[2] At the same time, however, the technologies that facilitate economic expansion also provide the only means to witness the global conditions of inequality and precarity and thus to act politically on these processes. These simultaneous functions of facilitating and uncovering the effects of globalization make it imperative to investigate the social and political conditions of communication networks. Investigating the conditions of representation is particularly crucial in the case of subjects who have been destabilized under globalization, as representation may expose these populations to more violence rather than serve to protect them.[3]

For these reasons, Judith Butler has argued that rather than seeking representation we must ask "about the conditions under which it becomes possible to apprehend a life or set of lives as precarious, and those that make it less possible, or even impossible" (2). As Butler defines it, precariousness is a basic human condition that is overcome through social bonds (14). When these bonds are weakened or the institutions of care, protection and welfare misaligned with social needs, used for political ends or simply torn down, subjects become exposed once again to precarious conditions. Any attempt to represent this state, however, is subject to what she calls the "framing" function of representation. Representation provides a means for recognition, but also identifies and differentiates subjects, sorting humanity into categories that potentially legitimate the further precarization of populations. As it is not possible to represent, visualize or create material and institutional connections without this function of framing, Butler suggests a goal of "apprehension" rather than recognition (3–5). For Butler, this "apprehension" of precarious life can only occur when there is a disjuncture between the frame and its subject. At this point, the frame itself becomes visible and the ontological ideology it has created can be undone (12).

The ethical dilemmas that Butler outlines for representing precariousness in the present also pertain to past contexts. The tendency to understand current global precarization as the unprecedented result of neoliberal governmental policies, global technology, and capitalist financialization has obscured ways in which many of these processes were already present in early globalization.[4] One of the clearest examples of the precarization of entire regional populations was the early transatlantic slave trade. During the sixteenth century European slavery was transformed from a local and relatively sporadic institution to commercialized chattel slavery. By the early seventeenth century the capture, imprisonment, and forced migration of hundreds of thousands of West Africans had already become the basis for labor in large swaths of the Americas and elsewhere. The commodification of human labor in a transatlantic market, by which Africans were geographically separated from their communities of origin, was supported by an ideology of what Orlando Patterson has called "social death." Even if in practice enslaved Africans were able to maintain familial and cultural ties and to create new ones during their arduous journeys, their lives were still ultimately determined by their legal status as commodities that could be bought and sold. The violent separation of Africans from their families and communities and from the networks and practices of meaning that sustained their lives in Africa is, indeed, a very early form of the extreme precarization of global labor.

The paltry documentation of the Atlantic slave trade also demonstrates the paradox of representing this precarity: the very ships that served as prisons for massive numbers of Africans on the Atlantic voyage and as conduits for the governmental and financial interactions that facilitated this human commodification, also carried witnesses to the trade. Yet while the brutality of the slave trade did not go entirely unnoticed at the time, there exist surprisingly few documents that detail the conditions of the imprisonment, sale, and Atlantic journey of enslaved Africans during the early period. The missing archive of the transatlantic slave trade has often been remarked and a long tradition of historiography has worked hard to overcome its limitations.[5] But given limited numbers of documents, it is all the more important to analyze with care the few exceptions to this archival silence. In the early period, almost all documents detailing the slave trade were written in complicity with the system of enslavement and therefore had little interest in documenting its systemic violence. Even fewer give expression to the enslaved, although again there are fascinating exceptions to this rule.[6] Documents that are written to defend the slave trade, however, can be read in such a way that the frameworks used to capture enslaved Africans in systems of representation and recognition can be denaturalized.[7] While the apprehension of precarious subjects in such an archive remains a challenge, we can more surely analyze the ideological scaffolding that framed this precarity and thus contributed to the rapid institutionalization of the transatlantic slave trade and slavery.

The Jesuit Alonso de Sandoval (1573–1651) has long been recognized as the author of one of the earliest and most extraordinary accounts of the Iberian slave trade. Sandoval's arrival in Cartagena de Indias in 1605 coincided with a surge in the trade that made the city one of the most important slave ports in the Americas. Not only did Sandoval decide to dedicate his ministry to the baptism and evangelization of the arriving Africans, but he also wrote an extensive treatise on the conditions of the transatlantic voyage and enslavement in the Americas. Published originally in 1627 as *Naturaleza, policia sagrada y profana, costumbres, ritos, disciplina y catechismo, de todos etiopes* and then again in a heavily revised version in 1647 with an additional title of *De instauranda Aethiopum salute*, the treatise was a missionary manual intended to outline the best practices for conversion as well as to convince other Jesuits to take on the same labor. Sandoval explicitly modeled his treatise on the Jesuit Jose de Acosta's two monumental works: the missionary manual *De procuranda indorum salute* (1588) and the highly successful natural history of the Americas, *Historia natural y moral de las Indias* (1593).[8]

While influenced by Acosta, however, Sandoval focused his ministry on a distinct context and population. Despite the century of interaction with sub-Saharan Africa, European accounts relied on classical and Biblical references and had little knowledge of the diversity of Africa and its people.[9] Sandoval draws on the same sources but supplements these with an extensive natural and human history of Africa drawn from contemporary accounts. Like Acosta, Sandoval discusses at length the moral and legal status of the subjects of his evangelization. However, the commodification and sale of human subjects required considerations quite distinct from those that determined indigenous policy in the Americas. Whereas the Spanish Crown had prohibited indigenous slavery in 1537, the context of African enslavement was deemed legitimate by the European doctrine of "just war" (Andrés-Gallego and García Añoveros 23). No commentator of the period questioned the premise of African slavery, although many critiqued the form in which enslavement was carried out.

Although like all other prominent commentators, Sandoval accepts the enslavement of Africans, he goes further than most in his critique of the violence of the trade. Most of the critique occurs in several chapters inserted within his geography of Africa and includes shocking descriptions of the conditions enslaved Africans had endured by the time they had arrived in Cartagena. As some of the only published representations of the violence of the middle passage from the period, these have rightly received scholarly attention.[10] However, scholars have not recognized the connection between these scenes and the rest of the treatise, particularly the first book in which they appear. In this first section of his treatise, Sandoval outlines an unusual geography in which he extends the racial category of blackness to link a number of peoples located around the globe to West Africans.[11] Read together, these unusual elements of Sandoval's treatise form part of a greater transition from sixteenth-century jurisprudence on "just war" to an incipient racial construction of globalized labor. As much as they are denunciations of the violence of the slave trade, Sandoval's graphic descriptions of scenes he witnessed in Cartagena are also crucial to a new ideological frame for slavery that avoids altogether the question of original capture.

It is no coincidence that a Jesuit provided this new frame. As an order with global pretensions and an extensive network of correspondents, it is quite possible that the Society of Jesus was the only early modern institution capable of systematically documenting the transatlantic slave trade. Jesuit practice combined the Christian and economic motives for engaging with chattel slavery: Jesuits not only served as missionaries along the path of the capture, commodification and sale of African slaves, but also the order itself owned slaves for both personal and plantation labor (Olsen 16). The Jesuits' global letter-writing network is an archive of the order's internal debates on the trade and labor regimes of enslaved Africans. While the published stances of prominent Jesuits such as Luis de Molina (1535–1600) became the most prominent theological justification of the transatlantic slave trade, the order's internal correspondence shows a more contentious debate on the subject (Alencastro 165–76). Sandoval's treatise can only be understood in this context. While apparently not fully apprised of the internal debate in the order, Sandoval includes verbatim epistolary correspondence with the Jesuit superior of Luanda, the port of origin of most slaves arriving in Cartagena de Indias. He also cites Jesuit authors as the source for most of his geographical information. Sandoval clearly intuited and made use of the order's ability to link points along the commodity chain of transatlantic slavery as well as the global dimension of its information network.

Jesuit sources, therefore, put Sandoval in a unique position to witness the transatlantic slave trade and particularly to question its structural violence. The fact that he did not ultimately take a stance against the trade, despite his critique of its excesses, has often been remarked as a sign of Jesuit accommodation of slavery (Davis; Vila Vilar; Blackburn; Olsen). Yet Sandoval provides more than just an apology for the trade. As a complex text located on the cusp of the mercantilist explosion of the slave trade, the treatise shows how framing slavery was crucial to dissimulating the effects of early global labor supplies. Sandoval represented the African enslaved as a miserable subject and thus established a means for the Christian recognition necessary for salvation. But this image of the effects of violence on the African body cut out the causal chain that produced this destitution. Sandoval's opening account of the global geography of blackness substitutes this missing causal chain and implicitly provides a racial logic for European slaving beyond Africa. Sandoval's act of witnessing, therefore, should not be viewed in isolation from the rest of his treatise. The frame that denounces the trade in local rather than global terms was a necessary prelude to the transition from the individualized jurisprudence of just war to a racial justification that met the needs of the large-scale slave commerce of the seventeenth century.

Alonso de Sandoval and Jesuit Global Correspondence

Born in Seville in 1576 and raised in Lima, where his father occupied a bureaucratic post from 1583 on, Alonso de Sandoval attended the Jesuit seminary during a period of upheaval in the justification and administration of the Spanish empire, especially the controversial Toledan reforms in Peru. In 1605 he was sent to Cartagena de Indias, in what was then the viceroyalty of Nueva Granada, to serve as a missionary in the recently inaugurated Jesuit college (Vila Vilar 27–29). At that time, Cartagena was becoming the most important primary destination of what has been termed the "second great wave" of the slave trade, when a series of factors on both sides of the Atlantic resulted in the rapid expansion in the numbers of Africans who were imported as enslaved labor in the Americas. During this period, the slave trade was an almost exclusively Iberian enterprise, as the Spanish Crown controlled much of the territory where slaves were destined and the Portuguese occupied the African coast where slaves originated. From the end of the sixteenth century, coincident with the unification of the Spanish and Portuguese crowns, the Spanish Crown awarded Portuguese traders a monopoly contract (*asiento*) over the trade. Until the entrance of the Dutch into the commerce, the Portuguese oversaw its expansion through this bifrontal network of coastal factories, ports, and American plantations. During the first half of the seventeenth century, Portuguese traders continued to account for nearly seventy-five percent of the slave trade to the Americas, delivering most slaves to Brazil or the Caribbean (Eltis and Richardson 25).

This expansion of slavery from a sporadic commercial enterprise to a key element in imperial mercantilism occurred in the final years of the sixteenth century. The reasons for what has been called the "first wave" of mercantilist slavery are likely multiple. It is clear that the *asiento* monopoly had an immediate effect on the trade, and that expansion of plantations in the Americas at the time of indigenous demographic collapse also sharply augmented demand for labor (Alencastro 79). On the African side, with the arrival in 1607 of a new governor in Angola, Manuel Pereira Forjaz, the Portuguese state was effectively able to expand the range of the slave trade and actively compete with the myriad of traders of Portuguese, Spanish and Dutch origin. By 1617, moreover, another new governor, Mendes de Vasconcelos, led an even more notable shift from a trade that depended upon African enslavement practices to a *de facto* policy of warfare waged for the purpose of taking slaves. As Linda Heywood and John Thornton have written, the result of these administrative reforms was a "flood" of slaves to Spanish American ports such as Cartagena (112, 116). Recently, David Wheat has supported this impression, providing additional detail. The first surge in captured Africans sold in the Americas occurred in the last decade of the sixteenth century, although between 1602 and 1616 the numbers arriving at Cartagena dropped sharply as the slave trade turned to Veracruz. In between the years 1617 and 1625, a "second wave" arrived in Cartagena. While in the first surge the majority of traded Africans were from the Upper Guinea coast, with a minority from Angola, in the second surge these numbers were reversed and Angola became the dominant place of origin. Between 1626 and 1640, Angola accounted for two-thirds of the slaves traded in Cartagena (Wheat 4, 22).

Having arrived in Cartagena in 1605, Sandoval was perhaps the member of the order best positioned to witness these dramatic increases in the Portuguese slave trade as well as the horrific conditions to which enslaved Africans were subjected during the middle passage.[12] Deemed unfit for higher theological tasks, Sandoval was assigned to minister to arriving Africans (Vila Vilar 29). The massive numbers of Africans and unclear conditions of Christianization in Africa led to the theological problem of whether or not to risk the rebaptism of those arriving. In 1611, Sandoval penned a short work defending baptism in Cartagena, given doubts that the Africans had been properly baptized in Luanda (Navarrete 50–51). This short work developed into a larger and complex treatise on the nature of the ministry itself, published in 1627 as *Naturaleza, policía sagrada y profana, costumbres, ritos, disciplina y catechismo, de todos etiopes*. While the immediate impetus of the shorter work was to argue in favor of the catechism and baptism of Africans arriving in Cartagena, the expanded work of 1627 had a much broader purpose of inducing other Jesuits to undertake the task of evangelizing newly arrived African slaves.

Sandoval's introduction to his work describes the treatise's purpose and structure. After exhorting his colleagues to dedicate themselves to what he portrays is a ministry among the world's most "miserable" subjects, Sandoval dedicates much of his text to describing how best to catechize and baptize Africans who have been subjected to the middle passage. The practical needs of this task would appear to account for the division of his text into three main parts: the first, a global geography of peoples he variously labels Ethiopians or blacks; second, a description of the benefits of evangelizing them when they arrive on the slave ships; and third, a practical manual on how to catechize and baptize enslaved Africans (Sandoval, *Un tratado*).[13] Sandoval draws heavily on his personal experience, especially to describe the linguistic and cultural particularities of the Africans who arrived in Cartagena. But he also incorporates numerous published sources that he researched in the Jesuit library during a short return to Lima between 1617 and 1619.

These written sources are particularly evident in the first book of the treatise, the majority of which is a geographical account similar to that which Acosta had used to frame his 1588 missionary manual, *De procuranda*, but later published separately as *Historia natural y moral de las Indias* in 1593. Like Acosta, Sandoval wades into the nature of the subjects of his ministry. Drawing on Jesuit authors, however, he applies the term "black" not only to Africans, referred to by

Europeans as Ethiopians, but to numerous peoples who inhabited an extensive geography of a global South. "Blacks," he finds, reside not only in Africa, but also in India, Asia, and the Americas. The uneven nature of Sandoval's geographical knowledge reflects differences among the quality of his sources. Whereas his information on the West African polities that were supplying the slave trade to Cartagena is detailed and reflects his personal interactions with African slaves and slave traders familiar with the region, the wider geography he includes appears subject to the published sources available to him.

The clearest difference among the populations he describes, however, is whether they are subject or not to the transatlantic slave trade. For this reason, Sandoval interrupts his detailed description of West Africa to dedicate several chapters to the justification of the transatlantic slave trade, a question that had provoked a series of theological considerations in the previous century. The juridical foundation of enslavement rested upon a doctrine of "just war" by which the victor maintained a right to enslave the vanquished. No sixteenth-century author debated the legitimacy of enslavement in itself, given the correct conditions. The debate on African enslavement focused, therefore, on the empirical question of whether or not an individual slave could be certified to having been captured in a "just war." The stakes of the loss of liberty were clear to sixteenth-century commentators, and thus, most commentators understood the importance of overcoming what was termed "scruples" (*escrúpulos*) about the justice of any individual enslavement (Andrés-Gallego and García Añoveros 105–6).

While slavery was juridically clear to Europeans, and had underwritten sporadic slavery from the classical period onward, the middlemen who conducted the new transatlantic slave trade could often not certify how any particular slave had been enslaved in Africa. Sixteenth-century skeptics often cited personal interactions with Portuguese slave traders who told of the messy reality of capture in Africa, at times the result of distant wars and at other times kidnapping without even the pretext of war. Once a trader had information of unjust enslavement, according to European jurisprudence, the question became whether or not to free those illegally enslaved.[14] The more difficult question was whether unjustified enslavement tainted the entire commerce. Carried out in the context of scholastic economic treatises on contracts, value, and pricing, the focus of controversy became the sale of slaves for whom the original conditions of captivity could not be determined. In what became effectively the final opinion on the issue in his 1593 *De iustitia et iure*, the Jesuit Luis de Molina argued that if slave traders believed in good faith that their cargo had been legitimately enslaved then they could proceed with the sale as if this were true (García Añoveros 326).

Writing well after Molina's judgment on the matter, Sandoval could easily have authorized his discussion with a short citation from the prominent Jesuit. However, judgment on the legitimacy of enslavement rested ultimately on empirical knowledge, even in Molina's cynical scenario in which a buyer could state that he had no empirical knowledge of the context of original capture. In a treatise built on personal experience, both his and others, Sandoval had the ability to return to the question of original capture and by the juridical terms of enslavement the moral obligation to do so. After protesting his own perplexity, Sandoval states that his own opinion will follow that of the *dotores* (scholars), most especially Molina:

> the great controversy that exists among Scholars about the justification of such an arduous and difficult business [would leave] me perplexed during a long time if I were to pass over it in silence; despite this I have decided to address it, leaving the determination of its justification to the Scholars, who have written about this question so eruditely, principally our own Doctor Molina [. . .] (142).

He follows this statement with a series of skeptical reports from slave traders that bring back the very doubts that Molina had tried to expel. Rather than coming to a conclusion himself, therefore, Sandoval leaves the reader in the place of judge: "I will limit myself to presenting to all what I have understood about this during the many years that I have undertaken this ministry so that each may take into consideration what they think most conforms to justice" (142).

Surely intuiting the difficulty of the question of what he calls "such litigious things" (cosas tan litigiosas), in his introduction Sandoval authorizes his oral testimony from slave traders by noting that they are honorable subjects, and therefore trustworthy, and that Molina had also consulted traders. This testimony allows him to examine the justice of enslavement in the main ports supplying Cartagena: Cacheo and Guinea ports, Cape Verde, São Thomé and Luanda. For each of these ports, Sandoval interrogates the basis for "scruples" concerning the trade. Those arriving from Cape Verde he declares to be the simplest case:

> because this island is not Ethiopian land, but rather is where they bring them from all the other ports, as the most principal marketplace among all of them; and in this way those that bring these blacks from this port, since they buy them there as the third, fourth or further possessor, are not subject to scruples, just as neither are those buyers here in our ports: for this reason, without entering into the intrinsic justification of the thing, we will go on to those that come from the port of São Thomé [. . .] (Sandoval 142–43).

He expresses more doubt about those from São Thomé. As evidence, he cites his own discussions with slave traders. A trader "who had made many trips to these parts" admitted that "all of them had notably weighed down his conscience" (Sandoval 143). Indeed, a king in São Thomé, Sandoval notes, had enslaved entire families of anyone who angered him. In this region, Sandoval concludes, the slave trade proceeds beyond the experience of the scholastic authorities and thus: "whoever inquires and investigates (principally in things so litigious in themselves and in discoveries of new kingdoms and unexamined captures that even the Doctors have not addressed since they are ignorant of them) does not err" (143). He reserves his greatest doubts, however, for the slaves coming from Cacheo. Without citing his sources, he asserts that there are a variety of forms of enslavement in Guinea, ranging from trade for fabric from Goa to punishment for crimes such as adultery. Other times, slaves are simply ambushed and captured at night. Declaring that "this variety of forms of capture has made me greatly reconsider this business," Sandoval confirms his suspicions with the confessions of slave traders themselves, including one who declares that the trade was instigating the very wars that were supplying the slaves (147).

To this extent, Sandoval's discussion follows the lines of sixteenth-century commentators on the trade. However, Sandoval includes an additional source that his predecessors had not: the direct testimony of a Jesuit superior in Africa. After completing his tour of other African ports, Sandoval declares "on the blacks that come from Angola etc. I have found better information (if it is not the case that these captures have been damaged as is often the case)" (143). This "better information" is contained in a letter he has received from Luis de Brandão, Jesuit superior in Luanda, in response to Sandoval's 1610 inquiry into the origin of slaves coming from the port. Unlike his anecdotal documentation of the slave traders' reports, moreover, Sandoval reproduces verbatim the superior's letter. This unusual inclusion of private correspondence between Jesuits in a work intended for publication and on a topic of such controversy merits special attention. Effectively, Sandoval gives voice to the superior as a direct authority on the question of enslavement.

In contrast to the doubts that Sandoval has previously uncovered in testimony from traders, Brandão expresses no ambivalence about the trade. The Portuguese Jesuit opens his short but pithy letter with an acknowledgment of Sandoval's work in catechizing slaves, sympathizing with the "extraordinary frustrations that he must have with these black people" since "we in this College are saddled even by the Portuguese-speaking blacks." As for Sandoval's inquiry into the legitimacy of African captivity, Brandão is decisive: "I believe that your Reverence should not have scruples about that." In the first place, he writes, referring to the Portuguese council dedicated to questions of morality concerning the trade, the *mesa de conciencia* (Council of Conscience) in Lisbon, "this is something that the Council of Conscience in Lisbon, composed of erudite men of good conscience, has never censured." Furthermore, he adds, "the Bishops in São Thomé, Cape Verde and this city of Luanda, who are all erudite and virtuous men, have never censured it." Finally, "we have been here forty years and there have been very erudite Fathers here as well as in the Province of Brasil where there have always been eminent Fathers from our Religion and they have never considered this commerce illicit" (143–44).

In Brandão's reasoning, then, the trade has been authorized by members of the order more eminent than Sandoval. Once authorized, moreover, the trade appears to justify itself "and thus we, and the Fathers of Brasil, have no scruples about buying these slaves for our service." If anyone should doubt the legitimacy of the act of enslavement it is those in Angola who are buying from "persons who have perhaps stolen them." But those who take part in the transatlantic commerce, he states, "know nothing of this and so buy them in good conscience and in good conscience sell them over there." Brandão does admit the possibility that some traveling to the Americas had been illegally enslaved but an inquiry into all cases would simply not be feasible given the staggering numbers who passed through the port:

> to search for a few badly captured among the ten or twelve thousand Blacks who leave from this port every year would be impossible no matter how diligent one is. And to lose so many souls that are sent from here, many of which achieve salvation, so that a few badly captured might not be sent, without even knowing which these are, would not seem to serve God, since those would be few and those that achieve salvation are many and correctly captured.

He also warns Sandoval not to question the slaves themselves "because they will always say that they were stolen and captured with illegitimate titles" and assures him that captivity occurs according to a myriad of African "laws and customs." Finally, he cuts short the discussion with a terse testament to the conditions of the Jesuit mission: "But on this I can't say more to your Reverence, since it is a complex question, and neither about their rites and customs, because I have neither time nor the health to do so, etc." (144).

In the midst of Sandoval's contradictory reports on the justice of the enslavement of Africans, Brandão's letter is of a different stature: a mandate from a Jesuit superior to desist in his inquiry into slaves' origins. Even so, the position of the letter is buried amid the contrary testimony from slave traders, including one who confesses his grave doubts about the origin of a cargo of nine hundred Africans he has brought to Cartagena. As evidence, the slave trader even cites a sermon denouncing the injustice of African captivity, pronounced by the same Luis de Brandão. When Sandoval protests that Brandão has written opposing information in his letter, the trader explains that the surge in unjust captives occurred in the context of a specific war at the time (145). This confluence of contradictory reports from Africa on the justice of African enslavement corresponds to Sandoval's original statement that he will simply present the evidence that he has gathered over his years in the ministry "so that each may take into consideration what they think most conforms to justice" (142). In the following chapter, directly before his well-known descriptions of horrific conditions of the slave warehouses in Cartagena, he repeats his suspension of judgment: "these blacks, captured by the justice known only to God . . ." (151).

Sandoval's suspension of judgment effectively endorses Brandão's equation of justice with the greater good when the superior states that the salvation of the majority is more important than finding a few *mal cautivos* (incorrectly captured). While many commentators had similarly defended African enslavement as a means to a justified end of Christian salvation, this had not been understood as a compensation for unjust enslavement but rather as an additional benefit for the justly enslaved (Andrés-Gallego and García Añoveros 28). In this sense, Brandão does not seek to deny the reports of injustice, but rather meets them with a distinct logic: first, that the trade has been established for a long time and that Jesuits themselves participated in it; and second, that injustice of original enslavement could be compensated by the just end of salvation. By suspending his own judgment on the matter of slaves' origins in Africa and turning to local evidence of excesses in their transport and treatment, Sandoval ends up heeding his superior's mandate. The inclusion of Brandão's letter serves as an authorization for a return to a local empirical perspective rather than an inquiry into the global chain that had resulted in the violent effects that Sandoval witnesses in Cartagena.

Jesuit Networks and the Framing of Slavery

Historians have often noted the inclusion of Brandão's letter in Sandoval's treatise but have never analyzed its purpose in the rhetorical structure of the work. In the most detailed examination of the passage to date, Luiz de Alencastro has placed Brandão's letter in the context of the Jesuit debate on the legitimacy of slavery, carried out not only in published works such as that of Molina but also in a more contentious epistolary correspondence internal to the order. Correspondence from Jesuits in Africa often commented upon the question of the legitimacy of the slave trade. It is clear Jesuits even acted upon their conscience to denounce the trade. In 1583, Jesuits in Angola complained that one of their peers, Miguel García, was threatening to withhold confession from persons engaged in the slave trade (Alencastro 165). García was returned to Spain and reports from other Jesuits in Africa provided more accommodating stances. One of the more successful versions of this accommodation was that of Balthasar Barreira, a Jesuit stationed in Sierra Leone whose missives were included in the edifying literature that circulated within the order in the years just before Brandão penned his response to Sandoval. Alencastro argues that Brandão's letter simply reproduces Barreira's arguments in defense of the slave trade, in a reflection of the influence these must have had in correspondence internal to the order (Alencastro 177). If it is the case that Brandão does not voice an individual stance, but rather repeats elements that had become quasi-official Jesuit discourse on slavery, then Sandoval by contrast appears to act on conscience and out of the necessity of clarifying his local practice in Cartagena.

The correspondence between Sandoval and Brandão, therefore, provides an example of the divergent possibilities within the particular practice of Jesuit letter-writing. Global correspondence among Jesuits was a necessary structure for an order for which, as Jerome Nadal declared, "the world is our house" (O'Malley 46). Precepts in the *Constitutions*, augmented by Loyola's own requests to be informed, had established the order's epistolary practice (Harris 299, 304–5). In theory, Jesuits were to communicate every week with their superiors if they were in close proximity, once a month if they were not (*Constitutions* 292). In practice, epistolary correspondence from some missionary regions could be much more sporadic. Nonetheless, the practice of letter-writing among Jesuits produced a wealth of documentation, in some cases impossibly extensive, as well as new administrative and archival techniques that rationalized and centralized this information (O'Malley 2–3; Friedrich). It also greatly marked the culture of the order, which selected letters to be read aloud among Jesuits as "edifying letters" or to be the basis of the published Annual Letters (Correia-Afonso 6).

In this way, Jesuits could communicate with one another across the globe, and serve as authorities for one another within a greater structure of centralized selection and distribution.[15] Recently, scholars have argued that this blend of capillary reach and disciplinary centers made Jesuit letter-writing an antecedent to modern communication networks. Drawing on Bruno Latour's work on networks in science, for instance, Steven Harris has argued that the Jesuits' unusually robust production of scientific texts followed from their unique combination of long-distance networks and centralized nodes of accumulation. While the "emissaries" in the field gathered and collected, Harris argues that administrative centers could be considered what Latour calls "centers of calculation" where documents from the field were housed, accumulated, and re-ordered (Harris 294–96). Building on Harris's work, Markus Friedrich has detailed the Jesuits' own policies on correspondence. According to Friedrich, the Jesuit emphasis on centralization sought not only to rationalize information, but also to exercise control through governance. By the late seventeenth century, he argues, centralization had become a precept for governing a global organization: "it is clear that a 'center' meant several things for the Jesuits: 'disengaged,' 'empirical' panoptism, and an understanding of politics as effective governance, including a rational, proactive steering of the body social. Thinking a 'center' along these lines ultimately was a conceptual tool used to refashion politics" (Friedrich 543).

Fewer scholars have addressed the fact that through these same global networks, Jesuits also participated in and disseminated the violence of early European, especially Iberian, imperialism. Ivonne del Valle's analysis of eighteenth-century Jesuit writings from the northern frontier of New Spain is one of the first systematic approaches to the question of frontier violence and its transformation by the information-chain leading to the imperial centers (del Valle *Escribiendo*). Her work on colonial violence in the Jesuit José de Acosta's missionary manual, *De procuranda indorum* (1588) also has important consequences for reading Sandoval's work (del Valle "Entre el realismo," "Violence and Rhetoric"). Not only was Acosta's work a direct influence on Sandoval's treatise, but structurally the two texts also engaged different poles of the same geopolitical and economic contexts of the late sixteenth and early seventeenth centuries. Developing and neutralizing Las Casas's ferocious critique of the excesses of Spanish colonialism, for instance, Acosta represented the Americas as a dystopian context in which a lack of centralized oversight had unleashed the despotic power of Spanish colonizers (del Valle "Entre el realismo"). Yet unlike Las Casas's final stance that the Spanish king should quit the Americas, Acosta's solution is a complete rationalization of colonial life and every subject in the colonies (del Valle "Entre el realismo"). As opposed to centralization, then, Acosta favors the fragmentation and governmental administration of violence through an ethical reform of all members of the political economy (del Valle, "Violence and Rhetoric" 58).

The effect of this pragmatics is, as del Valle argues, to disperse and distribute the original violence of colonization in an attempt to dissipate the radical calls for justice that were occurring even in Acosta's lifetime (del Valle, "Violence and Rhetoric" 64–65). In an argument that reached back to Francisco de Vitoria's *De indis*, Acosta noted that it was impossible to embrace absolute justice without undoing the entire economic system and, since Christian evangelization depended upon this economic system, doing so would be contrary to the greater good of salvation (Vitoria 291; del Valle, "Violence and Rhetoric" 60). Indeed, while focusing and centralizing information, the bureaucratic network also risked connecting a dispersed geography and exposing the violence of a global economic order in which it participated. The typically Jesuit combination of fragmentation and habit, individuation and education, accomplished the administrative goals of governance without giving visibility to the aggregated violence of the system as a whole (del Valle, "Violence and Rhetoric" 65). More than a panopticon as the guiding force for reform through individual habit, the Jesuit at the center of Acosta's *De procuranda* might be called an orchestrator.

While Sandoval appears to have taken initiative to inquire into a question of conscience, Brandão's letter to Sandoval supports both the centralizing and fragmenting disciplinary force also made possible by the network. On the one hand, he suggests that Sandoval leave questions of conscience for a centralized body, the *mesa de consciencia* in Lisbon or other eminent *dotores* of the order. On the other, he insists upon a fragmented consciousness, giving up on the prospect of searching through the thousands of Africans that passed through his port for the couple *mal cautivos* and asking Sandoval also give up this impossible task. Just as in Acosta's example, the violence of the slave trade becomes fragmented, concentrated in local phenomena rather than a systemic whole. Seen from the context of the Jesuit network, therefore, Brandão forcefully blocks Sandoval's attempt to connect points in the geography of the slave trade to determine its legitimacy. Sandoval's inclusion of the letter that blocks this inquiry in turn authorizes his decision to turn the majority of his treatise to the conditions he personally witnessed in Cartagena. Justice is also transformed under this intervention. Rather than a late Lascasian dream of an absolutely ethical conquest, Sandoval adapts what del Valle calls Acosta's third way of a mediated and pragmatic justice (del Valle, "Violence and Rhetoric" 67). Without denying the need to bring justice to the enslaved, Sandoval frames this justice as Christian compensation rather than liberation.

Sandoval establishes the framework for this compensation through the graphic descriptions of what he himself has witnessed in the Cartagena warehouses where Africans were kept before being sold. After dismissing any ability to judge the justice of the trade, Sandoval dedicates the following chapter to the conditions of those who arrive after the transatlantic passage. The images focus closely on the bodies of the enslaved, which become emblems of "misery," a lexicalized juridical concept designating the need for care (More 31).[16] The depiction of the violence of the slave trade works to a final crescendo in the parting image of the chapter:

> And to see so many so sick, so destitute, and with so little succor and protection from their owners, since they commonly leave them naked on the floor with no shelter or aid, causes great pity and compassion. And there they lie and there they often miserably pass away with no one to mourn their bodies or their souls and one could reasonably doubt whether the cause of their death is their great abandonment or their sickness. A good proof of this will be what I saw and wept with my own eyes: in some of the houses of these owners of the slave ships there are great rooms with planks at the edges where they divide the men and women and enclose them all night to sleep and where they appear in the morning the way one would expect after such bestial treatment. They had designated these as places with no remedy for those beyond hope. There they dumped them and in that misery and misfortune there they suffered and finally eaten by flies, some above and others below the planks, there they died. I remember that once I saw among them two who had already died, their naked bodies on the bare floor, as if beasts, their mouths open and facing upward full of flies, their arms crossed as if to signify the Cross of the eternal condemnation befallen on their souls for having died without the Holy Sacrament of Baptism, as no one had been called upon to administer it [. . .] (Sandoval 153).

To communicate the violence of slavery, Sandoval selects an image of dead African men with their arms crossed "as if to signify the Cross" for having died unbaptized. Sandoval's depiction of the violent excesses of slavery substitutes his confused critique of the original capture or the ongoing and everyday violence that characterized enslavement as a governance regime. In fact, Sandoval has an interest in the social death of those who arrive in Cartagena. The bodies are naked, signifying both the indignity of enslaved deaths, but also the symbolic stripping of their original social context during the transatlantic journey. To overcome this social death, Sandoval envisions the Africans in a Christian posture, as if the drama of enslavement was not capture, chains, and commodification, but the body as profane condemnation. Above all, these are images of bodies that cannot themselves give witness to the experience of slavery. Already dead, they must be framed to be understood and spiritually secured, a framing that Butler reminds us occurs with all forms of representation.

Again, the Jesuit context of Sandoval's treatise is evident. It is likely that the emphasis on visualization in the *Spiritual Exercises* required of Jesuits contributed to Sandoval's graphic coding of the dead African body in Christian terms. As in the *Spiritual Exercises*, Sandoval composes a scene that frames its subject but cutting it out of any previous context. This permits the intimacy of witnessing, which in the *Spiritual Exercises* effects an identification between the exercitant and the object of contemplation (Loyola). In Sandoval's treatise, the framing permits the recognition of humanity in people whom he says have been treated as if beasts. The isolated, emblematic scene, therefore, establishes a liminal space in which a witness not directly involved in the trade can inspect its consequences as an outsider. But through this framing function, the violence of slavery is also limited to the context of the transatlantic journey that has people made "bestial." The abjection of African bodies begins when they are crowded into the hulls of the ships where "there is no Spaniard who daring to place his head through the trap door does not become sick, nor can remain inside for an hour without risking grave illness. Such is the stench, lack of space and misery of that place" (152). They arrive, he says, "turned into skeletons" and are brought from the ship "as raw flesh" after which they are placed in warehouses until being sold.

As opposed to the complex trajectory of African subjects that he has previously uncovered through a network of correspondents, letters, and published works, the representation of slavery becomes condensed in a scene witnessed by Sandoval himself. Indeed, the dialectic between horror and salvation rests on the confines of the ship and holding house where Africans are physically segregated and equated through their shared condition of bodily suffering. Notably, this scene is the center of Sandoval's denunciation of the effects of the middle passage. Rather than insisting on his inquiries into the subject of African enslavement, Sandoval's framing of slavery perfectly complements the Luanda Jesuit's assertion that the reiterated practice of commerce itself has erased the need to find individual justifications for the enslavement. By including Brandão's authorized mandate, then, Sandoval neutralizes the potential that Jesuit correspondence could expose the violence of the transatlantic trade. His graphic vision of the warehouses stands in for an investigation into the transatlantic production of precarized labor and permits his pivot from the global context to the local practice of slavery that will occupy the majority of his treatise.

The Slave Trade and the Globalization of Blackness

To this extent, Sandoval's treatise neutralizes the potential that Jesuit networks could expose the effects of a new global economy. But this stripping away of the African context and focusing solely on the slaves who have survived the middle passage is at odds with missionary practice that must understand the cultural origin of subjects of evangelization. Like Acosta before him, Sandoval turns to natural history to understand the place of Africa in a new geopolitics. But unlike the older Jesuit who was describing a "new world," Sandoval must contend with the long relationship between Christianity and Africa. Much of his geographical description focuses on the areas that supplied the human cargo arriving in Cartagena and about which he provides details on distinctions in customs, politics, and history. Clearly Sandoval's communication with African slaves, traders, and Jesuits provides more information on these areas than others. But while detailing the known history of Africa and its diversity, Sandoval also includes a fragmented account of other areas in Asia and the Americas. He implicitly justifies these additional geographies through the nomenclature he uses to categorize them. From the beginning of his treatise, Sandoval has equated Africans with what he calls "blacks." When he turns to other regions, however, he extends the term to include populations in Asia and the Americas. Neither a global natural history, nor a description of the distinct peoples and languages that arrive in Cartagena, the first book of Sandoval's treatise can best be described as an attempt to create a natural history of "black" populations of the world.

Sandoval makes several logical leaps to arrive at this geography of "black" populations. He begins his treatise with a detailed discussion of the nature of "Ethiopians," which he initially equates with the color "black": "since we will need to talk about blacks, or Ethiopians, throughout this book, it would seem best to discuss their name and nature first, before going on." The equation is valid, he argues, since most agree that etymologically, the term "Ethiopian" is related to "burnt." Thus, he declares, "we will call all black nations Ethiopians, beyond the particularities that each one of them represents: such as Guincos, Caravalies, Ardas, Lucumies, Congos, Angolas, Cafres, Macuas, and others" (69). The use of the term "black," here presented as synonymous with Ethiopian, is further extended, however, in his introduction to the scope of his treatise in which he describes its sources as "that which grave and erudite men have published about Ethiopia and the other Empires and Kingdoms of blacks and that which the fathers of the Society who are located on these missions have written, the attribution to whose authorship will be noted in the margins throughout this work" (58). Here, the geography of Ethiopia, the principal association with blackness, has been supplemented by other "Empires and Kingdoms of blacks."

Sandoval's inspiration appears to derive from his access to the network of Jesuits stationed in distinct areas of the globe whose letters and published works detail the populations of these regions. These writings permit a new type of centralization in his work, despite the regional focus on Cartagena: a global gaze that categorizes peoples according to whether they can be defined as "black" or not. Whereas "Ethiopians" may be etymologically related to "burnt" and thus defined as "black," the inclusion of further peoples under this denomination is not similarly justified. Rather, Sandoval appears to reverse the logic of his etymological foundation for a nomenclature according to color: while his treatise is ostensibly about Ethiopians, it will also include those who by their skin color can be denominated "Empires and Kingdoms of blacks," whatever their other geographical characteristics. In a treatise on catechization of "Ethiopians," the original equation between Ethiopian and "black" has permitted a more expansive geography.

In a detailed exegesis of this oddity, Eduardo Restrepo has taken on the challenge of disentangling Sandoval's terminology of geography and color. As Restrepo remarks, despite his initial comments, Sandoval does not fully equate Ethiopian and "black" (124). In the first place, Sandoval notes the diverse physical characteristics of the Ethiopians. For instance, there are those who are of more of a cinnamon color, those who have straight rather than curly hair, and a "nation of gentile Ethiopians, called Maracatos, black as tar but which have marvelously straight hair and the facial features of gentlemen [*ahidalgadas*] such as those of Spaniards" (191). At one point, Sandoval admits that "although it is true that we commonly refer to all of these nations as black, not all are dark; rather within and among them there is great variety; some are blacker than others, others not as black; others are quince color, as they say, others are dark brown, or zambos, or yellowish brown, as mulattoes, of a burnt color" (136). Sandoval also notes the diversity of the West African nations arriving in Cartagena, calling them by their polities and stating that some are more sought after by Spanish slaveholders than others.[17] Sandoval's written sources on greater Africa provide an even more eclectic assortment of anecdotes, including those that tell of lapsed Christians who defend their rites against missionaries and others that recount the barbarity of the Bedouins who refuse even to allow foreigners in their midst (193).

As Sandoval turns to regions outside of Africa, however, he exclusively adopts the term "black." "In the territory of Peru," he declares, "some say that there are nations of blacks so uncivil and remote that they have not even come to our notice" (59). Of Filipinos, he writes "these blacks are not as dark colored as those from Guinea, nor as ugly" (95). Indeed, the phenotypical diversity of Africans most likely permits the extension of the term "black." If Ethiopians may be called "black," even in their diversity, then the term can justifiably apply to all the world's darker-skinned people despite a similar diversity. Perhaps picking up on the common designation of some Filipinos as "little blacks" (negritos), for instance, Sandoval distinguishes between the *indios* and the "blacks" of the Philippines. The term "black" itself, then, becomes the operative link between territories stretching across the global south.

For Restrepo, this categorization stops short of establishing a racialized system (174). Rather, he argues, Sandoval leans toward a version of biology by which accidental qualities become naturalized over time without, therefore, inhering to color. However, it is important to note that Restrepo, like many readers of Sandoval, bases his argument on the 1647 revision of the treatise.[18] In the original publication of 1627, Sandoval posits only two much more rudimentary possibilities for the origin of blackness. The first is classical climate theory, by which the heat of the tropics had led to darker skin. But in this case, he argues, Spanish in the tropics would also give birth to darker children. For this reason he finds the second possible cause more plausible: that Africans are the descendants of Ham "who was the first servant and slave in the world, and who contained this intrinsic heat such that it stained his children and descendants" (75). This mark had designated those who bore it to be forever condemned to servitude. In the following chapter, he argues that any diversity within nations, which he calls by the Aristotelian term "monstrosities," was due to the power of the imagination during conception. In the 1627 edition of Sandoval's treatise, the curiosities of albino "blacks" introduce the possibility that accidents could change nature without disturbing the basic commonality of dark skin among the many "blacks" of the world.

The differences between the 1627 and 1647 versions of Sandoval's treatise reflect their distinct contexts. In 1627 the slave trade had just expanded into a massive enterprise whose main port of entry to the American market was Cartagena. While seemingly random in its scope and odd in its shoehorning of diverse geographies under the rubric of blackness, this geographical extension provides the basis for a leap from a juridical argument to a global racial division as the justification for slavery. At no point does Sandoval declare that all those whom he calls blacks can be enslaved. But from the beginning of his treatise he defines blackness as the condition of being "miserable." Indeed, Sandoval's decision to favor the category "black" over "Ethiopian" in the treatise may follow from this association. If blackness was the "mark of Ham" that condemned its people to servitude, then the extension of blackness across points of the Iberian empire, where trade and evangelization were occurring simultaneously, implicitly provided a racial logic for further enslavement. This potential for precarization as a normal condition was exactly what would ensure its institutionalization, beyond a specific case of sacred guilt or "just war."

In 1627, this logic is still incipient. Yet it is still a decisive transformation of previous justifications of the enslavement of Africans, once the arbitrary circumstances of "just war" had been put into question by the sheer numbers of enslaved arriving in the Americas. The juridical contortions of the sixteenth century were the first step in providing a rationale for the enslavement of a specific group of people, determined by skin color. Even toward the end of the sixteenth century, the individualizing discourse of "just war," by which each case must be argued and debated, was giving way to a language of geography and natural law. Sandoval takes this justification further, perhaps because he is unwilling to embrace the sweeping generalizations it entailed. Thus, whereas in treatises such as Tomás Mercados's 1571 *Suma y Contratos*, Africans are described as peoples of such bestial barbarism that they naturally fell into slavery, Sandoval presents something more like a racial codification of the global south (Mercado 232; Andrés-Gallego and García Añoveros 106). Color, then, becomes a general sign that divides the globe into Europeans, "the smallest of the four parts of the world, but the greatest in nobility, virtue, and gravity, magnificence and number of political beings," and a patchwork of geographies whose association in Sandoval's treatise depends upon two arbitrary conditions: the whims of the expansion of Iberian empires, that provided cover for the global reach of the Jesuits, and the increasing association between "blackness" and enslavement.

Conclusion

Sandoval's treatise affords a singular view of the construction of a new framework for transatlantic slavery at the moment when the commerce was quickly becoming inextricable from the global economy. The rhetorical structure for this incipient ideology reflected conditions afforded by only the global Jesuit network. Although it was not synonymous with the geography of the Iberian empires in the period, this Jesuit network tended to accompany Iberian expansion. In the early seventeenth century, Iberian expansion provided the global commercial structure for the transatlantic slave trade and Jesuits were necessarily witnesses to all of the points along the chain of production of commodified humans. The Jesuit involvement in slavery may be considered another form of their practice of moral accommodation, a term usually applied to their acceptance of diverse cultural practices in their missions (Rubiés; del Valle "Violence and Rhetoric"). While defending Jesuit slave ownership is not the task Sandoval sets out for himself in the treatise, his ministry follows from the assumption that slavery cannot be undone as an institution despite indications of its unethical basis even in the juridical terms of the period. Sandoval's shocking descriptions of Africans arriving in Cartagena cannot be considered neutral and unadulterated testimonies of the slave trade. These images appear in the treatise at the moment when Sandoval breaks with his inquiry into the conditions of enslavement in Africa, and are important elements in the foreclosure of the discussion that had been the focus of sixteenth-century debates. His account subtly turns from the idea that slaves unjustifiably captured, by the European doctrine of "just war," should therefore be freed, to the idea that those already enslaved, "with the Justice known only to God" may only be saved through Christianity.

As if to seal this transition, or perhaps because he intuits that even the moral argument that slaves were cursed by the mark of Ham would ultimately be inadequate to meet the needs of the voracious labor market of imperial capitalism, Sandoval provides a preliminary attempt at racializing the global south. While Sandoval made use of what was perhaps the only means to witness the radical transformation in forced labor at the time—the Jesuit letter-writing network—his publication of Brandão's admonition also exposes the way in which this network policed itself and prevented individual Jesuits from conducting investigations of conscience. Thus, instead of exposing the structure of precarization, in the capture, transport and sale of Africans, Sandoval used his spiritual training and information drawn from his fellow Jesuits to frame enslaved Africans as miserable subjects in need of Christianity. Like current structures of precarization, by which the very economic forces with an interest in transforming state and community institutions first work to undermine these, Sandoval's treatise exposes a vested interest in the violence of the slave trade. Far from an incoherent set of positions, the first book of his 1627 treatise prepares for his detailed focus on local conditions. While apparently the pinnacle of the European denunciation of the violence of the slave trade, Sandoval's framing of the enslaved relegates the experience and expression of violent precarization to the lost archive of transatlantic slavery.

NOTES

1. This article benefitted from presentations of sections of it at Washington University, Stanford University, the Mexico City Seminar "The Colonial Roots of Globalization," and the Tepoztlan Institute. I would like to thank Stephanie Kirk, Lisa Surwillo, Ericka Beckman, Daniel Nemser, David Kazanjian and other interlocutors at these venues. I would especially like to thank my co-editors, Rachel O'Toole and Ivonne del Valle, for their insightful and persistent comments on several drafts. All remaining errors are my own.
2. Numerous studies have argued that neoliberalism has increased "precarity." To name some of the most evocative recent analyses of this precarity, Carlo Galli has called the new international order one of "global war," Saskia Sassen has analyzed an intersection of ecological, human and financial "expulsions," and Judith Butler has questioned the political rights of those who are neither defended nor mourned on a global scale. While distinct, these approaches appear to agree that a basic characteristic of contemporary globalization is the increase in the velocity and number of global exchanges (of information, goods, or capital) and a corresponding weakening of the state as a political and regulatory system. In her excellent

study of precarity form of governance, Isabell Lorey gives a concise summary of recent studies on precarity. Following Judith Butler's work, she makes the distinction between precariousness as a "socio-ontological dimension of lives and bodies," precarity as a differentially distributed political condition, and precarization as a governmental process linked to economic neoliberalism (Lorey loc. 211).

3. In her study of the politics of visuality in Israel and Palestine, for instance, Gil Hochberg makes the case that Palestinians are subject to visual regimes of governance and thus are not favored by greater representation. See also, Butler 2.

4. The literature on precarization as a process linked to neoliberalism takes post-fordism as a beginning point. Lorey is a good example of a solid analysis that acknowledges the fact that recognition of precarization depends upon a previous norm of stability, through wage-labor, citizenship, and the welfare state. Despite the fact that she acknowledges that these structures were always restricted, by taking Michel Foucault's account of eighteenth-century shifts in governmentality as her starting point, Lorey ends up inscribing the same periodization (loc 221). Of course, if we define precarization as an economic interest in the destabilization of communities, particularly for labor, precarization should be understood to be a process present since the beginning of capitalism and not just in its latest neoliberal version.

5. The most significant recent work on the transatlantic slave trade is the online *Voyages: The Trans-Atlantic Slave Database* and the linked *Atlas of the Transatlantic Slave Trade*, by David Eltis and David Richardson. Other studies have looked more closely at the slave ship itself and the commodification process to which traders subjected Africans. Nevertheless, work on the slave ship has tended to focus on later periods and documentation from English ships. For a meticulous attempt to reconstruct the process of commodification on an English slave route, for instance, see Smallwood. For the conditions of the Portuguese slave ships from Angola, see Caldeira 132–41.

6. For the Iberian context of slavery, scholars have done extraordinary archival work to reconstruct lives of the enslaved. See, for instance, James Sweet's recent work on a healer caught by the Portuguese Inquisition, Domingos Alvares, which is one of the most complete histories of an enslaved subject. Rachel O'Toole's detailed archival work has followed the lives of enslaved men and women in the Peruvian coastal city of Peru. See for instance, her chapter in this volume and her book.

7. Following Judith Butler's suggestion, as images circulate frames become dislodged and introduced into distinct contexts, thus denaturalizing them (12). Although she does not consider the possibility, historical distance causes a different type of disjuncture between the framework and its subjects that also permits a denaturalization.

8. The full title of Sandoval's treatise is *Naturaleza, policía sagrada y profana, costumbres, ritos, disciplina y catechismo, de todos etiopes*. The 1647 edition simply added the title to which it is commonly abbreviated. Vila Vilar's introduction to her edition of Sandoval's 1627 treatise, published under the title *Un tratado sobre la*

esclavitud, remains the best summary of his life. For Acosta's influence on Sandoval, see 36–37.
9. See, for instance, Bethencourt.
10. See, for instance, Nicole van Germeten's comments in the introduction to her translation of an abridged version of Sandoval's treatise.
11. In her analysis of Sandoval's treatise, for instance, Margaret Olsen recreates his map of global "black" populations. Her explanation for Sandoval's extension of blackness, that few Jesuits were working in "black" Africa and therefore his sources would assume blackness in other regions, does not answer the question of why he would include this geography in his treatise (Olsen 80).
12. While it is probable that his fellow Jesuits in Luanda could have had a similarly stark portrayal of mercantile slavery, the early mission in Angola was feeble and fragmented, its few members repeatedly decimated by disease (Alden 76).
13. From this point on, all references to Sandoval's text will cite Enriqueta Vila Vilar's 1987 edition of the 1627 treatise, which she published under the title *Un tratado sobre la esclavitud*.
14. In several spectacular cases slaves deemed to have been incorrectly enslaved were indeed returned and freed.
15. John Correia-Afonso categorizes Jesuit letters into four types: those to the superior; those written to the members in general; those addressed to general public; and those between personal friends within the society (8).
16. For a summary of the use of the term "miserable" to describe indigenous subjects in Spanish imperial jurisprudence, see More 31–32. For an early application of the term by Vasco de Quiroga, see Ivonne del Valle's article in this volume.
17. Thus, using the term "Guinea" to refer to West Africans, Sandoval writes "These Guineans to whom we will presently refer are the blacks most esteemed by the Spanish as those who work the hardest, cost more, and those who we usually refer to by law as 'good natives,' of sharp wit, beautiful [bodies] and well disposed; [they are] by nature lively and happy and do not miss any opportunity to make music, sing and dance, even while engaged in the hardest toil on earth" (110).
18. Restrepo is aware of the differences between the two editions and chooses to work with the 1647 edition, as it is "very useful for dissipating the ambiguities and vague references in the first" (166) (my translation). However, this turn to the second edition erases the specific context in which the first was written.

WORKS CITED

Alden, Dauril. *The Making of an Enterprise: The Society of Jesus in Portugal, Its Empire, and Beyond, 1540–1750*. Stanford: Stanford University Press, 1996.

Alencastro, Luiz Felipe de. *O Trato dos Viventes: Formação do Brasil no Atlântico Sul, séculos XVI e XVII*. São Paulo: Companhia das Letras, 2000.

Andrés-Gallego, José, and Jesús María García Añoveros. *La iglesia y la esclavitud de los negros*. Pamplona: Ediciones Universidad de Navarra, 2002.

Bethencourt, Francisco. *Racisms: From the Crusades to the Twentieth Century*. Princeton: Princeton University Press, 2014.

Blackburn, Robin. *The Making of New World Slavery: From the Baroque to the Modern, 1492–1800*. 2nd ed. London: Verso, 2010.

Butler, Judith. *Frames of War: When Is a Life Grievable?* London: Verso, 2009.

Caldeira, Arlindo Manuel. "Angola and the Seventeenth-Century South Atlantic Slave Trade." *Networks and Trans-Cultural Exchange: Slave Trading in the South Atlantic, 1590–1867*. Eds. David Richardson and Filipa Ribeiro da Silva. Atlantic World, Vol. 30. Leiden: Brill, 2014. 101–42.

The Constitutions of the Society of Jesus. Trans. George Ganss S.J. St. Louis: The Institute of Jesuit Sources, 1970.

Correia-Afonso, John. *Jesuit Letters and Indian History, 1542–1773*. Bombay: Oxford University Press, 1969.

Davis, David Brion. *The Problem of Slavery in Western Culture*. Oxford: Oxford University Press, 1966.

del Valle, Ivonne. *Escribiendo desde los márgenes: Colonialismo y jesuitas en el siglo XVIII*. México: Siglo XXI, 2009.

———. "José de Acosta: Entre el realismo político y disparates e imposibles, o por qué importan los estudios coloniales." *Estudios transatlánticos postcoloniales: Mito, archivo, disciplina: cartografías culturales*. Eds. Ileana Rodríguez and Joseba Martínez. Vol. II. Barcelona: Athropos/Universidad Autónoma Metropolitana, 2010. 291–324.

———. "José de Acosta, Violence and Rhetoric: The Emergence of the Colonial Baroque." *Calíope* 18:2 (2013): 46–72.

Eltis, David, and David Richardson. *Atlas of the Transatlantic Slave Trade*. New Haven: Yale University Press, 2010.

Emory University. *Voyages: The Trans-Atlantic Slave Trade Database*. 2013. www.slavevoyages.org. Web. December 26, 2016.

Friedrich, Markus. "Government and Information-Management in Early Modern Europe: The Case of the Society of Jesus (1540–1773)." *Journal of Early Modern History* 12 (2008): 539–63.

Galli, Carlo. *Political Spaces and Global War*. Trans. Elisabeth Fay. Minneapolis: University of Minnesota Press, 2010.

García Añoveros, Jesús María. "Luis de Molina y la esclavitud de los negros africanos en el Siglo XVI: Principios doctrinales y conclusiones." *Revista de Indias* 40:219 (2000): 307–29.

Harris, Steven. "Confession-Building, Long-Distance Networks, and the Organization of Jesuit Science." *Early Modern Science* 1:3 (1996): 287–318.

Heywood, Linda M., and John K. Thornton. *Central Africans, Atlantic Creoles, and the Foundation of the Americas, 1585–1660*. Cambridge, UK: Cambridge University Press, 2007.

Hochberg, Gil Z. *Visual Occupations: Violence and Visibility in a Conflict Zone.* Durham: Duke University Press, 2015.
Lorey, Isabell. *State of Insecurity: Government of the Precarious.* Trans. Aileen Derieg. London: Verso, 2015. Kindle ed.
Loyola, Ignacio de. *Ejercicios espirituales de San Ignacio de Loyola.* Trans. Pablo López de Lara. Mexico City: Ediciones Paulinas, 1988.
Mercado, Tomas de. *Suma de Tratos y Contratos.* Vol. 1. Madrid: Instituto de Estudios Fiscales, Ministerio de Economía y Hacienda, 1977.
More, Anna. *Baroque Sovereignty: Carlos de Sigüenza y Góngora and the Colonial Mexican Archive.* Philadelphia: University of Pennsylvania Press, 2013.
Navarrete Peláez, María Cristina. "Las cartas annuas jesuitas y la representación de los etíopes en el siglo XVII." *Genealogías de la diferencia: Tecnologías de la salvación y representación de los africanos esclavizados en Iberoamérica colonial.* Ed. María Eugenia Chaves Maldonado. Bogotá: Editorial Pontificia Universidad Javeriana, Instituto de Estudios Sociales y Culturales Pensar, Abya-Yala, 2009. 23–57.
Olsen, Margaret. *Slavery and Salvation in Colonial Cartagena de Indias.* Gainesville: University of Florida Press, 2004.
O'Malley, John. *The First Jesuits.* Cambridge, Mass: Harvard University Press, 1993.
O'Toole, Rachel Sarah. *Bound Lives: Africans, Indians, and the Making of Race in Colonial Peru.* Pittsburgh: Pittsburgh University Press, 2012.
Patterson, Orlando. *Slavery and Social Death: A Comparative Study.* Cambridge, Mass: Harvard University Press, 1982.
Sandoval, Alonso de. *De Instauranda Aethiopum Salute: Naturaleça, policia sagrada y profana, costumbres, ritos y cathecismo evangélico de todos los Aethiopes con que se restaura la salud de sus almas.* Seville: 1647.
———. *Un tratado sobre la esclavitud.* Ed. Enriqueta Vila Vilar. Madrid: Alianza Universidad, 1987.
———. *Treatise on Slavery.* Ed. and trans. Nicole Von Germeten. Indianapolis: Hackett, 2008.
Smallwood, Stephanie E. *Saltwater Slavery: A Middle Passage from Africa to American Diaspora.* Cambridge, Mass: Harvard University Press, 2007.
Sweet, James H. *Recreating Africa: Culture, Kinship, and Religion in the African-Portuguese World, 1441–1770.* Chapel Hill: University of North Carolina Press, 2003.
———. *Domingos Álvares, African Healing, and the Intellectual History of the Atlantic World.* Chapel Hill: University of North Carolina Press, 2011.
Restrepo, Eduardo. "El negro en un pensamiento colonial de principios del siglo XVII: Diferencia, jerarquía y sujeción sin racialización." *Genealogías de la diferencia: Tecnologías de la salvación y representación de los africanos esclavizados en iberoamérica colonial.* Ed. María Eugenia Chaves Maldonado. Bogotá: Editorial Pontificia Universidad Javeriana, Instituto de Estudios Sociales y Culturales Pensar, Abya-Yala, 2009. 118–76.
Rubiés, Joan Pau. "The Concept of Cultural Dialogue and the Jesuit Method of Accommodation: Between Idolatry and Civilization." *Archivium Historicum Societatis Iesu* 74:147 (2005): 237–80.

Sassen, Saskia. *Expulsions: Brutality and Complexity in the Global Economy*. Cambridge, Mass: Harvard University Press, 2014. Kindle ed.
Vitoria, Francisco. *Political Writings*. Trans. Jeremy Lawrance. Cambridge, UK: Cambridge University Press, 1991.
Wheat, David. "The First Great Waves: African Provenance Zones for the Transatlantic Slave Trade to Cartagena de Indias, 1570–1640." *African History* 52:1 (2011): 1–22.
Vila Vilar, Enriqueta. "Introducción." *Un tratado sobre la esclavitud*. Madrid: Alianza Editorial, 1987. 15–44.

CHAPTER SIX

Household Challenges
The Laws of Slaveholding and the Practices of Freedom in Colonial Peru[1]

Rachel Sarah O'Toole

The relationship of enslaved and free people to colonial law, and therefore their status within the Spanish colonial state, was ambiguous. Africans and their descendants claimed a corporate status as Catholics (Bennett 127-28; Bristol 116-7). In this capacity, enslaved men and women called on ecclesiastical courts to protect their marriages while, organized in religious confraternities, they buried community members (Tardieu 86, 217; Germeten 90). In the Spanish Americas, the enslaved also exercised judicial personas, serving as witnesses in colonial courts and initiating suits against abusive owners (Bryant 20; Palmer 94). At the same time, enslaved men and women were restricted juridically. In comparison to the corporate organizations assigned to Indians and Spaniards, Africans were not represented in their own *cabildos* or municipal councils. Free and enslaved people of African descent did not occupy a "republic," a legal location that entitled Indians and Spaniards to their own courts, parishes, and laws, as a civil collective (Lewis 99, Martínez 221, O'Toole 5). Spanish and Spanish-descent elites excluded women of African descent from the honorable status that would allow protections of property and family (Mannarelli 99). Restrictions, though, did not mean a lack of legal agency. Armed with a double sighted position or a location of double consciousness, enslaved and freed people combined their legal astuteness and a practice of the court's literate world (Bennett 2, 33–34; DuBois 5; Jouve Martín 80, 82). Enslaved and free women of African descent worked to define honor according to their own social and economic realities and free men claimed the positions of royal vassals through their loyal military service (AGI; Walker 395).

Given the way that enslaved and free people of African descent simultaneously occupied and were excluded from the judicial, this chapter pushes us to examine the nature of legality in colonial Spanish America. Colonial law implied imperial oversight. Yet, in seventeenth-century Spanish America there was no single legal code governing slavery or manumission, and the Crown did not dictate local or regional law. Legal mandates were not imposed from above, but generated from below (Herzog, *Defining* 203). In other words, colonial rule was expressed through performance of the king or in other manifestations that localized imperial control (Cañeque 133, 143). Likewise, through their legal activism, Africans and their descendants translated imperial policy into local practice. In doing so, enslaved and free people actualized connections between the global institution of Spanish law and the colonial judiciary. If Spaniards, *creoles* (Spaniards born in the Americas), and "Indians" chose when to invoke Crown orders, enslaved and free people engaged with both metropolitan and local powerbrokers, connecting the locations of imperial rule. This chapter posits that, if legal mandates emerged from the local, then in the seventeenth century, the household was necessarily central. The Spanish early modern state was modeled around a patriarchal structure with a father-king who oversaw his vassals as children that was replicated in viceregal and local authority with an emphasis on maintaining harmony over executing justice (Cañeque 52, 90, 220; Cutter 92; Herzog, *La administración* 31; Premo 11). Slaveholders held their authority over enslaved people as heads of households and activated their domestic relations with enslaved people, especially women. By examining how enslaved and free people engaged with a colonial law rooted in the household, this chapter illuminates intimate negotiations at the core of the early modern Spanish empire.

To examine how the local and the imperial coincided, I examine manumission agreements in the coastal city of Trujillo on the northern Peruvian coast. Manumission, or the ability to self-purchase, was encoded in Iberian law, but in practice, slaveholders preferred to keep the process within their purview. Slaveholders granted enslaved people the ability to pursue legal manumission and then often granted loans to facilitate the purchase of freedom. Legally freed people, then, owed former slaveholders who continued as patrons. As a result, in the Spanish Americas, owners of slaves favored legal practices that re-established manumitted people within their domestic sphere by continuing to profit from freed people following the legal manumission (Hanger 40; Hünefeldt 160; Proctor, "Damned" 164–65). Since the ability to achieve manumission depended on intimate relations among the enslaved, freed, and slaveholders, the method in this chapter is to examine domestic space as well as intimate interactions that constituted primary sites of slaveholding (Graham, *House* 4, 49; McKinley, "Till Death" 387). In order to gain access to this level of intimacy, I move away from the scholarship's dependency on judicial documentation to examine the colonial notarial archive where daily interactions were recorded. By piecing together the fragmentary evidence collected from Trujillo's extant uncatalogued notary books, I reconstruct how enslaved and freed people claimed their freedom by removing themselves from the discursive construction of the household, as well as the actual domestic space owned by slaveholders or patrons.

At stake was how the Spanish empire manifested in the early modern era. As Michelle McKinley has demonstrated, unequal concubinary unions threatened the racial order to such an extent that viceregal administrators intervened, policing extramarital relationships and "public" sex (McKinley, "Illicit" 206). Private life, in other words, was not separate from imperial rule. In her exploration of how the legal category of "minor" emerged in late colonial Lima, Bianca Premo illustrated the overlapping nature of public and private authority as well as the interrelations between private hierarchies and the execution of the law (5, 23). Ann Twinam convincingly argued that so-called private events such as pregnancy, heterosexual romantic relations, and co-habitation were fundamental to the social, political, and economic structures of elite colonial Latin American families (43, 46). More explicitly, freed women and men, or those in the process of securing their freedom, faced the additional difficulty of transitioning away from the intimate arena of the slaveholder. Enslaved and freed people needed to secure funds and legal representation in order to challenge slaveholders' civil claims to their slave status, including their wages or other debts. In these disputes, intimate relations and the site of the domestic could be exceptionally influential even if unrecorded or assumed in written documentation. Therefore, I argue, without much assistance from Crown regulations, freed people created alternative forms of official documentation outside of the courts in an attempt to distance themselves from the purview of their former owners. Records served as forms of an additional authority, as freed women (and men) insisted on a more explicit and permanent recognition of their manumission. Armed with paper, enslaved and freed people moved outside the domestic, and therefore legal imaginary of what constituted slavery, and into freedom, or a civil space.

Slave Holding within the Household

Iberian law equated the slaveholder with the patriarch of a household. The laws of slavery followed the *Siete Partidas*, promulgated by Alfonso X around 1265, and confirmed as law in the 1505 *Leyes de Toro* (McKinley, "Fractional" 753; Watson 42). Laws regulating slavery and manumission were contained primarily in the Fourth Partida, or the book pertaining to matrimony that included regulations of concubines, illegitimate children, adoption, and vassalage (R. Burns xxi). Intertwining slaveholding with domestic arrangements and locating the slaveholder as a patriarch, enslaved women as concubines could require slaveholding fathers to support illegitimate offspring as Title 13, Law 1 explained that when an owner married his concubine making their children legitimate, she became free (*Las siete partidas* 40). Underlining medieval and early modern Iberian concerns with descent as well as inheritance laws favoring men, the Fourth Partida recognized the broader household and indicated who would inherit the patriarch's position (Martínez 52). Thus, Iberian law formed the basis of colonial Spanish American legal practices and established the household as the most significant institution within slaveholding. Slaves served in a dependent role since the Fourth Partida ordered that enslaved people obey, protect, and assist their owners and the owners' family, giving up all they own to the slaveholder (R. Burns xxiv). These intimate controls of slavery extended into legal manumission. Title 22, Law 8 of the Fourth Partida indebted the former slave to the owner who, in turn became a patron to the freed person. The patron could re-enslave the former slave, now a debtor, if she or he was not properly deferent (R. Burns xxiv). Their actions could certainly be known in public, but the laws of Iberian slavery required negotiations among people of a shared household, or those who shared intimacies or privacies.

The demography of the Americas, combined with the expansion of a global colonial economy, transformed Iberian laws of slaveholding. Iberian laws assumed the enslaved were Muslim, rewarding slaves who married in the Catholic Church with manumission (Andrés-Gallego 60). In the Americas, the primarily sub-Saharan African enslaved population was not freed for contracting Christian marriages even as the Crown repeatedly mandated their evangelization (Watson 48). As the Spanish Americas became more dependent on enslaved labor rooted in a racialization of slavery, the Crown turned to public regulations of enslaved Africans and their descendants in the Americas. Royal mandates repeatedly prohibited African-descent people, and other non-indigenous people, from inhabiting indigenous colonial towns and listed extensive punishments of armed or fugitive slaves (*Recopilación* 200v, 285–290v). Royal orders expanded how slaveholders and their proxies could punish slaves. Certainly colonial slavery laws required the Christian evangelization of Africans and therefore inclusion into the Catholic colonial politic. In the colonial context, as in Iberia, enslaved people took their owners to court to enforce agreements, especially those regarding manumission (Watson 48, 50, 55). Slavery, however, included a distinct exchange in the Americas. Reflecting increasingly commercial transactions, the Spanish Crown allowed that enslaved people in the Americas could hold property and in this way purchase their own freedom (Andrés-Gallego 60). In the Americas, relations between slaveholders and enslaved added a distinct transactional quality.

A customary law, or how a community practices the law, of manumission developed in the Americas. Notably, the Crown did not issue specific legislation governing self-purchase until the nineteenth century (De la Fuente 662). The enslaved had the ability to purchase their freedom, or secure a notarized *carta de libertad*, or "freedom letter," that detailed their freed status and explained the monetary exchange or debt of their manumission. The Fourth Partida (of the *Siete Partidas*) allowed that an owner could free an enslaved person in their will, a practice that spread throughout the Spanish Americas (Bowser 274). Enslaved and freed people, in turn, employed colonial courts to hold owners to their promises of testamentary manumission or demand that heirs honor stipulations of inheritance agreements (Hanger 49; McKinley, "Fractional" 773; McKinley, "Till Death" 384; Proctor, *"Damned"* 159). Legally active enslaved and free people, with their legal representatives, made judicial arguments based on a multitude of laws, customs, and precedents.

In practice, the process of gaining manumission was rooted in an intimate give-and-take among enslaved people, their supporters, and slaveholders and their families. Whether these manumission agreements were voluntary, testamentary, or conditional, my reading of the notarial records and limited judicial cases in the small city of Trujillo on the Peruvian northern coast indicates that enslaved people, or their proxies, had to first obtain permission from their owners to pursue a legal manumission.[2] Slaveholders could put off this request, could agree but promise that an enslaved person could secure manumission once they were deceased, or there could be an indeterminate period of "exchange" (Hünefeldt 120–21). Enslaved people could threaten that they would no longer serve, or would not serve with the same attentiveness, or would ask a powerful proxy to intervene (Graham, "Writing" 628; Naro 63). Once a slaveholder or their family agreed that an enslaved person could engage in a process of manumission, a price had to be set (Dantas 121). Debt became a critical point of disagreement but also of entanglement. As many scholars have documented, enslaved people in Spanish America worked to earn money, secured loans, or exchanged their future labor in order to pay their price (Hanger 29; Hünefeldt 51, 109, 112; Proctor, *"Damned"* 166). To pay for their manumission, enslaved people borrowed from their former owners and indebted their labor as well as that of their family members. As a result, payments for freedom extended slaveholding as enslaved people regularly handed over small cash installments to their owners or patrons and continued to work in households where they had formerly been enslaved (Hanger 40, 42). Lastly, in these transitory states, written documentation of the legal manumission had to be secured; this was a notarized document formulaically authored by the slaveholder. Written records were often not possible since enslaved and freed people were often only able to extract an owner's verbal promise even if uttered multiple times (ADL. Co. Ords. Leg. 198. Exp. 1347 [1669], 1). From beginning to end, the process of manumission involved intimate exchanges among the enslaved and slaveholders.

Manumission, then, was contained within personal relationships, ones that were legally constructed as well as enacted in notarial offices. Certainly enslaved and freed people contested slaveholder control, but as Ira Berlin has reminded us, slaveholders often engaged in manumission for their own benefit (224, 279). Slaveholders exchanged freedom for life-saving favors, sex work, childcare or other intimate labor (Hünefeldt 132). Those who gained freedom, primarily enslaved urban women, performed household work such as washing laundry, tending to the elderly, preparing food, and performing other domestic tasks that were woven into slaveholders' daily affairs (Hanger 23). As vendors, traders, and laborers, enslaved and free women maintained the food supplies in colonial cities as well as infused the credit and pawn exchanges that made local economies function (Bowser 108; Mangan 52, 83). Women of color could work for wages, transforming their time into cash and credit to purchase their freedom and those of their families (Hanger 29; Hünefeldt 113, 117). Women of African descent were so successful in their earning capacities that they were able to purchase their legal manumission throughout the Americas, including Mexico and Lima at rates of nearly 35 percent, 31 percent higher than men of color (Proctor, "Gender" 310–11). At the same time, enslaved and freed women benefitted from intimate connections with slaveholders who relied on their essential contributions to domestic spheres (Brana-Shute 187, 189; Graham, *House* 46; Proctor, "Gender" 317). Still, for the enslaved, the process of manumission was arduous, extensive, and subject to changing conditions. On their deathbeds, fearful of a lengthy stay in Purgatory, owners agreed to free slaves with their families as a Catholic act of charity (McKinley, "Till Death" 382). Heirs of the slaveholders, in turn, contested these promised testamentary manumissions, and often divided free from enslaved family members (Hünefeldt 120; Proctor, *"Damned"* 163).

Enslaved people could capitalize on these private, and fragile, arrangements of manumission. Negotiations outside the courts, as the following example indicates, may have been where enslaved and freed families negotiated freedom. In 1659, the owner of seven-year-old Joseph de Matamoros apprenticed him to the boy's grandfather, a carpenter who had also paid for Joseph's freedom in Trujillo (ADL. Garcia. Leg. 165 [1659], 501, 501v). The manumission agreement promised Matamoros would gain his freedom when he turned twenty-five years old, or the age of majority. The notary identified Matamoros as a *mulato* but did not assign a *casta* to his grandfather who worked as a master carpenter constructing sugar mills in a valley neighboring the city of Trujillo (ADL. Viera Gutierrez. Leg. 259 [1656], 8–8v). Given this context, the arrangement was simultaneously a transfer of property, an agreement among adults about a minor, and a rare recognition of family ties between a free man of Spanish descent and an African-descent offspring. With his artisan grandfather providing an entry into lucrative work in the local sugar economy, combined with a notarized document outlining the agreement of his eventual freedom, Matamoros's future seemed assured (Ramírez 97). Eleven years later, however, when his grandfather (and protector) died, Matamoros's apprenticeship was transferred to another master carpenter. The grandfather's legitimate son, Miguel de Aguilar Matamoros, made the new labor arrangement but did not recognize his relation, either as an uncle or a father, to the *mulato* Joseph (ADL. Verde. Leg. 250 [1670], 71v). In fact, Miguel de Aguilar Matamoros downplayed his kinship with Joseph and emphasized their relationship as one between a master and apprentice. The legitimate son recognized the freedom clause in the young man's apprentice contract and reaffirmed that Joseph would gain his manumission at age twenty-five. Freedom arrangements, even when they appeared in court, were based on family ties that were discussed but not recorded in writing.

Like the young carpenter's apprentice, enslaved and free people relied on individual arrangements with slaveholders in order to gain freedom. As discussed above, slaveholders recorded their intentions to manumit enslaved people from their households with a line in their will or a codicil that they claim counted as the *carta de libertad* or manumission agreement (Hünefeldt 70–71). Enslaved people could be aware of these allowances and certainly invoked these documents as written proof of their freed status or ability to engage in a process of manumission (McKinley, "Till Death" 384). A testament, however, was designed to distribute property, collect debts, and arrange the deceased's funeral; in other words, financial and religious tasks were made legal by the form, the official paper, and the notary. Yet, these testamentary freedoms could easily be revised since unknown debts could arise in probate causing executors to sell slaves rather than free them as previously agreed and even recorded (Naro 110). In the case of Leonor Ramírez (also of Trujillo), the freed woman retained a copy of her *carta de libertad*. Because she had continued to serve after her legal manumission, however, Ramírez had not been recognized as free when her owner died and the heir attempted to sell her as a slave (ADL. Co. Pedimentos. Leg. 280. Exp. 3591 [1572], 4). Her freedom had not been recognized and the existence of public, formal documents could not prevent slaveholders from enacting their own interpretations of manumission.

Seizing on their positions as the new owners of inherited slaves, heirs sabotaged testamentary manumissions by disregarding previous arrangements of freedom (Hünefeldt 17). For example, in Trujillo, Francisco Arara explained that in exchange for five hundred *pesos*, his owner would free him. The agreement had been arranged within the slaveholder's household with enslaved witnesses, but also had been made more public when a priest and a notary had also witnessed his owner's intention (ADL. Ca. Ords. Leg. 30. Exp. 608 [1700], 5). The owner's heirs, however, contested Francisco's freed status by claiming that the enslaved man sold from the West African coast lacked a formal manumission agreement. Indeed, in the sealed will dated July 6, 1700, the owner explained that he left five hundred *pesos* to his son to execute a task that could have been manumitting Francisco Arara. In the will, the owner legitimately freed another enslaved man at the time of his death, but only listed Francisco Arara as his property (ADL. Cortijo Quero. Leg. 110 [1700], 401, 403v). In other words, the slaveholder had promised, but not formalized Francisco Arara's manumission. Testaments, where domestic politics and inheritance questions intersected, were a common means to record a manumission agreement. Since enslaved and freed people read more as property in these texts, slaveholders' testaments could prove to be unreliable documents for those working toward manumission.

By acting as rulers of their own "realms," or extended households, slaveholders and their proxies dictated terms of manumission and could derail enslaved peoples' attempts to gain freedom. Slaveholders formulaically claimed that their love for enslaved children trumped that bestowed by their biological parents or relatives. Slaveholders also cast older slaves in the roles of their surrogate mothers or fathers, also an affective construction (Premo 225, 227). As expected, manumission's notarized formula or judicial language created and reinforced slaveholders' positions as patriarchs or widows acting in this capacity. In their role as protectors, they erased the purview of African-descent men and women over their own families, making themselves into the fathers as well as household guardians (Premo 214, 215; Walker 395). In this domestic role, slaveholders promoted their authority over the enslaved, establishing their material ownership in affective claims.

Most importantly (and unsurprisingly), slaveholders attempted to extend their control over enslaved or freed people by awarding favors. In other words, if slaveholding was understood as paternalistic caretaking laced with ownership of property, then manumission extended these contradictory practices. Illustrating how slaveholders controlled enslaved and manumitted people through generous acts of "donating" or granting an enslaved person their manumission, a slaveholder gave Isabel del Carmen y Sousa her freedom while selling Isabel's twelve-year son for the cost of the slaveholder's funeral and burial, as well as putting up for sale Isabel's twin ten-year-old daughters. The slaveholder, Margarita Suarez de Deza y Sousa, a widow, was the head of household, and had profited extensively from the trade in tobacco, chocolate, cattle, and other "combustible goods" between the highlands of Guamanchuco and the regional markets in Chile. The payment for the enslaved household labor, however, was costly benevolence. The slaveholder declared that anyone who paid the price of Sousa's son or daughters could and would be obligated to free them (ADL. San Roman. Leg. 219 [1713], 152, 152v, 154, 154v). Again, the slaveholder took while giving. The testamentary charge was to the future owners of the enslaved daughters, since in this case, the slaveholder did not have heirs entangling manumission with inheritance (McKinley, "Till Death" 384). The clause allowed the slaveholder to engage in an act of charity (conditional manumission) but still profit since the will mandated selling all the children at the time of the slaveholder's death. Even after her death, the slaveholder would control members of her household.

In order to emphasize their personal control, slaveholders underlined their caretaking relations with enslaved men and women. For instance, a former slaveholder argued that because he had raised Petrona Zamudio and loved her, she was his slave. Moreover, he explained, Petrona Zamudio kept his wife company, often sleeping in her room or bed. The slaveholding couple claimed to have educated the girl in addition to tending to her sicknesses and maintaining her in their home as would parents with their child (ADL. Co. Ords. Leg. 220. Exp. 1777 [1728], 4). Like kinship relations, the affection, however, was not gratis. The rhetoric of familiarity extended the slaveholders' authority and financial gain (Dantas 114). Although Petrona Zamudio's father stated she was free, the slaveholding couple demanded payment for their expenses. In a similar extension of childrearing into manumission, a nun from Trujillo's Santa Clara convent promised freedom to Luisa del Christos and Maria Landa, both of whom, she explained, she had raised. In turn, the two enslaved young women would serve her or the convent for a required period (ADL. Nuñez de Valcera. Leg. 186 [1679], 387v). Another *beata* (lay religious woman) also explained that she was manumitting young Petronila and Melchora because she "had raised them in her arms" (ADL. Cortijo Quero. Leg. 107 [1697], 156). Still, the two young girls would serve other nuns for a period following her owner's death. In the notarized agreements of the slaveholders, the trade of manumission for continued labor was couched in intimate or domestic relationships often favoring the slaveholder. The rhetoric points to how owners attempted to keep manumission arrangements "in house" and the freed children, who would become adults, within their sphere of influence.

This benevolent paternalism embedded in the process of manumission could inhibit enslaved and freed people from constructing their own, autonomous families. As a freed woman, Isabel de Sousa paid her ex-owner's *tenedor de bienes* (legal custodian of bequeathed goods) for the freedom of one daughter. Calling on the original clause in Margarita Suarez de Deza y Sousa's will, Sousa also secured a *carta de libertad*, a critical document proving her daughter's legal freedom. Sousa's other daughter, Jacoba del Carmen, had been sold to an owner who refused to negotiate. As a result Sousa initiated a civil suit demanding that the owner authorize a *carta de libertad* in exchange for her payment, given the stipulation in the original will. In response, the new owner demanded that Sousa produce proof of her claim. In the process, Sousa hid her daughter, presumably as security against the slaveholder's threats to leave for the highlands (ADL. Co. Ords. Leg. 218. Exp. 1738 [1721], 2, 4v, 9). In short, the slaveholder Deza y Souza's "gift" was highly problematic for Isabel de Sousa. It appears that without the powerful widow's support, or her family's presence in Trujillo, another slaveholder could resist even a clearly written mandate such as the testamentary clause. Isabel de Sousa certainly was working her options. She had secured both daughters, physically, and one's legal manumission, and she had the legal and cultural literacy as well as financial ability to take a slaveholder to court (McKinley, "Illicit" 211, 214). The case remained unresolved. Perhaps Isabel de Sousa was able to secure a satisfactory arrangement by paying the current slaveholder what he was also demanding: her daughter's daily wages (ADL. Co. Ords. Leg. 218. Exp. 1738 [1721], 10). Regardless, by painstakingly matching the fragmentary evidence from the slaveholder's testament with the freed woman's civil case, I suggest that manumission arrangements appear to be taking place off the judicial stage. Even in this powerful example of a freed woman's capabilities, the legal and domestic arrangements of manumission allowed slaveholders to act according to their own interests.

Slaveholder control did not negate enslaved agency. Undoubtedly, enslaved and freed people employed notaries and legal representatives to contest and negotiate with owners (Graham, "Writing" 618). Still, slaveholders employed the laws of slaveholding and their customary practices to keep slaveholding "in house." In the case of Margarita, her notarized manumission agreement provided written evidence of her owner's promise of freedom but also documented continuing obligations. The slaveholder declared that after her death, Margarita would serve her niece as well as grand-nephew and then be freed. The slaveholder obligated Margarita, a freed woman, to sweep the Dominican chapel of Nuestra Señora del Rosario (ADL. Espino de Alvarado. Leg. 155 [1694], 862v). While many people of Spanish descent as well as those among the growing numbers of free people of color worshipped in this chapel, Margarita's labor constituted her former slaveholder's offering to the Dominicans and the confraternity. Like other freed people, Margarita then continued to serve her former slaveholders after she had achieved legal freedom (Hanger 40). Margarita's arrangement with her slaveholder was not unusual, but customary. Manumitted freedom in Spanish America reaffirmed patriarchal authority as practiced and legally manifested through the domestic household.

Challenging the Household

Slaveholders, in many ways, constituted an intractable authority for enslaved people who knew that even formal promises of manumissions could be contested. Juana de Alvarado, a freed *parda* (a woman of African descent) explained that her owner had granted a testamentary manumission, but the heir did not recognize the clause in the will. In an attempt to seek out a higher authority to the disputing slaveholder (a priest), Alvarado appealed her case from the Trujillo bishopric to Lima's archbishopric court (AAL). Unfortunately, the heir retained copies of the testament, and Alvarado appears to not have been able to gain access. Nonetheless, her strategy could also be read as an attempt to publicize her case and to widen her appeal to a public that extended beyond the reluctant slaveholder.

Proxies could often serve in place of slaveholders. In Trujillo, Pedro Angola explained that his owner had died too quickly to render his wishes in writing, but had declared in front of many people that the enslaved man should be freed. Pedro Angola provided witnesses such as Juana Jofre, an African woman who was tending to the infirm owner, and wealthy slaveholders, including a local notary. In addition, Trujillo's bailiff (also a slaveholder) testified that even though "there had not been paper," the dead man had added a clause to his will freeing Pedro Angola (ADL. Ca. Ords. Leg. 19. Exp. 407 [1646], 2). Pedro Angola's perseverance and expertise paid off. He had to wait two years before Trujillo's municipal magistrate (or *alcalde ordinario*) declared him to be a free man. Cognizant that a written codicil was necessary, Pedro Angola expanded the slaveholder's household to include pertinent witnesses in her petition.

To gain his freedom, Pedro Angola performed according to the paternalistic expectations of his dead owner and the accompanying slaveholders. According to Trujillo's bailiff, following the owner's granting of manumission, "the black Pedro came into the room . . . got on his knees and gave thanks to" his owner (ADL. Ca. Ords. Leg. 19. Exp. 407 [1646], 2). In doing so, Pedro Angola acknowledged the slaveholder's authority, even continuing after death. Pedro Angola was not alone, as enslaved men and women continued to benefit but also remain bound by the patronage of their former slaveholder or a proxy (Hanger 57). Slaveholders recalled enslaved people's loyalty, service, and obedience in the manumission agreements and judicial cases, emphasizing the owner's benevolence as reason for granting freedom (Velázquez Gutiérrez 149). For example, in Trujillo, a widow agreed to grant a two-year *quarterona* (a woman of mixed African and Spanish descent) daughter of her slave, Pasquala her manumission. She explained her motivations; the child had been born in her house and the mother had served willingly (ADL. Protocolos. Viera Gutierrez. Leg. 259 [1656], 367v). Likewise, another slaveholding widow signed a manumission agreement for *mulata* Juana de Miranda because the enslaved woman had been "loyal, lawful, and had served with love and care" (ADL. Protocolos. San Roman. Leg. 213 [1699], 613). In these and other notary records paid for by slaveholders, slaveholding women emphasized their patronage of enslaved women and children who were raised in their households.

Freedom, then, required that people such as Pedro Angola recall and feel gratitude for the generosity of an ex-owner, much like faithful vassals of a protective ruler offering gratitude on bended knee to a ruler who rewarded their loyalty. Undoubtedly, slaveholders throughout Spanish America favored grateful and obedient slaves, often requiring similar public demonstrations of appreciation and devotion (Bowser 274). In these performances, slaveholders played the role of the benevolent fathers who had the right to punish their slaves within the limits set by the state but also, like the king, could grant pardons and favors as evidence of their paternal love (Herzog *Defining* 31; Meiklejohn 189; Uribe-Uran 823). In effect, in their relations with enslaved and freed people, slaveholders mimicked the king's benevolence as they made Africans and their descendants perform the role of vassals.

Enslaved and freed people certainly employed the household's centrality in Iberian law to their own benefit, but a constant goal was to gain distance from or exit the slaveholder's household. The documentary process of manumission provided one entry, since each agreement had to include a slave's manumission price.[3] Many enslaved men and women often paid for their freedom and that of their kin, or arranged for a proxy to pay (Ferreira Furtado 107; Hanger 23). In the act of paying or arranging the debt, enslaved and freed people bargained over the cost. In these exchanges enslaved and freed people could also articulate their relationship to slaveholders. Rather than an exchange of affection or a promise to be fulfilled in the future, monetary or labor debt agreements could be made more concrete. In addition, enslaved and freed people employed notarial agreements to record how their debt would be paid. In other words, if slaveholders controlled the manumission agreement, enslaved and freed people worked to control the subsequent debt agreement, and challenge their place within the slaveholders' households.

Men and women who were in the process of paying for their manumission were vulnerable, and could be easily re-classified as enslaved by slaveholders or colonial authorities. In order to assure their legal positions, enslaved and freed people attempted to move discussions of money and their commercial relations with slaveholders into the written record. A slaveholder assumed the authorship of an official manumission agreement that was composed by a notary on paper with a royal seal signed by witnesses, so that enslaved and freed people had to seek external proof of the sum that they owed, had paid, or were in the process of paying. Freed people were in an even stronger legal and customary position when they paid for a separate notarized debt agreement that often followed their official manumission agreement in the notarial book's subsequent folios (Hanger 42). Authorship was a key distinction in these two types of documentation. Slaveholders officially executed the manumission agreement but the manumitting person (or their guardian) signed a subsequent debt agreement. With these and other documents, freed people could gain acknowledgement of their manumitted status and counter ex-slaveholders who attempted to change the agreed price of their freedom (Scott 1076). Freed people, even more importantly, authored debt agreements. Documenting exchanges of funds or agreements of debts and payments also allowed enslaved people to identify their relationship with slaveholders and ex-owners as more financial than familiar. Rather than a favor granted by a patron to a client, a notarized discussion of debt and repayment added the weight of a business transaction to a manumission agreement still in process. Certainly, notarized records could be falsified and scribes and witnesses could collaborate with slaveholders instead of serving enslaved and freed people (K. Burns 83). Nonetheless, a notarized agreement of the monetarized exchange extended manumission arrangements beyond slaveholders' households.

A certain level of daily autonomy or an honorable reputation could also be critical to helping enslaved and freed people prove their manumitted status. Valentín de Silva argued that he was free because he had been treated as such since the day he was born. The argument presented in this civil case recalled an idea from the *Siete Partidas* that those treated as free should eventually be considered legally manumitted (ADL. Co. Ords. Leg. 206. Exp. 1503 [1686], 1v, 57v). In the Iberian world more broadly, a person could become a particular status if people understood her or him as such, and more so if written documentation was generated testifying to the fact (Graubart 486, 494). This type of formalization of enacted status could work for either the enslaved or slaveholders. In another judicial dispute regarding a manumission petition, the slaveholder's witnesses argued that because the women in question paid their slave remittances and served domestically (such as buying provisions and cooking food), they were slaves and not freed women (ADL. Co. Ords. Leg. 196. Exp. 1319 [1663], 3v). In other words, a perception of the women's daily labor could also manufacture enslaved status (Naro 91, 111). Nonetheless, the enacted claims to status that required audience participation moved enslaved and freed people's contestation of slaveholding away from just the authority of the slaveholder. In a public performance, enslaved and freed people developed locations outside of the household to challenge the authority of slaveholders.

Documentation as Alternative Authority

The challenge that enslaved and freed people faced was dislodging manumission negotiations from the intimate exchanges with slaveholders. Enslaved and freed people could pay notaries to record their version of negotiations with slaveholders (Owensby 6–7). A wide range of witnesses could testify that large households and whole neighborhoods were aware that a slaveholder and an enslaved person had agreed to a manumission arrangement (McKinley, "Such Unsightly" 242). Still, given the tenuousness of written agreements controlled by slaveholders, enslaved and freed people worked toward creating and maintaining their own documentation.

Enslaved and free people understood that any written document was superior to oral testimony. For example, Santiago Gonzales, a formerly enslaved man, presented "a simple paper," or an un-notarized written document, in Trujillo to prove that his owner had freed him (ADL. Ca. Ords. Leg. 36. Exp. 707, [1717], 5v). Was Gonzales making a mistake by presenting an unofficial piece of paper to challenge his slaveholder? Given the ways that slaveholders rhetorically and actually attempted to contained enslaved and freed people within their domestic purview, Gonzales's move was very smart. By creating or having created a written record of his slaveholder's manumission, Gonzales produced an object that would have more legal weight than hearsay. At the same time, he moved away from the direct control of a slaveholder who so often wrote, supervised, or paid for the documentation that served as enslaved and freed people's petitions for freedom. In a similar move toward an alternative authority, Cristóbal de Berrio of *casta congo* (sold from the Kingdom of Kongo) and Rodrigo Santiago employed Cartagena's Inquisition court to argue that their owner had granted them their freedom. They presented an un-notarized written document and explained that due to professional animosities in the town of Tolu, their owner had been unable to secure a trustworthy notary (AHN. Inquisición. Exp. 8 [1717], 1). Appealing their impending sale by the heirs, Berrio and Santiago recalled sentiments that appear to be from the *Siete Partidas* stressing the natural state of freedom (Meiklejohn 182). In a document signed by Berrio, the legal representatives of the two men claimed that rather than slavery, "freedom was better for mortals and cannot be sold for all the gold in the world" (AHN. Inquisición. Exp. 8 [1717], 16v). In the Spanish Americas, slaveholders and enslaved people engaged in a transactional exchange of intimate labor and monetary exchanges to achieve or to deny manumission. Certainly, the freed men articulated their desires in the juridical language recognizable to the court. But, in this case, employing the venue of the ecclesiastical court, the freed men articulated their definitions of freedom. According to the man from West Central Africa and his *creole* companion, freedom, as opposed to manumission, did not have a monetary value and could not be transacted in the worldly markets.

Cognizant of the distinction between manumission and freedom, enslaved and free people understood the fragility of their position and were highly conscious that control of written documents constituted an avenue to confront slaveholders' revisionism. In a case from Mexico, the heirs of Pedro de Soto López with his executor argued against the freedom of Juan Clemente, Úrsula, Lucía, María de Soto, Clara de Soto with her children Juan Pedro and Thomas de Soto as well as Joseph de Soto and Sebastian de Soto. The owner had granted manumission with his word, in a patriarchal performance that underlined the intimate arrangements as well as the commercial value of the manumission. Pedro de Soto López's nephew testified that he and a priest were standing next to his uncle's bed when some of Clara's enslaved children entered, playing, as was usual during the period of his sickness. The priest asked Pedro de Soto López to free them. When his uncle did not respond, the nephew intervened, repeating the cleric's plea, adding that Pedro de Soto López had raised them and the act was a "trifle" as well as an act of charity. In response, his uncle blessed the children without saying a word and it was understood that he would manumit them. The judge's sentence of the civil case concurred, stating that Pedro de Soto López "had not left them absolutely free, but only in the case" that his estate could afford the cost, emphasizing the instability of testamentary manumission (AHN. Exp. 2 [1727], 121v). But, Juan Clemente and the rest of the enslaved household of Pedro de Soto López did not win their manumission in the court. Instead they had caused written documentation of an oral testimony to be produced regarding an act of granting manumission.[4] By filing a lawsuit, the enslaved people with their free kin (such as Clara de Soto's husband) had recorded the testimony of a priest and the deceased owner's nephew. They had created the manumission, even if it would be denied due to the heirs' lack of finances.

Enslaved and freed people also came to rely on ecclesiastical institutions to document their status. Clerics (like notaries) charged parishioners to record baptisms, marriages, and deaths in parish records. The price was worth it for enslaved and freed people who employed baptism records to counteract the documentary control of slaveholders. For example, María Jacinta pointed to her baptism in order to counter claims of ownership by María de la Garza. María Jacinta produced a certificate of her baptism in the nearby Chocope valley that had occurred seventeen years before. In the case of María Jacinta, the copied entry stated clearly that she had been baptized as a free black girl on July 19, 1711 proving that she was no longer a slave. The slaveholder contested the claim, asserting that she had not given permission for the baptism and stating that the "simple words said by a priest did not free" her. Boldly, de la Garza reduced clerical authority and Catholic baptism to an event of mere hearsay. The slaveholder's challenge did not sufficiently undermine the weight of a written document composed by ecclesiastical officials in front of multiple witnesses in the public space of a parish church. In the end, Trujillo's magisterial court recognized the authority of the baptismal record and ruled in favor of María Jacinta, declaring her to be free (ADL. Co. Ords. Leg. 220. Exp. 1789, [1730], 2, 7v, 38v). Marriage, baptism, and burial records provided a way to prove descent and inheritance in colonial litigation (Cope 68; Twinam 77). As a result, enslaved and freed people like María Jacinta and her family were therefore aware that parish records were useful to claim their transition from slavery to freedom.

Baptism records could replace and also challenge notarized manumission records. The cleric-executor of Luisa Pacheco's will employed a baptism record as proof of manumission. As the daughter of María *conga* and enslaved to Pacheco, in 1708 six year-old Juliana was left in limbo after the death of the slaveholder. In other instances, Juliana would have been sold to another owner

(McKinley, "Till Death" 384). In this case, the cleric-executor employed the entry of her baptism in the parish, recorded, in her owner's presence, that she had been christened as free and subsequently raised as such (ADL. Protocolos. Cortijo Quero. Leg. 118 [1708], 161v). Again, the wording of the baptismal record as copied into the notarized manumission agreement enacted Juliana's status. The participation of the slaveholder also most likely made this claim to free status less open to challenge. Nonetheless, like María Jacinta, Juliana was baptized in a rural community on the northern Peruvian coast. There, in the colonial indigenous town, clerics may have been more available than notaries and regional slaveholders may have been less likely to intrude into indigenous governance (K. Burns 131). At the same time, their example indicates that, composed by clerics and possibly sponsored by godparents, a baptism record could be a written tool that allowed parents and family members to establish the free status of an infant or child. This type of alternative record could later act as cornerstone for an adult's case for freedom.

In addition to creating written records that would serve in their petitions for freedom, enslaved and freed people also created their own public record. Historians have argued that Spanish American slaveholders (and those elsewhere) offered manumission to women who became their consensual or nonconsensual sexual partners (Rout 88; Townsend 113). Certainly, slaveholders made arrangements with enslaved women in their households for manumission based on exchanges of sex, but also in recognition of familial ties and intimate service (Naro 58). The problematic for enslaved women and their kin was that slaveholders rarely publicly and legally acknowledged a relationship with enslaved or freed women, since colonial elites dismissed the honor of African-descent women (Boyer 161). In addition to sexual and intimate exploitation, enslaved women and their families also faced the challenge of documenting the events or circumstances that slaveholders categorically denied or kept silent. In a rare judicial case, legal representatives of Isabel Angola explained that because she had sexual intercourse with her owner, she should be freed (ADL. Co. Ords. Leg. 181. Exp. 963 [1633], 5v). Feelings, family, or even reproduction were not part of the arrangement. Instead, sex was to be exchanged for manumission (Soulodre-La France 91). In these petitions, the legal representatives of enslaved and freed women and their kin avoided discussions regarding loyalty to the slaveholders' households or their role raising children (Arrelucea Barrantes 60). In its place emerges a transactional quality to slaveholding and manumission that enslaved women, in particular, attempted to employ.

Both slaveholders and enslaved people seized on the multiple legal means and the variety of customary practices that, in the seventeenth century, were available to them. Enslaved and freed people reached for alternative authorities to supersede, challenge, or merely work around the documentation and intentions of slaveholders. In some cases, the Catholic Church provided institutional support for enslaved and freed people to document their status, and therefore challenge slaveholders for their own manumission or that of family members. In others, enslaved and freed people expanded justifications based on making public their experiences as domestic workers or family members of slaveholders. In either instance, enslaved and freed people articulated standards to define freed status that differed from slaveholders' discourses of charity and patronage.

Conclusions

Enslaved and freed people in seventeenth-century Peru understood that slaveholders had an interest in controlling their property. The courts often required a written document to certify manumission. These same records could often specify long-term obligations that further tied freed people to their former slaveholders or new patrons. In effect, the written records of manumission could entrap enslaved and free people by establishing a judicial record. Enslaved and freed people, however, did not prefer traditional patronage or wish to rely on the supposed "good" word of their owners. As discussed in this chapter, men and women of African descent struggled to create alternative documentation, seizing on the tools of literacy for their own ends even as they remained aware of writing's traps.

Nonetheless, enslaved and freed people engaged with the practices of manumission, indicating their abilities to contract legal representation as well as understand the logic of early modern slavery. Their actions indicate that men and women of the African Diaspora maintained a "preoccupation with" a "striking doubleness" that Paul Gilroy has explained makes those of the black Atlantic "in an expanded West but not completely of it" (58). In other words, enslaved and free people were actors in the laws of slavery and manumission, but simultaneously excluded as full subjects given their status as property. As survivors of the transatlantic slave trade or free inhabitants without a collective corporate location within colonial Spanish American governance, Africans and their descendants understood the multiplicity of their locations. Enslaved and freed people were simultaneously part of colonial society, and violently excluded. In this capacity, they employed the tools of manumission while articulating their suspicions of its paternalistic logic.

Enslaved and freed people articulated visions of freedom that included separation, in a variety of forms, from their owners and patrons. Enslaved people understood that a legal manumission could allow them to decide where to raise their children or to engage in their own economic pursuits. Through leadership roles in confraternities and in their capacities as godparents and creditors in the seventeenth century, free men and women claimed *vecindad*, or municipal status, a category that had become obtainable officially only to Spaniards in Spanish America but also claimed in other forms by urban Andeans and the inhabitants of the early modern Spanish world (Graubart 487; Herzog, *Defining* 44–45). For free people of color, a *vecino* or *vecina*, or a municipal citizen who owned property, was (or had been) honorably married, and assumed a public or political role. Freedom, then, meant that a woman or a man was no longer a dependent or a member of another's household. A free person could be counted on to secure their own creditors, stand behind their own word, and answer for themselves and *their* household. Therefore, the attainment of freedom in colonial Trujillo was about a legal transaction, an exchange of funds, but also part of a lengthy process that could result in the establishment of a civil person, a free person, who wielded their own written archives and negotiated commercial transactions of affective labor.

To gain this position of free person, enslaved and freed people attempted to secure an audience for their legal customary actions and move the practice of gaining manumission away from the more intimate relations with their owners. By creating their own forms of documentation, freed people challenged the authority of slaveholders, and also, then, a foundational discourse of empire. They would also be patriarchs or heads of households, claiming these positions from colonial authorities or the customary law of local slaveholders. If the Spanish Crown relied on local elites to govern and customary practice to serve as colonial law, then enslaved and freed challenges to slaveholders struck at the everyday mechanics of empire. Enslaved and freed people shifted the negotiation of manumission into means of their own control. In this way, enslaved and freed people acted on their dual status of simultaneous insiders and outsiders to encourage a legal formalism within a horizontal empire (Gilroy 48). While Habsburg autonomy allowed enslaved and freed modification of customary practice, African Diaspora freedom would be articulated apart from a paternalistic state in fugitive kingdoms, religious practices, and domestic arrangements. Simultaneously, in the courts, notary offices, and municipal governments, men and women of the African Diaspora inserted themselves into the discourses that constructed the Spanish empire.

Notes

1. A 2010 Humanities Center Faculty Research Award (University of California, Irvine) provided funding for this research. For their comments and suggestions, I thank Karen Graubart, Ann Kakaliouras, Shoshanna Lande, Bob Moeller, Bianca Premo, and Tamara Walker as well as Anna More, Ivonne del Valle, and other participants of "The Colonial Roots of Globalization" seminar (2013) at the Museo Franz Mayer (Mexico City) funded by a Mellon-LASA Seminar Grant.
2. For example, see doña Antonia Galindo, a nun in Santa Clara, explanation that she granted legal manumission to the sons of Lorenza Galindo because their mother had asked, and paid. ADL. Espino de Alvarado. Leg. 151 (1690), 189v.
3. The *Siete Partidas* declared that a slaveholder needed to acknowledge receipt of a slave's actual payment of their manumission (*Las siete partidas* 741).
4. For other strategies involving not winning the judicial cases see McKinley, "Till Death" 389.

WORKS CITED

Archivo Arzobispal de Lima (AAL). "Trujillo. Juana de Alvarado, parda, sigue causa contra el licenciado don Fernando de Ayala, quien le niega su libertad, la cual se halla expresada en el testamento de dona Maria de Alvarado." 1709. Apelaciones de Trujillo. Legajo 25, Expediente 5. Lima, Peru. MS.

Archivo Departamental de La Libertad (ADL). "Provanza hecha por Pedro Angola, negro esclavo que fue del Maestro de Campo Martín de Basavil, difunto, en razón de su libertad." 1646. Cabildo, Causas Ordinarias. Legajo 19, Expediente 407. Trujillo, Peru. MS.

_____. "Expediente seguido por el negro esclavo Francisco Arara contra los albaceas del Capitán don Antonio de Samora vecino de Trujillo sobre el otorgamiento de libertad precio pago de 500 pesos." 1700. Cabildo, Causas Ordinarias. Legajo 30, Expediente 608. Trujillo, Peru. MS.

_____. "Expediente seguido por el señor comisario general de la Caballería don Joseph Joseph de Herrera y Sarsosa, alcalde provincial de la Santa Hermandad y Ordinario de Trujillo sobre otorgación de libertad de don Santiago Gonzales negro criollo esclavo de don Manuel Gonzales de Castro, difunto, 2 hermanos y sus padres." 1717. Cabildo, Ordinarias. Legajo 36, Expediente 707. Trujillo, Peru. MS.

_____. "Expediente seguido por Ysabel Angola, contra los bienes de Pedro Cortez, su amo, difunto; sobre su pretendida libertad, con lo demás deducido." 1633. Corregimiento, Causas Ordinarias. Legajo 181, Expediente 963. Trujillo, Peru. MS.

_____. Expediente seguido por Elena de Paz y Vela, mulata en la causa de demanda contra el maestro de campo don Juan de Herrera Salazar, alférez real y regidor perpetuo de Trujillo; sobre su libertad, de sus hijos y nietos con lo demás deducido. 1663. Corregimiento, Causas Ordinaras. Legajo 196, Expediente 1319. Trujillo, Peru. MS.

———. "Demanda de Isidro de Olivitos, negro criollo, con Manuel Díaz González, albacea y tenedor de bienes del Bachiller don Pedro Olivito y Guzmán, difunto, cura que fue de la parroquia San Sebastián de los Naturales de esta ciudad; sobre la otorgación de libertad." 1669. Corregimiento, Causas Ordinarias. Legajo 198, Expediente 1347. Trujillo, Peru. MS.

———. Demanda de Valentín de Silva, pardo mulato, esclavo contra Joan Sebastián de Torres y María del Rosario, hermanos, sobre su libertad. 1686. Corregimiento, Causas Ordinaras. Legajo 206, Expediente 1503. Trujillo, Peru. MS.

———. "Expediente seguido por Ysabel de Sousa, morena libre, madre legítima de Jacoba del Carmen su hija con el Capitán don Diego Manzano Dorador; sobre le otorgue a dicha su hija carta de libertad por la cual hace obligación de 150 pesos tal como lo estipula en su testamento doña Margarita Suárez de Deza y Souza." 1721. Corregimiento, Causas Ordinarias. Legajo 218, Expediente 1738. Trujillo, Peru. MS.

———. "Expediente seguido por don Juan Lorenzo Rizo, vecino de Trujillo, contra Bartolomé de Zamudio, oficial de carpintero; sobre pago de alimentos a una hija natural Petrona Zamudio, libertine." 1728. Corregimiento, Causas Ordinarias. Legajo 220, Expediente 1777. Trujillo, Peru. MS.

———. "Expediente seguido por María Jacinta, negra libre contra María de la Garza, parda; sobre pretender privarle de su libertad que estaba gozando." 1730. Corregimiento, Causas Ordinarias. Legajo 220, Expediente 1789. Trujillo, Peru. MS.

———. "Pedimento de Luis de Equino, en nombre de Leonor Ramírez, negra para que Diego Muñoz Ternero declare en la causa que trata con Diego Núñez de Paredes sobre su libertad." 1572. Corregimiento, Pedimentos. Legajo 280, Expediente 3591. Trujillo, Peru. MS.

———. Protocolos. Cortijo Quero. Legajos 107 (1697); 110 (1700); 118 (1708). Trujillo, Peru. MS.

———. Protocolos, Espino de Alvarado. Legajos 151 (1690); 155 (1694). Trujillo, Peru. MS.

———. Protocolos, Garcia. Legajo 165 (1659). Trujillo, Peru. MS.

———. Protocolos, Nuñez de Valcera. Legajos 186 (1679). Trujillo, Peru. MS.

———. Protocolos, San Roman. Legajo 213 (1699); 219 (1713). Trujillo, Peru. MS.

———. Protocolos, Verde. Legajo 250 (1670). Trujillo, Peru. MS.

———. Protocolos, Viera Gutierrez. Legajo 259 (1656). Trujillo, Peru. MS.

Archivo General de Indias (AGI). "Don Pedro de Toledo y Mendosa alcalde de Sta Hermandad desta ciudad de los reyes." 1645. Audiencia de Lima, Cartas y expedientes: personas seculares vistos o resueltos en el Consejo. Legajo 166. Seville, Spain. MS.

Archivo Histórico Nacional (AHN). "Pleito civil de Cristobal y Rodrigo, esclavos de Francisco de Berrio y Guzman." 1717. Inquisición. 1614, Expediente 8. Madrid, Spain. MS.

———. "Pleito civil de Juan Clemente y otros esclavos contra Pedro de Soto Lopez." 1661/1665. Consejo de Inquisicion, Pleitos Civiles. Legajo 1727, Expediente 2. Madrid, Spain. MS.

Andrés-Gallego, José. *La esclavitud en la América española*. Madrid: Ediciones Encuentro, 2005.

Arrelucea Barrantes, Maribel. *Replanteando la esclavitud: Estudios de etnicidad y género en Lima borbónica*. Lima: CEDET, Centro de Desarrollo Étnico, 2009.

Bennett, Herman. *Africans in Colonial Mexico: Absolutism, Christianity, and Afro-Creole Consciousness, 1570–1640*. Bloomington: Indiana University Press, 2003.

Berlin, Ira. *Many Thousands Gone: The First Two Centuries of Slavery in North America*. Cambridge, Mass: Belknap Press of Harvard University Press, 1998.

Bowser, Frederick P. *African Slave in Colonial Peru 1524–1650*. Stanford: Stanford University Press, 1974.

Boyer, Richard. "Honor among Plebeians." *The Faces of Honor: Sex, Shame, and Violence in Colonial Latin America*. Eds. Lyman L. Johnson and Sonya Lipsett-Rivera. Albuquerque: University of New Mexico Press, 1998. 152–78.

Brana-Shute, Rosemary, "Sex and Gender in Surinamese Manumissions." *Paths to Freedom: Manumission in the Atlantic World*. Eds. Rosemary Brana-Shute and Randy J. Sparks. Columbia: University of South Carolina Press, 2009. 175–96.

Bristol, Joan. *Christians, Blasphemers, and Witches: Afro-Mexican Ritual Practice in the Seventeenth Century*. Albuquerque: University of New Mexico Press, 2007.

Bryant, Sherwin, "Enslaved Rebels, Fugitives, and Litigants: The Resistance Continuum in Colonial Quito." *Colonial Latin American Review* 13:1 (June 2004): 7–46.

Burns, Kathryn. *Into the Archive: Writing and Power in Colonial Peru*. Durham: Duke University Press, 2010.

Burns, Robert I. "Introduction." *The Siete Partidas*. Trans. Samuel Parsons Scott. Ed. Robert I. Burns. Philadelphia: University of Pennsylvania Press, 2001.

Cañeque, Alejandro. *The King's Living Image: The Culture and Politics of Viceregal Power in Colonial Mexico*. New York: Routledge, 2004.

Cope, R. Douglas. *The Limits of Racial Domination: Plebeian Society in Colonial Mexico City, 1660–1720*. Madison: University of Wisconsin Press, 1994.

Cutter, Charles. *Legal Culture of Northern New Spain, 1700–1810*. Albuquerque: University of New Mexico Press, 1995.

Dantas, Mariana. *Black Townsmen: Urban Slavery and Freedom in the Eighteenth-Century Americas*. New York: Palgrave Macmillan, 2008.

De la Fuente, Alejandro. "Slaves and the Creation of Legal Rights in Cuba: *Coartación* and *Papel*." *Hispanic American Historical Review* 87:4 (Nov. 2007): 659–92.

Ferreira Furtado, Júnia. *Chica da Silva: A Brazilian Slave of the Eighteenth Century*. Cambridge, UK: Cambridge University Press, 2009.

Germeten, Nicole von. *Black Blood Brothers: Confraternities and Social Mobility for Afro-Mexicans*. Gainesville: University Press of Florida, 2006.

Gilroy, Paul. *The Black Atlantic: Modernity and Double Consciousness*. Cambridge, Mass: Harvard University Press, 1993.

Graham, Sandra Lauderdale. *House and Street: The Domestic World of Servants and Masters in Nineteenth-Century Rio de Janeiro*. Austin: University of Texas Press, 1988.

———. "Writing from the Margins: Brazilian Slaves and Written Culture." *Comparative Studies in Society and History* 49:3 (2007): 611–36.
Graubart, Karen. "The Creolization of the New World: Local Forms of Identity in Urban Colonial Peru, 1560–1640." *Hispanic American Historical Review* 89:3 (Aug. 2009): 471–99.
Hanger, Kimberly. *Bounded Lives, Bounded Places: Free Black Society in Colonial New Orleans, 1769–1803*. Durham: Duke University Press, 1997.
Herzog, Tamar. *La administración como fenómeno social: La justicia penal de la ciudad de Quito (1650–1750)*. Madrid: Centro de Estudios Constitucionales, 1995.
———. *Defining Nations: Immigrants and Citizens in Early Modern Spain and Spanish America*. New Haven: Yale University Press, 2003.
Hünefeldt, Christine. *Paying the Price of Freedom: Family and Labor Among Lima's Slaves, 1800–1854*. Berkeley: University of California Press, 1994.
Jouve Martín, José Ramón. *Esclavos de la ciudad letrada: Esclavitud, escritura y colonialismo en Lima (1650–1700)*. Lima: Instituto de Estudios Peruanos, 2005.
Lewis, Laura A. *Hall of Mirrors: Power, Witchcraft, and Caste in Colonial Mexico*. Durham: Duke University Press, 2003.
Mangan, Jane. *Trading Roles: Gender, Ethnicity, and the Urban Economy in Colonial Potosí*. Durham: Duke University Press, 2005.
Mannarelli, María Emma. *Private Passions and Public Sins: Men and Women in Seventeenth-Century Lima*. Trans. Sidney Evans and Meredith D. Dodge. Albuquerque: University of New Mexico Press, 2007.
Martínez, María Elena. *Genealogical Fictions: Limpieza de Sangre, Religion, and Gender in Colonial Mexico*. Stanford: Stanford University Press, 2008.
McKinley, Michelle. "Fractional Freedoms: Slavery, Legal Activism & Ecclesiastical Courts in Colonial Lima, 1593–1700." *Law and History Review* 28:3 (2010): 749–90.
———. "'Such Unsightly Unions Could Never Result in Holy Matrimony': Mixed-Status Marriages in Seventeenth-Century Colonial Lima." *Yale Journal of Law and the Humanities* 22:2 (2010): 217–55.
———. "Till Death Do Us Part: Testamentary Manumission in Seventeenth-Century Lima." *Slavery and Abolition: A Journal of Slave and Post Slave Studies* 33:3 (2012): 381–401.
———. "Illicit Intimacies: Virtuous Concubinage in Colonial Lima." *Journal of Family History* 39:3 (July 2014): 204–21.
Meiklejohn, Norman A. "The Implementation of Slave Legislation in Eighteenth-Century New Granada." *Slavery and Race Relations in Latin America*. Ed. Robert Brent Toplin. Westport: Greenwood Press, 1974. 176–203.
Naro, Nancy Priscilla. *A Slave's Place, A Master's World: Fashioning Dependency in Rural Brazil*. London: Continuum, 2000.
O'Toole, Rachel Sarah. *Bound Lives: Africans, Indians, and the Making of Race in Colonial Peru*. Pittsburgh: University of Pittsburgh Press, 2012.
Owensby, Brian. *Empire of Law and Indian Justice in Colonial Mexico*. Stanford: Stanford University Press, 2008.

Palmer, Colin A. *Slaves of the White God: Blacks in Mexico, 1570–1650.* Cambridge, Mass: Harvard University Press, 1976.

Premo, Bianca. *Children of the Father King: Youth, Authority, & Legal Minority in Colonial Lima.* Chapel Hill: University of North Carolina Press, 2005.

Proctor, Frank T., III. "Gender and the Manumission of Slaves in New Spain." *Hispanic American Historical Review* 86:2 (2006): 309–36.

———. *"Damned Notions of Liberty": Slavery, Culture, and Power in Colonial Mexico, 1640–1769.* Albuquerque: University of New Mexico Press, 2010.

Ramírez, Susan. *Provincial Patriarchs: Land Tenure and the Economics of Power in Colonial Peru.* Albuquerque: University of New Mexico Press, 1986.

Recopilacion De Leyes De Los Reynos De Las Indias. Madrid: Ivlian De Paredes, 1681.

Rout, Leslie. *The African Experience in Spanish America.* Princeton: Markus Wiener Publishers, 2003 [1976].

Scott, Rebecca. "Paper Thin: Freedom and Reenslavement in the Diaspora of the Haitian Revolution." *Law and History Review* 29 (Nov. 2011): 1061–87.

Las siete partidas del sabio rey Don Alonso el Nono, nueuamente glosadas por el licenciado Gregorio López . . . con su reportorio muy copioso assi del testo como de la glosa. Valladolid: Diego Fernandez de Cordova, 1587-88.

Soulodre-La France, Renée. "Socially not so dead! Slave Identity in Bourbon New Granada." *Colonial Latin American Review* 10:1 (June 2001): 87–103.

Tardieu, Jean-Pierre. *Los negros y la iglesia en el Perú: Siglos XVI-XVII.* 2 Vols. Quito: Centro Cultural Afroecuatoriano, 1997.

Townsend, Camilla. "'Half My Body Free, the Other Half Enslaved': The Politics of the Slaves of Guayaquil at the End of the Colonial Era." *Colonial Latin American Review* 7:1 (1998): 105–28.

Twinam, Ann. *Public Lives, Private Secrets: Gender, Honor, Sexuality, and Illegitimacy in Colonial Spanish America.* Stanford: Stanford University Press, 1999.

Velázquez Gutiérrez, María Elisa. *Mujeres de origen africano en la capital novohispana, siglos XVII y XVIII.* Mexico City: Universidad Nacional Autónoma de México, 2006.

Uribe-Uran, Victor. "Innocent Infants or Abusive Patriarchs?: Spousal Homicides, the Punishment of Indians and the Law in Colonial Mexico, 1740s–1820s." *Journal of Latin American Studies* 38: 4 (Nov. 2006): 793–828.

Walker, Tamara. "'He outfitted his family in notable decency': Slavery, Honor, and Dress in Eighteenth-Century Lima, Peru." *Slavery and Abolition: A Journal of Slave & Post-Slave Studies* 30:3 (Sept. 2009): 383–402.

Watson, Alan. *Slave Law in the Americas.* Athens: University of Georgia Press, 1989.

◆ CHAPTER SEVEN

The Reason of Freedom and the Freedom of Reason

The Neo-Scholastic Critique of African Slavery and Its Impact on the Construction of the Nineteenth-Century Republic in Spanish America

María Eugenia Chaves
Holly Jackson, translator

The idea that human beings are free by nature and that people have the right to defend and preserve their freedom was a constant theme in the erudite debates that, from the sixteenth century onward, accompanied Iberian campaigns of conquest and colonization on both sides of the Atlantic. In these debates, the loss of natural freedom was justified solely as a consequence of certain causes regulated by so-called *ius gentium*, ("law of nations").

The *ius gentium* appears when it becomes necessary to extend positive law beyond the frontiers of individual societies. From the sixteenth century on, the European powers engaged in extended wars to gain control of the seas and to secure maritime trade routes. In this context, the importance of the *ius gentium* grew. The colonization of the Americas and the rise of African enslavement, based on the expansion of evangelization and the development of the triangular slave trade established a set of conditions from which a new globalized world order emerged. The *ius gentium*, then, may be considered an extremely refined product of Spanish theologians and jurists (instituted during the sixteenth and seventeenth centuries), or more specifically a juridical and theological framework that would justify the exploitation of subjected populations and maintain peace between the major hegemonic powers in a community that they conceived of as universal (Pereña, "La tesis," and "La génesis"). Yet, the colonial practices of invasion, conquest, and slavery that accompanied this expansion tended to break all the norms of natural law (Brion Davis 192–217). As a result, the work of the so-called School of Salamanca proved to be fundamental in consolidating the authority of the imperial *ius gentium*. The Dominican theologian Francisco de Vitoria planted the seed for this development in his *Relectiones* (notes on the courses he gave at the University of Salamanca).[1] In this way, the *ius gentium* that developed throughout the colonial period gradually undermined scholastic natural law.

Building on Cicero's idea of natural law (the first century BCE), Thomas of Aquinas developed Christian doctrinal natural law in the thirteenth century CE, establishing that as an effect of the law of "nature," all things created tended to fulfill the ultimate purpose for which God created them.[2] Human beings not only fulfilled this mandate but also had the ability to make decisions regarding their own conduct and that of the rest of creation. For Aquinas, "this participation of the eternal law in the rational creature is called natural law" (I, II question 91 article 2). According to Aquinas, the exercise of human reason could establish particular principles (I, II question 91 article 3), thus producing human law, later called positive law. However, dictated by the free exercise of human reason, positive law was subject to two conditions: that of seeking the good of the community, and that of being in harmony with the universal principles of natural law, "but if in any point it deflects from the law of nature, it is no longer a law but a perversion of law" (I, II question 95 article 2). Insofar as human laws respond to the particular circumstances of the societies that issue them, their authority is limited (Barcala 297).

In what follows, I argue that the conflict between natural law and *ius gentium*, arising along with the colonial process in the sixteenth century, had a long-lasting effect on how creole elites defined freedom, until as late as the early nineteenth century. Put another way, any attempt to justify or condemn indigenous or African slavery, either in the colonial or in the republican era, was at the same time an intervention in the discourses regarding the conditions of freedom and sovereignty within the political community.[3]

From 1811 on, creole revolutionaries begun to search for a solution to deal with the difficulties that African slavery presented to nations founded on the political ideal of natural freedom. In this context, a critique of African slavery gained momentum, including some proposals to manumit slaves (Chaves, "El oxymoron"). The argument against slavery, however, was not new. Already in the seventeenth century, important treatises had been written that condemned the enslavement of Africans and demanded its abolition. In this essay, I analyze two texts that denounce the injustice of African slavery. The first, written by the Aragonese Capuchin Francisco José de Jaca in 1681, constitutes one of the earliest and most radical abolitionist treatises (López García 123–76; Jaca 3–70). The second, a text written in 1821 by Félix de Restrepo, an insurgent lawyer from the Viceroyalty of New Granada, introduces a law of gradual manumission, called the law of "free wombs" (Restrepo 82–132).

I intend to use the temporal as well as contextual distance between these texts for methodological purposes. The comparative reading proposed here is employed as a methodological device to establish whether the aforementioned long-term conflict between natural law and *ius gentium* could function as a pertinent hypothesis. The temporal leap from the seventeenth to the nineteenth century allows me to illustrate, first, that the efforts of the political and intellectual elite to define a free political community were deeply influenced by the way in which they conceived and justified the enslavement of indigenous and African people; and second, that this long-term influence was articulated in the conflict between the tenets of natural law and *ius gentium*.

I begin my analysis with a review of Francisco José de Jaca's abolitionist position, a description of the context in which he wrote, and the intellectual traditions with which he was in dialogue. A summary of Restrepo's text occupies the second part of this article. I conclude with some reflections concerning the relation between the two texts.

A Mission in Tierra Firme

The neophyte missionary Francisco José de Jaca arrived on the Caracas coast in 1678 and, over the course of three years, developed his ministry in the Misión de los Llanos de Caracas. In this region, the Spanish conquest had been bloody as well as destructive, and different practices of enslavement were imposed on indigenous people and Africans (López García 32–46; Peña González, "Estudio Preliminar"). The cruel exploitation of the conquest must have clashed strongly with the sincere desire of the young Capuchin to rescue new souls for the Christian community and for the Kingdom of God.

The Misión de los Llanos, along with the other two missions on what is today the Venezuelan coast, was dedicated to the evangelization and resettlement of the indigenous population into *reducciones de indígenas* (colonial Indian towns) using violent methods. Native people defended themselves by engaging in a permanent state of war against the invaders (De Carrocera).[4] However, war with the indigenous population was not the only problem Hispanic authorities faced. By the end of the seventeenth century, communities of runaway slaves (*cimarrones*), allied with native peoples, resisted colonial power in the region, threatening to destabilize the structure of colonial society dependent upon various forms of slavery.[5]

Upon arriving in the "New World," Jaca passed through Cartagena, the largest port of entry for enslaved Africans into Spanish America. Here he witnessed how African men and women arrived after the infamous voyage: abused, humiliated, and subjected to indescribable violence. Later, in the Misión de los Llanos, he had the opportunity to see rebelling Africans and natives at war, sometimes winning and other times pursued and murdered for defending their freedom.[6] Most likely, Jaca's intellectual efforts to oppose slavery and to claim unconditional abolition were inspired by this experience.

A Resolution

Jaca unwaveringly maintained his critique of the enslavement of Africans in his sermons and during ongoing confrontations with the authorities, demanding its abolition.[7] After a short stay in the Misión de los Llanos, he was instructed to return to Spain, allegedly because of the controversies caused by his sermons. On his return journey through Havana (July 1681 to September 1682), he continued preaching against slavery. He met a fellow Capuchin missionary the Frenchman Epifanio de Moirans, who shared his ideas and joined in his efforts to condemn slavery.[8] In December of 1681, both of them were excommunicated, handed over to secular authorities, and imprisoned.

All evidence indicates that prior to being imprisoned for the first time, Jaca had finished writing *Resolución sobre la libertad de los negros y sus originarios, en estado de paganos y después ya cristianos* (*Resolution on the freedom of blacks and their forebears, in a state of paganism and later as Christians*). This text is comprised of two parts. The first brings together a set of propositions proving that the enslavement of Africans is contrary to natural law, common to all humans as children of God. The second part is dedicated to establishing that Christians involved in slavery or slave trading act in disobedience of the law of God and of the Church. Jaca's text is scholastic in nature and, as such, presents and proves its arguments using commentaries from the Bible, teachings of Christian and pagan philosophers, and opinions of contemporary erudite writers. The themes that the *Resolución* puts forward reveal the argumentative framework that would later enable any radical discourse in favor of freedom and against the enslavement of Africans. The main objectives of the text are, first, to denounce and to argue against the contradiction that slavery poses with regard to natural law, Christian doctrine, and Biblical texts, and second, to advance a critical and rigorous examination of the conditions sanctioned by the *ius gentium* to legitimize slavery.[9]

The first part of the text is a defense of "human rights." Following the Thomistic principles of natural law, Jaca begins by explaining that although divine wisdom possesses an absolute power over "the rational being," God bestowed upon human beings the power of freedom. Hence, if God is the primary cause of the rationality and freedom that define human beings, it is unacceptable that they would contradict these conditions (Jaca Part I, titles 1 and 2). Having established that the primary cause of freedom is God, Jaca devotes himself to demonstrating that the justifications the *ius gentium* instituted in order to accept slavery go against the natural freedom originated in God´s will (Jaca Part 1, title 6).

Propositions 6 through 16 constitute an attack, with extensive documentation, against three of the main arguments with which *ius gentium* justifies slavery: a) the legitimacy of the wars that the Portuguese and Spanish made against African peoples; b) the legitimacy of the wars that supposedly existed between African peoples; and c) the "invincible ignorance" slave traders claim to have regarding the origin of these wars. One by one, Jaca exposes and annuls the authority of these reasons and denounces the enslavement, purchase, sale, resale, and possession of Africans as absolutely illegitimate.

Jaca opens the discussion of the first argument with the question: "What reason for just war is there between Spaniards and blacks [. . .] who, being slaves, suffer much violence, ignominy and tyranny in order to be as they are, sold and resold from their native lands to these and others more remote with such mistreatment?" (Jaca Part 1, title 6).[10] He responds that there exists no justification for slavery, because the violence with which it is executed goes against the first principle: "*Quod tibi non vis, alteri ne feceris*" (Jaca Part 1, title 6) (Do not unto others that which you would not wish them to do unto you).[11] Regarding the second point, Jaca argues that it is unlikely that the wars between African peoples are just, and he develops explanations. The first is that no one had provided true witness accounts of the fact. His second reason has to do with the barbaric nature attributed to Africans:

> How could any halfway competent person miss the fact that barbaric peoples, whose blindness constantly tramples upon the law of God, living like beasts could have or have reached justified foundations for such wars (if they could conceive of them) (Jaca Part 1, title 7)?[12]

Jaca makes an important distinction between wars in which states are involved, and wars between peoples of a single state, or between families or bands, as were the case of wars among Africans. *Ius gentium* legitimated the former and the enslavement that followed, and sanctioned as illegitimate the latter. Following this distinction he concludes that in the case of wars between Africans the practice of slavery was illegitimate:

> [. . .] even if it were true that, given that these [Africans] in their seditious disturbances live like beasts, they could be sought out (as Aristotle says) in order that they may live in human society, this could in no way be under the oppression of such contemptible servitude, because though this may improve *quirito* or political law, it would be a detriment to natural law, which is the foundation of the other laws (Jaca Part 1, title 9).[13]

In the titles that follow, from 10 to 15, the author takes up once more the fundamental argument that the rationality and freedom bestowed by God in man are natural law because they come from the first principle that is God. He explains that because of this principle, man in "su intrínseco ser" ("his intrinsic self") must not be alien to himself, but rather to be of his own, which amounts to being, for the rational man, free, and for the free man, rational (Part 1, title 10).[14] In this, Jaca shows that the slavers can allege neither ignorance of these first principles nor "good faith" in the sale and resale of Africans, since a principle that comes from God is general and cannot be debated on the basis of particular situations like those that would justify slavery. The Capuchin describes these assumptions with which *ius gentium* tries to justify slavery as "errors," and critiques them severely. Among these errors he refers to the justification of slavery as necessary for the conversion of Africans to Christianity (Part 1, title 11) and to the acceptance of slavery as legitimate punishment for a crime committed. Commenting on the latter he explains that because slave dealers have no certainty of proving the crimes allegedly committed by enslaved Africans, the doubt would be enough to annul any possibility of legitimizing slavery. Based on these reasons, Jaca concludes this first part, accusing the slave dealers of "being bestial people, deserving of mortal punishment" (Part 1, title 16).[15]

In the second part of his *Resolución*, Jaca shows the contradiction produced by the enslavement of Africans in the Christian community, understood as a free political community. Before moving on to this point it is necessary to reveal more about the intellectual currents with which Jaca dialogues to compose his work. This analysis allows me to define the contours of a discursive field that from the sixteenth century until the nineteenth century made possible the enunciation of a radical defense of natural freedom. By opposing the principles of *ius gentium* that legitimized slavery, this radical discourse put into question the foundations of a global order which, strongly dependent upon the slave system, sustained the whole colonial process.

Just War, Slavery, and Possession

The contours of the debate about the slavery of indigenous people were defined by the works of a group of sixteenth-century scholars who took it upon themselves to collect and to reinterpret the Greek and patristic texts on slavery.[16] These authors produced their works in an intellectual context of renewed scholasticism, developed by the so-called School of Salamanca and its leading figure Dominican Francisco de Vitoria, who posed the doctrine of *ius gentium* as the axis of the debate.[17] If natural law was understood to be an expression of divine will, *ius gentium*, although determined by the former, was considered an unwritten positive right of a consensual sort. *Ius gentium* rights were to be sustained by custom (which could be shared by all nations) in order to organize relations regarding commerce, war, the spreading of the Christian faith and, more generally, power relations and forms of subjugation and their limits. Vitoria defined these *ius gentium* rights as the core principles of what he called the law of "society and natural communication" (Vitoria 129–50). For Vitoria, if indigenous people were to violate this fundamental law, war against them, including their enslavement, would be justified as a legitimate Spanish response.[18]

As of the second half of the sixteenth century, when large contingents of enslaved Africans began arriving to the Caribbean islands and Tierra Firme, this discussion would expand to include a justification of African slavery. Dominicans Domingo de Soto and Tomás de Mercado, and the Jesuit Luis de Molina were among the authors who made important contributions to this issue.[19] Although they rejected Aristotle's understanding that there existed a "natural slavery," these authors accepted that there existed conditions imposed by *ius gentium* that justified slavery, and they took on the task of analyzing whether in the case of Africans these conditions had been met.[20] They concentrated mainly on three causes: just war, punishment for a serious crime, and having sold oneself or one's children voluntarily into slavery. Soto established that given the doubts that emerged regarding this matter and the inconsistencies that arose in the enslavement of Africans, the business was a mortal sin that ought to be terminated. Mercado and Molina developed the issue more thoroughly. Both authors recognized and condemned the violence involved in the enslavement of Africans; however, as they accepted that *ius gentium* could justify slavery and slave trading, their efforts concentrated in examining whether the causes therein dictated were being met (Obregón; Peña González, "Entre la encomienda" 263–78). First, they confirmed that the wars between the Portuguese and African peoples were just and the resulting slaves legitimate. Thus, they concluded that the slave trade warranted no objections.[21] For Molina, the slavery imposed on Africans by their own authorities as punishment for crimes committed was also legitimate; he likewise considered the enslavement of boys and girls legal when their parents had sold them to middlemen due to penury. He reasoned, displaying a surprising cultural relativism, that these customs, though barbaric, should be respected and, as such, those slaves did not pose a moral problem for the slave traders (Molina, *De Iustitia*, volume 1, second treaty, argument 35, cited in Costello 189–90; García, "Luis de Molina" 199–200).

As long as these authors considered Africans to be savage, tyrannical, and ignorant, they also had to accept that the wars between them were unjust. Consequently, legitimizing slavery in these circumstances was inconceivable.[22] In these cases, the slave traders were to check the origin of slaves and if they were illegitimate they ought to restore their freedom and make reparations for damages caused (Mercado 103 r.–104 v.; Molina, *De Iustitia*, volume 2, argument 35, fourth conclusion, cited in Costello 192–93). Thus, both Mercado and Molina advised slave traders not to intervene in a business deal that seemed suspect.

Up to this point, Molina and Mercado had treated only the initial purchase; however, continuing on to analyze subsequent transactions, especially those produced after the Middle Passage, they entered a more complicated terrain. Mercado abstained from taking a stance. Molina, on the other hand, confronted the problem and concluded that it is impossible for the second and third buyers to check if the slaves were legitimate or not. Faced with this doubt, the Jesuit established that the buyers' right to possession had to be privileged as well as their supposed "good faith" (Molina, *De Iustitia*, volume 1, second treatise, argument 36, cited in Costello 195–98). In spite of recognizing that slavery is at odds with natural law, with this conclusion privileging *ius gentium*, Molina instated a gap between the legitimacy of enslavement and the legitimacy of possession, making it feasible to maintain slavery as a right to property.

A century before Molina, fray Bartolomé de las Casas articulated a contrary argument. Las Casas, in his defense of the freedom of indigenous people, used the metaphor of blindness to describe the incapability of authorities and prelates to recognize the justice of natural freedom. In an *Opusculum* probably written in 1556, included by Las Casas in his manuscript of *History of the Indies*, he opposes the enslavement of Africans in similar terms.[23] In this document, Las Casas summarized the history of the Portuguese invasion of Africa. In contrast to what Molina would conclude years later, Las Casas affirmed that the enslavement of

Africans amounted to a great sin and has no justification because it went against natural law and the teachings of the Gospel. He insisted upon the liberation of enslaved Africans and in order to correct the current injustice, he demanded that owners monetarily compensate freed slaves.[24] Las Casas's *Opusculum*, although unpublished along with the rest of the manuscript until the nineteenth century, is important for two reasons: first, it shows a change in the Dominican's opinion about the legitimacy of African slavery; second, it corroborates the fact that the pronouncement regarding the freedom or enslavement of Africans hinges on a discursive confrontation between, on the one hand, the assumptions of natural law and, on the other, the principles of *ius gentium*.

It is important to note that scholars who followed the path marked by Vitoria and by the authority of *ius gentium* rejected the existence of a universal empire governed by a natural divine law common to all and controlled by a single religious authority such as the Pope or the prince (Vitoria 87–105). Las Casas and Jaca adopted a position to the contrary, because in defending the absolute primacy of natural law they accepted the absolute authority of the Church, insisting on evangelization as the vehicle for integrating the world into the Christian community, understood as a universal political empire (Pagden, *Señores* 73–86). As I will discuss below, this difference will be important to understanding Jaca's position regarding first, the responsibilities that the political community as a whole must assume in order to recognize the historical damage slavery had inflicted to its fundamental principles, and second, to accept the consequences that abolition would impose on its members.

More than a century later, following in the footsteps of Las Casas, Jaca appears to have refuted all of the premises elaborated by the most important scholars from the sixteenth century onwards to justify the possession of slaves at the same time as they condemned slavery, a contradictory position with long-term consequences as we shall see further on. Throughout his *Resolución*, Jaca returns many times to the metaphor of blindness used by the Bishop of Chiapas in order to express the slave owners', authorities', and clergymen's permanent denial of natural divine law (Part 2, titles 19, 22, 27, 45, 62).[25]

Fellow Citizens of the Saints and Relatives of God

The second part of the *Resolución* aims to demonstrate, in sixty-four chapters the following: "Considering Apostle Saint Paul we are sealed in holy baptism with the blood of Jesus Christ, he tells all of the faithful that we are not to be children of slavery, but rather of our own freedom" (Jaca Part 2, title 1).[26] Inspired by the

Pauline writings, Jaca establishes that the baptized "are no longer strangers nor foreigners, but rather fellow citizens of the saints and relatives of God," (Part 2, title 1) and remarks that as citizens and Christians they form a political community, the *Cives Sanctorum*, "so that no one may dare bind [...] being citizen with being a slave, nor being a member of the Church with accepting slavery within it" (Part 2, title 1).[27] In these chapters the Capuchin explains the nature of the relationship between the Christian political community and its "citizens," making evident that the origin of this relationship is baptism. Jaca then equates the relationship between the Church and its "citizens" with that of a mother and her children. This simile allows him to demonstrate that the relationships among the baptized as well as the unity of the community as a political whole are conditioned by the *filia* that is brotherhood. The Capuchin also used the simile to explain that freedom is transmitted from the Church to the baptized since the legal status of the offspring follows that of the mother's womb: *partus ventrem sequitur* (the condition of the offspring follows the condition of the womb) (Part 2, title 8). By applying this norm instituted by Roman law, the Capuchin was able to make a strong case to demonstrate that freedom, a fundamental characteristic of the Church, was also that of those who through baptism have become children of her womb and members of the Christian community. The enslavement of some members of this free community would clearly contradict this premise.[28] However, as the author shows, since early Christianity, the question of how to integrate the recently baptized into the *Cives Sanctorum* as free people and enjoy the privileges of citizens was a matter of discussion because to some, they were considered Christians in name only. Therefore, it was assumed that they would remain for a time in the capacity of "servants" (Part 2, title 9).

In his *Resolution* Jaca challenged this tradition. He made evident that the majority of Africans were baptized and, as such, shared with the rest of the Church the *filia* that sustains the political community. Given this condition, Africans should be integrated into the community as free people. The contrary, that is the enslavement of Africans, would be a sin and a contradiction, both highly damaging for the community as a whole. The Capuchin goes further in his critique and claims that natural freedom should be extended even to those who had not been baptized, because the *filia* existed as a potential capacity, waiting for the moment of salvation in order to emerge (Part 2, chapter 39).

To close his argument in favor of Africans' natural freedom, he compelled the Church to exercise its power not only to "interpret and declare some things with regard to natural law" (Part 2, title 14) but above all to oppose the increasing influence of *ius gentium*, which accepts slavery.[29] Having established the injustice that slavery represents for the religious and political community, Jaca closed his thesis demanding immediate economic, social and political reparations for the Africans who were victims of this crime. Jaca remarked that these acts of restitution were the responsibility of the community as a whole, not just of some of its members, because the existence of slavery had inflicted harm upon the "common good" and not just upon the individual good. In this sense, Jaca demanded that slaves should be freed and receive restitution even if these acts of reparation would endanger public peace and owners' economic interests (Part 2, titles 39 and 51). As we can see, Jaca's *Resolución* contradicted the arguments of Molina, who had justified possession "in good faith" on the part of the second and later buyers, considering that both the right to property and the public order should prevail over the right to natural freedom.

Although in early nineteenth-century Spanish America the matters defined by Jaca were present in abolitionist rhetoric, a discourse so radically in favor of natural freedom did not repeat itself. What emerged were several projects to emancipate the children of female slaves whose wombs were declared legally freed while the rest of their bodies remained enslaved, as were the rest of the slaves. These projects bore a contradiction between the necessity the creole elites felt to resolve the problem of slavery in a nation built upon the rhetoric of natural freedom, and the impossibility of abolishing slavery without jeopardizing the economic interest of the owners. In what follows I will give a brief review of one of these discourses in order to analyze this discrepancy and to arrive at certain conclusions.

From Jaca's Natural Freedom to Creole Abolitionism in the Nineteenth Century[30]

Some of the constitutions that began to appear in 1810 as a result of the processes of Spanish American independence were preceded by a declaration of rights stating that freedom was a natural right concerning all human beings.[31] In some cases, these declarations prompted some slaves to claim their freedom (Chaves, "'Nos los esclavos'"; Bragoni). In order to confront the contradiction that slavery imposed in the heart of these young republics elites establish processes of gradual emancipation. These measures sought to neutralize the potential for slave revolutions avoiding at the same time the dismantling of slavery. Such was the case in the republic of Antioquia, in the former Viceroyalty of New Granada.

In 1814, a year after declaring its independence and two years after sanctioning a republican constitution, the government of Antioquia passed the "Ley sobre la manumisión de la posteridad de los esclavos africanos y sobre los medios de redimir sucesivamente a sus padres" ("Law on the manumission of posterity of

African slaves and on the means of successively freeing their parents"). Preceded in South America only by similar initiatives in Chile (1811) and Río de la Plata (1813), the law freed "the wombs" of female slaves and as such, the children born after its passage.

The Antioquian Félix de Restrepo presented the initiative years later to the Congress of Cúcuta, in 1821 (Restrepo 82–132). He introduced his project with a lengthy speech in which he denounced the enslavement of African descendants as a political inconsistency in a republic, and a fatal contradiction in a Christian community:

> The Christian Religion is so far from protecting slavery that nothing could be more contrary to it. The Gospels completely proscribe it: *Love your neighbor as yourself* [...] *Do not unto another that which you would not want done unto you*, dictates this same religion, and it is the duty of man in society, as the governments of Europe and America have enthusiastically repeated (Restrepo 104, italics in original).[32]

According to Restrepo, maintaining slavery was a mortal sin in a Christian republic and deserved divine punishment. He feared that this punishment could be expressed in a renewed political subjugation to Spain, a condition he associates with a state similar to that of slavery.

Having established this initial proposition, Restrepo devotes a large part of his speech to showing that African slavery lacked a legal basis. For this task he follows the same argumentative logic established by Jaca in order to oppose the norms of *ius gentium* that legitimized this practice, therein "doing violence" to natural law. Restrepo concentrates on three of these assumptions: the legitimization of slavery as a consequence of just war; the idea that African slavery existed prior to European intervention and thus presented no problems of conscience to the traders; and the assumption that conquest and slavery were initial steps not just to the salvation of the souls of Natives and Africans, but also to their integration into the Christian community through baptism. Restrepo considers this last argument, "barbaric" (108). Up to this point, his discourse closely follow the opposition between natural law and *ius gentium* that Jaca articulates in his *Resolución*, and his conclusion shapes up just as forcefully as Jaca's:

> I have said it a thousand times, and now I repeat it in the presence of this Sovereign Body: if the independence from Spain is to cause us a single injustice; if it is necessary to continue the oppression of humanity in order to sustain the Republic, may it perish, may there be no gold, may we be slaves of the Spaniards, but may we be virtuous (Restrepo 111).[33]

Resting on the defense of natural law, this speech allowed the Antioquian to denounce African slavery as a violence imposed by *ius gentium*. However, he was to introduce three ideas that would transform the course of his conclusions. The first has to do with the fear of a general slave rebellion that was considered imminent in a republic that maintained slavery; the second refers to the doubts generated by the integration of freedmen into the republic; and the third is the sensitive matter of owners' property rights. Given these considerations, abolition, although posed as the only antidote for the ills that slavery could lead to in the republic, is presented as an equally dangerous measure, because although it would reduce the risk of a slave uprising, it would generate great social instability that would be even more pernicious to the social order:

> I agree to the principle that slavery should be destroyed without destroying the owner [. . .]; not granting freedom is brutality; granting it all at once is hasty. Social freedom has gradations and requires a certain disposition of those who receive it in order to not be dangerous [. . .] On the other hand, whites who under the authority of existing laws have employed their fortune in a type of commerce, no matter how unjust it be [. . .], should not be ruined at once by another error of legislators. We are in a situation in which we cannot be entirely just (Restrepo 124).[34]

The way out of this contradiction was the application of the so-called law of "free womb." This republican law was inspired by the same Roman Law tradition used by Jaca and defined the legal status of the children as dependent upon the status of the mother. However, as we shall see, Restrepo applies this norm in an entirely divergent way. Freeing the wombs of female slaves the republican law, in its 1814 version as well as the version approved by the Congress of Cúcuta in 1821, granted manumission to the infants born after its proclamation. Nevertheless, in order to protect the property rights of owners, the law required manumitted infants to work as slaves for the owners of their mothers until adulthood. However, after this time their freedom was not granted immediately, but was subject to further examination. A group of "virtuous men," were to judge whether the manumitted complied with norms of good conduct in order to deserve freedom and a place in the republic. Moreover, the law ordered that the manumission of the rest of the enslaved population required the disposition of public funds in order to repay owners. In this sense, the law defended by Restrepo, contrary to his initial statements, resisted the application of freedom as a natural right and denied any chance of considering it as a political right guaranteed by the free community.

Final Reflections

The purpose of this article has been to examine a hypothesis suggesting that Jaca's revolutionary abolitionist proposal outlined the discursive themes that, from the end of the seventeenth century to the moment of the construction of the modern nation, were used to enunciate the defense of freedom as a natural and unconditional right. Conceived as a divine mandate, the natural freedom constituted the basis of the Christian republic and drew its argumentative force from the defense of natural law and from a consistent critique of *ius gentium*. Jaca's *Resolución* adds to this critique and constitutes a radical response to the scholars of the School of Salamanca and their followers, whose efforts contributed to the consolidation of the authority of *ius gentium* as the necessary discursive framework to sustain a colonial order, the global and transnational logic of which turned out to be profoundly dependent upon African slavery.

More than a century later, in the context of the Spanish American war of independence, the long-lasting influence of Jaca's argumentation to denounce *ius gentium* and to defend natural freedom is evident in Restrepo's discourse against slavery. In spite of his initial opposition, however, Restrepo ended up concocting a proposal to manumit the offspring of female slaves while maintaining slavery.

The key issue, present in the discourse of both Jaca and Restrepo, was the transforming character the womb of the mother had on the identity of those considered as citizens of the political community, be it the *civis sanctorum* or the independent republic. These authors reinterpreted, in their own way, the particular Roman legal law of *partus ventrem sequitur*. Jaca associated the Church with a free female womb. As such, the Church as a free mother guarantees the political freedom to those who, through baptism, become its children and citizens of the *civis sanctorum*. The conclusion that follows is that all Africans who were baptized in the Christian faith are free not just as a consequence of the first principle of natural law, but also because they belong to a political community that guarantees that freedom. They are also citizens because as children of the Church participate of the *filia*, the brotherhood relationship that constitutes the republic. Using these arguments, Jaca was able to place the responsibility for the injustice committed in the enslavement of naturally free people and the costs of reparation the abolition entailed on the body politic (the community of citizens as children of the Church), as a whole.

Contrary to Jaca's discourse, Restrepo applied the Roman law of the *partus ventrem sequitur* literally. The law of "free womb" in its 1814 version, as well as the version approved by the Congress of Cúcuta in 1821, replaced the body politic of the Church with the body of individual female slaves and in doing so, Restrepo was able to take the idea of freedom out of the realm of politics, and introduce it into the realm of private and domestic life. In this context, the meaning of freedom became naturalized in the body of individual female slaves, and lost its condition of natural right, pertaining to the Christian political community as a whole. Accordingly, Restrepo's speech construes freedom as a philanthropic act. Moreover, it privileges economic reparations to the owners over economic reparations to the slaves, thereby producing the least impact possible on private interests and on those of the nascent creole republic.

The comparison this article has undertaken between Jaca's radical discourse in favor of slave abolition and Restrepo's proposal of gradual manumission reveals the political denial on which the colonial global order was structured. This denial that continued to guarantee the function of slave systems far into the republican era allowed the creole elite to postpone the recognition of fundamental political rights to the population of African descent. In this sense, the intellectual efforts of Jaca, though apparently futile in their time, constitute a lasting legacy of discourses in defense of radical natural freedom as the central element of the political communities, a powerful tool that the creole elite of the global colonial empire and of the independent republic endeavored to reduce and domesticate through the principles of *ius gentium*.

NOTES

1. Francisco de Vitoria's ideas were especially prevalent in *De indis posterior sive de iure belli* (1539).
2. For the development of natural law in imperial Rome, see: Schiavone, *Ius. La invención del Derecho en Occidente* 331–55.
3. On the debate about slavery in the development of the Atlantic revolutions see James 62–144; Dubois 155–221; and Pope Melish 50–83.
4. On the importance of the Spanish *misiones* (missions) during the process of conquest and colonization in general, see Stern.
5. See Pollak-Eltz; Sánchez 77–99; Landers 93–101; Navarrete; Cáceres.
6. In 1680 a royal decree authorized the Capuchin order to "reduce" *cimarrones* to colonial towns. See De Carrocera, *Misión de los Capuchinos* 430–31. However, some communities of *cimarrones* reached a deal with the colonial authorities to support the missionaries in the *reduccciones*. For the case of Cartagena, see Tardieu 169–81.
7. The biographical information on Jaca outlined here is based on Peña, "Estudio Introductorio"; and López 32–46.
8. Moirans, *Servi liberi seu naturalis mancipiorum libertatis iusta defensio*, translated from Latin to Spanish, annotated and published in: Peña González, *Epifanio de Moirans*. See also López García, 177–298.

9. On the sources of laws justifying the enslavement of Africans see García, *El pensamiento* 115–30; Gallego and García Añoveros.
10. "¿Qué razón de guerra justa hay entre españoles y negros [. . .] que por esclavos con tanta violencia, ignominia y tiranía de sus naturales tierras a éstas y otras más remotas para ser como son, vendidos y revendidos con los maltratamientos que constan?"
11. According to Jaca this mandate connects the first principle (the will of God) with the second principle (human will), the latter understood as the source of *ius gentium*. Pagden, *La caída* 94–97 offers a discussion of the concepts of natural law and *ius gentium* in relation with the first and second principles.
12. "¿A quién de mediano discurso se le ha de esconder, que gentes bárbaras cuya ceguedad atropella a cada paso con la ley de Dios, viviendo como fieras han de tener, ni alcanzar fundamentos justificados, para dichas guerras (caso que las fraguaran)?"
13. "[. . .] aunque fuera verdad, dado que los tales [africanos] en sus sediciosos disturbios vivan como fieras, pueden ser buscados (según dice Aristóteles) para que vivan en sociabilidad humana, pero de ninguna manera con la opresión de tal y tan vilipendiosa servidumbre, porque si mejorara el derecho quirito o político, empeoraban el natural que es el fundamento de los otros."
14. ". . . sino ser de él mismo, lo que constituye en ser de hombre, por lo racional libre y por lo libre racional."
15. ". . . gente bestial, digna de mortal castigo."
16. See Hanke; Maestre Sánchez 91–134; Pagden, *La caída*; Brion Davis 165–91.
17. See Abellán; Pérez Luño 27–42; and Pagden "Human Rights."
18. Vitoria 129–50; See the discussion about this matter in Pagden, *La caída* 113–16; Pérez Luño 89–92; Añaños 525–96; Peña, "Los Derechos Humanos."
19. For a discussion of Soto's opinions, see Peña González, "Entre la encomienda" 263–78; and Tomás de Mercado, *Suma de tratos y contratos* 102r.–107v. Luis de Molina deals with this matter in *Seis libros de justicia* initially published in 1593. On his arguments, see García, "Luís de Molina" 307–29; and Costello 163–98. See also Obregón 424–52. In 1588, Molina published *Concordia liberi arbitrii cum gratiae donis, divina scientia, praescientia, providentia, praedestinatione*. This work would trigger one of the biggest theological controversies of the era, for its defense of the role of human freedom in interpreting natural law and grace. The influence of this work contributed to the authority of *ius gentium* to be imposed over the authority of natural law. On the matter see Costello 207–18. On the development of the theory of *ius gentium* in Francisco Suárez see Pereña, "La génesis."
20. Ginés de Sepúlveda and Francisco de Vitoria agreed that the concept of "natural servitude" of the barbarians, as defined by Aristotle, does not mean slavery or the privation of natural freedom, but rather the exercise of a political control of the wisest over the weak and savage. Notwithstanding this coincidence, their conclusions differ. While Sepúlveda alleges that just war and the control over the savage is licit under natural law, Vitoria, using the authority of *ius gentium*, explains that harm suffered is the only cause that justifies war, and he shows that the "savages"

of the New World have harmed the Spaniards in many ways, particularly opposing the "law of free communication" and, consequently, deserve war and slavery (Sepulveda 81–85, 163; Vitoria, "Sobre los indios" 129–50, and "Sobre el derecho a la Guerra" 173–212). See also Pagden, *La caída* 93–150. For a historical review of the matter of barbarism and slavery in Greek and medieval Christian philosophies, see Brion Davis 60–102. For Aristotle's position on the matter, which has been considered rather incoherent, see Millet.

21. Following Vitoria, Molina claims that the wars of the Portuguese against Africans in Angola are just because they are a response to harm received. Vitoria also maintained that the wars between African peoples were as just as any other war and that the slaves resulting from these wars should be accepted as legitimate. See Pagden, *La caída* 52, 58; and Costello 174–85.

22. Tomás de Mercado 103r.–104v. See Molina's opinion in *De Iustitia et Iure*, volume 2, argument 34, cited in Costello 177. See also García, "Luís de Molina" 319. Jaca adopts a similar position, as we have seen (quote above).

23. See Las Casas; Almeida de Souza 58–86; Peña González, "Entre la encomienda," 263–78.

24. "[. . .] "nunca perjudicaron ni injuriaron a la fe, ni jamás impedirla pensaron y aquellas tierras tenían de buena fe porque nunca nos despojaron [. . .] ¿pues con qué razón y justicia podrán justificar ni excusar tantos males y agravios, tantas muertes y cautiverios, tantos escándalos y perdición de tantas ánimas como en aquellas pobres gentes aunque fuesen moros hicieron los portugueses? ¿nomás de porque eran infieles? Gran ignorancia y damnable ceguedad ciertamente fue esta" (Las Casas 67) ([. . .] "they never harmed or jeopardized the faith, nor did they think of banning it, and they possessed those lands in good faith because they never robbed us [. . .] so with what reason or justice can the Portuguese justify or excuse so many ills and insults, so many deaths and captivities, so many scandals and the perdition of so many souls among those poor people, even though they were blacks? Just because they were infidels? This was surely great ignorance and damnable blindness."

25. One of these authors was the Jesuit Alonso de Sandoval who during his mission in Cartagena of the Indies wrote a treatise to establish an appropriate technology for the evangelization of Africans that arrived as slaves to that port (Sandoval, *De instaurata*; Chaves, *Genealogías*). Jaca read and cited Sandoval's work (Jaca Part 2, title 43). However, his intentions were diametrically opposed to those of Sandoval's.

26. "Considerándonos el Apóstol San Pablo sellados en el santo bautismo con la sangre de Cristo Jesús, nos dice a todos los fieles no ser hijos de esclavitud sino de peculiar libertad."

27. ". . . ya no son extraños ni forasteros, sino conciudadanos de los santos y familiares de Dios" and "para que nadie ose encuadernar [. . .] el ser ciudadano con el ser esclavo, y serlo de la Iglesia con la esclavitud en ella."

28. Francisco de Vitoria, inspired by Aristotle, defines the *civis* as the space in which natural man is transformed into civil man, in full use of all of his faculties and

abilities to rule over the world and defines those who, despite possessing the potential ability to do so, have not managed to overcome their natural state as "savages." In the final part of "Sobre los indios" and in "Sobre el derecho a la Guerra," Vitoria justifies the Spaniards' control over the Natives, with reasons from *ius gentium* (55–149, 151–212). Jaca seems to redefine the political concept of the *civis*, therein distancing himself from Vitoria.

29. "... ser intérprete y declarar algunas cosas acerca del Derecho Natural..."
30. For a more complete analysis of Restrepo's speech and its relationship to other contemporary discourse, see Chaves, "El oxymoron," wherein some of Jaca's arguments are briefly reviewed.
31. Some of the first Spanish American republics wrote constitutions even before declaring their independence. Thus there was included a formula by which the links of subordination to the absent Spanish Monarchy were maintained, to varying degrees. On the particular case of the New Kingdom of Granada, see Uribe-Urán, "La Eclosión" and "Insurgentes" 17–48. Between 1810 and 1820, these constitutional texts, although inspired by the Constitution of the United States, conceived of natural freedom through the Hispanic neo-scholastic tradition associated with divine natural law. See Stoetzer.
32. "Tan lejos está la Religión Cristiana de proteger la esclavitud, que nada hay más contrario a ella. El Evangelio lo prescribe enteramente: *Amarás a tu prójimo como a ti mismo* [...] *No hagas a otro lo que no quisieras que se hiciese contigo*, dicta la misma religión, y es un deber del hombre en sociedad, como lo han repetido con entusiasmo los gobiernos de Europa y América."
33. "Mil veces lo he dicho, y ahora lo repito a presencia de este Cuerpo Soberano: si la independencia de España nos ha de costar una sola injusticia; si es necesario continuar la opresión de la humanidad para sostener la República, perezca ésta, no haya oro, seamos esclavos de los españoles, pero seamos virtuosos."
34. "Convengo en el principio de que la esclavitud debe destruirse, sin destruir al propietario [...]; no conceder la libertad es una barbarie; darla de repente es una precipitación. La libertad social tiene grados y necesita cierta disposición en los que la reciben para que no sea peligrosa [...] Por otra parte los blancos que, bajo la autoridad de las leyes existentes, han empleado su caudal en una especie de comercio, por más injusto que sea [...], no deben ser arruinados de repente por otro nuevo error de los legisladores. Estamos en un caso en que no podemos ser enteramente justos."

WORKS CITED

Abellán, Joaquín. "El vínculo entre la tradición y el mundo moderno: Las teorías políticas de Derecho Natural, 1600–1750." *Historia de la Teoría Política*. Vol. 2. Ed. Fernando Vellespín. Madrid: Alianza Editorial, 1995. 7–68.

Alcacer, Antonio. *Las Misiones capuchinas en el Nuevo Reino de Granada, hoy Colombia (1648–1820)*. Bogota: Ediciones Seminario Seráfico Misional Capuchino, 1959.

Almeida de Souza, Juliana. "Guerra justa y gobierno de los esclavos: La defensa de la esclavitud negra en Bartolomé de las Casas y Alonso de Sandoval." *Genealogías de la Diferencia: Tecnologías de la salvación y representación de los africanos esclavizados en Iberoamérica colonial*. Ed. María Eugenia Chaves. Bogota and Quito: Editorial de la Pontificia Universidad Javeriana y Abya-Yala, 2009. 58–86.

Añaños, María C. "El título de 'sociedad y comunicación natural' de Francisco de Vitoria: Tras las huellas de su concepto a la luz de la teoría del dominio." *Anuario Mexicano de Derecho Internacional* 12 (2012): 525–96. Web. May 2014.

Aquinas, Tomas de. *The Summa Theologica, First Part of the Second Part*. Trans. Fathers of the English Dominican Province. New York: Benziger Bros. edition, 1947. Web: dhspriory.org/thomas/english/summa/FS/FS091.html#FSQ91OUTP1. September 2016.

Avendaño, Diego de. *Corregidores, encomenderos, cabildos y mercaderes: Thesaurus Indicus*. Vol. I, Tit. VI–IX (1668). Edited, introduced, and translated by Ángel Muñoz García. Colección de Pensamiento Medieval y Renacentista 93. Pamplona: Ediciones Universidad de Navarra. 2007.

Baraibar, Álvaro, Bernat Castany, Bernat Hernández, and Mercedes Serna, eds. *Hombres de a pie y de a caballo: Conquistadores, cronistas, misioneros en la América colonial de los siglos XVI y XVII*. New York: IDEAS, IGAS, 2013.

Barcala, Andrés. "La Edad Media." *Historia de la Teoría Política*. Vol. 1. Ed. Fernando Vellespín. Madrid: Alianza Editorial, 1995. 217–324.

Bragoni, Beatríz. "Esclavos insurrectos en tiempos de revolución (Cuyo 1812)." *"Negros de la Patria": Los afrodescendientes en las luchas por la independencia en el Antiguo Virreinato del Río de la Plata*. Eds. Silvia Mallo and I. Telesca. Buenos Aires: SB, 2010. 113–31.

Brion Davis, David. *El problema de la esclavitud en la cultura occidental*. Bogota: Ancora Editores, 1996.

Cáceres, Rina. "Mandingas, congos y zapes: Las primeras estrategias de libertad en la frontera comercial de Cartagena, Panamá siglo XVI." *Afrodescendientes en las Américas. Trayectorias sociales e identitarias: 150 años de la abolición de la esclavitud en Colombia*. Eds. C. Mosquera, M. Pardo, and O. Hoffmann. Bogota: Universidad Nacional de Colombia, Instituto Colombiano de Antropología e Historia, 2002. 143–69.

Chaves, María Eugenia. *Genealogías de la Diferencia: Tecnologías de la salvación y representación de los africanos esclavizados en Iberoamérica colonial*. Bogota and Quito: Editorial de la Pontificia Universidad Javeriana y Abya-Yala, 2009.

———. "Nos los esclavos de Medellín." *Nómadas* 33 (2010): 43–55.

———. "El oxímoron de la libertad: La esclavitud de los vientres libres y la crítica a la esclavización africana en tres discursos revolucionarios." *Fronteras de la Historia* 19:1 (Jan.–June 2014): 174–200.

Copleston, Frederick. *Historia de la Filosofía*. Vol. 3: De Ockham a Suárez. Barcelona: Ariel, 1989.

Costello, Frank B. *The Political Philosophy of Luis de Molina, S.J. (1535–1600)*. Rome: Institutum Historicum S. I.—Gonzaga University Press, 1974.
De Carrocera, Buenaventura (capuchino). *Misión de los Capuchinos en los Llanos de Caracas*. Tomo 1. *Introducción y Resumen Histórico. Documentos (1657–1699)*. Caracas: Biblioteca de la Academia Nacional de Historia, 1972.
Dubois, Laurent. *A Colony of Citizens: Revolution and Slave Emancipation in the French Caribbean 1787–1804*. Chapel Hill: University of North Carolina Press, 2004.
Gallego, Andrés, and José García Añoveros. *La Iglesia y la Esclavitud de los Negros*. Navarra: Universidad de Navarra, 2002.
García Añoveros, Jesús María. *El pensamiento y los argumentos sobre la esclavitud en Europa en el siglo XVI y su aplicación a los indios americanos y a los negros africanos*. Madrid: Consejo Superior de Investigaciones Científicas, 2000.
———. "Luís de Molina y la esclavitud de los negros africanos en el siglo XVI: Principios doctrinales y conclusions." *Revista de Indias* 60:219 (2000): 307–25.
Hanke, Lewis. *All Mankind is One: A Study of the Disputation Between Bartolomé de Las Casas and Juan Ginés de Sepúlveda in 1550 on the Intellectual and Religious Capacity of the American Indians*. DeKalb: Northern Illinois University Press, 1974. Translators Jorge Avendaño-Inestrillas and Margarita Sepúlveda. Mexico City: Fondo de Cultura Económica, 1985.
Jaca, Francisco José. *Resolución sobre la Libertad de los Negros y sus originarios, en estado de paganos y después ya cristianos: La primera condena de la esclavitud en el pensamiento hispano*. Edited, introduction, and annotated by Miguel Anxo Peña González. Madrid: Consejo Superior de Investigaciones Científicas, 2002.
James, C. L. R. *The Black Jacobins: Toussaint L'Ouverture and the San Domingo Revolution*. New York: Vintage Books, 1989.
Landers, Jean. "Conspiradores esclavizados en Cartagena de Indias en el siglo XVII." *Afrodescendientes en las Américas. Trayectorias sociales e identitarias: 150 años de la abolición de la esclavitud en Colombia*. Eds. C. Mosquera, M. Pardo, and O. Hoffmann. Bogota: Universidad Nacional de Colombia, Instituto Colombiano de Antropología e Historia. 2002. 93–101.
Las Casas, Bartolomé de. *Brevísima relación de la destrucción del África. Preludio de la Destrucción de Indias: primera defensa de los guanches y negros contra su esclavización*. Ed. Isacio Pérez Fernández. Salamanca: Editorial San Esteban, 1989.
"Ley sobre la manumisión de la posteridad de los esclavos africanos y sobre los medios de redimir sucesivamente a sus padres." *Gazeta Ministerial de la República de Antioquia* Año segundo de su independencia, Numero 2, semestre 1 (domingo 2 de octubre de 1814): 6–7. Biblioteca Nacional de Colombia, Sala Samper, BGN VFDU 1–477, no. 8. Bogota, Colombia. MS.
López García, José Tomás. *Dos defensores de los esclavos negros en el siglo XVII (Francisco José de Jaca y Epifanio de Moirans)*. Caracas: Universidad Católica Andrés Bello, 1982.
Maestre Sánchez, Alfonso. "'Todas las gentes del mundo son hombres': El gran debate entre Fray Bartolomé de las Casas (1474–1566) y Juan Ginés de Sepúlveda (1490–1573)." *Anales del Seminario de Historia de la Filosofía* 21 (2004): 91–134. Web. May 2014.

Mercado, Tomás de. *Suma de Tratos y Contratos: Dividida en seis libros.* Seville: Casa de Fernando Díaz, 1587.
Millet, Paul. "Aristotle and Slavery in Athens." *Greece & Rome,* Second Series, 54:2 (Oct. 2007): 178–209. Web. February 2014.
Molina, Luis. *De iustitia et Iure tomi sex.* Vols. 1–6. Maguncia, 1659.
_____. *Seis libros de justicia y derecho.* Trans. Manuel Fraga Iribarne. Madrid: Consejo Superior de Investigaciones Científicas, 1947.
_____. *Concordia del libre arbitrio con los dones de la gracia y con la presciencia, providencia, predestinación y reprobación divinas.* Translation to Spanish, introduction, and annotation, Juan Antonio Hevia Echevarría. Oviedo: Biblioteca Filosofía en Español, Fundación Gustavo Bueno, 2007. Versión digital en: filosofia.org/cla/mol/index.htm.
Mosquera, Claudia, Mauricio Pardo, and Odile Hoffmann, eds. *Afrodescendientes en las Américas. Trayectorias sociales e identitarias: 150 años de la abolición de la esclavitud en Colombia.* Bogota: Universidad Nacional de Colombia, Instituto Colombiano de Antropología e Historia. 2002.
Navarrete, María Cristina. *Cimarrones y palenques en el siglo XVII.* Cali: Universidad del Valle, 2003.
Obregón, Liliana. "Críticas tempranas a la esclavización de los africanos." *Afrodescendientes en las Américas. Trayectorias sociales e identitarias: 150 años de la abolición de la esclavitud en Colombia.* Eds. C. Mosquera, M. Pardo, and O. Hoffmann. Bogota: Universidad Nacional de Colombia, Instituto Colombiano de Antropología e Historia. 2002. 424–52.
Olsen, Margaret. *Slavery and Salvation in Colonial Cartagena de Indias.* Gainesville: University Press of Florida, 2004.
Pagden, Anthony. *La caída del hombre natural: El hombre americano y los orígenes de la etnología comparativa.* Madrid: Alianza Editorial, 1988.
_____. *Señores de todo el mundo: Ideologías del imperio en España, Inglaterra y Francia (en los siglos XVI, XVII y XVIII).* Barcelona: Península, 1995.
Peña González, Miguel Anxo. "Estudio Preliminar." *Resolución sobre la libertad de los negros y sus originarios, en estado de paganos y después de cristianos: La primera condena a la esclavitud en el pensamiento hispano.* Ed. Miguel Anxo Peña González. Madrid: Consejo Superior de Investigaciones Científicas, 2002. xxiii–xcviii.
_____. *Francisco José de Jaca: La primera propuesta abolicionista de la esclavitud en el pensamiento hispano.* Salamanca: Universidad Pontificia, 2003.
_____., ed. *Epifanio de Moirans. Siervos libres. Una propuesta antiesclavista a finales del siglo XVII.* Madrid: Consejo Superior de Investigaciones Científicas, 2007.
_____. "Derechos Humanos en la Escuela de Salamanca." *Derechos humanos en Europa.* Coord. José Román Flecha Andrés. Salamanca: Universidad Pontificia de Salamanca—Instituto de Estudios Europeos y Derechos Humanos, 2009. 51–78.
_____. "Entre la encomienda de los naturales y la esclavitud de los africanos: continuidad de las razones." *Hombres de a pie y de a caballo: Conquistadores, cronistas, misioneros en la América colonial de los siglos XVI y XVII.* Eds. Baraibar, et al. New York: IDEAS, IGAS, 2013. 263–78.

Pereña, Luciano. "La génesis saureciana del Ius Gentium." *De Legibus*. Vol. IV. Estudio preliminar. Francisco Suárez. Madrid: Corpus Hispanorum de Pace, CSIC, 1973. xix–lxxii.

———. "La tesis de la paz dinámica." *Relectio De Jure Belli, O, Paz Dinámica: Escuela Española De La Paz Primera Generación, 1526–1560*. Francisco de Vitoria. Madrid: Consejo Superior de Investigaciones Científicas, 1981. 29–94.

Pérez Luño, Antonio Enrique. *La polémica sobre el Nuevo Mundo: Los clásicos españoles de la Filosofía del Derecho*. Madrid: Trotta, 1992.

Pollak-Eltz, Angelina. *La esclavitud en Venezuela: Un estudio histórico-cultural*. Caracas: Universidad Católica Andrés Bello, 2000.

Pope Melish, Joanne. *Disowning Slavery: Gradual Emancipation and "Race" in New England, 1780–1860*. Ithaca: Cornell University Press, 1998.

Restrepo, Félix. "Discurso sobre la manumisión de esclavos, pronunciado en el soberano Congreso de Colombia reunido en la Villa del Rosario de Cúcuta en el año de 1821." *Vida y escritos del doctor José Félix de Restrepo*. Ed. G. Hernández de Alba. Bogota: Imprenta Nacional, 1935. 82–132.

Sánchez, Sandra. "Miedo, rumor y rebelión: La conspiración esclava de 1693 en Cartagena de Indias." *Historia Crítica* 31 (Jan.–June 2006): 77–99.

Sandoval, Alonso. *Naturaleza, policía sagrada y profana, costumbres y ritos, disciplina y catecismo evangélico de todos Etíopes*. Seville: Francisco de Lira Impresor, 1627.

———. *De instaurata aethiopum salute: Historia de AEthiopia. Dividida en 2 tomos*. Madrid: Alonso Paredes, 1647.

Schiavone, Aldo. *Ius: La invención del Derecho en Occidente*. Buenos Aires: Adriana Hidalgo, 2009.

Sepúlveda, Ginés. *Tratado sobre las justas causas de la guerra contra los indios* [*Democrates Alter De Iustis Belli causis apud indos*, c. 1547]. Trans. Manuel García Pelayo. Mexico City: Fondo de Cultura Económica, 1996.

Stoetzer, Carlos. *Las raíces escolásticas de la emancipación de la América española*. Madrid: Centro de Estudios Constitucionales, 1982.

Tardieu, Jean-Pierre. "Un proyecto utópico de manumisión de los cimarrones del 'palenque de los montes de Cartagena' en 1682." *Afrodescendientes en las Américas. Trayectorias sociales e identitarias: 150 años de la abolición de la esclavitud en Colombia*. Eds. C. Mosquera, M. Pardo, and O. Hoffmann. Bogota: Universidad Nacional de Colombia, Instituto Colombiano de Antropología e Historia. 2002. 169–81.

Uribe-Urán, Víctor Manuel. "La Eclosión Constitucional en la Nueva Granada y el Constitucionalismo Atlántico en la Década de 1810." *Coloquio Internacional Independencias y Constituciones: Otra Mirada al Bicentenario*. Cartagena: Corte Constitucional de Colombia—Centro de Estudios Históricos—Universidad Externado de Colombia, November 8–10, 2010.

———. "Insurgentes de provincia: Tunja, Nueva Granada, y el constitucionalismo en el mundo hispánico en la década de 1810." *Historia y Memoria* 5 (July–Dec. 2012): 17–48.

Vitoria, Francisco de. *Sobre el poder civil* [*De potestate civili* 1528]. *Sobre los indios* [*De indis prior* 1538–1539]. *Sobre el derecho a la Guerra* [*De indis posterior sive de iure belli* 1539]. Ed. Luis Frayle Delgado. Madrid: Tecnos, 1998.

Stern, Steve. "Paradigms of Conquest: History, Historiography, and Politics." *Journal of Latin American Studies: The Colonial and Post-Colonial Experience. Five Centuries of Spanish and Portuguese America* 24 (1992): 1–34. Web. May 2014.

◆ CHAPTER EIGHT

Jesuits and Indigenous Subjects in the Global Culture of Letters

Production, Circulation, and Adaptation of Missionary Texts in the Seventeenth and Eighteenth Centuries[1]

Guillermo Wilde
Payton Phillips Quintanilla, translator

Beginning in the early seventeenth century, the Society of Jesus developed a missionary program among the indigenous communities of the South American Lowlands in an effort to expand the control of the Catholic monarchy over remote regions. The initiative resulted in a new autonomous Jesuit province called Paracuaria, which covered a wide territory represented by the jurisdictions of Río de la Plata, Tucumán, Asunción, and Chile. In that region, the Jesuits founded several dozen mission towns or reductions (*reducciones*), the majority of which survived even after the expulsion of the order from all Spanish dominions in 1767. In addition to integrating indigenous subjects into the colonial system, the missions sought to defend the territory, thus contributing to an autonomous sociopolitical, economic, and military organizational structure constituted almost exclusively of indigenous peoples under the supervision of the Jesuit priests. The missions formed part of a constellation of Jesuit establishments that, during a period of more than 150 years, housed successive generations of missionaries arriving from different parts of Europe and the Viceroyalty of Peru, as well as slaves of African descent and thousands of native speakers of diverse indigenous languages.

Although these spaces functioned as points in their own networks for the circulation of peoples, texts, and objects, it is only recently that historiography became interested in the connections that were maintained among them. Classic studies on the history of the church tended to treat the missions in this part of South America as isolated spaces unconnected to one another, and their indigenous inhabitants as passive recipients of the Gospel imposed from the centers of ecclesiastical authority.[2] Marked by a clearly institutional focus, traditional historiography centered almost exclusively on the factual reconstruction of the establishment of these most distant missions, and of the career trajectories of specific Jesuits, mainly Europeans, who were sent there. Since the 1970s, new historiographic currents have sought to reintegrate these spaces into regional and global networks, reconstructing the economic and political connections among types of Jesuit establishments.[3] Although this turn in the literature was fundamental to the new academic agenda, it suffered from two limitations. First, by prioritizing the economic and practical aspects of the missions, it left by the wayside an analysis of the cultural and symbolic. Second, it conceived of the indigenous population as passive participants in the formation and consolidation of the mission towns. From the 1990s forward, the discovery of new primary sources and the development of new critical approaches produced an interpretative turn that highlighted the importance of the cultural dimension and of indigenous agency. Studies on the role of the Society of Jesus in the expansion of the Iberian empires and in the worldwide dissemination of the arts and sciences acquired particular relevance for this turn, as did ethno-histories concerned with the interactions between priests and indigenous peoples in local missionary contexts. These two levels of analysis of missionary activity, however, have not been sufficiently placed in dialogue until now.[4]

This chapter proposes their simultaneous consideration based on an analysis of one aspect of missionary culture: textual production. Since the founding of the order, the Ignatians placed great importance on the circulation of reports about their overseas missions, which they recorded through diverse types of texts, manuscripts, and printed works. These texts were supported by a centralized and hierarchical system of data collection that the order promoted from Rome and the principal European metropolises, to which letters flowed from geographically isolated regions. Within the large repertoire of circulating texts it is possible to identify, on the one hand, those oriented toward the description and establishment of typologies and classifications of the indigenous groups targeted for conversion—in other words, generalizations and abstractions useful to colonial administration and the organization of missionary activity—, and, on the other hand, practical texts directly concerned with pastoral work and answering the daily demands of the missions. While the first type of text manifested the capacity of the Jesuits to construct a global missionary order, uniting diverse pieces (the non-Christian societies of the world) within a single frame that had as its center the Society of Jesus, the second type of text expressed adaptations to the specific contexts of local customs, placing in evidence not only the negotiations between priests and indigenous subjects, but also the direct participation of the latter in the texts' production.[5]

I am interested in analyzing both levels of textual production—that of the abstract, centralizing typologies, and that of the practical texts—as part of a single process in which knowledge was generated and then constantly updated during the seventeenth and eighteenth centuries. I will analyze the characteristics of these texts and the ways in which they were interconnected in the same missionary endeavor. I suggest that while one type of text promoted detached but administratively useful cultural and political classifications based on the abstraction of direct missionary experience and the treatment of indigenous subjects as mere objects of conversion, the other expressed the concrete negotiations that priests maintained with the indigenous population brought into the space of the mission, and the limits that this negotiation imposed on the rigid application of metropolitan models. This apparent opposition between types of texts reveals complementary and simultaneous orientations in Jesuit missionary print production as promoted by the order: one that was centralizing, hierarchical, abstract, and intended to reinforce a corporate identity before a European audience; and another that was adaptive to local contexts and designed to facilitate communication with, and the indoctrination of, indigenous peoples.

In each case, their function and practice differed. The texts based on a typological knowledge of the indigenous population were oriented toward organizing missionary activity from the top down, as well as facilitating communication among different parts of the Jesuit corporation (and the colonial administration in general). The texts based in practical experience proposed to make evangelization of, and interaction with, the indigenous population more effective, an objective that necessarily demanded increased flexibility in the ostensibly rigid regulations imposed by the centers of power; or, in certain cases, an acceptance of orders without the intention of following them. Although the general framework of the production and circulation of texts was dictated by the central authorities of the order, indigenous peoples, as we will see, actively participated in shaping both their forms and uses, thereby contributing to their transformation. If these indigenous subjects indeed became integrated into a global culture by adopting the codes and conditions imposed by the colonial process, they also acquired autonomy within that process. For their part, the priests, although they defended a coherent corporate identity and culture in their most widely circulated texts, not only accepted but also encouraged indigenous autonomy in the creation of missionary texts, reflecting an adaptive attitude that followed the Jesuit "way of proceeding."[6]

Typologies and Classifications

Missionary spaces were connected to each other in diverse ways and formed part of a greater network to which urban schools and residences also belonged. However, while priests located in cities established strong social, political, and economic ties with the local elites, the rural spaces fomented productive activities and commercial networks that extended throughout the entire viceroyalty of Peru. In turn, each province of the order participated in wider transatlantic connections.[7] As part of the administrative policies of the order, priests had to circulate through various missionary establishments, alternating posts and positions, and were not permitted to stay in any one of them for a prolonged amount of time. This regional circulation of people drove the spread of information that connected diverse Jesuit spaces. With the objective of obtaining benefits from the monarchs, recruiting new missionaries, and informing the order's Superior General of their provinces' needs, specific Jesuit provinces periodically sent priests named procurators (*procuradores*) to Rome and the European courts. As Markus Friedrich has shown, the bureaucratic system that supported these information and communication networks required a high level of formalization and verticality in which the order's Roman administration fulfilled a fundamental role, although the different provinces distributed throughout the world also had a certain margin of autonomy in decision-making.[8]

All of the Jesuit provinces operated in a similar manner. The production of texts of various types was the primary method of communication between the numerous Jesuit establishments, as well as the principal mechanism employed by the Jesuit Superior General in Rome to centralize the activity of the order and monitor the performance of priests spread throughout the world. Standing out among the salient characteristics of the order's internal circulation of information was the hierarchical organization, centralization, and regulation of writing. Nonetheless, the Jesuits that inhabited the frontier missions enjoyed a wider margin of liberty in decision-making and writing activities, given the concrete circumstances of their posts: long distances and isolation, unstable economic conditions, and persistent dangers.

Throughout the entire period of Jesuit action in the overseas territories, there was a constant flow of information that encompassed all aspects of missionary work, from the purely administrative to the "scientific." Print production based in exploratory travels multiplied with the growth of the order, giving the impression of an inexhaustible effort to reach the farthest corners of the world. In the eighteenth century, especially, the order published collections of letters and administrative documents in formats destined for a broad public; relating the experiences of Jesuits from diverse European provinces in missions overseas, these texts were widely embraced by European readers.[9] In this manner, the Jesuit press acquired a leading role in the emergence of a "world consciousness" that contributed to the monumentalization of the order in the expansion of the Catholic world.

The texts that constructed and standardized classifications and typologies of the societies targeted for conversion occupied a prominent space in this missionary corpus. Frequently, the Jesuit texts of greatest circulation compared peoples that populated the various spaces of the mission, including them in general classifications according to their ways of life, their religion, and their customs. Although we know from the Jesuits' less-circulated registers that local realities were much more nuanced and complex, most official chronicles, as we will see, favored the idea of an ordered and homogenous missionary space. The Jesuits did not waiver in crystalizing that image with the goal of emphasizing the efficacy of their work, generating among European readers a solid imaginary of the order and the good governance of its provinces.[10]

Jesuit representations were concerned not only with describing the religious beliefs of each society but also the sphere of their civil and political practices, which were to be respected as long as they did not threaten the Christian religion. There is no doubt that the ultimate goal of the priests was always the conversion of the natives, which is why the supposed ethnographic interest of these texts should always be approached with caution. The high period of Jesuit evangelization was marked by directives from the Third Council of Lima, which established much more rigid and uniform doctrinal models than those that had characterized an initial period of evangelization more open to local beliefs.[11] In any case, it is fair to point out that in many instances the Jesuit texts allowed a certain anthropological curiosity about—and even secular reflections on—indigenous societies to surface, especially in reference to native languages or civil practices that posed no threat to Christianity.[12]

A search for the earliest attempts at a "comparative ethnology" leads inevitably to the work of the Jesuit José de Acosta (1540–1600), who constructed a typology of peoples as differentiated into three classes. The first class possessed a stable political regime, public laws, fortified cities, magistrates, commerce, and writing. The second class, which included American peoples (*naciones*) such as the Incas and the Aztecs, had governmental systems, fixed settlements, administrative and military policies, and a certain religious splendor. The third class, located at the bottom of the scale, included populations that were considered and commonly referred to in the era as "without law, without king, and without faith" (*sin ley, sin rey, y sin fé*). The various peoples of the lowlands of South America among which the Jesuits began to develop missionary activities were included in this category. Guillaume Boccara suggests that Acosta's typology didn't necessarily describe the concrete reality of the groups in question, but rather communicated "above all a policy of representation, colonization, and pacification" (105). In the politics of the mission, the great cultural and political classifications, such as Acosta's, were the first instruments used to determine the populations that were to be the objects of conversion.[13] In subsequent centuries, other writings would reproduce this hierarchy, with some variation, emphasizing the distinction between sedentary agricultural societies and nomadic hunting societies. Pedro Guevara, in his *History of Paraguay*, refers to "types of nations" that, "[in] addressing their ways of life and sustenance, we can divide into two castes and generations, one of laborers that cultivate the land to sustain themselves with its fruits and roots, and the other peoples that seek nourishment from fishing and hunting, and from some wild fruits." While the first had "permanent establishments," were "subject to their chief (*cacique*)," and took great pains to obtain results from their "industry and hard work," the second were a cast of "vagabonds" that lacked permanent housing (Guevara 539).

In this same period, classificatory mechanisms gave way to the systematic association between cultural or linguistic traits ("nations") and well-defined territorial circumscriptions. The organization of missionary undertakings began with the identification of "nations" denominated by ethnic names that corresponded to the languages supposedly spoken by all of their members.[14] At the end of the sixteenth century, the Jesuit José de Barzana (1530–1597), on his way from the Andes to Paraguay, recognized the Guaraní as speakers of "one single language" (Furlong, *Alonso de Barzana* 93). Two centuries later, the Jesuit José Peramás (1732–1793) wrote that the Guaraní were "one single type of people" that spoke "just one language that was and still is [the prevailing language] in most parts of South America" (Peramás 37). What is not clear in the letters is that the Jesuits were the ones promoting linguistic homogenization. Initially they were concerned with identifying languages and ethnic groups in all of their diversity. But, once the population had been congregated into towns, they pushed "linguistic reduction" based on the selection of the language most commonly spoken in those towns, which was then standardized by means of vocabulary books and grammar guides. In this process, certain languages were lost straightaway in favor of the expansion of a general language. This policy logically facilitated the development of the missionary town, conceived up until then as an unmanageable Babel.[15]

Missionary activity itself produced texts and discourses that became progressively standardized through descriptions of a more general character, influencing in turn the design of policies and methods of conversion to be applied in other regions. Reports about the successes and failures of the missions in different parts of the world circulated with a certain fluidity among the members of the order, who zealously systematized them, protected them in archives, and disseminated them in works printed *ad hoc* and deposited in the libraries of the order. In one text from 1747 titled "Difficulties in the conversion of the unfaithful of this province of Paraguay and the means to conquer them," the Jesuit José Cardiel (1704–1781) proposed a plan to convert numerous peoples that inhabited the region of Río de la Plata by creating amongst them colonies of sedentary Indians that would serve as good examples. According to Cardiel, the plan could not fail because it had been previously applied with success to a Chichimeca population in northern Mexico, in which sedentary colonists from other regions had been implanted. In the same text, Cardiel distinguished nations "on horse" from nations "on foot," and wrote that the most barbarous Indians "on horse" did not have "farms" or houses, "nor [did they have] villages," but lived "like vagabond Gypsies" (Cardiel). As the foundation for the elaboration of his own plans, Cardiel not only utilized the group classifications prevalent during his era, but also provided examples from other faraway missionary experiences about which he had read.

The expulsion of the Society of Jesus from all of Iberia's dominions in 1767 inaugurated a new era in Jesuit textual production. From this moment on, the Ignatians exiled in the Pontifical States began to produce texts that recalled their missionary experiences. These writings, which were now oriented toward readers outside of the order (benefactors as well as detractors), sought to valorize the missionary experience through personal testimony. But above all—and this is perhaps one of the key markers of post-Jesuit writing—, they toiled to demonstrate the "scientific" nature of their affirmations, paying special attention to the presentation of proof and the meticulous corroboration of evidence.[16] Much of this work sought to establish dialogues or polemics with the enlightened philosophers that were writing against the Society of Jesus during this era. Standing out among the texts dedicated to Paraguay is another piece by José Cardiel that defends the Guaraní missions against the diffusion of rumors about the creation of an independent Jesuit "Republic," as well as a tract by Peramás comparing those same missions with Plato's *Republic*. The declaration of having personally been in the places described tended to be an effective rhetorical tool of the works in question, and this was the case of both Cardiel and Peramás, who had been missionaries in the same region. The occasional disparities presented between their works responded above all to the interlocutors with whom they dialogued.

In European exile, German Jesuits such as Martin Dobrizhoffer (1717–1791) and Florian Paucke (1719–1780) wrote chronicles on the Indians of Chaco of great ethnographic value. Another Jesuit, Sánchez Labrador (1717–1798), wrote about the botany, zoology, and linguistics of the region of Paraguay. Some of these texts were published posthumously. Paucke wrote about his experiences among the Mocobí, accompanying the manuscript with a series of his own illustrations that depicted images of daily life in the reductions. Dobrizhoffer published a history of the Abipón Indians (the Latin version is from 1784), in which he also reports on other indigenous populations of the region of Chaco and the city of Asunción. Sánchez Labrador, whose work was partially published only in the twentieth century, is of great interest. He worked in the Guaraní reductions between 1746 and 1758, was sent to teach theology as a professor in Asunción in 1759, and departed again the following year to the Mbaya Indian mission of Chaco where he founded the reduction of Belén. From this location he set out to find a road that would lead to the Chiquitos region, and when he returned he was surprised by the order of expulsion. He then took up residence in Ravenna, where he died in 1798. Other Jesuits, including Domingo Muriel and Lorenzo Hervás y Panduro, used information from Sánchez Labrador's reports in their own works.

The accumulation and verification of previously written records was a common strategy among the Jesuits in exile. At the end of the decade of 1780, the publication of the Catalan Jesuit José Jolis's (1728–1790) writings on the region of Chaco was announced.[17] Jolis's work apparently aimed to correct and complement that of Jesuits who had previously written about Chaco, including Pedro Lozano, Nicolás del Techo, or François Xavier Charlevoix. But in contrast to these figures, Jolis had personally been to the region and had had Indians under his charge. As he himself confesses, the previous works were useful to him in as much as he could personally verify their contents.[18] In the same era the Jesuit Joaquin Camaño (1737–1820) prepared a work of comparative ethnology, which never reached publication, based on a methodology in which questionnaires were sent to exiled ex-Jesuit missionaries, requesting information about different indigenous societies.[19] In addition, Camaño produced a large quantity of maps, plans, and historical essays during his exile in Faenza, and he wrote texts about the indigenous populations that inhabited the region of Chaco. In line with previous Jesuit publications, the texts identify indigenous "nations" and "tribes" (*parcialidades*) by their respective ethnic names (Furlong, *Joaquín Camaño* 125). Shortly before the expulsion, Camaño developed missionary activities in Chiquitos and maintained correspondence about American languages with the well-known Spanish Jesuit Lorenzo Hervás y Panduro, who prepared among other works of interest, the widely disseminated *Catalogue of Languages*.[20]

In short, the expulsion of the Jesuits did not constitute a radical departure from the previous period in respect to the general orientation of their writing. The exiled Jesuits tended to systematize in the most meticulous manner previous writings, consolidating and distilling a classificatory schema that already existed from before. In this sense, they not only reaffirmed the "scientific" character of their texts but also their political nature, since through them they highlighted the role of the Society of Jesus in the development of good governance, both civil and Christian, among the indigenous populations of America. The continuous communication that the Jesuits maintained among each other in exile, always looking to confirm information, reinforced their preoccupation with presenting a respectable image of intellectuals to a European audience that was largely hostile to the order.[21] Therefore, the transcontinental circulation of texts about missionary experiences continued to contribute to the fortification of the corporate identity of the order. As Steven Harris points out, it permitted it to function as an organic whole in which the parts were connected to one another despite the large geographic distances between them.[22] The typologies proposed an "understanding of the global" in which each culture and region had its place within a single Jesuit tree whose branches reached the entire world.

Appropriations and Adaptations

Jesuit textual production had to adapt to local contexts. For this reason, a good part of the corpus, handwritten and printed, was subject to modifications that reveal negotiations with the recipient indigenous population. Indigenous participation in textual production did not consist solely of the contribution of local elements to a prearranged global schema, but gave form to singular texts that resulted from the growing ability and autonomy of these populations as they acquired literacy skills. This section will explore some examples.

Within the missions, the production of texts was inextricably related to factors such as the practice of reading and writing, in which the indigenous parishioners had an important role. Although not all of them knew how to read and write, literacy in the missions advanced rapidly within the indigenous elite. This occurred both among local council (*cabildo*) officials who needed to transcribe acts and sign documents, and among church employees, from sacristans to musicians and singers, whose work included reading and copying sheet music and doctrinal texts. At the beginning of the eighteenth century a diversity of papers written by Indians were already circulating that reveal the existence of a lettered missionary culture. The creation of a missionary press at the beginning of the eighteenth century was, in this sense, an emerging element within a larger framework of indigenous writing practices that had already reached an important degree of autonomy.[23] In fact, the press coexisted with the production of hand-copied manuscripts, which was the previous customary method.[24] Within these writing practices the creation of manuscript catechisms was common, largely in the form of dialogues, which incorporated new elements into the existing versions. We also know of voluminous books of sermons and even historical "diaries" or narratives—the latter of which often related the events of violent conflicts—which have been attributed to indigenous authors, though for the most part they are anonymous. These texts were not uniform. In general, they introduced elements of local linguistic variability and signaled an important level of diversity in missionary styles, related in great measure to the presence of Jesuits who supervised translations in collaboration with indigenous subjects, or the tendency, large or small, of the natives of certain towns to reinforce their local linguistic customs. The fundamental characteristic of these texts is their instructional character, that is, the fact that they had to be useful for everyday preaching in the missions; they were efficient, practical, and up to date, especially from a linguistic point of view, but also from a doctrinal and iconographic standpoint.

A series of doctrinal books was published and circulated in the missions, a large number of which compiled or synthesized previous texts, while others were completely developed *in situ* according to the necessities of the catechistic, liturgical, and sacramental activities. This permits an understanding of the existence of manuscripts and printed texts dedicated to updating previous works that were no longer completely relevant. This is the case of strictly linguistic works published at the missionary press, such as the *Vocabulary* (1722) and *Art of the Guaraní Language* (1724). Both texts are attributed to the Italian Jesuit Paulo Restivo (1658–1740), but in reality they are updated versions of the linguistic labors of the Jesuit Antonio Ruiz de Montoya (1585–1652), published a century before. In his edition, Restivo indicated numerous changes in linguistic customs introduced during a century of missionary activity, which necessitated the collaboration of literate indigenous informants. In a similar manner, another work, this time a manuscript titled *Selected phrases and ways of speaking favored and used in the Guaraní Language* explicitly signals "various words and modes of speech not used" in certain towns, and claims to be a useful guide for missionaries undertaking pastoral activities (see Petrovio, introduction). This work is also polemically attributed to Restivo, who signed with the anagram Blas Petrovio. It is supposed that it was also Restivo who in 1733 translated to Guaraní a classic from missionary history, *The Spiritual Conquest*, redacted by the Jesuit Antonio Ruiz de Montoya a century before and relating the vicissitudes the missionary experienced in the conversion of the region of Guayrá.[25] It seems reasonable to believe that, with this translation, Restivo sought to divulge and reaffirm an historical consciousness among his indigenous audience about the contribution of their ancestors to evangelization.[26]

A Guaraní version of the treatise *On the Difference Between the Temporal and the Eternal*, by the Spanish Jesuit Eusebio Nieremberg (1595–1658), emerged from the missionary press of Paraguay in 1705. This book, designed to explain the futility of life on earth and inculcate the fear of God in the people, was first printed in Madrid in 1640, and then reprinted many times in Spanish and other languages. In 1684, the first illustrated edition appeared in Amberes with engravings by Bouttats, which included images representative of diverse scenes in the text. The Jesuit José Serrano (1634–1713) undertook the translation to Guaraní alongside, as it can be supposed, a group of anonymous indigenous collaborators. Apparently, the translation of the work was ready to be remitted to Europe for printing when a Jesuit printer arrived at the missions from Europe to establish a printing press in the region. Serrano writes to the Superior General of the order, Tirso González: "in this way the imprint, like the many illustrations that adorn it, has been the work of the hand of God, and how much more admirable when the instruments are poor Indians" (Furlong, *Orígenes del arte tipográfico* 140). The same Jesuit tells us of translations to Guaraní of other useful works for missionary activity, such as the *Flos Sanctorum* of Ribadeneyra, published later by the same press. The general congregations engaged in discussions and the Jesuits continuously inquired to the general priest of the order in Rome about all the subjects pertinent to the development of the missions, including the publication of texts, illustrating both an imposition of norms and a certain liberty of decision-making within the missions.

Nieremberg's missionary text presents a series of particular characteristics, especially in its visual aspects, which reveal preferred adaptations to the local context. First, it includes a notably larger number of images than the original European imprint, one of which even carries the signature of an indigenous engraver named Juan Yaparí. Second, it incorporates local zoological and botanical motifs that replace elements included in some of the images of the European original. Third, it subtly introduces visual modifications that, it stands to reason, sought a greater impact among indigenous readers. In some images the effects of depth are diminished and the proportions of natural formations, such as mounds, waves, and clouds, are increased. Although the only indigenous name that appears on these engravings is that of Yaparí, judging by the variation and lack of regularity in the visual modifications that were introduced, it is possible that other indigenous artists intervened in the creation of the images contained in the book. Some missions were particularly well known for the quality of their artisans and the existence of workshops where numerous indigenous artists worked. The appearance of a single indigenous name on only one of the images of the series is striking, however, since most visual missionary production tended to remain anonymous. For the moment we cannot advance much further in the interpretation of the indigenous role in the process of selection of motifs. Nonetheless, it stands to reason that, inside the workshops, there was a certain amount of negotiation between the missionaries and the indigenous artisans around what images would best illustrate passages of the text and what local elements were at once effective and innocuous enough to transmit the evangelical message.

Other research has been able to confirm the inspiration of certain models for the images in the book. In addition to the obvious reference to the engravings of Bouttats, one could mention illustrations included in the *Evangelicae Historiae Imagines* by Jerónimo de Nadal, Bernadino Passeri, Marten de Vos, and Anton Wierix.[27] But the text reflects a certain pragmatism, in accordance with the Jesuit "way of proceeding," that permitted a relatively free handling of available models and sources, much like the recourse to visual adaptations for the images in which indigenous collaborators clearly participated.[28]

Of particular impact are the images representing the cycle of hell and its punishments, nonexistent in the European original. The "mouth of hell" is one of the iconographic themes most recognizable in other previous and contemporary works, since it was utilized frequently for preaching and catechism in the modern age, as much in Europe as in America. A contemporary representative example is the *Disabuse of sinners necessary to all types of persons very useful to missionaries, and enlightened preachers* (1724), by the Italian Jesuit Alejandro Perier (1651–1736), which is dedicated to describing the punishment and torments of those condemned to hell. According to a study of Fernando Gil, Perier remained in the Brazilian missions for more than thirty years and illustrated his book with an image of the mouth of hell similar to the one included in the Guaraní translation of Nierembeg. Perier, for his part, turns to Italian sources like Segneri and Pinamonti, known for their missionary sermons. But beyond these possible influences and connections, it can be assumed that the incorporation of the images of hell contributed to the reinforcement of sermons and a visual discourse that already had validity in the missions. In effect, the subject of the devil and the agonies of hell were commonly exploited by missionaries in their preaching.[29]

We do not know the exact criteria that guided the translation of these texts into an indigenous language, as they varied from one region to another, nor the way in which the indigenous population, principally the elite, intervened in their re-elaboration. There existed another translation of Nieremberg's book to the Chiquitana language in the region of the missions of the same name, which seems to indicate a coordinated policy of translations in missionary areas in close proximity. One could conjecture that, with the promotion of these translations, the Jesuits sought to exploit to the highest degree the linguistic possibilities inherent to the native languages, and at the level of the most sophisticated theological discourses of the Catholic religion.

Translation to the vernacular was not limited to doctrinal treatises and manuals, but also reached the whole span of knowledge that was necessary for missionary activity *in situ*. In these types of texts in particular, the direct dependence of the Jesuits on local knowledge held by the indigenous populations is revealed; without these local informants, it was very difficult, if not impossible, to acquire this knowledge. Some research has put emphasis on the traffic of "profane" information about medicine and botany that the Jesuits obtained, as much through the personal assimilation of knowledge and skills that were previously acquired by others, as through the persistent interaction with indigenous informants willing to collaborate.[30] This information was rarely organized or captured in treatises that reached publication. Instead, the Jesuits could spend numerous decades in the meticulous accumulation of detailed facts and the consultation of extant bibliographies in the libraries of the order.

Although it was not covered in the Jesuit "Plan of Studies," the *Ratio Studiorum*, knowledge of medicine was central to the practical development of the mission. It was therefore required that missionaries possessed this knowledge, and that it circulated in the form of the canonical texts of the discipline in the different libraries of the order. The medical and botanical treatises produced in the missions sometimes made explicit references to indigenous collaborators from whom they obtained first-hand information about the properties and usages of the plants of the jungle. In this type of textual production, the relationship between different spaces of knowledge became particularly intense since any applications of botanical medicine produced on the Iberian Peninsula or in other parts of America had to be put to the test in the concrete spaces of the missions. Out of this process they obtained additional knowledge to augment and modify those practices. In his botanical treatise, *Missionary Medical Material*, the Jesuit Pedro de Montenegro (1663–1728) remembers the difficulties that he had to confront upon collecting information during his twenty-five years of residency in the missions of Paraguay, and accuses "witch doctors" and "sorcerers" of obstructing his work ("Plantas de misiones" 13–14). Other treatises were written directly in Guaraní, like that of Marcos Villodas, penned in 1725 with the title, *Pojha Ñaña, Missionary Medical Material or Herbarium of the Guaraní Reductions*.[31] We also know of a "Medical Treatise" written by the Jesuit Segismund Aperger (1678–1772) in 1720, who found himself at the missionary press that very year. According to the Jesuit Speth, in those days Aperger was ready to "edit a work of great utility" (Furlong, *Historia y bibliografía* 347). Treatises like that of Aperger, just like those of his antecessor Montenegro, are preserved in exemplary manuscripts that exhibit signs of local interactions and adaptations.

It is deceiving to refer to the authority of these texts since in most cases they were the result of collaborations between various people, and circulation through various hands, following the suggestions of councils, synods, congregations, and, logically, practical necessities. In this sense, the authorship tended to be undefined or multiple. It is important to highlight the explicit indigenous participation in their composition insomuch as it indicated limits to the pure and rigid imposition of a metropolitan textual model (as much from the point of view of content as from form).

Once the missionary system was established, the Jesuits began to promote not only the adoption of doctrine by their indigenous parishioners through repetition and memorization, but also the production of original texts and the formation of a theological framework among members of the native elite. Two missionary imprints of the same era explicitly illustrate this point: the *Explanation of the Catechism* and *Sermons and Examples*, both written by the native chief and musician Nicolás Yapuguay, under the direction of the Jesuit Restivo. In the introduction to the exemplar of the *Explanation*, Restivo presents a tribute to the Indian: ". . . renowned and superior to that which fits an Indian is the capacity of this Nicolás Yapuguay, *cacique* and musician of Santa María, and, with reason, his person is highly praised by all for the command, clarity, and elegance with which he happily explains himself, even in subjects dealing with God, which is not so easy to find in other Indians" (Yapuguay VII). In official writings, this type of Jesuit appreciation for the capacities of the Indians is not common. However, members of the elite apparently reached an important level of autonomy in the composition of doctrinal texts. We do not know the details surrounding the intellectual relationship between Restivo and Yapuguay, but judging from the same text, they maintained a constant and fluid interchange for the definitive composition of the book, which contained ideas that were ultimately authorized and filtered by the Jesuit. Although authors employed European models in the development of the material for the explanation of the catechism (particularly the version of Bellarmino, Turlot, Mercader, and Pomey), they also included locally elaborated treatises and doctrines in which they introduced, for example, a sermon on the

Passion of Christ, or a table with the degrees of kinship or other relationships that constituted impediments to ecclesiastic matrimony (Melià, *La lengua guaraní* 316).

Apparently such collaborations were common in some towns, where the indigenous subjects made writing a relatively autonomous exercise. The Jesuit Peramás mentions the indigenous man named Vázquez, from the reduction of Loreto, who dedicated himself to writing and embellishing sermons that he had heard from the priest. In the reduction of Corpus Christi, he adds, there was also an Indian named Melchor who wrote a type of historical work, and in San Francisco Javier, another indigenous author composed a *History* of his town. According to the account of Peramás, the elaboration of the texts of sermons resulted from a process of creative listening on the part of indigenous writers:

> The mode in which [an Indian] composed this volume [of sermons] was the following: every Sunday he paid close attention to what the Priest, or the Priest's assistant, presented about the Gospel of the day, and what he added later, exhorting, here, reprimanding there, with the goal of improving customs. Meditating on these things the Indian went to his house and, once there, reproduced the sermon, and put it in pure Guaraní language (Yapuguay VI).

An initial oral emission by the priest was transcribed and rewritten by hand by the indigenous parishioner who heard it. He returned his embellishment to the priest, who sometimes used it again. This reference reveals the dependence of the Jesuit on indigenous linguistic knowledge in the preparation of oral pieces. Even more, it indicates that a strategy (or method) of the mission consisted in promoting indigenous participation in the production of texts that, although they responded to a more or less standardized model, like the sermons, necessarily had to adapt to local customs, and specifically to indigenous orality. This required a relaxation of the models and the exercise of an important level of pragmatism.[32]

Nonetheless, the increasingly solid command of writing attained by indigenous parishioners began to constitute a risk for the Jesuits to the extent that Indians could make autonomous use of writing and escape the control of the priests. In some documents from the eighteenth century, Jesuits express the need to attentively monitor the writing activity of indigenous subjects, penalizing acts of contempt and inappropriate habits. This point manifests an interesting irony. The expansion of the global mission had promoted the dissemination of writing among indigenous inhabitants in this part of America, standardizing linguistic habits and forms of preaching, translating works of high doctrinal value, and developing experts in theology among members of the elite. Nevertheless, the complete adoption of this lettered culture by the same indigenous populations ended up favoring their autonomy to a greater level than that which their promoters, the Jesuit priests, considered acceptable. In certain circumstances, the technology of writing began to be utilized by a sector of the indigenous population beyond the control of the priests.[33] Even after the expulsion of the Jesuits, numerous regions of missionary action maintained their previous textual practices, now entirely disentangled and constantly recreated by indigenous writers. In certain regions like Moxos, Chiquitos, and Guaraníes, administration of the documents (and full control of the writing) passed to indigenous hands, and the practice of telling local stories and recording collective and individual memories grew side by side with contact with non-indigenous society.[34] Although indigenous subjects would continue to be included in the great typologies inherited from the Jesuit era, they also would not abandon the position they had attained in the writing of their own history.

Final Reflections

Within the enormous corpus of texts produced in, for, and from the missions, I have focused on the analysis of two types. One is composed of texts that formalized and crystalized classifications of indigenous societies that were the objects of religious conversion. The other is constituted by texts with a clearly practical orientation, destined for daily use in the missions. The texts in question show two simultaneous, parallel, and, in appearance, contradictory orientations of the Catholic missionary territories overseas, one tied to the reinforcement of a missionary identity of the Jesuits as "apostles of evangelization" and experienced experts on the American missions, the other related to the capacity to adapt to concrete spaces and to interact with the indigenous populace, who intervened explicitly in their production. The analysis of both facets or orientations, permits identification of the intrinsic tensions of the global missionary expansion that had to respond simultaneously to the requirements and audiences of the European metropolises and the exigencies of daily interaction with indigenous peoples who, in this same process, gained autonomy and agency. This double circulation of texts does not appear to exhibit explicit contacts or mutual influences, but it reveals nonetheless two sides of the same coin. These are texts produced by members of the same religious order, influenced by implicit or explicit indigenous collaboration, and while they represent two distinct types of documents that apparently function independently of one another, together they reinforce, from different angles, a single mission.

NOTES

1. I am grateful to the organizers of this volume for their kind invitation to participate in the workshop that gave origin to this text, and for the meticulous work of commentaries and revisions that they made to early versions of this chapter.
2. Among the works most representative of the history of the evangelization, see Borges Morán; and the many works of Furlong.
3. On the political and economic networks established by the Jesuits in the region, see the classic works of Magnus Mörner; and Juan Carlos Garavaglia.
4. The subject of the missions, the expansion of the Iberian Empires, and the circulation of knowledge has been the object of some important works in the last twenty years. Among the most representative are celebrated research volumes like that of working groups, such as those organized by Vincent and Fabre; Corsi; Kawamura and Veliath; Coello, Burrieza, and Moreno; Castelnau, et al.; and Wilde, *Saberes de la conversion*. Of particular relevance to the subject of the Jesuits and their global connections are the books of Alden; Clossey; and Molina. For an ethno-historical perspective, see Barbara Ganson; and Guillermo Wilde, *Religión y poder*. The question of Jesuit writing and printing has acquired a particular relevance in recent studies, which clearly reflect an articulation of the global and the local, such as those of Valle; Kohut and Torales Pacheco; Pietschmann, Ramos Medina, and Torales Pacheco.
5. Although I revisit here a distinction proposed in Wilde (*Saberes de la conversion*), Ivonne del Valle had previously oriented her reflections in a similar direction concerning Iberian margins. The author writes:

   > it is important to highlight, on one hand, the economy of written production and a knowledge both colonialist (tools in the possession and the administration of said territories) and imperial (in the sense in which they constructed an empire, a system based in science, an economy) that attempted to control the peripheral zones, and on the other, to elucidate, based on the organization of said economy, the exact impact that the territory and the indigenous groups had on it, even as it sought to impose specific systems on them (10).

6. The "Jesuit way of proceeding" is founded in the missionary and apostolic vocation of the order from its origins, from the spiritual exercises of Ignacio, to the missionary practice promoted by Francisco Xavier. This way of proceeding involved a non-dogmatic approach to particular situations of cultural and political interaction and a decisions-making process based in cases. On the subject, see Zatyrka Pacheco. The recent book by J. Michelle Molina advances the question of Jesuit spirituality in a global perspective.
7. The reconstruction and tracking of the movement and careers of certain Jesuits through South American spaces, as well as their motivations in the moment of formation of the order's first provinces, is a subject that still needs to be studied.

For an approximation to the problematic of "mission desire," see Maldavsky. On the procurators, see Zubillaga; and Martínez-Serna.

8. Friedrich also highlights general aspects of Jesuit correspondence, such as its classification, standardization, serialization, and hierarchical ordering ("Communication and Bureaucracy"). From the same author, see also "Government and Information." It should be clarified that the centralization of information facilitated the work of the historians of the order who, since the seventeenth century, had written and published histories of the missions in different parts of the world. In the eighteenth century, the accumulation of information was such that a Jesuit like François Xavier Charlevoix was capable of writing detailed histories on the Society of Jesus in New France, Japan, and Paraguay without leaving Rome, by resorting to the archives of the order. Another well-known French Jesuit and contemporary of Charlevoix, Lafitau, was also able to access information on Japan without ever having been in the archipelago. On this subject, see Takao Abé. On the level of decision-making, the order granted certain autonomy to its different provinces. In a recent study, Fabian Fechner sustains, against the argument of a supposed rigid verticalism, that decision-making was based in a process of decentralized communications, making way for peripheral overseas spaces and the possibility of creating unregulated spaces, which tolerated respect for diverse local situations.

9. In his analysis of the Jesuit print production of the German countries, Borja González affirms that, "Jesuit imprints formed an integral part of the cultural horizon of German readers in the seventeenth and eighteenth centuries" (170). For his part, Steven Harris calls attention to the contrast between the global reach of the administration and movement of the missionaries, and the geographic and corporate concentration of the final sites of the production of texts (226).

10. In addition to annual letters, which contained accounts that were accessible to European readers, beginning in the seventeenth century a series of documentary collections were published that included transcribed letters from Jesuit missionaries carrying out activities, principally in the Asian world, but also in the Americas. Among the most important are the *Lettres édifiantes e curieuses*, published by the French Jesuits Charles LeGobien and Pierre du Halde between 1701 and 1776, and *Der Neue Welt-Bott*, published by the Bavarian Jesuit Joseph Stöclein between 1726 and 1761. On the subject, see the studies, already mentioned, by Borja González; and Harris. To track the work and trajectory of Jesuits that acted in New Spain, see Ivonne del Valle's book, already cited; and the studies of Bernd Hausberger.

11. Juan Carlos Estenssoro notes that the III Council of Lima (1582–1583), where the Jesuits had a preponderant role, marked a new phase in the evangelization of South America in which certain religious practices promoted in the prior period were condemned, even as heretical, in a push to identify native forms of Christianity. Sabine MacCormack discusses the dilemmas that they faced in designing missionary methods during this period, which passed from a paradigm based in persuasion to one based in the force and reason of state.

12. This secularizing displacement was a characteristic that marked above all the Jesuit

missions of Asia where the Jesuits explicitly developed the method of adaptation to local cultures, which required that they define beforehand the boundary between civil practice and pagan rites. On the subject, see the excellent discussion introduced by the research of Joan Pau Rubiés, "The Concept of Cultural Dialogue," and "¿Diálogo religioso"; Ines Zupanov; and Elisabetta Corsi.

13. On the "comparative ethnology" of Acosta, see the work of Anthony Pagden. Concerning Jesuit classifications, Rubiés affirms that they should be understood "in the light of their selective portrayal of one culture to another for the sake of the missions" ("The Concept of Cultural Dialogue" 243).

14. I have been able to focus with more detail on the problematic of the classifications in Wilde, "De las crónicas jesuíticas".

15. For a panorama of the linguistic diversity in regions like Chiquitos and Jesuit Moxos, see respectively Tomichá Charupá; and Saito, "Fighting against Hydra." The latter analyzes in detail the phenomena of the disappearance of languages as a result of the Jesuit program of homogenization.

16. Even during the Jesuit era, the reflections of some Jesuits were occasionally subject to revisions by their colleagues in the order. Successors of Acosta tended to recriminate him for his lack of ethnographic rigor. Such is the orientation that some Jesuit works of the eighteenth century acquired, on the basis of "ethnographic" information systematically compiled during almost two centuries of missionary action. Prieto notes that, although Acosta affirmed that his reflection on America was based on his own experience, a good part of his *Natural and Moral History* had been written in Spain and not in America. The Jesuit Bernabé Cobo (1580–1657), by contrast, "proudly announced that he had composed his book piecemeal, writing about each region while residing in it" (Prieto 169–70).

17. Among the extant documentation in the Catalan archive of the Society of Jesus exists a list of Jesuits exiled in Faenza. The name Jolis has an interesting footnote that reads as such:

> Don Joseph Jolis, who escaped alive from Chaco, and its Barbarians, real, true, and living, came to die in Faenza due to Chaco and its *paper* Indians: the partially-printed history of Chaco took his life: and the long and weak First Volume ended up wrapping sardines, since there was no one (and there were many) who would face the Second, even though the deceased had left much waste (AHSIC).

I thank Akira Saito for access to this important documentation.

18. The complete title of the only work of Jolis is *Saggio/ sulla Storia Naturale / Della Provincia / del Gran Chaco / e sulle pratiche, e sun´costume dei/ Popoli che l bitano/ insieme Con tre Giornali / Dil altrettandi viaggi fatti alle interne / contrade di que ´Barbari/ Composto / Dal Signor Abate / D. Giuseppe Jolis / Tomo 1/ In Faenza, MDC-CLXXXIX / Per Lodovico Genestri / Con licenza de ´Superiori*. The work should have a total of four parts, but only the first was printed (Cardozo 353).

19. On the Jesuit Camaño, see Furlong, *Joaquín Camaño S.J.*

20. The well-known linguistic work of Hervás formed part of a larger collection of twenty-one volumes written between 1778 and 1787 known as *Idea dell'Universo*. The catalogue of languages already mentioned contained the largest compilation of data on the languages of the world in a historical-comparative perspective. In said work, Hervás proposes an integrated classification of the American languages, stemming from information gathered and sent to his Jesuit colleagues in exile, in addition to other published references, also Jesuit. Although the linguistic explanation was usually mixed with theological interpretation, Hervás, in a rationalist impulse uncommon among the anti-Enlightenment figures of the era, emphasized the necessity of distinguishing the human spirit from sensual nature (Hassler). For more information on the life of Hervás, see the recent edition of his *Jesuit-Spanish Library (Biblioteca jesuítico-española (1759–1799)* (Hervás y Panduro).
21. On the intellectual activity of the Jesuits in exile, see Niccolò Guasti.
22. Concerning the local-global relationship, Borja González signals: "While the missionary letters redounded in local narratives, the discursive, visual, and material homogenization permitted the reader to recognize not only their Jesuit character but, above all, reminded them of the interdependence between the parts and the whole, and in this way the universality of the Catholic project" (184).
23. On missionary printing activity, see Furlong (*Orígenes del arte tipográfico*; *Historia y bibliografía*).
24. For a number of texts produced by indigenous authors, see Bartomeu Melià, "Escritos guaraníes"; and Eduardo Neumann.
25. For more detailed references to these documents, see Furlong, *Antonio Ruiz de Montoya*; and Melià, "Fuentes documentales". On the linguistic actualizations proposed in the eighteenth century, see Obermeier and Cerno.
26. In a study dedicated to another missionary imprint from Paraguay, also attributed to Restivo, Palomera Serreinat identifies modifications clearly meant to adjust to local use. Inserted at the end of the *Manual Ritual (Un ritual bilingüe en las reducciones del Paraguay)*, published in 1721 in the reduction of Loreto, are forty penitential exhortations in the Guaraní language which enumerate common sins among the missionary Indians, followed by a series of standardized questions and answers.
27. Some of these influences are identified by Bailey. For a detailed analysis of the visual aspects of the work, see González and an erudite article by Obermeier.
28. The missionary workshops still require deeper study. The only known work on the subject belongs to Furlong (*Artesanos*).
29. The Austrian Jesuit Anton Sepp explicitly relates how he exploited the subject in his mission: "On both lateral walls of the church I made them [the Indians] paint the four ends of man [death, judgment, hell, glory], of which hell has a particularly horrible appearance, so that my Indians give up sin for fear of punishment if heaven's love doesn't make them change" (257).
30. In this sense, the seventeenth century correspondence maintained between Nicolás Mascardi, Jesuit missionary in Chile, and his teacher, Athanasius Kircher in Rome, on the geography, botany, and astronomy of the austral region becomes paradig-

matic. On the subject, see Furlong, *Nicolás Mascardi, S.J.*; the recent complication of Constanza Acuña; and the book by Prieto.
31. In addition to the manuscript of Villodas that is conserved in the Wellcome Library, in the national Library of Madrid there is a codex titled "Book of medicine in the Guaraní language" that accompanies "a book on medicine in alphabetical order in Spanish" (*un libro de medicina por orden alphabetico en español*) by Gregorio López, which confirms that the work of López circulated through the Jesuit reductions in a Guaraní version. On the subject, see Martín Martín and Valverde.
32. On the mission sermon in a comparative perspective, see the study of Perla Chinchilla.
33. A critical moment in which this manifests was the so-called "guerra guaranítica," an armed uprising of the Guaraní against the crowns of Spain and Portugal, which had signed a treaty that obligated the evacuation of seven Jesuit missions. In the commotion of this conflict, the rebel Guaraní began to circulate letters amongst themselves to communicate information and directives. The investigation of Eduardo Neumann centers specifically on this aspect.
34. On these phenomena in the missionary region of Moxos, see Saito, "Las misiones y la administración."

WORKS CITED

Arxiu Històric Societatis Iesu, Sant Cugat (AHSIC). "Catalogue of the province of Paraguay from the intimation of the arrest in Julio de 1768. Contains the dead, and alive, the expelled, secularized, and married, with the place in which they made the arrest. There are also the members of the last mission, although some of them had not even embarked; they were already assigned to that Province = in Faenza." July 1780. Archivo Tarragonense de la Compañía de Jesús. ACPE 18. Sant Cugat, Spain. MS.
Abé, Takao. *The Jesuit Mission to New France: A New Interpretation in the Light of the Earlier Jesuit Experience in Japan*. Leiden: Brill, 2011.
Acuña, Constanza, ed. *La curiosidad infinita de Athanasius Kircher*. Santiago: Ocholibros, 2012.
Alden, Dauril. *The Making of an Enterprise: The Society of Jesus in Portugal, Its Empire, and Beyond, 1540–1750*. Stanford: Stanford University Press, 1996.
Bailey, Gauvin A. *Art on the Jesuit Missions in Asia and Latin America, 1542–1773*. Toronto: University of Toronto Press, 1999.
Boccara, Guillaume. "Antropología política en los márgenes del Nuevo Mundo: Categorías coloniales, tipologías antropológicas y producción de la diferencia." *Fronteras movedizas. Clasificaciones coloniales y dinámicas socioculturales en las fronteras americanas*. Ed. C. E. Giudicelli. Mexico City: Colegio de Michoacán/Casa de Velázquez, 2010. 103–35.

Borges Morán, Pedro. *Métodos misionales en la cristianización de América, siglo XVI.* Madrid: Consejo Superior de Investigaciones Científicas (CSIC), 1960.

Borja González, Galaxis. "Las narrativas misioneras y la emergencia de una conciencia-mundo en los impresos jesuíticos alemanes en el siglo XVIII." *Procesos: Revista ecuatoriana de historia* 36 (2012): 169–92.

Cardiel, José. "Difficultades que hay en la conversión de los infieles de esta Provincia del Paraguay, y medios para vencerlas." 20 August 1747. Colección Biblioteca Nacional. Vol. 289, Pieza 4310/2, Pliego 1 vuelta. Archivo General de la Nación, Buenos Aires, Argentina. MS.

Cardozo, Efraím. *Historiografía paraguaya.* Mexico City: Instituto Panamericano de Geografía e Historia, 1959.

Castelnau, Charlotte de, Marie L. Copete, Aliocha Maldavsky, and Ines G. Zupanov, eds. *Missions d´évangelisation et circulation des savoirs, XVIe–XVIIIe siècle.* Madrid: Casa de Velasquez-EHESS, 2011.

Chinchilla, Perla. *El sermón de misión y su tipología: Antología de sermones en español, náhuatl e italiano.* Mexico City: Universidad Iberoamericana, 2013.

Clossey, Luke. *Salvation and Globalization in the Early Jesuit Missions.* Cambridge, UK: Cambridge University Press, 2008.

Coello, Alexandre, Javier Burrieza, and Doris Moreno, eds. *Jesuitas e imperios de ultramar, Siglos XVI–XX.* Madrid: Sílex Ediciones, 2012.

Corsi, Elisabetta. *Órdenes religiosas entre América y Asia: Ideas para una historia misionera de los espacios coloniales.* Mexico City: Colegio de México, 2008.

Dobrizhoffer, Martin. *Historia de los Abipones.* 3 vols. Resistencia: Universidad Nacional del Nordeste, [1784] 1967.

Estenssoro, Juan Carlos. *Del paganismo a la santidad: La incorporación de los indios del Perú al catolicismo, 1532–1750.* Lima: IFEA-Pontificia Universidad Católica del Perú, Instituto Riva-Agüero, 2003.

Fechner, Fabian. "Las Tierras Incógnitas de la administración jesuita: Toma de decisiones, gremios consultivos y evolución de normas." *Histórica* 38:2 (2014): 11–42.

Friedrich, Markus. "Communication and Bureaucracy in the Early Modern Society of Jesus." *Scweizerische Zeitschrift für Religions und Kulturgeschichte* 101 (2007): 49–75.

———. "Government and Information-Management in Early Modern Europe: The Case of the Society of Jesus (1540–1773)." *Journal of Early Modern History* 12 (2008): 539–63.

Furlong, Guillermo. *Artesanos Argentinos durante la dominación hispánica.* Buenos Aires: Editorial Huarpes, 1946.

———. *Orígenes del arte tipográfico en América, especialmente en la República Argentina.* Buenos Aires: Editorial Huarpes, 1947.

———. *Historia y bibliografía de las primeras imprentas rioplatenses, 1700–1850.* Vol. I. Buenos Aires: Guarania, 1953.

———. *Joaquín Camaño S.J. y su "Noticia del Gran Chaco" (1778).* Buenos Aires: Librería del Plata, 1955.

———. *Nicolás Mascardi, S.J. y su Carta-Relación (1670).* Buenos Aires: Ediciones Theoria, 1963.

———. *Antonio Ruiz de Montoya y su carta a Comental (1645)*. Buenos Aires: Ediciones Theoria, 1964.

———. *Alonso de Barzana, S.J. y su carta a Juan Sebastián (1594)*. Buenos Aires: Ediciones Theoria, 1968.

Ganson, Barbara. *The Guarani under Spanish Rule in the Rio de la Plata*. Stanford: Stanford University Press, 2003.

Garavaglia, Juan Carlos. *Mercado interno y economía colonial*. Mexico City: Grijalbo, 1983.

Gil, Fernando. *De la diferencia entre lo temporal y eterno: Crisol de desengaños con la memoria de la eternidad, postrimerías humanas y principales misterios divinos de Juan Eusebio Nieremberg S.J*. Buenos Aires: Bolsa de comercio, 2010.

González, Ricardo. "Textos e imágenes para la salvación: La edición misionera de la diferencia entre lo temporal y eterno." *ArtCultura, Uberlândia* 11 (2009): 137–58.

Guasti, Niccolò. "Rasgos del exilio italiano de los jesuitas españoles." *Hispania Sacra* 61:123 (2009): 257–78.

Guerra, Francisco. *Historia de la materia médica hispano-americana y filipina en la época colonial: Inventario crítico y bibliográfico de manuscritos*. Madrid: Afrodisio Aguado, S. A, 1973.

Guevara, Pedro. "Historia del Paraguay, Río de la Plata y Tucumán [1764]." *Colección de obras y documentos relativos a la historia antigua y moderna de las Provincias del Río de la Plata*. Vol. I. Eds. Pedro de Angelis, and Andrés M. Carretero. Buenos Aires: Editorial Plus Ultra, 1969.

Harris, Steven J. "Mapping Jesuit Science: The Role of Travel in the Geography of Knowledge." *The Jesuits: Cultures, Sciences, and the Arts, 1540–1773*. Eds. John W. O'Malley, Gauvin A. Bailey, Steven J. Harris, and T. F. Kennedy. Toronto: University of Toronto Press, 1999.

Hassler, Gerda. "Teoría lingüística y antropología en las obras de Lorenzo Hervás y Panduro." *Los jesuitas españoles expulsos: Su imagen y su contribución al saber sobre el mundo hispánico en la Europa del siglo XVIII*. Ed. Manfred Tietz. Frankfurt: Iberoamericana-Vervuert, 2001.

Hausberger, Bernd. *Jesuiten Aus Mitteleuropa Im Kolonialen Mexiko: Eine Bio-Bibliographie*. Wien: Verlag für Geschichte und Politik/Oldenbourg, 1995.

———. "La vida cotidiana de los misioneros jesuitas en el noroeste novohispano." *Estudios de historia novohispana* 17 (1997): 63–106.

Hervás y Panduro, Lorenzo. *Catálogo de las lenguas de las naciones conocidas y numeracion, divisio, y clases de estas segun la diversidad de sus idiomas y dialectos*. Vol. 1: *Lenguas y naciones americanas*. Madrid: Imprenta de la Administracion del Real Arbitrio de Beneficencia, 1800.

Kawamura, Shinzo and Cyril Veliath. *Beyond Borders: A Global Perspective of Jesuit Mission History*. Tokyo: Sophia University Press, 2009.

Kohut, Karl, and María Cristina Torales Pacheco, eds. *Desde los confines de los imperios ibéricos: Los jesuitas de habla alemana en las misiones americanas*. Madrid/Frankfurt: Iberoamericana/Vervuert, 2007.

López, Gregorio. *Libro de medicina en lengua guaraní; Libro de medicina por orden alphabetico, en español*. MSS/22992. 1601–1700? Spain National Library, Madrid, Spain. MS.

MacCormack, Sabine. "'The Heart Has Its Reasons': Predicaments of Missionary Christianity in Early Colonial Peru." *The Hispanic American Historical Review* 65 (1985): 443–66.

Maldavsky, Aliocha. "Pedir las Indias: Las cartas *indipetae* de los jesuitas europeos, siglos XVI–XVIII, ensayo historiográfico." *Relaciones* 132 (2012): 147–81.

Martín Martín, Carmen, and José Luis Valverde. *La farmacia en la época colonial: El arte de preparar medicamentos*. Granada: Universidad de Granada, Editorial Monográfica, 1995.

Martínez-Serna, J. Gabriel. "Procurators and the Making of the Jesuits' Atlantic Network." *Soundings in the Atlantic World: Latent Structures and Intellectual Currents, 1500–1830*. Eds. Bernard Bailyn, and Patricia L. Denault. Cambridge, Mass: Harvard University Press, 2009. 181–209.

Melià, Bartomeu. "Fuentes documentales para el estudio de la lengua guaraní de los siglos XVII y XVIII." *Suplemento Antropológico* 5:1–2 (1970): 113–61, 287.

———. *La lengua guaraní en el Paraguay colonial: La creación de un lenguaje cristiano en las reducciones de los guaraníes en el Paraguay*. Asunción: Centro de Estudios Paraguayos "Antonio Guasch," 2003.

———. "Escritos guaraníes como fuentes documentales de la historia paraguaya." *Nuevo Mundo Mundos Nuevos* 6 (2006). Web. 27 February 2015.

Millones, Luis, and Domingo Ledezma. *El saber de los jesuitas: Historias naturales y el Nuevo Mundo*. Madrid: Iberoamericana, 2005.

Molina, J. Michelle. *To Overcome Oneself: The Jesuit Ethic and Spirit of Global Expansion, 1520–1767*. Berkeley: University of California Press, 2013.

Montenegro, Pedro de. "[Plantas de misiones]." Before 1715. JCB Manuscripts. Codex Sp 36. John Carter Brown Library, Providence, Rhode Island. MS.

Mörner, Magnus. *Actividades políticas y económicas de los jesuitas en el Río de la Plata*. Buenos Aires: Hyspamérica, 1985.

Neumann, Eduardo. "Razón gráfica y escritura indígena en las reducciones guaraníticas." *Saberes de la conversión: Jesuitas, indígenas e imperios coloniales en las fronteras de la cristiandad*. Ed. Guillermo Wilde. Buenos Aires: Editorial SB, 2011. 99–130.

Obermeier, Franz. "Der argentinische Erstdruck Nierembergs *De la diferencia* in Guarani im Kontext der Bilderzyklen in Lateinamerika im 18. Jahrhundert." *ART-Dok: Digital Repository Art History* 154 (2006). Web: archiv.ub.uni-heidelberg.de/artdok/154/. 21 August 2015.

Obermeier, Franz, and Leonardo Cerno. "Nuevos aportes de la lingüística para la investigación de documentos jesuíticos del siglo XVIII." *Folia Histórica del Nordeste* 26 (2013): 33–56.

O'Malley, John W., Gauvin A. Bailey, Steven J. Harris, and T. Frank Kennedy, eds. *The Jesuits: Cultures, Sciences, and the Arts, 1540–1773*. Toronto: University of Toronto Press, 1999.

Pagden, Anthony. *The Fall of Natural Man: The American Indian and the Origins of Comparative Ethnology*. Cambridge, UK: Cambridge University Press, 1982.

Palomera Serreinat, Lluís. *Un ritual bilingüe en las reducciones del Paraguay: El manual de Loreto (1721)*. Cochabamba: Editorial Verbo Divino, 2002.

Paucke, Florián. *Hacia allá y para acá o una estada entre los indios Mocobíes, 1749–1767*. Edición de Edmundo Wernicke. Vol. 4. Tucumán: Universidad Nacional de Tucumán, [1829] 1942–1944.

Peramás, José Manuel. *La república de Platón y los guaraníes (1793)*. Buenos Aires: Emecé Editores, 1946.

Perier, Alexandre. *Desengano dos peccadores Necesario a todo genero de Pessoas, Utilissimo aos Missionarios, e aos Pregadores desenganado, que só desejao a salvação das Almas/ Obra composta em discrusso Moraes pelo padre Alexandre Perier da Companhia de Jesus*. Rome: Missionário da província do Brasil, 1725.

Petrovio, Blas [Restivo, Paulo]. "Phrases selectas y modos de hablar escogidos y usados en la Lengua Guaraní sacadas del Thesoro escondido que compuso el venerable padre Antonio Ruiz de nuestra compañía de Jesús para consuelo y alivio de los fervorosos misioneros principiantes en la dicha lengua, 1687." Reference 14/4/41. Museo Mitre, Buenos Aires, Argentina. MS.

Pietschmann, Horst, Manuel Ramos Medina, and María Cristina Torales Pacheco, eds. *Alemania y México: Percepciones mutuas en impresos, siglos XVI–XVIII*. Mexico City: Universidad Iberoamericana, 2005.

Prieto, Andrés I. *Missionary Scientists: Jesuit Science in Spanish South America, 1570–1810*. Nashville: Vanderbilt University Press, 2011.

Rubiés, Joan Pau. "The Concept of Cultural Dialogue and the Jesuit Method of Accommodation: Between Idolatry and Civilization." *Archivum Historicum Societatis Iesu* 76 (2005): 237–80.

———. "¿Diálogo religioso, mediación cultural o cálculo maquiavélico? Una nueva mirada al método jesuita en oriente, 1580–1640." *Jesuitas e imperios de ultramar, Siglos XVI–XX*. Eds. Alexandre Coello, Javier Burrieza, and Doris Moreno. Madrid: Sílex Ediciones, 2012. 35–63.

Saito, Akira. "Las misiones y la administración del documento: El caso de Mojos, siglos XVIII–XX." *Senri Ethnological Studies* 68 (2005): 27–72.

———. "'Fighting Against a Hydra': Jesuit Language Policy in Moxos." *Beyond Borders: A Global Perspective of Jesuit Mission History*. Eds. Shinzo Kawamura and Cyril Veliath. Tokyo: Sophia University Press, 2009.

Sánchez Labrador, José. "El Paraguay Católico." 2 vols. *Homenaje de la Universidad Nacional de La Plata al XVII Congreso Internacional de Americanistas en su reunión de Buenos Aires en mayo 16 a 21 de 1910*. Buenos Aires: Imprenta de Coni Hermanos, [1770] 1910.

Sepp, Antonio S.J. *Continuación de las labores apostólicas*. Vol. II. Ed. Werner Hoffman. Buenos Aires: Editorial Universitaria de Buenos Aires, 1973.

Tomichá Charupá, Roberto. *La primera evangelización en las reducciones de Chiquitos, Bolivia (1691–1767)*. Cochabamba: Editorial Verbo Divino, 2002.

Valle, Ivonne del. *Escribiendo desde los márgenes: Colonialismo y jesuitas en el siglo XVIII*. Mexico City: Siglo XXI Editores, 2009.

Villodas, Marcos. "Pojha ñaña. Materia médica misionera o Herbario de las Reducciones Guaraníes. Misiones. Año de 1725 por Marcos Villodas S.J." Reference MsAmer31. Wellcome Library, London, England. MS.

Vincent, Bernard, and Pierre-Antoine Fabre, eds. *Missions religieuses modernes: "Notre Lieu est le monde."* Rome: École Française de Rome, 2007.

Wilde, Guillermo. *Religión y poder en las misiones de guaraníes*. Buenos Aires: Editorial SB, 2009.

———. "De las crónicas jesuíticas a las 'etnografías estatales': Realidades y ficciones del orden misional en las fronteras Ibéricas." *Nuevo Mundo, Mundos Nuevos* (Nov. 2011). Web: nuevomundo.revues.org/62249?lang=es. 20 August 2015.

———., ed. *Saberes de la conversión: Jesuitas, indígenas e imperios coloniales en las fronteras de la cristiandad*. Buenos Aires: Editorial SB, 2011.

Yapuguay, Nicolas. *Sermones y Exemplos en lengua guarani / Por Nicolas Yapuguay / Con direction / de vn religioso de la compañía / de Iesus*. Edición facsimilar de la edición principe del año 1727. Buenos Aires: Editorial Guarania, 1953.

Zatyrka Pacheco, Alexander Paul. "El 'modo nuestro de proceder' en la práctica misionera de Francisco Xavier. Una impronta al método jesuítico de misión ad gentes." *San Francisco Javier entre dos continentes*. Ed. by I. Arellano Ayuso, A. González Acosta, and A. Herrera Curiel. Madrid: Iberoamericana Vervuert, 2014.

Zubillaga, Félix. "El procurador de la Compañía de Jesús en la corte de españa (1570)." *Archivum Historicum Societatis Iesu* 16 (1947): 1–55.

◆ CHAPTER NINE

The Iridescent *Enconchado*

Charlene Villaseñor Black[1]

Enconchado paintings—multimedia artworks created in colonial New Spain in the late seventeenth and early eighteenth centuries—combine oil painting on wood panel with iridescent mother-of-pearl inlay. So far, several hundred have come to light, all made in Mexico City, with production peaking between 1690 and 1710 (Bargellini 187–89; Castelló Yturbide 149). Documents have been discovered identifying artists by name—most notably, members of the González family, along with important viceregal painters such as Nicolás Correa, Agustín del Pino, and others (Bargellini 187; Tovar de Teresa, "Documentos"; Tovar de Teresa, "Los artistas").[2] In some cases, scholars have identified patrons—all members of the elite, including the viceroy and high-status creoles. A significant number of *enconchados* ended up at the Spanish court, including twenty-four panels for King Charles II; others in the homes of Spanish nobility; and even some in Spanish churches and convents (García Sáiz, "Nuevos materiales" 135; García Sáiz, *La pintura* 5 6).[3] Based on analysis of commissioning documents and inventories recording *enconchados*, eminent art historian Clara Bargellini has suggested that most of these works were made for domestic settings, an idea supported by their dimensions (187). *Enconchados* are diminutive in size compared to larger works such as altarpieces, but can be as much as three to four feet tall and two to three feet wide.

These works have only recently become the object of sustained inquiry, a result of current interest in materiality in art history and the humanities. Previously, scholars overlooked *enconchados* because of their composite construction and the artists' use of shell mosaic, which made the works seem more like decorative, rather than fine, art. Additionally, the growth of technical art history, an interdisciplinary field that joins conservation science and traditional art historical study, has focused attention on the material construction of artworks. Thriving interest in global trade during the early modern period is an additional factor in the current attention to *enconchados*.[4]

This essay is inspired by these trends, and furthermore seeks to consider the works in the context of early modern Iberian globalization. *Enconchados* are the perfect vehicles for this inquiry since, despite advances in their study, tracing the origins of and the artistic influences on *enconchados* has been a complex and confounding endeavor for art historians. Much attention has focused on the Asian origins of the technique of mother-of-pearl inlay and on conjecture as to the ethnicity of the objects' creators. To complicate the question of artistic sources, mother-of-pearl inlay has been used around the world and over the centuries to create material objects; possible sources for *enconchados* include the ancient Americas, Europe, and the Middle East. Such speculation about ultimate visual precedents or sources of inspiration, and attempts to establish the ethnicity of makers based on style, expose the limitations of the language of art history to account for the complex cultural products of the global early modern world.

In fact, *enconchados* bring to mind the sort of objects discussed by Alessandra Russo in her recent book *The Untranslatable Image*, in the introduction to which she presents for consideration an altar cloth from San Miguel Tzinacantepec, Mexico, dating from the seventeenth or eighteenth century (Tepotzotlán, Viceregal Museum). Crafted of feathers affixed to cotton and depicting a variety of human figures, animals, flowers, and other decorative motifs, this altar cloth has thus far challenged scholars to securely pin down its style, its iconography, even its date. Russo writes, "Its images intersect so much that it seems impossible to identify any of its 'ancestors'" (*The Untranslatable* 12). Is it indigenous, or derived from European popular art? Russo's suggestion of "untranslatable" as a label to categorize such objects seems apropos. Influenced by Aby Warburg's theorization of "difficult objects," Russo borrowed the term from French philosopher and philologist Barbara Cassin, who writes, "to speak of untranslatable does not signify that these terms . . . are not or cannot be translated—the untranslatable is rather what one never stops (not) translating" (Warburg 293–330; Cassin xvii; Russo, *The Untranslatable* 6). Russo proposes this new qualifier, "untranslatable," as a corrective to the current art historical vocabularies used for colonial art, which she rightly deems inadequate (1-15). The *enconchados* of viceregal New Spain, similar to Russo's altar cloth, exemplify the notion of untranslatability, or unfixability. In an attempt to move beyond the impasse of untranslatability, I focus in this essay on the materiality of *enconchados*, on their shiny amalgamated surfaces, created from shell, oil paint, and colored varnishes. Indeed, their iridescent surfaces have motivated my methodology, inspiring me to rethink art historians' quests for ultimate visual precedents, neatly articulated genealogies, and definitive artistic sources. Instead, what can a focus on surfaces tell us about such early modern artifacts? I return to this question in my conclusion, as I propose a new way to think about early modern art and globalization.

(Dis)locating Origins

To date, most scholars have focused on the Asian roots of the Mexican *enconchado* technique of shell inlay. Mother-of-pearl inlay originated in China during the Song period (960-1127), then spread to Thailand, India, Japan, and Korea. An example from China—a sumptuous twelve-panel screen, *Spring Morning in the Han Palace*, from the Qing dynasty, Kangxi period, which dates from between 1662 and 1722 [Fig. 9.1], roughly contemporaneous with the Mexican *enconchados*—can be considered representative of the technique. Constructed from wood, the screen is covered with black lacquer and embellished with mother-of-pearl mosaic, crushed shell, and gold foil inlay (Leidy 9-50, especially 40-41). The screen's artist used iridescent shell to create all parts of the scene represented—figures, architecture, and landscape elements.

Although the technique originated in China, most scholars have singled out Japanese influence on Mexican *enconchados* because of Spanish attempts to missionize, colonize, and conduct trade in Japan in the early modern period.[5] A number of researchers have published research on these connections, linking *enconchados* to Nanban objects, Japanese exportware imported to New Spain via Manila galleons beginning in 1573 (Armella de Aspe 12; Castelló Yturbide 140-42; Rivero Lake and Vallarino 246; and Rivero Lake). "Nanban" translates as "Southern barbarians" (i.e., Europeans, referring specifically to Portuguese and Spaniards). Nanban artworks reflect some European influence and were intended for use by missionaries or to be traded. Such objects are documented in European royal inventories beginning in the sixteenth century (Leidy 9). Typical Nanban works are made of lacquered wood and include liturgical objects such as lecterns, portable altars, furniture, and other decorative arts [Fig. 9.2]. Many Nanban works imported into Mexico use shell mosaic, and sometimes tortoise-

FIGURE 9.1. *Women in a Palace*, detail from *Spring Morning in the Han Palace*, Qing dynasty, Kangxi period (between 1662 and 1722), 9 ft. 4 5/8 in. × 24 ft. 8 1/16 in. (286.1 × 752 cm), purchase, The Vincent Astor Foundation Gift, 2001, The Metropolitan Museum of Art, New York.

shell, and look somewhat similar to *enconchados*, thus suggesting Nanban art as a possible source of inspiration.

In fact, Mexican antiquarian Rodrigo Rivero Lake has suggested that Japanese Nanban artists who had immigrated to New Spain made *enconchados*. Miguel and Juan González, who signed a series of *enconchados* that represent scenes of the Conquest, were supposedly Japanese. Rivero Lake extrapolates from several notarial documents published by Guillermo Tovar de Teresa in 1986. One of them, a lease for a house in Mexico City, names father and son artists Tomás and Miguel González. The former is described as a "maestro de pintor de maque" (master of lacquer painting), and his son as an "oficial de dicho arte de pintura" (official of said art of painting). The notary of another document, a contract commissioning a series of artworks, "láminas de pintura y embutida, de concha" (sheets of painting and inlay, of shell), names Juan González, Miguel's brother, as a creator of *enconchados* (Tovar de Teresa 1986, 98–100). From the reference to lacquer in the first document, Rivero assumes that Tomás and Miguel were Japanese. Lacquerware was, and is, an art traceable to Japan (among other places),

FIGURE 9.2. Lectern, Japan, Momoyama period (first third of the seventeenth century), wood, mother-of-pearl inlay (*enconchado*), and lacquer, dimensions unknown, Cathedral, Pontevedra (Tuy), Spain, Archivo Oronoz, Madrid.

and it was especially popular in western Mexico, the probable entry point for Japanese immigrants, so it is not impossible to believe that artists working in lacquer may have been of Japanese descent. Furthermore, Rivero Lake suggests that Christianized Japanese immigrants to Mexico frequently took "González" as a last name, based on "embarkation records" from ships traveling from Japan to Mexico, but unfortunately he does not reproduce or cite any of these documents (Rivero Lake 156–60, 297).[6] Rivero Lake's argument about Japanese artists in Mexico is suggestive but calls for additional verifying documentation. Other scholars have uncovered various documents recording the presence of Japanese immigrants in colonial New Spain, an intriguing link that could help confirm Japanese influence on viceregal art.[7]

Building on the thesis that Nanban art is the major artistic source of inspiration for *enconchados*, recent research by Mexican art historian Sonia Ocaña Ruiz draws on the material evidence of the artworks themselves. Focusing on the floral decoration of *enconchado* frames, she has identified striking similarities to Nanban art (Ocaña Ruiz, "*Enconchado*" 129). The closest source for Mexican *enconchados* does, then, seem to be Nanban objects, at least for the frames. The major scenes themselves, though, depart significantly from Japanese Nanban and other Asian models in the privileging of both iridescence and "reality effects," to borrow Roland Barthes's term for strategies to suggest reality or facticity, in early modern Europe and the Americas, as I shall demonstrate (Barthes 141–48). Another fruitful avenue to explore is the possibility of Korean influence, a prospect mentioned briefly by Rivero Lake and others (Rivero Lake; Ávila). Preliminary comparison to Korean mother-of-pearl inlay reveals compelling similarities that merit closer consideration. The most likely avenue of transmission was Korean influence on Japanese artists producing Nanban artworks.[8]

The extent of global trade and the mobility of people and objects in the early modern world further complicate attempts to trace lines of influence (Álvarez and Villaseñor Black 267–75). Style and the use of specific artistic techniques such as inlay seem insufficient for identifying the origin of an artwork in the case at hand. Can we really discern the ethnicity and geographic origin of an object's creator through stylistic analysis?[9] Furthermore, mother-of-pearl inlay was also employed in Indo-Portuguese objects, some of which copy works from other regions. Rivero Lake, for example, has published Colombian copies of Mexican works that imitate Nanban, objects that, like Russo's altar cloth, seem to defy categorization (Rivero Lake 304–5). Current art historical language that defines and traces stylistic influence and visual precedence—still major tasks of the art historian—seems insufficient to explain the genesis of such visually complex works, whose intersecting, interfolding array of possible influences confounds art historical discourse. On the question of visual sources, one of the leading authorities on *enconchados* has observed, "Viceregal Mexico did not play a passive role in the reception of Asian art, but reworked features of Asian objects into its own distinctive production of folding screens, ceramic and lacquer objects, and the paintings on wood inlaid with mother-of-pearl known today as *enconchados*" (Ocaña Ruiz, "*Enconchado*" 129). Her observation is important because it rejects the interpretation of colonial art as merely imitative of imported sources. In the process, it also challenges the idea that the early modern world comprised a network of privileged sites of cultural generation that influenced other, peripheral locales, such as New Spain, the colonized, passive recipient of European or Asian thought.

Besides, is "Japanese influence" a sufficient explanation for the creation and popularity of these unusual artworks in viceregal Mexico? In contrast to the shell pieces in Nanban works, and the use of shell more generally on Asian screens and even in European examples, Mexican artists seem to have been more strategic about their use and placement of shell pieces. This observation raises a number of questions about these unusual works that remain unanswered in the current art historical literature. How and why did Mexican artists choose to employ iridescent shell fragments in these scenes, and where in the compositions were they placed? Did this strategic use of shimmering shell inflect the meaning of the images? In addition, what can be suggested about the materiality of *enconchados*? What is known of the shell employed, and where did it come from? I also address the links between *enconchados* and other artworks that privilege iridescence—notably, featherworks and textiles. How was this fascination with shifting, ephemeral reflections and glowing, iridescent colors linked to new interests in natural science? These are the questions I pose, bypassing the urge to fix a stylistic origin or genealogy for *enconchados*. While my approach is similar to Russo's in its deemphasis of stylistic influence and its recognition of the complexity of the early modern visual world, I take a strong cue from the objects' materiality in an attempt to advance historical, contextual understanding. I hope to shift focus to a close examination of the surfaces of *enconchados*— to their materiality—in an attempt to demonstrate how they produced meaning in the global early modern Hispanic world. I call this approach a methodology of iridescence, and, like the glinting surfaces of *enconchados* creating ceaseless reflections, it generates multiple destabilizing questions and, as we shall see, new understandings of previously opaque art objects.

The Materiality of Shells

Let us begin with close inspection of the material construction of *enconchados*. Scientific analysis conducted in Mexico on the famous Conquest series of panels in Argentina and Madrid's Museo de América has clarified the process of creation. Artists combined oil painting on wood panel (or sometimes canvas) with shell mosaic, which was enhanced with drawing and finally covered with shiny layers of varnish or oil glaze. In some cases, the artist(s) inserted a layer

FIGURE 9.3. Miguel González, *Virgin of Guadalupe*, circa 1698, oil on canvas on wood with mother-of-pearl inlay (*enconchado*), 49 × 37 in (124.46 × 95.25 cm), Los Angeles County Museum of Art, Los Angeles.

FIGURE 9.4. Miguel Gonzalez, *Virgin of Guadalupe*, late seventeenth century, oil on canvas on wood with mother-of-pearl inlay (*enconchado*), dimensions unknown, Museo de América, Madrid.

of cardboard or paper (*cartón*) on top of the wood, a technique clearly derived from Asian screens. The final layers of glaze and varnish created the translucent, glowing surface seen on many Mexican *enconchados*, as did the variegated pieces of shell, which are colored in a variety of hues ranging from golds, whites, and tans to pinks, blues, and greens (González; Escalera Ureña and Rivas Díaz).[10]

This essay focuses on one of the panels of the aforementioned Conquest series, one of the best-known and most closely studied sets of *enconchados*, as well as on three images of the Virgin of Guadalupe, the most common sacred subject depicted by *enconchado* artists, all by the most prominent masters of the genre, Miguel and Juan González (Armella de Aspe 82). In addition, I examine a scene of the Education of the Virgin recently acquired by the Los Angeles County Museum of Art (LACMA), and specifically its handling of drapery and architectural details [Figs. 9.3, 9.4, 9.5]. These works, like most other *enconchados*, selectively employ the mosaic technique.

LACMA's recently acquired Virgin of Guadalupe, dated to around 1698, is signed by Miguel González [Fig. 9.3] (Katzew, "The Virgin"). In this example, the standard four Guadalupan apparitions surround Mary's luminescent figure, depicting her three appearances to Juan Diego and the culminating revelation of her image to the archbishop of Mexico City. The dove of the Holy Spirit appears above, balanced below by the symbol of the founding of Tenochtitlán, an eagle perched on a cactus. This *enconchado* preserves its original frame, which was an integral part of the design, as it is decorated with symbols of the Immaculate Conception.

The other two *enconchados* of the Virgin of Guadalupe, both from the Museo de América in Madrid, date from 1697 and were collaborations of Miguel and Juan González (Vargaslugo 119–55). In the simpler variant, [Fig. 9.4], the artists attempted to replicate the original *tilma* (cloak) in shell mosaic, while Mary appears surrounded by delicate roses, petals picked out in shiny pink and white nacre.

At her feet is the site of Tepeyac, its architectural details differentiated in luminescent white shell. In the final depiction [Fig. 9.5], portraits of saints surround the Virgin, with God the Father at the top and a rare representation of Jesse at the bottom; this latter is an allusion to the Tree of Jesse, a shorthand indicator of the genealogy of Jesus, and a reference to Isaiah 11.1: "And there shall come forth a rod out of the root of Jesse, and a flower shall rise up out of his root." Saints Joachim and Anne, Mary's parents, flank her figure at the top, with two depictions of St. Francis below, the one on the left revealing the saint's stigmata and the one on the right representing the miracle of the crucifix at San Damiano. At the bottom, the two Saint Johns appear, the Baptist on the left and the Evangelist on the right.

FIGURE 9.5. Miguel González, *Virgin of Guadalupe with Saints*, 1692, oil on canvas on wood with mother-of-pearl inlay (*enconchado*), 34 1/4 × 27 in. with frame (87 × 69 cm), Madrid, Museo de América, Album / Art Resource, NY.

FIGURE 9.6. Miguel González and Juan González, *Moctezuma Offering Gold Presents to Hernán Cortés*, detail from *The Conquest of Mexico*, 1698, oil on canvas with cardboard and mother-of-pearl (*enconchado*), 80 8/10 × 48 in.; 38 1/5 × 20 4/5 in. (205 × 121 cm; 97 × 53 cm), Madrid, Museo de América, Album / Art Resource, NY.

In LACMA's *enconchado* representing the Education of the Virgin, which dates from the late seventeenth century, a partial, although illegible, signature can be detected in the bottom left (Katzew, "The Education"). In this unusual scene, the child Virgin appears in the classroom in the temple, learning with the other girls. The unidentified artist used shell to create the draperies and details of the architecture. The final *enconchado* considered in this essay [Fig. 9.6] is a detail of one of the Conquest series of screens showing Moctezuma offering gold presents to Hernán Cortés, dated to 1698 and signed by both Juan and Miguel González (Vargaslugo). Because the artwork appears in Spanish King Charles II's inventory from the year 1700, scholars have assumed he commissioned it (Ocaña Ruiz, "Nuevas reflexiones" 129). The González brothers used shell both in the designs on the frame and to evoke the shiny armor of the Spanish and Aztec soldiers.

Close examination of these works and others as well as comparison to other possible sources in Asian, European, and Middle Eastern art demonstrate several key points about Mexican *enconchados*. Unlike their possible sources of artistic inspiration, *enconchados* almost never use shell for figures' faces or bodies but instead use it most frequently for drapery and to replicate metal, stone, flower petals, or feathers, as in the case of depictions of armor, architecture, roses, or angels' wings. In other words, in the body of these works, shell tends to be used to represent shiny, iridescent materials. Thus, the use of mother-of-pearl is not solely decorative, as in many of the Japanese Nanban works and other potential sources. This is a notable deviation from other examples of shell inlay, and a major innovation by New Spanish artists. Furthermore, the color of the shell varies considerably in Mexican *enconchados*, in contrast to most other examples, which clearly privilege either luminous white pearl shell or naturally occurring iridescent pinks and greens. In these examples, artists employed shells of all the same color, a more abstract approach to creating the image that is less interested in creating reality effects—that is, in suggesting facticity or reality. Mexican *enconchados* demonstrate a greater variety of colors thanks to the use of varying colors of shell and the application of an oil glaze and/or varnish brushed over the mosaics.

Careful inspection of the shell in *enconchados* reveals Mexican artists' unique visual strategies in its deployment. But what was the source of the shell used, identified as mother-of-pearl, or *madreperla*? Was it the same as the shell used in Nanban works? While on the surface this seems like a straightforward question, the answer is not obvious, since mother-of-pearl is derived from common mollusk shells, which can be found around the globe, in both fresh and saltwater (Leidy 9). Produced by the mollusk itself, mother-of-pearl results from the secretion of layer upon layer of lustrous calcium carbonate, which create its hard,

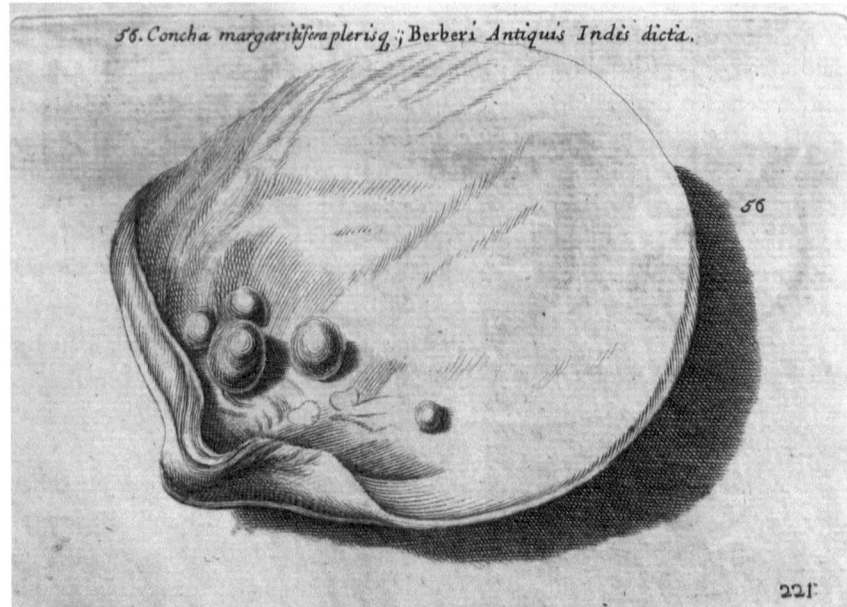

FIGURE 9.7. Martin Lyster, "Pinctada Mazatlanica," *Historiae Conchyliorum*, 1670, 498001, Huntington Library, San Marino, California.

protective shell. Mollusk genetics, food, and water conditions influence the shells' varying color, thickness, and iridescence. Over the centuries and around the globe, artists cut away the naturally iridescent interior parts of mollusk shells, polished them, and finally trimmed them for use in mosaic.

In the case of Mexican *enconchados*, the source of the shell was Mexico itself, specifically the Pacific coast of Baja California, according to documents and other reports, and possibly also the coast near Oaxaca. Both were important pearl fishing areas. Shells, the discarded by-product of the search for pearls, began to be sold to supplement income from the pearl fisheries in Mexico as early as the seventeenth century. A document from 1737, around the time of the production of *enconchados*, indicates that 92 *arrobas* of shells (about 2,300 pounds) were shipped to Seville from Veracruz in May of that year (Castelló Yturbide).[11] Other early sources indicate that the shells were sold to make up for lost profit as pearl production decreased (Kunz and Stevenson 238–39).[12] The 1737 document identifies the shells being sold. Of the two kinds of mussel shells that contained pearls, only one possessed a shell thick enough to be cut and reused, whereas the other was very fragile. The shell used in *enconchado* paintings thus derives from *Pinctada mazatlanica*, also called the La Paz pearl oyster, which is found in the eastern Pacific from Baja California to Peru [Fig. 9.7] (Landman and Mikkelson 32–33; Armella de Aspe 22, 24).[13]

Interestingly, this same shell has been identified by archeologists in pre-Columbian objects recovered in Mexico, and more work needs to be done on the possible links between pre-Columbian and colonial shellwork.[14] Shellwork was a highly developed art form in the ancient Americas, as evidenced by objects made from the beautiful, colorful *Spondylus* shell. *Spondylus* was so valued that the Aztecs gathered it as tribute, as seen in the Codex Mendoza, a manuscript created around 1540–42 by an indigenous artist.

Attention to the materiality of shells sheds new light on our understanding of *enconchados*. The work of conservation scientists, for example, clarified the material construction of the artworks. Close examination of how artists in New Spain employed shell mosaic to replicate shiny, iridescent materials revealed the innovative nature of their creations, particularly in comparison to possible artistic sources, such as Asian art. The source of the shell was discovered to be Mexico itself, a fact that inspires the search for meaning in the local milieu of New Spain, a topic to be addressed in the next section. Other work, however, remains to be done, such as investigation into possible continuities with pre-Columbian shellwork, as well as additional archival investigation, particularly focused on Oaxaca. Finally, consultation with malacologists, zoologists who specialize in mollusks, might reveal information on mollusk genetics along the Pacific coast to help explain the variations in shell used.

The Meaning of Iridescence

As archival documents have clearly demonstrated, mollusk shells were readily available in colonial Mexico, but easy access is not enough to explain why artists chose to employ them to create *enconchados*. Why did viceregal artists make paintings that incorporated shiny shell fragments, and how did their use of shell produce meaning? I have pursued various avenues as I attempt to answer these questions, taking account of patronage, looking at documentary and literary sources of the period, investigating the history of science, and comparing analogous artworks such as feather paintings and textiles to the *enconchados* themselves. My approach is inspired by the iridescent sheen of the *enconchados* and rooted in the local sourcing of the mollusk shell.

The monumental Mexican baroque poem, *La grandeza mexicana*, penned by Bernardo de Balbuena in 1604, has been a major source of information for understanding the meanings associated with pearls and mother-of-pearl in viceregal New Spain. In this laudatory epistolary poem, Balbuena catalogues the riches of New Spain—its arts, natural resources, and trade—including a number of references to Mexico's pearl industry. In fact, both "lustrous nacre" and pearls of the "mar del Sur," the "South Sea" or Pacific Ocean, are praised in the second stanza. Mother-of-pearl reappears, along with pearls, at various other times throughout the poem, and again in the closing chapter (Balbuena 91). One of the final stanzas reads: "y de sus playas en los más profundos / senos lucir los nácares preciosos, / que de perlas te dan partos fecundos" (122) (And from its beaches in its deepest bays / shine precious pearl shells, / that give you abundant births of pearls). Elsewhere in his work, Balbuena singles them out again, associating them with "heroic beauty" and "deep knowledge" gifted to humans: "Oh tú, heroica beldad, saber profundo, / que por milagro puesta a los mortales / en todo fuiste la última del mundo; // criada en los desiertos arenales, / sobre que el mar del Sur resaca y quiebra / nácar lustroso y perlas orientales" (63) (Oh you, heroic beauty, deep knowledge, / by a miracle given to humans / in all you were the last of the world; // raised in desert sands, / on which the Pacific recedes and breaks / lustrous nacre and oriental pearls). Balbuena's poem makes two points clear: first, that mother-of-pearl was associated with the pearl industry in New Spain, and second, that pearl shell was singled out as a valued, distinctive natural product of Mexico.[15] It is clear that period viewers valued mother-of-pearl as an important natural resource of New Spain and associated it with the riches of pearl fishing, pointing to the significance of pearl shell mosaic in Mexican *enconchados*.

This appreciation of shell demonstrated by the *enconchados* and Balbuena's poem can also be situated within the larger arena of the history of science. The seventeenth century was the great era of interest in shells, as evidenced by the first major publication cataloging shells from around the world, the *Historia Conchyliorum*, with more than 1000 print illustrations, published in 1685–92 by Martin Lister [Fig. 9.7], and other related texts, such as Philippo Buonanni's *Recreatio mentis et oculi* (1684) and Georg Eberhard Rumpf's *D'Amboinsche Rariteitkamer* (1705), as well as the invention of the discipline of conchology, the study of mollusk shells.[16] Shells were also a popular item in *kunstkammern*, or cabinets of curiosity. Notable collectors of seashells, signifiers of European imperialism, the exotic, and scientific interests, can be documented throughout Europe in the sixteenth and seventeenth centuries (Dance; Dietz 369–75). By the eighteenth century, three major European centers had emerged for shell collecting: the Netherlands, Paris, and England (Dietz 369–70). As indicated by period sources, the most beautiful, rare, and collectible shells came from Asia or the Middle East. Striking specimens became the object of shell still lives, the specialty of Netherlandish artists such as Adriann Coorte, who worked in the city of Middleburg, and others (Slive). In contrast, collectors did not hold shells from the Americas in high esteem (Dietz 373–44).

Not particularly collectible, surplus Mexican mussel shells were transformed by artists into *enconchado* mosaics, made into pearl buttons, cut into delicate spoons, and used as decorative inlay in furniture, according to period sources.[17] Another context in which to think about *enconchados*, then, is within baroque meditation on notions of culture and the role of human ingenuity in the crafting of cultural artifacts from naturalia, theorized by such people as Anthony J. Cascardi.[18] Additional work needs to be done on this subject and others. For example, how did *enconchados* produce meaning within the context of seventeenth- and eighteenth-century interest in optics and Westerners' burgeoning knowledge of the mechanics of human vision?[19] But the most important context in which *enconchado* shell mosaic produced meaning is the history of textiles. The strategic placement of shiny shell fragments to mimic drapery in *enconchados* brings to mind iridescent fabrics such as changeable silk, or shot silk, known as *tornesol* [Fig. 9.8].

Translated by textile historian Elena Phipps as "turns to the sun," *tornesol* was fashionable among the upper classes beginning in the sixteenth century in Spain and elsewhere in Europe (Phipps 221).[20] Created by employing two different colors of thread, one in the weft and another for the warp, the fabric becomes iridescent, especially when in motion, seeming to change color as it moves. Surviving *tornesol* fabrics from the period are rare; an example of a man's suit from 1790, employing purple and black threads, gives an idea of the shimmering effect [Fig. 9.8]. Early modern painters such as El Greco also represented *tornesol* fabrics, and one can glean an impression of their sheen from period paintings [Fig. 9.9]. Note the draperies worn by the kneeling adolescent angel in the top left foreground of El Greco's *Assumption*, a shiny *tornesol* woven from purple and yellow threads.

The effect of the shell draperies in *enconchado* paintings is not dissimilar to that of *tornesol* silk, and, in fact, Mexican artists enhanced the luminescence of the shell fragments by brushing pigments suspended in glazes or colored varnishes over the surface, a technique unique to Mexican art. The viewer beholds moving reflections, glimmering and shifting lights, sparkles and luminosity, not unlike *tornesol* fabrics in motion. These scintillating light effects must have been even more pronounced when these works were seen in their original settings—interior spaces lit by candlelight.[21] Imagine the effect of flickering light reflecting off their gleaming surfaces, light sparkling, refracting off the luminous pieces of shell. How differently the viewer today perceives these works, on display in museums, under strong, uniform light.

FIGURE 9.8. Man's suit, 1790 (altered 1805), silk plain weave (shot taffeta) with sequins and metallic-thread embroidery, coat center back length 45 1/2 in. (115.57 cm); breeches side length 26 1/2 in. (67.31 cm), purchased with funds provided by Suzanne A. Saperstein and Michael and Ellen Michelson, with additional funding from the Costume Council, the Edgerton Foundation, Gail and Gerald Oppenheimer, Maureen H. Shapiro, Grace Tsao, and Lenore and Richard Wayne, Los Angeles County. Museum of Art, Los Angeles, www.lacma.org.

FIGURE 9.9. El Greco, *Assumption of the Virgin*, 1577–79, oil on canvas, 158 3/4 × 83 3/4 in, (403.2 × 211.8 cm), Art Institute of Chicago, Chicago / Art Resource, NY.

FIGURE 9.10. Agustín del Pino, St. Ignatius Loyola, circa 1700, oil on wood with mother-of-pearl inlay (*enconchado*), 43 1/2 × 33 1/8 in. (110.49 × 84,1375 cm), Denver Art Museum Collection, Denver, Gift of the Collection of Frederick and Jan Mayer, 2013.302. Photography courtesy of the Denver Art Museum.

Viceregal artists used shell to recreate draperies in *enconchado* paintings. In fact, the very first *enconchado* painting still extant, a *Salvator Mundi* dating from the sixteenth century, employs crushed shell in the draperies to mimic textiles—in this case, probably in imitation of brocade, with its golden or silvery threads. Similar strategies can be seen in any number of *enconchados*, including a seventeenth-century example representing St. Anthony, where crushed shell was used to create a glittery, textured brocade.[22] In a stunning example by Agustín del Pino from the eighteenth century, depicting St. Ignatius of Loyola, the pieces of shell were deployed to suggest richly embellished draperies [Fig. 9.10].

Balbuena's *La grandeza mexicana* had much to say about the textiles of New Spain, including silks and brocades, catalogued at three different places in the poem. In one stanza, in fact, the author seems to single out *tornesol*: "Telares de oro, telas de obra primar, / de varias seda, de colores varias, / de gran primor, gran gala y grande estima; / el oro hilado, que con las voltarias / hebras que el aire alumbran entretienen / mil bellas manos y horas solitarias" (Balbuena 81–82) (Looms of gold, fabrics of premium work / of various silks, of various colors / of great beauty, great finery, and great esteem; / spun gold, that with ever-changing threads that illuminate the air / a thousand beautiful hands and solitary hours).[23]

The first dictionary of Castillian, Sebastián de Covarrubias's *Tesoro de la lengua Castellana, o Española*, published in 1611, includes a discussion of *tornesol* textiles (here spelled *tornasol*) in an entry dedicated to *tornasol* plants and flowers, thus establishing a link between such textiles (and the *enconchados* imitating them) and scientific inquiry into heliotropic plants. Let us examine Covarrubias's dictionary entry: "TORNASOL, yerua conocida, llamada de los Griegos Heliotropio. Diósele este nombre porque sus flores y ramas se van conuirtiendo con el mouimiento del Sol, desde que nace hasta que se pone. . . . Ay cierta tela de seda y lana deste nombre, por tener diuersos visos puesta al Sol." (1338) (TORNASOL, a known plant, called Heliotrope by the Greeks. It was given this name because its flowers and branches turn with the movement of the Sun, from dawn to sunset. . . . There is a certain fabric of silk and wool of this name, because it has a different sheen when facing the sun). Covarrubias thus links period taste for these iridescent fabrics, their glinting sheen reflecting the movement of light, to plants that follow the sun. Scientific texts documenting the flora of the New World, in fact, carefully describe heliotropic plants. The most famous example was, of course, the sunflower, called *girasol*. Flemish baroque artist Anthony Van Dyck memorialized it in his *Self Portrait with Sunflower* of about 1630 (private collection), a painting that employs cochineal, another New World product, to tint the reddish costume, according to Barbara Anderson ("Evidence" 365). A number of botanical prints can be cited. Flemish artist Joris Hoefnagel gracefully illuminated the "marvel of Peru" (also

FIGURE 9.11. Artist Unidentified, *Christ (Salvator Mundi)*, feather mosaic, sixteenth century, 30 1/2 × 27 1/2 in (85 × 70 cm) (without frame), Mexico, Museo Virreinal, Tepozotlán, Archivo Fotográfico "Manuel Toussaint," Instituto de Investigaciones Estéticas.

FIGURE 9.12. Juan Bautista Cuiris, *Christ as a Young Man*, feather mosaic, circa 1590/1600, 10 × 7 1/6 in (25.4 × 18.2 cm), Kunsthistorisches Museum, Vienna.

called a "four o'clock," the *Mirabilis jalapa*) in *Mira Calligraphiae Monumenta* (Vienna, 1561–1562 and 1591–1596), on folio 32, and produced another engraving of the same flower, entitled *Ipsa Dies Aperit: Conficit Ipsa Dies* (One Day Brings It Forth and the Same Day Ends It) in *Archetypa Stvdiaqve Patris Georgii Hoefnagelii* (Frankfurt, 1592), plate 9. Amsterdam artist and herbalist Emanuel Sweerts produced an engraving of a sunflower in his *Florilegium amplissimum et selectissimum*. *Mira Calligraphiae Monumenta* (Most Ample and Select Gathering of Flowers. Model Book of Calligraphy) by Joris Hoefnagel (Frankfurt, 1612), part 2, plate 25.[24]

As these various artworks and texts reveal, iridescence was a prominent cultural interest, one associated with heliotropism in plants—that is, the movement of plants in response to the sun. Artists in New Spain valued iridescence in other artistic genres: for example, in feather paintings, particularly those that employed glinting hummingbird feathers [Figs. 9.11 and 9.12].[25] In both of these works, produced by indigenous artists in Mexico in the sixteenth century, iridescent hummingbird feathers produce a shimmering effect. Notice, in particular, the iridescent green globe held in Christ's hand in the *Salvator Mundi* [Fig. 9.11] or the shimmering green background in the portrait of Christ [Fig. 9.12].

Writing in Mexico in the 1550s, Dominican friar Bartolomé de las Casas, in his *Apologética historia sumaria* (Apologetic History of the Indies), singled out such featherworks for their iridescence in an extensive passage:

> [P]or una parte mirándola parece ser dorada, sin tener oro; por otra parte parece tornasol; por otra tiene lustre verde, no teniendo principalmente verdura; por otra, mirada al través, tiene otra hermosa color, y por otra, otra, y así de otras muchas, todas con lustre y maravillosa gracia; de aquí es que se suele un oficial de éstos estar sin comer sin beber un día entero, poniendo y quitando plumas, según que vee más convenir los matices, y para que la obra cause más diferencia de lustres y colores y más hermosura, mirando, como dije, de un parte y después de otra; una vez mirándola al sol, otras a la sombra, otras de noche, otras de día o casi de noche, otras con poca lumbre, otras con mucha, otras al través y por sosquín, otra por el contrario y al revés. (qtd. in Russo 86)

> *It appears to be gilded, without containing any gold; elsewhere, it has a sheen; on the other it has a green luster, without being really green; on the other, when viewed from one side, it has a different beautiful color, and from another, a different one, and so on from many others, all with a luster and wonderful grace; thus it is common for a tradesman working on these to go without eating and drinking for a whole day, while adding and removing feathers, according to how he sees the shades concentrating, and so that the work produces a greater variety of luster and color and more beauty, as I*

said, when viewed from one side and then the other; now looking at it in the sun, then in the shade, then at night, then in the day or the twilight, at other times with low light, at others in strong light, at other times from the side and at an angle, at others from a different one and on the reverse.[26]

All of these cultural products—iridescent *enconchados, tornesol* fabrics, shimmering feather mosaics—can be linked to broader scientific interest in heliotropism. Moreover, all demonstrate the valorization of light effects, reflections, and changeability in the period.

The frequent depiction of the Virgin of Guadalupe in *enconchado* paintings, several of which are presented in this article, raises another issue [Figs. 9.3, 9.4, 9.5]. Is iridescence relevant to sacred subject matter? Among sacred *enconchados,* the most frequent theme represented is the Virgin of Guadalupe (Armella de Aspe 82). The frequency of her depiction indicates the importance of creole devotion to her figure as well as her popularity throughout the Spanish empire, as *enconchado* images of her can be found not only in New Spain but also in Spain and other former possessions. The taste for this subject reflects the predilections of elite creole and Spanish patrons. In fact, Mexican *enconchados*, in general, exhibit a high incidence of unusual, learned iconographies. Examples include scenes picturing the Credo, a representation of Mary and St. Joseph looking for lodging, and the unusual depiction of the Virgin's Education in the Temple that shows the actual classroom where the temple girls learned.[27] These are erudite iconographies, not subjects that typically appear before the general populace in paintings or sculptures in churches. Privileged patronage of the *enconchados* can explain these iconographic anomalies and the frequent portrayal of the Virgin of Guadalupe. In fact, *enconchados*, because they were mostly created for elite domestic spaces, provide an index of the religious themes most popular among the creoles. María Concepción García Sáiz, curator at the Museo de América, has commented that *enconchados* clearly appealed to the learned ("Nuevos materiales" 139).[28]

Another possible explanation for these pearl shell images of the Virgin of Guadalupe is the traditional association of the Madonna with pearls, symbolism that dates back to the Middle Ages. Like the mussel, which miraculously produces a pearl, Mary miraculously generated the baby Jesus.[29] In Renaissance Europe, pearls were seen as symbolic of Mary's virginity, and hence, a woman's purity (de Jongh 69–97). An early nineteenth-century source comments specifically that in Mexico Mary was associated with pearls (Hardy). This association of Mary with pearls suggests that the iridescence of the pearl shell in these paintings evoked specific religious meanings. Could the material used here—pearl shell—have been intended to embody Mary's miraculous body, the shell of the pearl that was Christ?

The LACMA *enconchado* [Fig. 9.3] makes this association with purity explicit in its representation of Immaculist symbols in its frame. The Immaculate Conception, the belief that Mary herself was conceived without sin in the womb of her mother, St. Anne, was extremely popular in the early modern Hispanic world, although it did not receive papal approval until 1854. The subject appears frequently in art in New Spain and Spain beginning in the 1500s, the result of Franciscan promotion of the cult. The subject of the Virgin of Guadalupe is related to the Immaculate Conception, and its iconography derives from the same sources in the Book of Revelation and the Song of Songs. In the *enconchado*, we see the full-length standing Madonna floating against a bright golden sky (i.e., the *mandorla* or aureola), standing on a crescent moon, giving visual form to the description in Revelation 12.1 of the apocalyptic woman "clothed in the sun with the moon under her feet." Various Immaculist symbols appear in the frame around her: the sun and moon, the stairway to heaven, the spotless mirror, the tower of David, the lilies of purity, the *porta coeli* (door to heaven), and the well of living waters.[30] The foliage may refer to the enclosed garden or *hortus conclusus*, symbolic of Mary's virginity. The ship, seen on the right side of the frame, surely refers to Mary as "Stella Maris," or star of the sea, an important Marian advocation during the era of global maritime exploration and trade. One of the Madrid *enconchados* similarly emphasizes Mary's role as the pure vessel that bore Christ, in its articulation of the Tree of Jesse iconography [Fig. 9.5].

These intriguing associations between the Virgin Mary, pearls, and pearl shell indicate that not only does materiality matter to art historians and conservators today, but it also mattered to colonial creators and viewers. This idea is bolstered by a specific reference to mother-of-pearl that appears in a *villancico* by Felipe Santoyo García from 1690, a date that coincides perfectly with the production of *enconchado* images. Sung at matins on the Virgin of Guadalupe's feast day in Mexico City's cathedral, the song praises the miracle of "la Flor de Guadalupe," noting in one stanza how heaven gave the miraculous painting its blues, the lily gave it white, and the rose its shining mother-of-pearl: "Allí al mirar el prodigio de la / Flor de Guadalupe, no hay / diciembre que no acabe ni / Abril que flor no tribute / Para tan alta pintura del Cielo / da sus azules, la Azucena para / el blanco, la Rosa su nácar / pule" (qtd. in Armella de Aspe n.p.) (There, looking at the wonder of the / Flower of Guadalupe, there is no / December that ends nor / April which does not pay tribute in flower / To such a high painting, Heaven / gives it blues, for white, / the Lily, the Rose its nacre / shines).[31] This suggestion is given material form in depictions of the Virgin of Guadalupe, such as the examples in Madrid, in which the miraculous roses that encircle Mary are constructed of shiny, delicate petals crafted from shell, which match her iridescent draperies [Figs. 9.4 and 9.5].

Pearls are, of course, an expansive, elastic signifier. References to them abound in the Gospels and in other sacred texts. There are two famous references in the Gospel of Matthew: the parable of the pearl of great price, in Matthew 13.45–46, and the famous reference to casting pearls before swine in the Sermon of the Mount in Matthew 7.6. Both have traditionally been interpreted as referring to the kingdom of heaven and the word of God. According to St. Augustine, the pearl is a symbol of Christ; others have described it as a signifier of salvation, or of faith (de Jongh 76). The Book of Revelation refers to the "pearly gates" of heaven. Thus, it is not surprising that pearl shell would be invested with theological significance.

Pearls are also reminders of the riches of the New World, considered by Europeans to be one of the most significant finds in the Americas. A number of famous pearls had been found there, such as "La Peregrina," reportedly recovered by an African slave in the Gulf of Panama in the sixteenth century. King Philip II gave it to Mary Tudor and memorialized it in a portrait by Spanish court artist Anthonis Mor [Fig. 9.13]. This famous treasure reappears over the centuries in other royal portraits—for example, in court artist Juan Pantoja de la Cruz's painting of Margaret of Austria from 1606 (Madrid, Museo del Prado) and in Diego Velázquez's rendition of Queen Elizabeth on horseback from the 1630s (Madrid, Museo del Prado). Eventually, actress Elizabeth Taylor wore the pearl, a gift from Richard Burton. Pearls thus also represented the riches of European imperialism, plundered splendors of a New World.

Conclusions: Iridescence as Methodology

Iridescent Mexican *enconchado* paintings, when compared to their possible artistic sources, are unique in their selective use of pearl shell to mimic draperies, metals, stone, and feathers. They formed part of a web of relationships between luminous textiles, shimmering featherworks, and heliotropic plants. The origin of the shell was Mexico itself, and specifically the Pacific coast. Literary sources such as Balbuena's *La grandeza mexicana* help recover some of the images' original meanings. Other notable characteristics emerged: the prevalence of *enconchados* with religious subject matter depicting the Virgin of Guadalupe, and the presence of obscure, learned iconographies.

But to return to one of the issues with which I began this essay: Can we explain or even convincingly identify the complex network of sources that inspired the creation of Mexican *enconchados*? I admit: I am confounded. No art historical language seems to exist to explain adequately the genesis of these

FIGURE 9.13. Anthonis Mor, *Portrait of Queen Mary I of England (Tudor)*, 1554, oil on wood, 42 9/10 × 33 in (109 × 84 cm), Museo del Prado, Madrid, Erich Lessing / Art Resource, NY.

objects. Like Russo's altar cloth, referenced at the beginning of this essay, the origins of these artworks can be situated in multiple locales and temporalities; such works demonstrate that it is impossible at times to use style to trace an object's origins. Furthermore, to describe *enconchados* as "hybrid" seems inappropriate if we retain the term's original political sense of describing objects that employ visual tactics to oppose colonization, strategies of indigenous agency.[32] The current use of "hybrid," focused on indigenous-European mixtures, also skirts the complexity of the potential sources here. *Enconchados* can be linked to Japanese Nanban art, Korean and Chinese art, shellwork in the indigenous Americas, and Islamic-influenced and Indo-Portuguese artworks as well as European sources. More importantly, *enconchados* seem to constitute new inventions by artists in New Spain.

These various challenges offer inspiration to reflect on early modern globalization. In the case of *enconchados*, the prevalence of shell mosaic (both geographically and chronologically ubiquitous), the scope of world trade, and the early modern movement of peoples and objects around the globe render traditional comparative strategies of visual analysis inadequate to establish a complete visual or chronological genealogy. Instead, by focusing on the surface and on the materiality of *enconchados*, we discovered that while *enconchados* clearly have some roots in Asian art, the mollusk shell originated in Mexico itself. *Enconchados* thus embody local innovation, materials, and meanings. They are both powerfully global and profoundly local.

The complexity of their genesis, and the challenge of explaining their creation, led me to Gilles Deleuze's *The Fold: Leibniz and the Baroque*, which employs the great mathematician Leibniz's theories of folds, pleats, curves, twisting surfaces, curvature, and movement as a model for thinking about the world. In my mind, folds, pleats, and curves represent ideas that cannot be pinned down, that do not constitute straight lines, concepts that muddle separation—analogues to the *enconchado* paintings. Such an approach, one could argue, also exerts its interpretive energies on the surface, eschewing the "depth" of traditional art history, by which I mean attempts to pinpoint sources, or identify artists' intent. Instead of attempting to isolate "sources" for the *enconchados* or identify the ethnicity of the artists, this article has chosen to focus on the *enconchados'* surfaces of iridescent shell, their scintillating reflections and glinting highlights. Cascardi has argued that this engagement with the surface is typical of the baroque and, furthermore, that baroque surfaces are composite, created from the juxtaposition of different art forms, similar to *enconchados'* mixed construction technique of shell mosaic and oil painting. He notes that "one of the concerns of the baroque was to build a rich and meaningful surface from the juxtaposition of material forms," adding, "The model is not one of surface and depth, but one of effects that are answered by other effects, none of which can be traced back to a determinate cause" (96, 101). Cascardi brings this interpretation to bear on Diego Velázquez's *Las Hilanderas* (*The Weavers*; Madrid, Museo del Prado, circa 1657)—a "synaesthetic" artwork that combines oil painting with tapestry and mythology—noting its baroque interest in the composite: "Composition, the technique of putting things together in a place, yields a fusion of media and forms" (103). According to Cascardi, the embrace of operations on surfaces represents Deleuze's theory of the baroque (105), with its endless folding, divisions, and echoes, analogized by the limitless possible sources and endlessly iterated reflections of *enconchados*. By embracing a different viewpoint—the surface—I relinquish the impulse to identify cause, intent, or origin.[33]

Deleuze and Leibniz's model for thinking about such complex relationships is the monad: two floors separated by a fold; the inside and the outside interpenetrate, time and space are compressed; the whole world is contained within. Cascardi analogizes the monad to the Solomonic column, like those employed in Gianlorenzo Bernini's famous Baldacchino, in the crossing of St. Peter's in the Vatican (1623–1644). In their twisting forms, "Bernini's pillars mark a moment when ornament turns the difference between 'inside' and 'outside' on its head, for the structure and function of the inside as themselves enfolded in the surface" (Cascardi 96). This model seems suggestive for thinking about Mexican *enconchados*, formed from fragments of the interior of mollusk shells, and about the mollusk shells themselves—created from layer upon layer of lustrous calcium carbonate.

The fabrication of *enconchados* in New Spain—with so many potential sources of inspiration, so many layers—shows how the early modern world was folded; how all was folds, unfolds, and refolds; how the whole world was connected; how time and space can become compressed. *Enconchados*, then, have the potential to deterritorialize art history, to shrink the early modern world. As such, they provide a new model for thinking about what has been called globalism before globalization.[34]

NOTES

1. Versions of this essay were presented at the University of Zurich (2012); Mexico City, Franz Mayer Museum (2013); the Getty Research Institute (2014); and UC Riverside (2014).
2. Other artists include Pedro López Calderón and an artist who simply signed his work "Rudolpho" (Ocaña Ruiz, "Nuevas Reflexiones," 128).

3. *Enconchados* were also owned by the Dukes of Moctezuma and the Infantado, and displayed in their palaces. Others have been identified in private hands. They can be found in convents such as the Descalzas Reales, Madrid, and also in Valladolid, Toledo, Guadalajara, and Castellón. García Sáiz ("Nuevos materiales" 139) discusses the patrons, who included creoles, peninsular Spaniards (*peninsulares*), and "some cultured elites" (*unas elites cultas*). For information on the patron Viceroy José Sarmiento y Valladares, Count of Moctezuma, who commissioned *enconchados* during his rule and after, see Virginia Armella de Aspe, "Preface," *La concha nácar en México* 9–10. After finishing his tenure as viceroy of New Spain, he returned to Spain and commissioned *enconchados* through his son, Vicente Juan Sarmiento. Additional information on patronage can be found in García Saiz, *La pintura* 5–6. The first person to mention *enconchados* in Spain was Antonio Ponz, who recorded having seen them in elite collections. He specifically referred to conquest and battles scenes owned by the Dukes of the Infantado. In the nineteenth century, additional references appeared.
4. On materiality, see Rosler et al. On the growth of technical art history and global trade, see Álvarez and Villaseñor Black.
5. On the topic, see Bailey 57–69; Rodríguez; and Sanabrais, "The Biombo." Dana Leibsohn is also working on the topic and has presented a number of talks on her research. Although this research is not yet published, an idea of her theoretical framework can be gleaned from her volume, coedited with Jeanette Favrot Peterson, *Seeing across Cultures in the Early Modern World*, and especially her "Introduction: Geographies of Sight" 1–20.
6. He reports having seen these manifests in various archives but unfortunately does not reproduce any in his book.
7. All of the documents are reviewed in Sanabrais, "'The Spaniards of Asia.'"
8. Many thanks to my colleague Burglind Jungmann, who first suggested this possibility to me and directed me to Beatrix van Ragué's article on shell inlay work in China and Korea.
9. See the discussion of this topic in the award-winning article by Carolyn Dean and Dana Leibsohn, "Hybridity and Its Discontents" (especially 11, 22). I also discuss the issue, expanding it to the realm of Spanish art, in my article "Race and the Historiography of Colonial Art."
10. The best general study of these panels is García Sáiz, "La conquista militar y los enconchados."
11. The document is reproduced in Castelló Yturbide and was originally published by Abelardo Carrillo y Gariel.
12. For more on the efforts to exploit pearl fishing and shells for economic benefit in Mexico, with special reference to shells from California, see Ortiz de Ayala 40 (qtd. in Castelló Yturbide 151); Mosk; Gerhard; Bueno Jiménez; and Perry. In 1908, the fisheries around La Paz produced a million pounds of shells, and, as of 1911, most of the discarded shells were sent to San Francisco (Pilsbry and Lowe, especially 34–35, 140). Pilsbry and Lowe note that as of 1929, "[m]any tons of shells are still

sent from La Paz annually to Paris and London markets for fine manufacturing purposes; and some of the choicest black pearls are still found here" (140). Most likely, some of these shells became mother-of-pearl buttons, which were made by hand until the mid-nineteenth century, when they began to be produced by machine (Lindbergh 51). Bueno Jiménez (100), citing Bernabé Cobo's *Historia del Nuevo Mundo*, writes of the sixteenth-century nacre industry, singling out the production of delicate white spoons from leftover shells. Already in the seventeenth century, pearl production in Baja California was declining (Gerhard 246).

13. Two different mussels produce pearls along the Pacific coast of Mexico: *Pteria sterna* and *Pinctada maztlanica*. Both shells were used by pre-Columbian cultures to make artifacts.
14. For examples, see Fields and Pohl.
15. Also see: "aquel pródigamente darlo todo, / sin reparar en gastos excesivos, / las perlas, oro, plata y seda a todo" (Balbuena 77) (that prodigious giving to all, / without care for excessive costs, / the pearls, gold, silver, and silk to all).
16. On the emergence of conchology, see Dietz, especially 365–9; she mentions the noted texts on 367.
17. The spoons and buttons are referenced previously; the use of decorative shell inlay in decorative art objects or furniture can be detected through examination of existing objects and is referenced in Covarrubias Orozco, s.v. "Nacar" 560.
18. My thanks to Ivonne del Valle for bringing Cascardi's text to my attention.
19. Dietz discusses these developments in the context of shell collecting.
20. The terms appear in colonial documents. The word was first used for fabrics in Spain in the 1330s (Phipps 22). It was a fabric favored by the nobility in Spain. Phipps cites inventories recording fabrics, crediting María del Carmen Martínez Melendoz, *Los nombres de tejidos en castellano medieval*.
21. I have been inspired by studies of lighting in colonial American (US) domestic architecture. See Leviner; and Huang. To my knowledge, no similar studies of colonial Mexico have been done.
22. Both are reproduced in *La concha nácar en México*. See Armella de Aspe.
23. Balbuena includes another list of textiles late in the text: "telas, sedas y brocados" (89) (fabrics, silks, and brocades).
24. All three of these were exhibited in the Getty Research Institute show curated by Barbara Anderson in 2008, *The Marvel and Measure of Peru: Three Centuries of Visual History, 1550–1880*, and all three works are part of the Getty collections.
25. On the *Salvator Mundi*, see Alessandra Russo, "Plumes of Sacrifice"; an expanded version of her arguments can be found in chapters 4 and 7 of *The Untranslatable Image*, 83–108, 171–96. She is the editor, along with Gerhard Wolf and Diana Fane, of *Images Take Flight: Feather Art in Mexico and Europe*. On the feather Christ in Vienna, half of a pair that also includes the Sorrowing Virgin Mary, see Estrada de Gerlero 96–97; and Pierce, Ruiz Gomar, and Bargellini, cat. 2, 102–4. I thank the audience at the Getty Research Institute in 2014, and in particular Daniela Bleichmar, who pushed me to further articulate the connections I saw between iridescent feathers and heliotropism.

26. The translated passage is quoted in Russo, *The Untranslatable Image* 86, with the original Spanish in n. 9 (translation by Eric Bye).
27. For the more normative iconography, see Charlene Villaseñor Black, "Paintings of the Education of the Virgin Mary."
28. García Sáiz sees the sets of *enconchados*, especially the historical and allegorical ones, as very learned. She even suggests that Carlos de Sigüenza y Góngora may have been the author of the ideas behind the Conquest series in the Museo de América (García Sáiz, "La conquista" 139) because of his influence on the friar Agustín de Vetancurt, whose history of New Spain, *Teatro mexicano*, she links to the *enconchados* (117).
29. See the discussion of Thomas Usk's (d. 1388) *The Testament of Love*, a text written in England during the reign of Henry VIII, on the following website, which catalogues and excerpts references to pearls in ancient and medieval texts, beginning with Pliny: d.lib.rochester.edu/teams/text/shoaf-usk-testament-of-love-appendix-1. For sixteenth- and seventeenth-century understandings of this idea, see de Jongh 76.
30. For the symbolism of the Immaculate Conception, refer to Stratton-Pruitt. Katzew correctly notes that these symbols refer to the Litany of the Virgin: collections.lacma.org/node/222405.
31. For more on the creole baroque and the Virgin of Guadalupe, see More 90–109.
32. See the thoughtful critique of the term by Dean and Leibsohn, especially 5, 7–9, 13–15.
33. I am inspired by Cascardi when he writes, "This specific condition might be called a belief in the manifest intelligibility of *surfaces*, and that entails relinquishing certain notions of cause as it relates to meaning, or accepting the possibility of meaning without the proof or verification of cause" (109). On the same page: "The culture of the baroque excels in the cultivation of just this kind of surface tension, producing energies that can't be reduced to any underlying cause."
34. This phrase was inspired by Yiengpruksawan et al.

WORKS CITED

Álvarez, Mari-Tere, and Charlene Villaseñor Black. "Art and Trade in the Age of Global Encounters, 1492–1800." *Arts, Crafts, and Materials in the Age of Global Encounters, 1492–1800*, special edition. *Journal of Interdisciplinary History* 45.3 (2014): 267–75.

Anderson, Barbara, curator. *The Marvel and Measure of Peru: Three Centuries of Visual History, 1550–1880*. Getty Research Institute, Los Angeles, CA. 8 July–19 October 2008. Museum exhibit.

———. "Evidence of Cochineal in Painting." *Journal of Interdisciplinary History* 45.3 (2015): 337–66.

Armella de Aspe, Virginia, et al. *La concha nácar en México*. Mexico City: Gutsa, 1990.
Ávila, Julieta. *El influjo de la pintura china en los enconchados de Nueva España*. Mexico City: Instituto Nacional de Antropología e Historia, 1997.
Bailey, Gauvin Alexander. "Asia in the Arts of Colonial Latin America." *The Arts in Latin America 1492-1820*. Ed. Joseph Rishel and Suzanne Stratton-Pruitt. New Haven: Yale University Press, 2006. 57-69.
Balbuena, Bernardo de. *La grandeza mexicana*. Ed. Luis Adolfo Domínguez. Mexico City: Porrúa, 1985.
Bargellini, Clara. "Juan González, *Saint Francis Xavier Embarking for Asia*." *Painting a New World: Mexican Art and Life, 1521-1821*. Ed. Donna Pierce, Rogelio Ruiz Gomar, and Clara Bargellini. Denver: Denver Art Museum, 2004. 187-89.
Barthes, Roland. "The Reality Effect." *The Rustle of Language*. Trans. Richard Howard. Oxford: Blackwell, 1986. 141-48.
Bueno Jiménez, Alfredo. "La 'granjería de perlas' en el Nuevo Mundo." *Cuadernos americanos* 142 (2012): 83-111. Web. 29 July 2015.
Las Casas, Bartolomé de. *Apologética historia sumaria* [1555-1559]. Ed. Edmundo O'Gorman. 2 vols. Mexico City: Universidad Nacional Autónoma de México, 1967.
Cascardi, Anthony J. "Philosophy of Culture and Theory of the Baroque." *Filozofski Vestnik* 22.2 (2001): 87-110.
Cassin, Barbara, ed. *Vocabulaire européen des philosophies: Dictionnaire des intraduisibles*. Paris: Le Seuil, 2004.
Castelló Yturbide, Teresa. "Los artesanos artistas." *La concha nácar en México*. Ed. Virginia Armella de Aspe et al. Mexico City: Gutsa, 1990. 137-81.
Cobo, Bernabé. *Historia del Nuevo Mundo*. Madrid: Atlas, 1964.
Covarrubias Orozco, Sebastián. *Tesoro de la lengua castellana, o española*. Madrid: Luis Sanchez, 1611. Web. 29 July 2015.
Dance, S. Peter. *Shell Collecting: An Illustrated History*. London: Faber and Faber, 1966.
Dean, Carolyn, and Dana Leibsohn. "Hybridity and Its Discontents: Considering Visual Culture in Colonial Spanish America." *Colonial Latin American Review* 12.1 (2003): 5-35.
Deleuze, Gilles. *The Fold: Leibniz and the Baroque*. Trans. Tom Conley. Minneapolis: University of Minnesota Press, 1993.
Dietz, Bettina. "Mobile Objects: The Space of Shells in Eighteenth-Century France." *The British Journal for the History of Science* 39.3 (2006): 363-82. Web. 29 July 2015.
Escalera Ureña, Andrés, and Estefanía Rivas Díaz. "Un ejemplo de pintura 'enconchada.' La Virgen de la Redonda: Estudio radiográfico." *Anales del Museo de América* 10 (2002): 291-305. Web. 29 July 2015.
Estrada de Gerlero, Elena Isabel. "La plumaria, expresión artística por excelencia." *Mexico en el mundo de las colecciones de arte, Nueva España*. Ed. Elisa Vargaslugo et al. Vol 1. Mexico City: Grupo Azabache, 1994. 73-80.
Fields, Virginia, and John Pohl. *Children of the Plumed Serpent: The Legacy of Quetzalcoatl in Ancient Mexico*. Los Angeles: Los Angeles County Museum of Art, 2012.
García Sáiz, María Concepción. "La conquista militar y los enconchados: Las peculiari-

dades de un patricinio indiano." *El origen del Reino de la Nueva España, 1680–1750.* Mexico City: Instituto Nacional de Bellas Artes, 1999. 108–39.

———. "Nuevos materiales para nuevas expresiones." *Los Siglos de Oro en los virreinatos de América 1550–1700.* Ed. Joaquín Berchez. Madrid: Museo de América, 1999–2000. 127–39.

———. *La pintura colonial en el Museo de América (II): Los enconchados.* Madrid: Ministerio de Cultura, 1980.

Gerhard, Peter. "Pearl Diving in Lower California, 1533–1830." *Pacific Historical Review* 25.3 (1956): 239–49. Web. 29 July 2015.

González, Miguel. *Los enconchados de la Conquista de México: Colección del Museo Nacional de Bellas Artes de Argentina.* Mexico City: Museo del Carmen, 1998.

Hardy, R. W. H. *Travels in the Interior of Mexico, in 1825, 1826, 1827, and 1828.* London: Henry Colburn and Richard Bentley, 1829.

Huang, Nian-Sheng. "Franklin's Father Josiah: Life of a Colonial Boston Tallow Chandler, 1657–1745." *Transactions of the American Philosophical Society* 90.3 (2000): i–viii, 1–155. Web. 29 July 2015.

Jongh, E. de. "Pearls of Virtue and Pearls of Vice." *Simiolus: Netherlands Quarterly for the History of Art* 8.2 (1975–1976): 69–97.

Katzew, Ilona. Curatorial note displayed with Miguel González's *The Virgin of Guadalupe* (*Virgen de Guadalupe*). Latin American Art Collection, Los Angeles County Museum of Art, Los Angeles, CA. 2010. Web. 29 July 2015.

———. Curatorial note displayed with *The Education of the Virgin* (*La educación de la virgin*). Latin American Art Collection, Los Angeles County Museum of Art, Los Angeles, CA. 2013. Web. 29 July 2015.

Kunz, George Frederick, and Charles Hugh Stevenson. *The Book of the Pearl: The History, Art, Science, and Industry of the Queen of Gems.* New York: The Century Co., 1909.

Landman, Neil H., and Paula Mikkelson. *Pearls: A Natural History.* New York: Harry N. Abrams and the American Museum of Natural History, 2001.

Leibsohn, Dana, and Jeanette Favrot Peterson, eds. *Seeing across Cultures in the Early Modern World.* Burlington: Ashgate, 2012.

Leidy, Denise Patry. *Mother-of-Pearl: A Tradition in Asian Lacquer.* New York: Metropolitan Museum of Art, 2006.

Leviner, Betty Crowe. "'Luminous and Splendid': Lighting Colonial Virginia Interiors by Candlelight." *Association for Preservation Technology Bulletin* 31.1 (2000): 17–20. Web. 29 July 2015.

Lindbergh, Jennie. "Buttoning Down Archaeology." *Australasian Historical Archaeology* 17 (1999): 50–57. Web. 29 July 2015.

Martínez Meléndez, María del Carmen. *Los nombres de tejidos en castellano medieval.* Granada: Universidad de Granada, 1989.

More, Anna. *Baroque Sovereignty: Carlos de Sigüenza y Góngora and the Creole Archive of Colonial Mexico.* Philadelphia: University of Pennsylvania Press, 2013.

Mosk, Sanford A. "The Cardona Company and the Pearl Fisheries of Lower California." *The Pacific Historical Review* 3.1 (1934): 50–61. Web. 29 July 2015.

Ocaña Ruiz, Sonia. "*Enconchado* Frames: The Use of Japanese Ornamental Models in New Spanish Painting." *Asia and Spanish America: Trans-Pacific Artistic and Cultural Exchange, 1500–1850. Papers from the 2006 Mayer Center Symposium at the Denver Art Museum*. Ed. Donna Pierce and Ronald Otsuka. Denver: Denver Art Museum, 2009. 129–49.

———. "Nuevas reflexiones sobre las pinturas incrustadas de concha y el trabajo de Juan y Miguel González." *Anales del Instituto de Investigaciones Estéticas* 35.102 (2013): 125–76. Web. 29 July 2015.

Ortiz de Ayala, Simón Tadeo. *Resumen de la estadística del Imperio Mexicano*. Mexico City: Herculana del Villar, 1822.

Perry, W. J. "The Pearl-Fishing Industry of the Americas." *Journal of the Royal Society of Arts* 59.3051 (12 May 1911): 670–71. Web. 29 July 2015.

Phipps, Elena. *Looking at Textiles: A Guide to Technical Terms*. Los Angeles: The J. Paul Getty Museum, 2012.

Pierce, Donna, Rogelio Ruiz Gomar, and Clara Bargellini, eds. *Painting a New World: Mexican Art and Life, 1521–1821*. Denver: Denver Art Museum, 2004.

Pilsbry, H. A., and H. N. Lowe. "West Mexican and Central American Mollusks Collected by H. N. Lowe, 1929–1931." *Proceedings of the Academy of Natural Sciences of Philadelphia* 84 (1932): 33–144. Web. 29 July 2015.

van Ragué, Beatrix. "Zu Chinesischen Perlmuttlacken des 14. Jahrhunderts." *Artibus Asiae* 38 (1976): 128–38.

Rivero Lake, Rodrigo. *Namban: Art in Viceregal Mexico*. Mexico City: Turner, 2005.

———, and Roberto Vallarino. *La visión de un anticuario*. Mexico City: Américo Arte, 1997.

Rodríguez, Etsuko Miyata. "The Early Manila Galleon Trade: Merchants' Networks and Markets in Sixteenth- and Seventeenth-Century Mexico." *Asia and Spanish America: Trans-Pacific Artistic and Cultural Exchange, 1500–1850. Papers from the 2006 Mayer Center Symposium at the Denver Art Museum*. Ed. Donna Pierce and Ronald Otsuka. Denver: Denver Art Museum, 2009. 39–57.

Rosler, Martha, et al. "Notes from the Field: Materiality." *The Art Bulletin* 95.1 (2013): 10–37.

Russo, Alessandra. "Plumes of Sacrifice: Transformations in Sixteenth-Century Mexican Feather Art." *RES: Anthropology and Aesthetics* 42 (2002): 226–50.

———. *The Untranslatable Image: A Mestizo History of the Arts in New Spain, 1500–1600*. Trans. Susan Emanuel. Austin: University of Texas Press, 2014.

———, Gerhard Wolf, and Diana Fane, eds. *Images Take Flight: Feather Art in Mexico and Europe*. Chicago: University of Chicago Press, 2015.

Sanabrais, Sofia. "The Biombo or Folding Screen in Colonial Mexico." *Asia and Spanish America: Trans-Pacific Artistic and Cultural Exchange, 1500–1850. Papers from the 2006 Mayer Center Symposium at the Denver Art Museum*. Ed. Donna Pierce and Ronald Otsuka. Denver: Denver Art Museum, 2009. 69–106.

———. "'The Spaniards of Asia': The Japanese Presence in Colonial Mexico." *Bulletin of Portuguese-Japanese Studies* 18–19 (June–Dec. 2009): 223–51.

Slive, Seymour. *Dutch Painting, 1600–1800*. New Haven: Yale University Press, 1995.
Stratton-Pruitt, Suzanne L. *The Immaculate Conception in Spanish Art*. Cambridge, UK: Cambridge University Press, 1994.
Tovar de Teresa, Guillermo. "Documentos sobre 'enconchados' y la familia mexicana de los González." *Cuadernos de Arte Colonial* 1 (1986): 97–103.
———. "Los artistas y las pinturas de incrustaciones de concha nácar." *La concha nácar en México*. Ed. Virginia Armella de Aspe et al. Mexico City: Gutsa, 1990. 103–35.
Usk, Thomas. *The Testament of Love*. TEAMS Middle English Texts Series, University of Rochester. Ed. Alan Shoaf. Kalamazoo: Medieval Institute Publications, 1998. Web. 29 July 2015.
Vargaslugo, Elisa. "La pintura de enconchados." *Mexico en el mundo de las colecciones de arte*. Vol. 4. Mexico City: UNAM/Consejo Nacional para la Cultura y las Artes, 1994. 119–55.
Villaseñor Black, Charlene. "Paintings of the Education of the Virgin Mary and the Lives of Girls in Early Modern Spain." *The Formation of the Child in Early Modern Spain*. Ed. Grace Coolidge. Burlington: Ashgate, 2014. 93–119.
Warburg, Aby. "Memories of a Journey through the Pueblo Region." *Aby Warburg and the Image in Motion*. Ed. Philippe-Alain Michaud. New York: Zone Books, 2004 [1923]. 293–330.
Yiengpruksawan, Mimi, et al. "Roundtable: The Global before Globalization." *October* 133 (Summer 2010): 3–19. Web. 29 July 2015.

◆ CHAPTER TEN

"Idolatrous Images" and "True Images"

European Visual Culture and its Circulation in Early Modern China

Elisabetta Corsi
Benjamin Cluff, translator

The purpose of this essay is twofold: to analyze some aspects of European visual culture that were transmitted to foreign Catholic missions, in particular to China,—the focus of our study—and the manner in which this culture was partially adopted by natives and readapted in contexts that differed from those that the missionaries expected.[1] Before proceeding to this analysis we will examine the attitudes of Jesuit missionaries toward the images, painted or sculpted, that they found in local temples, showing how their attitudes, while initially intolerant, gradually became more receptive, though still preferring distinct aspects of Chinese culture, in particular those intimately connected to Confucianism that came to be considered adequate for incorporation into Christianity. In other words, I want to offer a more nuanced version of this process, which has come to be known as "accommodation policy."[2] In the first place, it seems to me that such an analysis is fundamental to demonstrating how, during the first phase of modernity in Europe, there existed distinct perceptions of images according to whether they were associated with pagan cults or the Catholic world. In particular, the Jesuits, as distinguished members of the European intellectual elite, recognized gradients of paganism. This permitted, for example, missionaries to "tolerate" a statue of Confucius more than a statue of a Buddhist deity. In the case of Confucius (551–479 BCE), this occurred because the Jesuits emphasized his moral and ethical positions, purging his thought of all religious connotation, and interpreting the Confucian rites as simple ceremonies whose purpose was not transcendental but mundane, necessary in order to preserve the bureaucratic Chinese state's integrity.

Second, though China is my focus, where it seems appropriate I want to extend my analysis to other mission sites, in particular New Spain, with the purpose of emphasizing the connections between two worlds, connections facilitated precisely by the circulation, promoted by the Jesuits, of religious books and images, given that such items were essential instruments of evangelization. This way of understanding and carrying out evangelization through the written word and engraved images is not exclusive to the Jesuits, since it was also practiced by the Franciscans in the Spanish colonies.[3] However, in case of the Jesuits, this practice acquires a special connotation, as determined by the *Spiritual Exercises* of Ignacio de Loyola (1544). Essentially, an analysis of the iconographic dimension of Jesuit evangelization cannot fail to mention the very foundation of the Society's visual culture: the *Spiritual Exercises*. In this manual of instructions for "imparting the exercises," Loyola proposes a path to spiritual conversion in which the exercitant should, through a process called *composition loci* ("composing [seeing] the place"), imagine the key moments in the life of Christ as if he had been present at the moment in which they occurred.

> *The first prelude* is a mental image of the place. It should be noted at this point that when the meditation or contemplation is on a visible object, for example, contemplating Christ our Lord during His life on earth, the image will consist of seeing with the mind's eye the physical place where the object that we wish to contemplate is present (54).

Although the first editions of the *Exercises* did not have images, illustrated versions began to circulate, the purpose of the prints being to assist the exercitant in his imaginative efforts. The images, therefore, had a didactic and not an aesthetic objective; they were "iconotexts" and their purpose was to be meditated, read as if they were texts (Clunas 180).[4] Their efficacy consisted in provoking an emotional response (*application sensum*) in the one who was viewing them in order to, thus, foment religious zeal and piety.

These didactics of the visual imagination, established in the *Exercises*, constitutes the context from which we analyze the missionary's attitudes toward images belonging to the people toward whom they directed their evangelizing work.

Let us examine, for example, this assertion by José de Acosta in the *Natural and Moral History of the Indies* (Seville 1590):

> Although there is great offense to God in the kinds of idolatry I have described, in which mere creatures are worshiped, the Holy Spirit condemns and abominates much more another kind of idolater, those who worship only figures and images made by the hands of men, although they are mere stones or sticks or metal and have only the shape bestowed on them by the artist who made them (269).

These words are extremely significant as they indicate what the European colonizers thought of the images associated with cults with which they had contact, both in Asia and the New World. The missionaries, the focus of this essay, refer to "idolatrous images," since the native cults were not considered "religions" but sects, so that the images employed were not thought of as "true images," but rather as simulacra, the product of their creator's fantasies.[5] It is not for reasons of iconoclasm that the Catholic missionaries condemned these images; on the contrary, it was because they considered them to be pure materiality and not figures of the divine: "mere stones or sticks or metal," as Acosta affirmed.

A few years later, on the other side of the globe, Scipione Amati, an interpreter for Japanese nobles who arrived in Rome to pay homage to Pope Pablo V, called the images of Japanese idols, "deaf, dumb, blind" and "futile" to the faith of those who worship them (Amati 15).[6] Acosta's and Amati's observations, in fact, reflect the theoretical posture assumed by renowned theologians of the time: for example, the Jesuit Saint, Cardinal Robert Bellarmine (1542–1621); and Cardinal Gabriele Paleotti (1522–1597). In the *Quarta Controversia generalis* (*The Fourth General Controversy*), Bellarmino demonstrates the distinction between images and idols, and how the former are true while the latter are false, therefore "falsa similitudo idest rapresentat id, quod revera non est" (false images should not be revered for what they represent). In particular images legitimize the cult of saints, since they are true, as it is in the case of "vera rei similitudo: ut cum pingimus hominem equum" (Bellarmino 473) (an image of true things as when we paint human beings and animals [horses]).

In the work *Discorso intorno alle imagini sacre et profane* (*Discourse Around Sacred and Profane Images*), Gabriele Paleotti introduces the theory of religious painting with a basis in the extremely stark commands of the Council of Trent: a religious, moral, and aesthetic theory that is centered on the concept of *decorum*, understood as "expediency" and "just measure."[7] According to Paleotti there is no risk that a Christian might be "unable to discriminate between the figure and the figured, or the image and the object" like a gentile would, given that "there is ordinarily no one with the use of reason among the Christian folk who would make the mistake of believing that a statue of stone was a real saint" (Discourse 140). On the other hand:

> Being principally for the spirit, it necessarily follows that sacred pictures are pleasing to it, or rather, that they are formed with signs of religion and sanctity such that those who have already made their habit in the spirit and are called spiritual take pleasure in viewing them, as things proportioned to themselves; while the others, gazing at them and perceiving the dissimilarity to themselves, feel compunction and resolve to heighten their devotion (Discourse 313).

From these quotes we can clearly see that, for Bellarmino as much as for Paleotti, it is fundamentally important to oversee the works of art so that their educational purpose is sufficiently explicit. Although it is unlikely that Christians might mistake "the figure and the figured," since they are rational beings, unlike the idolatrous pagans, it is expedient to stay away from any excess (this is the meaning of *decorum*), so as to avoid any risks.

Idolatrous Images

Let us now ask what were the inevitable consequences of such scornful attitudes, manifested by José de Acosta and Scipione Amati, toward the images employed in native cults. It is well known that in New Spain, the missionaries, like the Spanish conquistadors, had no qualms about destroying religious images and sites and using the resulting materials to construct their settlements and churches.

However, regarding the attitude that the missionaries in Asia, in particular the Jesuits, had toward the native sites and places of worship, scholars have generally adopted a very indulgent point of view with the purpose of emphasizing the notion of *accomodatio* (or accommodation) instead of intolerance. Although evangelization in China was not carried out within the context of colonial conquest, and the missionaries were subjected to Chinese bureaucracy in order to obtain authorization to evangelize, nonetheless the testimonies offered by missionary accounts—such as the *Annual Letters*, as well as other historical narratives, such as Daniello Bartoli's, which we will analyze below—sometimes evoke the same destructive practices toward the native religious culture that the historiography conventionally associates with the evangelization of the New World. For this reason it is important to note that the supposed tolerant attitude of the

Jesuits was quite selective. In other words, it did not extend to all aspects of Chinese material and visual culture, but only to that which the missionaries considered suitable for their purposes. As mentioned, given that the local religions were not "true religions," there could not have been a dialogue between equals and, therefore, Christianity could not simply insert itself into a set of practices that it considered to be idolatrous. It should be remembered that the presence of "religions" different from Christianity was considered to be the result of demonic action in the world. In particular, missionaries reacted with suspicion to any pious or ritual practice that was similar in form to Christian devotional practices since it was believed that the devil used similarity or imitation in order to more effectively deceive humankind. Likewise, the images of non-Christian cults were considered to be much more diabolic when the represented figures seemed to evoke Christian symbols and motifs. I will return to this point later; now I will examine what occurs in the case of Confucianism.

It should be remembered that according to the form of religious syncretism that predominated since at least the beginning of the Ming Dynasty (1368–1644), Confucianism, Buddhism, and Taoism were not mutually exclusive in the sense that they could be practiced during distinct moments of one's life, or even at the same time, according to one's needs. In effect, the sources refer to *sanjiao yijiao* 三教一教 (the three religions are one and the same), recognizing common foundations of all three. The Jesuit missionaries rejected this syncretic approach though they accepted Confucianism and assigned it a superior status in relation to other philosophical currents and religious doctrines. However, this was only possible by purging Confucianism of those same religious elements, above all, anything concerning ritual practices, which were the very elements that allowed Confucianism to be considered one of the *sanjiao* (three religions). In the chronicles and other documentary sources, for example *Confucio Sinarum Philosophus* (a collective work composed by various Jesuit missionaries residing in China and published in Paris in 1687 under the auspice of Louis XIV), Confucianism was presented as more of a founding ideology of the Chinese bureaucratic state, composed of a combination of ethical and moral precepts. In Confucianism religious and "superstitious" elements would be absent, thus, it could not be considered a pagan cult.[8]

Let us now consider Daniello Bartoli's account of Matteo Ricci's arrival to Beijing in 1610, above all in connection with the destructive attitude toward local images to which I have already referred. In this narrative it is appropriate to emphasize the manner in which the missionaries, assisted by Chinese converts, carried out the destructive work "in a diligent and careful manner" (Bartoli 369). This means that before painter Jacobo Niva started to paint the altarpiece, it was necessary that all images related to pagan cults be destroyed. Nonetheless, because the building had been granted to the Jesuits by the Emperor himself, the Jesuits, as advised by "Mandarin friends" and otherwise fearing a violent reaction on the part of the Emperor, recognized his munificence in beautiful Chinese characters engraved in stone in the building's entrance hall:

> I Padri, con esso altri di casa, in colà di ventesimo d'Ottobre, diroccaron gli altari, e gl'idoli, dati perciò allo stratio d'alquanti giovani Christiani, che arsero que di legno e ve ne havea non pochi in un altra stanza più dentro, e sminuzzarono que di terra, facendone diligentemente, che trovandone, era loro avventura. . . . Cio' fatto consacrarono alla Reina degli Angioli la cappella gia' promessale in voto: e per lo nuovo altare della maggiore che si apprettavam il F. Niva Iacopo, prese a dipingere un Salvatore maestosamente in atto di insegnare agli Apostoli che gli stavano a' piedi, e sopra lui un cielo aperto in disposizione conveniente al mistero. Così ben si avverò la fino allora falsa iscrizione dell'Eunuco, che l'avea intitolato, Tempio di Buona Dottrina. Ma non per tanto i Padri consigliativi dal Dottor Lione, e da altri Mandarini amici, fecero a grandi e bei caratteri sculpire in fronte della porta maggiore, "Quel palagio esser dono fatto loro della magnificenza del Re" (Bartoli 369)

> *The priests, and with the others of the house, on the 20th day of October, cast the altars and idols to the ground, so that the young converts might destroy them, and they burned those that were made of wood, and there were many more in another interior room, and they broke to pieces those that were made of clay. They carried out the work in a diligent and careful manner. After this, they consecrated the chapel for the Queen of Angels, as had been vowed, and they entrusted the altarpiece of the new altar to brother Jacobo Niva, who began to paint a Savior majestically in the act of teaching the Apostles, who were at his feet, and above him the sky opened in response to the ministry. In this manner, the Eunuch's inscription was revealed to be true, which, until then, had been false, having named it: Temple of Good Doctrine. Yet, in short order, the priests, following to the council of Doctor León [Xu Guangqi], and of other Mandarin friends, had the following phrase engraved on the vestibule, with large and beautiful characters: "this palace is a gift of the King's munificence."*[9]

In this passage we can also see that not only were the "idolatrous images" destroyed but they were replaced by other, "true images" as well; that is, images that, due to the ontological status granted them by the missionaries, had enough charisma to ratify as truth, reify, or substantiate the inscribed name of the temple as the temple of the Good Doctrine (Zheng Dao 正道). The persistence of this conception about the efficacy of Christian images as vehicles to encourage religious piety can more fully be understood if, for example, we analyze the comments of one of the thinkers who, in the field of hermeneutics, has most contributed to molding our understanding of visual culture and delineating a field of study known as iconology: Hans-Georg Gadamer. I am referring in particular to his reflections on the ontological regulations of religious imagery, their "mode of being a picture" (Gadamer 130–71).

In his magisterial discussion on the ontology of the work of art, Gadamer analyzes the relationship between the image and that which is represented through it. He affirms, "[h]ence presentation remains essentially tied to the original represented in it. But it is more than a copy. That their representation is a picture—and not the original itself—does not mean anything negative, any mere diminution of being, but rather an autonomous reality." Given that the original and its representation are bound in an indissoluble relationship by way of the image, although it maintains an autonomous reality, "the picture . . . comes to presentation in the representation." Every representation of this type reflects the ontological status of the represented. Owing to the fact that the content of the image is an emanation of the original, the latter is not diminished in the representation but rather, "this means that being increases." It is a characteristic of emanation that its product is derived from an overabundance. As such, that which emanates is not diminished. The development of this Neoplatonist philosophical notion, which overcomes the substantialist limits established by Greek philosophy, establishes the ontological status of the image. The fact that the original is not impoverished by the "outflow of many from it . . . means that being increases" (Gadamer 141–42).[10]

Gadamer is correct in recalling that Greek fathers used this doctrine to reject the iconoclastic stances in the Christology that were derived from the Old Testament. In the very act of the Lord's *kenosis* (a Greek term through which, in theological language, incarnation is indicated—it literally means "emptying") they recognized the value of sensible likeness and hence, a justification for artistic representations. To these considerations, Gadamer adds a very significant passage about religious images:

> [O]nly the religious image displays the full ontological power of the picture. For it is really true that the divine becomes picturable only through the word and image. Thus the religious picture has an exemplary significance. In it we can see without any doubt that a picture is not a copy of a copied being, but is an ontological communion with what is copied. It is clear from this example that art, as a whole and in a universal sense, increases the picturability of being (143).

Gadamer's assertions have been essential to the development of theories of response; however, these assertions are limited to the notion of the religious image within Christianity.[11] For this reason, the supposed universality of the notion of increase of being in the image must be considered with much caution, given that in the process of formulating it, Gadamer does not consider the problem of perceiving images that belong to other cultures and distinct religions. Further, it is always appropriate to contextualize the dynamics of the production of images, as they presuppose that the principles and ideologies that underlie their creation are shared: Christian images are interpreted as such by individuals who possess the tools sufficient to decodify them.

For the missionaries, the only religious images were those in which the relationship between the being and its representation was effective, that is, Christian images. On the contrary, with "pagan images" there was no increase in the being, only its absolute absence: to cite Acosta once more, "they are mere stones or sticks or metal" (269). In this sense, strangely, the missionaries appear to be Gadamer's precursors.

On the other hand, Serge Gruzinski postulates that the missionaries may have presumed that the indigenous peoples were unable to distinguish between "signifier" and "signified," to such a degree that the idol and the divinity were conflated (47). In fact, this position, as we saw earlier in this essay, was part of the theoretical argument regarding religious painting set forth by Paleotti. According to the missionaries, this attitude could lead indigenous people to manifest devotion to their own divinities and show dread when presented with Christian images. On the other hand, the dangerous proximity between "signifier" and signified" was also an essential component of a particular type of Christian images, which, as Hans Belting demonstrates, had a resurgence in the seventeenth century, as they were considered very effective for fomenting parishioners' devotion. I am referring to the so-called miraculous or acheiropoietic images (from the Greek *a-cheiro-poiēton*, rendered in Latin as: *non manufactum*, that is, not created by human hands).[12] By choosing this type of image for use in evangelization, in fact, the missionaries were running the risk that the natives would respond with an attitude similar to that which Paleotti condemned. Serious misunderstandings that resulted from this choice are studied below. However, before turning to that subject, it is necessary to reflect, even if briefly, upon the context that produced the miraculous or acheiropoietic images, in particular as it concerns their resurgence in the seventeenth century.

FIGURE 10.1. "Salus Populi Romani," engraving in Wilhelm Gumppenberg, SJ (1609–1675), *Atlas Marianus sive de Imaginibus Deiparae per Orbem Christianum Miraculosis*. Ingolstat, Typis Georgii Haenlini Typographi Academici, 1657.

Acheiropoietic Images as True Images

Indeed missionaries considered miraculous or acheiropoietic images, in particular the image of the Virgins of Saint Sixto or of Saint Mary the Great (attributed in legend to the apostle Luke), the most appropriate for evangelization [Fig.10.1].

Given that this special category of images had significant circulation in the overseas Catholic missions, it is worth examining.[13] One of the earliest references to the Virgins of Saint Luke is found in the work of Giulio Mancini (1558–1630), *Alcune considerationi appartenenti alla Pittura come di Diletto di un Gentilhuomo*, one of the first theoretical treatises on painting that, even in manuscript form, was widely read in the sixteenth century.[14] Mancini speaks of "Molti immagini miracolosi che si dicono di S. Luca ... come quella di S. Maria in Via Lata, cavata da quella cappella dove S. Luca, stando in Roma, faceva oratione, e, come si crede, scrisse gl'Atti degli Apostoli" (Vol. I, 55) (Many miraculous images that are said to be painted by Saint Luke ... such as the one in Santa María in Via Lata, where the chapel in which Saint Luke, while in Rome, would pray and, it is believed, wrote the Acts of the Apostles was located).[15]

Given that Luke was a physician and not a painter, the legend attributed the veracity of the portrait, and therefore its miraculous efficacy, to the intervention of Mary herself as well as the Holy Spirit. The miraculous power of these images was such that it could be transmitted to the copies, following a process that is the inverse of that which occurs in works of art. If in the reproduction of objects we witness a weakening of the subject in the copy, as Walter Benjamin has indicated in his famed essay about the work of art in the age of mechanical reproduction in regards to photography, the apotropaic character of the icon is preserved in its replicas to the extent that a sacred quality is attributed to the archetype.[16]

When this typology of images returned to its zenith, following the Council of Trent, and their devotion became an essential part of the Catholic renovation of spiritual life, the missionaries began to request copies to be employed as instruments of conversion. The Jesuit historian Daniello Bartoli notes that toward the end of January 1601, after finally arriving in Beijing and having been admitted to the Court, Matteo Ricci had showed the Emperor Wan Li "two portraits of the Savior and his divine Mother," and perhaps a copy of *Salus Populi Romani*, one of the famous acheiropoietic images that, according to tradition, had been painted by Saint Luke due to the "inspiration" of the Virgin herself.[17] Upon seeing them, the ruler had been so impressed that he did not want to keep them, deciding instead to send them to the Empress Mother. As narrated by Bartoli, Emperor

Wan Li affirmed upon seeing them, "This is the living God!" and was "unable to bear the presence of the two images, [which were] so natural that they terrified him, as though they were alive" (363).

The ruler was similarly upset when he saw the icons and, according to Bartoli, said that "next to this living God their idols seemed dead" (363).[18] The Jesuit historian's account shows that the missionaries were convinced that the charisma of these images was so powerful that, in spite of the dread the images had generated in the ruler and his venerable mother, they had been recognized as "images of the living God," that is, as we discussed in the first pages of this essay, "true images."

At times, however, the sacred images could cause dangerous misunderstandings, as occurred in this other account:

> Non così avvenne delle imagini di Nostra Signora, e del Divin suo Figliuolo a lei in braccio, poste sopra l'altare della lor nuova chiesa: peroche, come non tutti udivano la distinzione, la dignità, la natura de' personaggi ch'elle rappresentavano, si cominciò a bisbigliare nel popolo, che il Dio de gli Europei, era Donna: ed altri non bene affatto intendevano, come non fossero due. Perciò al primo saperne, i Padri ne corsero al riparo, come solo in que'principi si poteva: e fu togliendo quell'inciampo d'avanti a' ciechim già che non era lor conceduto d'uscire in publico ad illuminarli con la predicazione del vero. Toltane dunque d'in su l'altare quella male intesa, vi riposero in sua vece un'altra imagine, che gran ventura fu haverla, del Salvatore (Bartoli 179)

> *The same did not occur with the images of Our Lady with the Divine Child in her arms, which were placed above the altar of the church. Because not all present understood the distinction, the dignity [and] the nature of the personages that they represented, a rumor began to spread among the people that the God of the Europeans was a woman. And others did not understand that one must distinguish between the two [images]. For this reason, the priests resorted to the only remedy available to them, that is, the removal of said trickery from view, since they were not permitted to go out in public in order to enlighten the people with their preaching of the truth. They removed, then, the misunderstood image and replaced it with another image, that of the Savior, that by happenstance they had with them.*[19]

It is very probable that the Chinese, upon seeing the image of the Virgin with the Holy Child in her arms, associated it with a representation of Bodhisattva Guan Yin (觀音) and, in effect, in many plastic representations of Guan Yin in

FIGURE 10.2. Anonymous Dehua craftsman, Guan Yin sitting on a lotus throne, holding a child (c. 1725–1750), Qing period (1644–1911), Dehua (Fujian), white porcelain, made for export, Rome, © National Museum of Oriental Art, inventory no. 15766/22613.

FIGURE 10.3. Anonymous Chinese Painter, Copy of the Madonna of St.Lucas, (last quarter of the sixteenth century, beginning of seventeenth century), Ming period (1368–1644), Xi'an (Shaanxi), watercolor on silk, 120 × 55 cm., Chicago, © The Field Museum of Natural History (catalog no. 116027, photo archive identifier A114604_02).

Dehua porcelain (Fujian Province), made at the beginning of the eighteenth century [Fig. 10.2]. It is possible to detect a strong cultural contamination, as so many of the iconographic elements are borrowed from the conventional representation of the Virgin with the Child in her arms.[20]

The iconographic model of the *Salus* only depicts the bust of the Virgin, while the Dehua statues reproduce the figure in its entirety. This is also the case with the oldest Chinese version of the Virgin of Saint Luke [Fig. 10.3]. Given the singular character of this work, it seems pertinent to pause and reflect on it. Berthold Laufer acquired the work in 1910 for the Chicago Field Museum. The renowned art historian and museologist bought it from a Xi'an city official. In the lower right-hand side there is a signature by famed painter Tang Yin 唐寅 (1470–1524); however, the pronounced derivation from the European prototype suggests that the work was painted by an artist who was close to the missionaries residing in China.[21] The principal difference between the *Salus Populi Romani* [Fig. 10.1] and this Chinese version, consists of the fact that the figure of the Virgin has been painted in her entirety and wrapped in a white cloak, her arms crossed in order to support the Child. The Child maintains the same gesture of giving a blessing with the right hand, while the left hand has a book, totally Sinicized in the binding and format. The head of the Child is shorn except for the *ushnisha* (knob) of hair on top, a symbol of wisdom, according to the ancient Buddhist custom. Notwithstanding the fact that the two figures are completely Sinicized and reflect the iconography of Guan Yin, it is extremely unusual that the Virgin has been portrayed with bare feet, given that this practice goes against the gender conventions of traditional Chinese society in which, as it is well known, female feet possessed a strong erotic appeal.

In the prior account we saw that the image of the Virgin had provoked misunderstandings among the Chinese, as some had believed that she was the goddess whom the Europeans worshipped. In contrast, in this other account, Ricci explains that displaying a beautiful icon of the Virgin would risk fomenting religious sentiment among the neophytes:

> Frattanto, volendo dar qualche rimedio alla freddezza della gente di quella città in volere udire le cose della nostra Santa Fede, volse provare se poteva farli venire a casa et affetionarli alle cose de Iddio. Era il loro anno novo [25 gennaio 1591]: per questo si risolse di ponere quella bella ancona che era venuta dalla Nova Spagna—che sempre estava nella cappella di dentro e non la potevano vedere né le donne né altra gente della plebe—in pubblico nella chiesa a vista di tutti per alcuni giorni. Et, adornando molto bene l'altare e tutti i muri di essa con vitrij, quadri e molte spere,

e candele, la pose nell'altare, faccendo una divota vista; il che, saputo dalla gente, cominciò a concorrere di tutte le parti, come a cosa che tutti desideravano vedere (D'Elia, *Fonti ricciane*, 305)

> *Meanwhile, hoping to remedy the indifference of the people of that city, who did not want to hear anything concerning the new Faith, he pondered having them come to the house and attempting to help them develop a fondness for the things of God. It was Chinese New Year (January 25th, 1591): for this reason he decided to put that beautiful icon, which had arrived from New Spain—which was always in the interior of the chapel where no women, nor other people considered to be vulgar could see it—in the public space of the church, within view of all, for a few days. Further, adorning the altar very well and all walls with glass, paintings, and many orbs, and he put candles upon the altar, creating a devout scene, so that, when the people entered in, they began to arrive from all parts, as if it were something that all wanted to see.*[22]

My hypothesis is that the icon of which he speaks in this account is a copy of the acheiropoietic image of the Virgin of Guadalupe. Given that the apparition of Mary supposedly took place in 1531, it is very important, given the primary purpose of this edited volume, to explore the distinct articulations of early globalism, since in 1591 copies of that holy image were circulated in the far off missions of the East. The principal foundation of my hypothesis is that the narration leads us, once again, to the importance of the copies made of the *acheiropoietai*, owing to the fact that they can maintain, and even augment, their aura of sacredness. In fact, not only did Ricci shelter the precious icon in an interior chapel of the church, in the most protected and sacred place, but he also showed it in a very selective manner; since "no women, nor other people considered to be vulgar," could see it, it is likely that he only showed it on the occasions when high-ranking mandarins visited the Jesuit residence. However, so that the icon could exercise its power of persuasion upon the unreceptive people of that village, acting more effectively than the words of preachers, Ricci moved the icon to the public space, "within view of all, for a few days." The manufacture of copies of religious icons also invites us to reflect upon distinct gradients of adoption of the represented images, that is, the distinct forms through which the archetypes were appropriated and transformed: just as the goddess Toci-Tonantzin was gradually transformed into the acheiropoietic image of the Virgin of Tepeyac in New Spain, in China the image of the goddess Guan Yin gradually acquired the semblance of the Virgin carrying the Child in her arms.[23]

The "Universal" Semiotics of Catholic Images

In the chronicles analyzed above we see how missionaries utilized acheiropoietic images of the Virgin with the Son in a very cautious and selective manner. Regarding this aspect, other documents allow us to add to our comprehension of the typology of images required for the missionaries' work. In a letter to the Society General, Claudio Aquaviva (1543–1615), dated February 18, 1598, in Peking, Niccolò Longobardi (1565–1655), future Superior of the Jesuit mission in China and successor to Ricci, stated the following:

> Quella necessità che habbiamo di libri, habbiamo anche di imagini per potere consolare et aiutare i nuovi cristiani: et così confidatici nell'istessa pietà et zelo di codesti ss. vi li supplichiamo parimenti che vogliamo cooperare alla conversione di queste anime, mandandoci alcune imagini così di pennello come di stampa. In particolare saranno molto accomodate in questi principii le immagini del Salvatore, et della B. Vergine, alla quale tengono tutti i Cinesi ancor Gentili molto grande devotione, et li fanno profondissima reverenzia, battendo la testa in terra, et chiamandola Xim Mu Mian Mian, che vuol dire: Santa Madre et Regina delle Regine. Sopra tutto ci sarano qui di singolar consolazione et profitto un paio di quei libri che fece il Nso Padre Natale con li Mysterii e considerationi della vita di Christo, perché quando vengono questi mandarini tirati dalla fama degli Europei, gli possiamo mostrar cosa che ci dia subito occasione di seminare quel che si pretenda in queste Missioni. Et per aiutare partamente li idioti usiamo assai a proposito alcuni libretti dozzenali, dove si rapresentano con figure li misterii della fede, li Comandamenti, li peccati mortali, li sacramenti etc. Quali tutti li stimano qui per molto artificiosi e sottili, e haver quell'ombra che non tengono le pitture Cinesi. Onde i giorni passati venne qua uno di questi Governanti, et vedendo un libretto colli misterii della vita di Xsto n. Si.re ne restò stupito, et in fine voleva che gliene facesse un presente: ma parendomi che non conveniva darlo in mano d'un Gentile, li dissi che questo era libro del nostro Jau [Jiao], cioè della legge che noi altri professiamo, per il che non poteva dispensarsene. Al che egli rispose che io haveva raggione, chiedeva pure che gline dasse alcun altre che non mi fosse tanto necessario: et così li presentai le favole d'Esopo figurate, quale lui ricevette con ambe le mani et dandomi molte grazie, come se fosse stata la miglior opera ch'ha di Friandra (ARSI, Jap.Sin., 13, f.117a)

> *Just as we need books, we also need images that will allow us to comfort and aid the new Christians. Trusting to the piety and zeal of these gentlemen, we request that you participate in the conversion of these souls by sending us images, painted and printed.*[24] *Images of the Redeemer, as well as those of the Blessed Virgin, will be most welcome. The Chinese, Gentiles though they may be, show great respect and devotion to her and*

bow deeply before her, touching their foreheads to the floor and calling her Xim Mu Mian Mian.[25] *Above all, it would be of great consolation and most beneficial if you could send a few of those books created by our own Father Nadal containing the Mysteries and considerations of the life of Christ, so that when these Mandarins, attracted by stories about the Europeans, visit us, we might show them something that will immediately open to us the opportunity to sow the seeds intended by these missions.*[26] *In order to help the illiterate specifically, we make advantageous use of some ordinary books* (dozzenali) *containing images which represent the mysteries of the faith, the Commandments, the deadly sins, the sacraments, and so forth. These illustrated books are, in everyone's view, quite artistic and subtle, as [their images] comprise shadows that no Chinese painting possesses. For example, in recent days one of those Mandarins came and, seeing a small book about the mysteries of the life of Christ our Lord, he was amazed and eventually asked that it be given to him as a gift. But I thought it unwise that it should be put in the hands of a Gentile, and so I told him that this book was part of our Jau, meaning the law that we profess, and therefore we could not do without it.*[27] *He then replied that I was correct and therefore asked that we give him another [book] that was not so essential. And so I presented him with the illustrated fables of Aesop, which he received with both hands, thanking me profusely as if it were the best of all the works in Flanders.*

In this story, Longobardi showed a clear understanding of the way in which he would employ the prints and engravings he requested: those from the renowned Plantin press in Antwerp, such as those that illustrated the work of Jerónimo Nadal (1507–1580), *Evangelicae Historiae Imagines*, dedicated to various moments in the life of Christ in accordance with the liturgical year, most likely went to the literate upper class; for commoners, the ordinary books (*dozzenali*) that used images to explain the dogmas of the faith, the Decalogue, and the sacraments would suffice. This is a clear reference to the *idiotarum libri* (books for the illiterate), which played an important role in medieval catechism and regained their popularity during the Reformation. Longobardi emphasizes the fact that the presence of shadows constitutes a boon to the work of evangelization.

The missionaries' trust in the educational and persuasive value of sacred images may have its source in the notion of the communicative effectiveness of images, their ability to be read according to a universal semiotics that transcends linguistic barriers. According to this idea, when shown to the uneducated or uninitiated, images were supposed to be directly intelligible, reaching the heart more than the mind. This is why Agostino Mascardi (1591–1694), the famed historiographer and professor at the Sapienza of Rome, drew a paternalist comparison between didactic paintings and a kind of "mute history":

> Painting in its materiality has been defined as if the people were its master, but the opposite can also be said, that painting is the people's master, because the unlettered are lacking in comprehension and learning, as are little children, and should be considered in the same category, given the fact that they have no books other than paintings (275–76).

Mascardi continued by addressing the moral importance of the image as a means to induce goodness in the minds of the people. Likewise, Federico Borromeo (1564–1631), in his treatise *De Pictura Sacra* (On Sacred Painting), writes of the pedagogical function of images as a medium that makes the mysteries of the Christian faith more intelligible and allows them to be perceived by the senses (3).

As we have seen, this process was well known to missionaries; Matteo Ricci tried to move the hearts of the Chinese by employing an image of the Virgin from New Spain, despite the risk of generating misunderstandings regarding the nature of the represented figure. Images, thanks to their properties as *muta predicatio* (silent preaching), were quite useful in reinforcing the preached word in foreign missions where strange tongues formed significant barriers.

Buddhist preaching also employed images, especially those that emphasize the soteriological aspects of the doctrine. Francisco Xavier himself provided a vivid description of monks' sermons in Japan, which were accompanied by paintings of Buddhist hell (339).[28] Another similar practice which was sure to call the missionaries' attention was the introduction of relics for consecration.[29] The spread of relic worship gained momentum with the canonization of Francisco Xavier, Ignatius Loyola, Philip Neri, Teresa of Ávila and Isidore of Madrid in 1622. As the hagiography of these saints began to develop, iconographic symbols from important events of their lives increased in use. In the case of Xavier, for example, the most popular iconography depicted him at the pinnacle of ecstasy, in the act of opening his soutane with both hands. This image was normally accompanied by the phrase *Satis est, Domine, satis est* (It is enough, O Lord, it is enough).[30] Xavier was the epitome of the apostolic ideal aspired to by the Society of Jesus from the start and obviously this aspect was reflected in representations of the saint. The oil paintings in the Profesa Jesuit School in Mexico City, painted by Chinese converts residing in Macao, emblematize the dissemination of the cult of this saint in China and New Spain.[31]

The growing importance of the relationship between relics, images, and religious practices in the history of Christianity in Asia might lead us to forget the constant tension between divine absence and the very presence in the mystagogy (introduction to Christian mystery) of the sacramental liturgy that lies at the heart of Christianity: God reveals himself through the word and the word is assimilated by hearing and reading, not by seeing. In Gutenberg's time, the word of God was available, in principle, to both the Protestant and Catholic worlds, in Bibles printed in Latin and in the various vernaculars. This new circumstance had a great effect on preaching, because it originated instruction manuals on how to preach sermons. The danger implicit in the excessive use of images in rituals provoked continual negotiations regarding their symbolic value, bringing us, according to Belting's ideas, to the crisis of the old image and a different usage of the image (14–16).

A set of documents in the General Archives of the Nation in Mexico City provides evidence of this fact. The documents discuss cases of the Inquisition and narrate false miracles attributed to the martyrs of Nagasaki.[32] The Holy Office had issued an order regarding corrections to be made to paintings that showed Jesuits who were martyred (AGN). Despite the highly circumspect reaction to the images and relics of the martyrs of Nagasaki, their propagation could not be curtailed, as demonstrated by the innumerable reproductions in New Spain, particularly those connected to San Felipe de Jesús, the creole saint who became the patron saint of Mexico. Such relics, attributed to the martyrs of Nagasaki, were rumored to be held in the school of San Pablo in Macao (Yuuki 292–94).

The idea that images had to be employed carefully and selectively is found in a document that predates somewhat Longobardi's letter (discussed above). The *Memorial of things to come for the present that is to be sent to the King of China* was written in Macao in 1588 by Alessandro Valignano, the Visitor of the Jesuit mission in Asia. It was directed to General Claudio Acuaviva. In points 19, 22, and 25 Valignano requests:

> Some of the best-printed books of architecture that can be found. Also you shall send other books of faces and other beautiful figures, richly illuminated, all of which shall show joyful countenances, not of martyrs, nor wars, nor the mysteries of the Passion of Our Lord, because for now they do not suit our purposes, and it would be especially good to send a book of all the Supreme Pontiffs, and another of the Emperors and Kings, the best that have been printed in Italy or Spain, which should be excellently illuminated with various colors. A few large paintings by some great artist, such as one of Jesus Christ Our Lord in great glory, surrounded by many angels, and one of the Assumption of Our Lady, perfect and glorious with her child in her arms, or skillfully painted standing with her son in her arms, surrounded by angels and in great glory. Some paintings of old Rome and new Rome as they are printed and illuminated with fine inks and gold, and on parchment would be best, by which we may help the Chinese understand the greatness of His Holiness and the city where he dwells if one might find or commission some engraving that might be printed of a solemn procession ... of cardinals, bishops, prelates, etc., a thing of great worth which we intend to communicate to

the Chinese regarding the Holy Roman Church, and if this were done, it should be painted in a manner very pleasing to the eye of the Chinese, achieved by painting a long road enclosed on the right by a stockade, painting behind this an infinite number of people kneeling with their hands raised, and on the other side painting ... arranged for a procession ... an organ and an excellent Flemish clavichord, beautifully adorned.[33]

Two important points stand out in reading this document. First, as mentioned above, there was a need to make selective use of images, considering not only their recipients but also their content, because in China it was necessary to avoid propagating bloody images like those that represent the Passion of Christ, "because for now they do not suit our purposes." Therefore, Valignano is completely aware of the fact that the Chinese had a low tolerance for displays of nude and bloodied human bodies. The image of God incarnate and crucified truly was a scandal for many educated Chinese, who shared a more pneumato-centric view of God, that could be assimilated to the concept of *Tian* 天 (heaven), associated with that of *Qi* 氣 (energy, *pneuma*). The image of a crucified God raised serious criticisms and led to intolerance, and its worship provoked massive incarcerations and executions in the 1660s. However, among the congregations shepherded by the Jesuits in China, the existence of the Congregation of the Passion of Christ, whose statutes are conserved in the Roman archive of the Society, is also documented (ARSI, Jap.-Sin. I, 173.2b). It is logical to imagine that, given the aversion to bloodied images among the Chinese, the forms of worship promoted by the acolytes of the Congregation did not include the use of images that reproduced the passion of Christ, nor would they perform live representations of the Passion, as occurred in New Spain.

Secondly, Valignano insisted on acquiring images of pontiffs and monarchs, suggesting that his target audience was the highest strata of Chinese society. He also requested that they send him scenes that were markedly ritualistic, a characteristic in tune with a Chinese society imbued with rites at every level. Essentially, the processions that he requested needed not to be scenes of religion but rather of ritual, of protocol, in that they depict "an infinite number of people kneeling," worshiping "cardinals, bishops, prelates," and not statues of saints as was usually the case in religious processions that, in the late sixteenth century, had reached their peak as an important part of the worship practices encouraged by the Church among the people, both in Europe and in the colonies. The request for musical instruments should be understood in the same light—Ricci really did receive the clavichord—because it points to the importance of music within Chinese social practices.

Valignano requested maps of Rome because he understood the Chinese people's prowess in urban development and cartography and he wanted to show them that European cities, especially Rome as the capital of Christianity, were by no means inferior to Chinese cities.[34] We must remember that Chinese society during the late Ming dynasty was a highly self-referential society. Although it may not be defined as "xenophobic," the imperial authority viewed foreigners with suspicion and limited their movement within the empire. Merchants were not allowed to reside outside of the commercial port areas and missionaries needed authorization from the local Mandarins before they could establish a residence and build a church. As Valignano's letter demonstrates, he was able to glimpse a strategy based in ritual and culture that captured the Mandarins' attention, even though at that time he did not yet have an in-depth understanding of the complex structure of Chinese society with its upper echelon occupied by literate bureaucrats. When compared to processions that took place during the same period in New Spain, characterized by pathos in their live performances of the Passion of Jesus, it should come as no surprise that more formal and solemn processional forms developed in China, though the latter were limited to the periods when Christians enjoyed more religious freedom. However, the second aspect that characterizes the document cited above did not escape Valignano's attention: the importance that Chinese civilization placed on the written transmission of knowledge, through books, and the way in which the creation of private libraries was in itself a symbol of power and social capital.

Traditional Chinese society placed fundamental importance on literati culture; the very origin of the word that designates a written text, *wen* 文, maintained a sacred aura that discouraged the inappropriate disposal of written pages. It is interesting to note that just as the term *textum* originally designated a "texture," the grapheme *wen* 文 recalls the same textile metaphor because the archaic pictogram that originated this word was written with the radical "silk" (*si* 絲), e.g., *wen* 紋, indicating thus a mark or a drawing upon fabric. Writing is thus intimately linked to the materiality of the media that made it possible: silk and later paper, two Chinese inventions that would soon become universal resources.

Printing, which as we know was invented in China around the seventh century C.E., boomed during the second half of the Ming Dynasty (1368–1644), when Matteo Ricci arrived in China (1581). This flowering of print lent remarkable momentum to the spread of the culture of the book, as well as the formation of a community of readers whose socio-economic conditions differentiate them somewhat from the class that, traditionally, had dominated classic culture. The missionaries were able to take advantage of the emerging community of readers, consisting in equal parts of mid-level functionaries and rural bourgeoisie. They soon realized that producing written texts would guarantee a certain impact, stimulating a demand that was already growing.

It is therefore at the level of what is referred to as "cultural civility" that the Jesuit missionaries identified themselves with the Chinese "men of letters" (*wenren* 文人), constructing an image of themselves that was quite different from the general perception in Catholic Europe. It is at the level of bibliophilia, collecting, and exegesis where the Jesuit Italians and the Chinese literati were able to meet and dialogue. The former would soon learn to define themselves as *Litterati Europæi*, hoping thus to emphasize an intrinsic affinity with the latter, the *wenren* 文人, as seen in a handwritten document that I found in the Provincial Archive of the Society of Jesus in Mexico City (Grimaldi and Pereira). It seems highly significant to me that a copy of this report, of which other copies obviously exist, should have been sent to the Jesuit missions in Mexico as well. Additionally, the document's contents addressed key issues connected with Confucius and the cult of Heaven—which in just a few years would determine the controversy surrounding rituals—thus guaranteeing that even in the distant Viceroyalty of Mexico these concepts would be debated as points of reference to judge superstitious practices. It may be that this attitude eventually caused a weakening of the missionaries' own identity, a sense of ripping and laceration, but that is an argument that we will leave for an as yet unwritten history of missionary psychology. At the same time, the missionaries would help reinforce the identity of a parallel and antagonistic group, that of European clerisy, as suggested by the publication of an oft-reprinted book about the figure of the erudite man, *L'uomo di lettere difeso ed emendato* (*Defense and forgiveness of the erudite gentleman*), by the aforementioned Jesuit historian Daniello Bartoli.[35]

This intellectual horizon provides the contextual framework in which all missionary activity in China, characterized by the two elements of diplomacy and cultural mediation, should be understood. Erudition was the common ground of self-refinement. In China it is called *xiushen* 修身, based on a concept taken from *Daxue* 大學 ("The Great Learning"), while in Europe it is *la coltura d'ingegni* ("the cultivation of the intellect").[36]

In effect, when Ricci arrived in Nankin, the city was one of the centers of production for xylographic prints as well as the home to one of the two National Academies of China, which themselves became notable producers of very fine prints. The production of books was also enriched by editorial activities in local academies, religious institutions, and private printing houses. The fact that Ricci was able to interact with the city's intellectual circles is demonstrated by the presence of copies of engravings, taken from the aforementioned work of Jerónimo

Nadal, in *Chengshi moyuan* 程式墨苑 (*Mr. Cheng's Garden of Inksticks*, 1606) compiled by Cheng Dayue 程大約 (1541-1616?), a renowned typographer and ink cake producer.[37] A catalogue of illustrations for molds used in the fabrication of ink sticks, the book belongs to the genre that, together with catalogues of models of letter-writing paper (such as the famous *Shizhuzhai jianpu* 十竹齋牋譜, "Epistle Paper Manual for the 'Ten Bamboo Workshop'"), is highly appreciated for its exquisite technique not only with the engraving of molds but also in polychromatic printing processes. Within the context of the visual and lettered culture of China at the time, the request made by the missionaries for books and engravings points us to another way of understanding the "cultural imperative" theorized by the renowned Dutch sinologist Erik Zürcher (Standaert 51–53).[38]

It does not really matter if, in the end, works such as *Chengshi moyuan* were produced within a culture that was designated *zhangwu* 長物, or that which is "superfluous," as objects closely linked to erudite pastimes of the literati and the collectors of the time. But what were religious images doing among "superfluous" objects? Could it be that the pastimes of Chinese literati were related, in the minds of the missionaries, with the approved recreation of the lettered European male, "in conversation with God and nature," to paraphrase another of Bartoli's popular books? Or did Ricci, trusting blindly in the universal power of those images, the "true images" with which this essay begins, believe in their capacity to transmit to whomever viewed them something of the message they contained? Or was Ricci a skilled simulator, perhaps joining in the game in order to enter in the good graces of those in power at the time, to the point of running the risk of a blasphemous usage of those revered images? It may be that all these interpretations hit near the mark, but one seems to hold true: the missionaries' attempt to colonize the religious-cultural horizon of the Chinese by promoting the use of religious images in diverse contexts actually translates into a decontextualization of those images and not into an "increase of being," as suggested by Gadamer. This means that promoting Christianity in China led to the secularization of the images and objects related to religious worship or, even worse, to their appropriation—as in the case of the Guan Yin with a child in her arms—by a Buddhism that was totally opposed to Christianity. Indeed, in the same way that the Jesuits had emphasized the secular aspects of Confucianism to adapt it to their missionary strategy, Christian images, stripped of their original religious content, were perceived by the Chinese as exotic and "curious" vestiges, suitable for the enjoyment of the lettered and the collector.

NOTES

1. Given the need to clarify some sinological aspects, I have used some of my recently published texts and others still in progress. See Corsi, "Constructores de fe" ("Masons of Faith"), and "La retórica" ("The Rhetoric"). My analysis here is limited to the first period of the Chinese mission's establishment, after Matteo Ricci's arrival in Nanchang toward the end of the sixteenth century. During this period the majority of religious images circulated in print form, as illustrations in books and as engravings. Thus, this essay does not take into consideration works by artists such as Giovanni Gherardini and Giuseppe Castiglione, or the diffusion of scientific imagery and linear perspective, subjects I have explored in other publications.
2. On the "accommodation policy" adopted by the Jesuits of the China mission, see Standaert 50–53, 310.
3. See, for example, Duverger 167–71.
4. Here Clunas is using Peter Wagner's sense of "iconotexts." See Clunas (180); and Wagner. Clunas argues that it was precisely the combination of text and image, which the Jesuits considered necessary to a proper understanding of the meaning of an engraved scene, that conflicted with the Chinese notion of painting held by the literati elite of late Ming (1368–1644). He, therefore, dismisses the possibility of an influence of European imagery on Chinese painters and engravers. Indeed, according to the Chinese scholar-painters of the time, the expression of the artist's individuality was far more important than the subject of the painting itself (Clunas 186). Following the path opened by James Cahill (71–105), I argue that, despite being shared by the majority of the elite members of the late Ming society, this self-conscious, intellectualized attitude toward painting did not prevent the distribution of religious images and illustrated books, ranging from fiction to Confucian educational aids, as well as popular art, among the middle-class gentry with whom the missionaries mostly interacted. Taking advantage of the provincial gentry's favorable disposition toward a diversified range of imagery, as opposed to the literati's exclusive predilection for calligraphy and landscape painting, the Jesuits were able to turn their curiosity toward Western images drawn in *chiaroscuro* and according to the tenets of linear perspective, although, as we will see over the course of this essay, their effort did not produce the results the Jesuits expected.
5. As is well known, in the sixteenth century, the term "religion" was applied to Catholic religious orders and congregations. The idea of a plurality of religions that are as esteemed as and on par with Christianity is very modern and not universally accepted. Conservative Catholic theologians continue defending, even today, the notion of Christianity as the *only religion*. On the other hand, the recent events in many Mediterranean Islamic countries oblige us to reflect again upon fundamentalism and religious intolerance (under any sign) as grave threats to humanity. In this sense, Evonne Levy, in *Propaganda and the Jesuit Baroque*, has already noted

sinister parallels and prefigurations of Nazi cultural propaganda in the iconographic projects of the Jesuits.
6. The bibliography on the Japanese missions is enormous, though it still lacks a study that examines their presence in the printed works of the time. In fact, the prince's diplomatic expedition to Europe was soon incorporated into a narrative designed to disseminate knowledge about Japan in Europe, as is the case with Amati's *Historia*.
7. The decree of the Council of Trent can be consulted in *Canone et decreta sacrosanti ecumencici Concilii Tridentini* (*Canons and Decrees of the Holy Ecumenical Councils of Trent*) 205 "Sessio vigesima quinta" ("Twenty-fifth session"). The work of Paleotti was recently reprinted under the direction of Stefano Della Torre. See Paleotti, *Discorso* (2002), and *Discourse*. The classic reference work on Paleotti's text is by Prodi, "Ricerche," reprinted in *Arte e pietà nella Chiesa tridentina*. See also Prodi, *Il Cardinale Gabriele*, vol. II, 527–62; and Jones. More recently, Lina Bolzoni and Mary Carruthers have each studied the connection between images and preaching.
8. Much has been written about this interpretation, which the Jesuits also developed in order to promote their missionary efforts in Europe. For some of the most important studies on the topic, see Jensen; and Mungello. I follow Paul Rule's use of the term "interpretation" because I do not agree with Jensen's position on Confucius and Confucianism, according to which they were a Jesuit construct that the missionaries utilized in a metonymic sense, that is, in order to represent Chinese civilization in its entirety ("considered the foundation of the Chinese religion to be Confucius and his doctrine," Jensen 117). In effect, they did not consider Confucius and his thought to be the founder and foundation of Chinese religion, simply because, as I have already mentioned, in that era the notion of religion outside of Christianity did not exist. On the contrary, the Jesuits emphasized the civil and moral character of Confucian doctrine, at the cost of ritual and religious aspects, in order to demonstrate that it was a philosophical system (and not an idolatrous sect) within which Christianity could function and flourish, as had already occurred with the Western classical tradition. On the topic of the consonance between the classical tradition and the Chinese philosophical tradition, see Goodman and Grafton.
9. Translation my own. It is worth noting that some years before the episode narrated by Bartoli, the Protestant Reformation in Northern Europe gained momentum precisely through the destruction of sacred images in the churches in response to Martin Luther's condemnation of some "papist" practices as idolatrous. Regarding this matter, see Belting 458–70.
10. For a discussion of some Gadamerian theories I have cited here, in the context of theory of response, see Freedberg 76–78. Although we know that Gadamer never adhered to Nazi ideology, it is also known that he was a disciple of Martin Heidegger. This coincidence seems to contribute to Evonne Levy's thesis, presented in her important work, *Propaganda and the Jesuit Baroque*, in which she demonstrates, while not addressing philosophical questions, that the same propagandistic purposes determine an unsettling proximity between Jesuit architecture and the

architectural projects designed by Albert Speer for the Third Reich (see chapter 2 in particular).
11. For a concise synthesis of the theory of response see Moxey.
12. For more on the archetypal images of the seventeenth century, see Belting 47–77, 436–57. The relationship between "signifier" and "signified" in acheiropoietic images is "dangerous" inasmuch as Catholic parishioners can show excessive devotion to them. Calls for "decorum" and sobriety in the use of devout images are, as we have seen, quite frequent in the religious literature of the Counter-Reformation. In reality, the missionaries must have been excessive in their use of miraculous images both in European and non-European missions if a century later Ludovico Antonio Muratori (1672–1750) was still lamenting the excessive use of religious images that the missionaries used to promote a rustic devotion and argue that it was necessary to "avisar ancora destramente il popolo, che s'intende di parlare all'originale, allorché si parla alla pittura o all'Immagine di stucco" (1472) (give the people a subtle reminder that the intent is to speak to the original when one speaks to a painting or a clay image).
13. Two beautiful copies of the *Salus Populi Romani* and of the *Madonna del Popolo*, also considered to be the work of Saint Luke, can be found in the old Jesuit school, the Seminary of San Martín in Tepotzotlán (in the State of Mexico).
14. *Alcune considerationi appartenenti alla Pittura come di Diletto di un Gentilhuomo* ("Remarks on Painting as a Delightful Occupation of the Gentleman") is often published as *Considerazioni sulla pittura* ("Remarks on Painting").
15. Translation my own. The Via Lata, today, is the Via del Corso in Rome.
16. See Benjamin.
17. See also Freedberg's discussion on the same, 126 and 231–35.
18. On the topic of Marianist acheiropoietic images, see Freedberg 99–135.
19. Translation my own. It is possible that he is referring to an image of *Salvator Mundi* (*Savior of the World*), that is, the iconography of Jesus performing a blessing with an orb in his hand. It was one of the favorite images of the Jesuits and was widely distributed among the missions. The same account is narrated in Ricci 366; and in D'Elia, *Le origini*, 32–33. See also Bailey, *Between Renaissance* 87; and Bailey, *Art on the Jesuit Missions* passim, especially 77, 79–80.
20. Guan Yin is the seventh-century female manifestation of Bodhisattva Avalokiteshvara (literally: "The Lord that looks down"). Known as the Buddhist goddess of mercy, Guan Yin is the subject of special worship by women who wish to have children. This confluence justifies the assimilation, in sculpture as well, of the Virgin Mary; however, the problem of circulation, appropriation, and transformation of Catholic iconography by Chinese artists is quite complex and presents various facets that are not yet clear. See Arnold, who specifically rejects the stereotype according to which maternal love was supposedly expressed universally, which would justify as pure coincidence the similarity between the two images. Indeed there is a direct dependence on Christian models that are appropriated and reinterpreted by the natives within a completely distinct religious sphere.

21. Concerning Tang Yin see Goodrich and Chaoying Fang, vol. II, 256–59.
22. Translation my own.
23. Regarding the miraculous power of the image in New Spain, see Motolinía, 140–41. On the topic of the apparition of the Virgin at Tepeyac, consult Brading.
24. The original is very difficult to comprehend (see note 27). It is likely that here, Longobardi is referring to European patronage that supported the overseas missions, also through donations of books and engravings.
25. This passage reflects a different attitude toward the previous narrative in which Ricci is forced to substitute the image of the Virgin with that of the Savior in order to avoid misunderstandings; it would appear that, in this case, there is no risk of the image of the Virgin being identified as that of God. There are not enough years separating Ricci's and Longobardi's stories to be able to attest that the process of assimilation—the Chinese Guan Yin adopting the iconographic motifs of the Salus with the Child in her arms—had taken place. On the other hand, *Shen Mu* 神母 could refer to Xi Wang Mu 西王母, "la Gran Madre de Occidente, [the Great Mother of the West]" the Taoist goddess who is the progenitor of the universe. In any case, syncretic assimilation to local cults would seem inevitable.
26. The *Evangelicae Historiae Imagines*, by Jerónimo Nadal, S.J. (1507–1580), related the most noteworthy episodes of Jesus's life, arranged according to the liturgical calendar. The volume, printed several times beginning in 1593 in the typography of the Plantin-Moretus family in Antwerp, was beautifully illustrated with engravings by the Wierix brothers: Jan (1549–c.1618), Antoon (c.1555–59–1604), Hieronymus (c.1553–1619); and also Karel van Mallery (1571–1635), Jan Collaert (1566–1628), and Adrian Collaert (1560–1618). The engravings were based on drawings by Giovanni Battista Fiammeri, S.J. (1530–1609) and Bernardino Passeri (1540–1596). The content and the iconographic apparatus of this work, which was translated many times and had significant circulation in Jesuit missions, have been disseminated by the following Chinese works: *Song nianzhu guichneg* 誦念珠規程 (*Instructions for Praying the Rosary*), by João da Rocha, S. J. (1583–1623); *Tianzhu jiangsheng chuxiang jingjie* 天主降生出像經解 (*Illustrated Explanation of the Lord of Heaven*), by Giulio Aleni, S.J. (1582–1649); *Jincheng shuxiang* 進呈書像 (*Illustrated Text Presented to His Majesty*), by Johann Adam Schall von Bell, S.J. (1592–1666). For an outline of the connections between Jesuit missionaries in China, the Plantin press and the Antwerp School, see Golvers.
27. The term *jiao* 教, literally "teaching," is also used in modern language to communicate the concept of "religion."
28. Letter dated June 2nd, 1549, in Malacca.
29. According to the seminal research conducted by André Grabar, relic worship is intrinsically related to the expansion of the religious image in the context of Catholicism. Unfortunately, I have thus far been unable to locate documents that address the rituals of inserting relics into church altars in China. That said, I believe there is a wide horizon to explore the response of Chinese converts to this kind of new, ritual object, although some had become familiar with the consecra-

tions of *tankas* (religious paintings belonging to Lamaist Buddhism, in the form of vertical scrolls) and of statues of Buddha and Bodhisattvas, precisely through the insertion of relics. For more on the consecration of Buddhist images, see Gombrich.

30. See Osswald.
31. For excellent reproductions of these works, allow me to refer to my article "*Dar a otro*" 30–43. Lamentably, these works are not cited in O'Malley, S.J. and Bailey or Bailey 1999 or Bailey 2003.
32. The documents are about missionaries, Franciscans for the most part, martyred during the antichristian persecutions in Nagasaki at the turn of the seventeenth century.
33. A reference to this memorial can be found in an epistle to General Acquaviva dated November 10, 1588, in Macao, (ARSI, Jap.-Sin. 11, I, ff. 1–9r). The epistle was well known but the memorial was thought to be lost. It was wonderful to discover it in the Fondo Gesuitico of the ARSI, mis-catalogued in a lot of documents belonging to a later date. The text has been edited for clarity.
34. For a discussion about the measures adopted by Ricci for presenting European cartography to Chinese intellectuals displacing the topographical center in order to make it coincide with China (*Zhongguo* 中國, literally "the central state"), even though Rome continued to be the center of Christianity and, thus, of the "civilized" world, see Mignolo 219–58.
35. Regarding the problem of the professionalization of knowledge, see Burke. I have used the Italian translation: *Storia sociale della conoscenza. Da Gutenberg a Diderot* (*A Social History of Knowledge. From Gutenberg to Diderot*), 43–46.
36. Zhu Xi 朱熹, Sishu jizhu 四書集注, f. 9r.
37. For more on Cheng Dayue see Goodrich and Chaoying Fang, vol. I, 212–15.
38. By "cultural imperative", Zürcher intended the pervasive power of Chinese culture by which foreign missionaries had been affected to the extent of losing their own identities.

WORKS CITED

Archivo General de la Nación (AGN). Disposición del Santo Oficio. Inquisición. Vol. 263, Record 1 L; Vol. 223, Folio 494/4; Vol. 419, Number 20, Folios 226–234v. Mexico City, Mexico. MS.

Archivum Romanum Societatis Iesu (ARSI). Jap.-Sin. 13, Folio 117a. Rome, Italy. MS.

_____. Jap.-Sin. I, 173.2b. Rome, Italy. MS.

_____. Jap.-Sin. 11, I, Folios 1–9r. Rome, Italy. MS.

Acosta, José de. *Natural and Moral History of the Indies*. Ed. Jane E. Mangan. Trans. Frances López-Morillas. Durham: Duke University Press, 2002.

Aleni, Giulio. *Tianzhu jiangsheng chuxiang jingjie* 天主將牲出像經解, *Explicación ilustrada del Señor del Cielo*. Jinjiang (Quanzhou), 1637.

Amati, Scipione. *Historia del regno di Voxv del Giapone, dell'antichita, nobilta e valore del svo re Idate Masamvne, delli favori, c'ha fatti alla Christanità, e desiderio che tiene d'esser Christiano, e dell'aumento di nostra santa Fede in quelle parti. E dell'Ambasciata che hà inviata alla S.ta di N. S. Papa Paolo V. e delli suoi successi, con altre varoe cose diedificatione, e gusto spirituale de i Lettori. Dedicata alla S.ta di N. S. Papa Paolo V. Fatta per il Dottor Scipione Amati Romano, Interprete, & Historico dell'Ambasciata.* Rome: Appresso Giacomo Mascardi, 1615.

Arnold, Lauren. "Folk Goddess or Madonna? Early Missionary Encounters with the Image of Guanyin." *Encounters and Dialogues: Changing Perspectives on Chinese-Western Exchanges from the Sixteenth to Eighteenth Centuries*. Ed. Xiaoxin Wu. Sankt Augustin: Monumenta Serica Institute; San Francisco: The Ricci Institute of Chinese-Western Cultural History at the University of San Francisco, 2005. 227–38.

Bailey, Gauvin Alexander. *Art on the Jesuit Missions in Asia and Latin America, 1542–1773*. Toronto: University of Toronto Press, 1999.

———. *Between Renaissance and Baroque: Jesuit Art in Rome, 1565–1610*. Toronto: University of Toronto Press, 2003.

Bartoli, Daniello. *Dell'Historia della Compagnia di Giesù: La Cina. Terza parte dell'Asia descritta dal P. Daniello Bartoli della medesima Compagnia*. Rome: Stamperia di Varese, 1663 (1ª ed. Roma: Lazzari, 1659).

Bellarmino, Roberto. *Quarta Controversia generalis. De Ecclesia Triumphante, sive de gloria et cultu sanctorum*, in *De Controversiis christianae fidei. Adversus huius temporis Haereticos*, 1586–1593, repr. in *Opera omnia*, vol. II, Naples: G. Giuliano, 1856–1862. 413–557.

Belting, Hans. *Likeness and Presence: A History of the Image before the Era of Art*. Chicago: The University of Chicago Press, 1994.

Benjamin, Walter. "The Work of Art in the Age of Mechanical Reproduction." *Illuminations*. New York: Schoken Books, 1988 (1ª ed. 1936). 217–51.

Bolzoni, Lina. *La rete delle immagini: Predicazione in volgare dalle origini a Bernardino da Siena*. Torino: Giulio Einaudi Editore, 2002.

Borromeo, Federico. *De Pictura Sacra*. Ed. C. Castiglioni. Sora: Pasquale Carlo Camastro, 1932.

Brading, David. *Mexican Phoenix: Our Lady of Guadalupe: Image and Tradition across Five Centuries*. Cambridge, UK: Cambridge University Press, 2003.

Burke, Peter, *Storia sociale della conoscenza. Da Gutenberg a Diderot*. Bologna: Società editrice il Mulino, 2002 (original ed. *A Social History of Knowledge. From Gutenberg to Diderot*. Cambridge-Oxford: Polity Press-Blackwell, 2000.

Cahill, James. *The Compelling Image: Nature and Style in Seventeenth-Century Chinese Painting*. Cambridge, Mass: Harvard University Press, 1982.

Canone et decreta sacrosanti ecumenici Concilii Tridentini, Augustae Taurinorum, Typographia pontificia et archiepiscopalis: Marietti, 1890.

Carruthers, Mary. *The Craft of Thought: Meditation, Rhetoric, and the Making of Images, 400–1200*. Cambridge, UK: Cambridge University Press, 1998.

Clunas, Craig. *Pictures and Visuality in Late Imperial China*. Princeton: Princeton University Press, 1997.

Corsi, Elisabetta. "Constructores de fe: Imágenes y arquitectura sagrada de los jesuitas en el Pekín imperial tardío." *Historia y grafía*, special issue on *Espacio, imágenes y retórica de las devociones* 26 (2006): 141–70.

———. "'Dar a otro modo y orden' (EE, 2,1) Wu Li's Education in Christian Visuality." *Culture, Art, Religion: Wu Li (1632–1718) and His Inner Journey*. Ed. Yves Camus, S.J. Macau: The Macau Ricci Institute, 2006. 113–127.

———. "La retórica de la imagen visual en la experiencia misional de la Compañía de Jesús en China (siglos XVII–XVIII): Una evaluación a partir del estado de los estudios." *Escrituras de la modernidad: Los Jesuitas entre cultura retórica y cultura científica*. Ed. P. Chinchilla Pawling and A. Romano. Mexico City: Universidad Iberoamericana, Paris: École Française des Hautes Etudes, 2008. 69–104.

Couplet, Philippe, Prospero Intorcetta, Christian Herdtrich, and François Rougemont. *Confucio Sinarum Philosophus sive Scientia Sinensis Latine Exposita* (*Confucio, filósofo chino, o sea la Ciencia china expuesta en latín*). Apud Danielem Horthemels, Paris 1687.

Da Rocha, João. *Song nianzhu guichneg* 誦念住規程: *Instrucciones para rezar el rosario*. Nanjing, 1619.

De Laurentiis, Valeria. "Immagini ed arte in Bellarmino." *Bellarmino e la Controriforma. Atti del Simposio internazionale di studi. Sora 15–18 ottobre 1986*. Ed. R. De Maio, A. Borromeo, L. Giulia, G. Lutz, and A. Mazzacane. Sora: Centro di Studi Sorani "Vincenzo Patriarca," 1990. 581–608.

D'Elia, Pasquale. *Le origini dell'arte cristiana cinese (1583–1640)*. Rome: Reale Accademia d'Italia, 1939.

———. *Fonti ricciane*. 3 vols. Rome: Istituto Poligrafico dello Stato, 1942.

Duverger, Christian. *La conversión de los indios de Nueva España: Con el texto de los Coloquios de los Doce de Bernardino de Sahagún (1564)*. Mexico City: Fondo de Cultura Económica, 1987; reprint 1996.

Freedberg, David. *The Power of Images: Studies in the History and Theory of Response*. Chicago and London: The University of Chicago Press, 1989.

Gadamer, Hans-Georg. *Truth and Method*. Trans. Joel Weinsheimer and Donald G Marshall. London: Bloomsbury Publishing, 2013.

Golvers, Noël. "The XVIIth-century Jesuit Mission in China and its 'Antwerp Connections': I. The Moretus Family (1660–1700)." *De Gulden Passer* 74 (1996): 57–188.

Gombrich, Richard. "The Consecration of a Buddhist Image." *Journal of Asian Studies* 26 (1966–1967): 23–26.

Goodman, Howard L., and Anthony Grafton. "Ricci, the Chinese and the Toolkit of Textualists." *Asia Major* 3 (1990–1991): 95–148.

Goodrich, Luther Carrington, and Chaoying Fang, eds. *Dictionary of Ming Biography, 1368–1644*. 2 vols. New York: Columbia University Press, 1976.

Grabar, André. *Martyrium: Recherches sur le culte des reliques et l'art chrétien antique*. 3 vols. Paris: Collège de France, Fondation Schlumbeerger pour les Etudes Byzantines, 1943–1946.

Grimaldi, Francesco, and Tomás Pereira, *et al. Brevis Relatio eoru, qua spectant ad Declarationem Sinarum Imperatoris Kam Xi circa Cœli, Cumfucij*. Beijing, 1700. Mexico City: Archivo Provincial Societatis Jesu, f. 3r. MS.

Gruzinski, Serge. *Images at War: Mexico from Columbus to Blade Runner (1492–2019)*. Trans. Heather MacLean. Durham: Duke University Press, 2001.

Ignacio de Loyola, *The Spiritual Exercises* (*Ejercicios espirituales*, 1544. MS). Trans. Anthony Mottola. New York: Image Books Doubleday, 1989.

Jensen, Lionel M. *Manufacturing Confucianism: Chinese Traditions and Universal Civilization*. Durham: Duke University Press, 1997.

Jones, Pamela M. "Art Theory as Ideology: Gabriele Paleotti's Hierarchical Notion of Painting's Universality and Reception." *Reframing the Renaissance: Visual Culture in Europe and Latin America, 1450–1650*. Ed. C. Farago. New Haven: Yale University Press, 1995. 127–39.

Levy, Evonne. *Propaganda and the Jesuit Baroque*. Berkeley: University of California Press, 2004.

Longobardi, Niccolò. "Epístola 28 de febrero de 1598." Jap.-Sin. 13, Folio 117r. Archivum Romanum Societatis Iesu, Rome, Italy. MS.

Mancini, Giulio. *Considerazioni sulla pittura*. Ed. A. Marucchi. 2 vols. Rome: Accademia Nazionale dei Lincei, 1956.

Mascardi, Agostino. *Dell'Arte Historica: Trattati Cinque*. Venice: s.e., 1660.

Mignolo, Walter D. *The Darker Side of the Renaissance: Literacy, Territiorialities and Colonization*. Ann Arbor: The University of Michigan Press, 2003.

Motolinía. *Memoriales o cosas de la Nueva España y de los naturales de ella*. Ed. E. O'Gorman. Mexico City: Universidad Nacional Autónoma de México, 1971.

Moxey, Keith. "Response." *Kritische Berichte*, special volume on "Mythen der Kunstwissenschaft—Art Historical Mythologies" 35 (2007): 28–30.

Mungello, David E. *Curious Land: Jesuit Accommodation and the Origins of Sinology*. Honolulu: University of Hawai'i Press, 1989 (1st ed. 1985).

Muratori, Ludovico Antonio. "Prima lettera al Segneri sulle missioni, 12 giugno 1712." *Epistolario di Ludovico Antonio Muratori*. Ed. M. Campori. Vol. I (1711–14). Modena: Società tipografica modenese, 1902. 1471–80.

Nadal, Jerónimo. *Evangelicae Historiae Imagines*. Antwerp: Excudebat Martinus Nutius, 1593.

O'Malley, John, and Gauvin A. Bailey, eds. *The Jesuits and the Arts, 1540–1773*. Philadelphia: Saint Joseph's University Press, 2005.

Osswald, María C. "The Iconography and Cult of Francis Xavier, 1552–1640." *Archivum Historicum Societatis Iesu* 71 (2002): 259–77.

Paleotti, Gabriele. *Discorso intorno alle imagini sacre et profane, diuiso in cinque Libri. Dove si scoprono varij abusi loro, Et si dichiara ilo vero modo che cristianamente si doueri nel porle nelle chiese, nella case, & in ogni altro luogo. Raccolto & posto insieme ad vtile delle anime per commissione di Monsignore Illustruss. & Reverendiss, Card. Paleotti Vescouo di Bologna*. Al popolo della Città & Diocesi sua, Bologna. 1582.

———. *Discorso intorno alle immagini sacre e profane*. Ed. Stefano Della Torre. Vatican City: Libreria Editrice Vaticana, Cad & Wellness, 2002.

———. *Discourse on Sacred and Profane Images*. Trans. William McCuaig. Introd. Paolo Prodi. Los Angeles: The Getty Research Institute, 2012.

Parker, Peter. *Reading Iconotexts: From Swift to the French Revolution*. London: Reaktion Books, 1995.

Prodi, Paolo. "Ricerche sulla teorica delle arti figurative nella Riforma cattolica." *Archivio italiano per la storia della pietà* 4 (1965): 123–212.

———. *Il Cardinale Gabriele Paleotti (1522–1597)*. 2 vols. Rome: Edizioni di Storia e Letteratura, 1967.

———. *Arte e pietà nella Chiesa tridentina*. Bologna: Il Mulino, 2014.

Ricci, Matteo. *Opere storiche del P. Matteo Ricci, S.I.* 2 vols. Ed. P. Tacchi Venturi. Macerata: F. Giorgetti, 1911–1913.

Rule, Paul. *K'ung-tzu or Confucius?: The Jesuit Interpretation of Confucianism*. Sydney: Allen and Unwin Australia, 1980.

Schall von Bell, Johann A. *Jincheng shuxiang* 進呈書像 (*Illustrated Text Presented to His Majesty*). Beijing, 1640.

Standaert, Nicolas. *L'«autre» dans la mission: Leçons a partir de la Chine*. Brussels: Lessius, 2003.

Valignano, Alessandro. "Memorial de las cosas que han de venir para el presente que se ha de enviar al Rey de la China." Fondo Gesuitico. 722/2, Folios 1–9r. Archivum Romanum Societatis Iesu, Rome, Italy. MS.

Wagner, Peter. *Reading Iconotexts: From Swift to the French Revolution*. London: Reaktion Books, 1995.

Xavier, Francisco. *Cartas y escritos de san Francisco Javier*. Ed. Félix Zubillaga. Madrid: Biblioteca de autores cristianos, 1996.

Yuuki, Diego. "El Colegio de San Pablo de Macao y la Iglesia de Japón." *Religion and Culture: An International Symposium Commemorating the Fourth Centenary of the University College of Saint Paul*. Eds. J. Witek and Michel Reis. Macao: Instituto Cultural de Macau; San Francisco: Ricci Institute for Sino-Western Cultural Relations, University of San Francisco, 1999. 277–97.

Zhu Xi 朱熹, Sishu jizhu 四書集注 (XII century), f. 9r. Taipei: Yiwen Yinshuguan, 1996.

◆ CHAPTER ELEVEN

Barlaam and Josaphat in Early Modern Spain and the Colonial Philippines

Spiritual Exercises of Freedom at the Center and Periphery[1]

Jody Blanco

> Mas, sea verdad o sueño
> obrar bien es lo que importa.
> Si fuere verdad, por serlo;
> si no, por ganar amigos
> para cuando despertemos
> (What's more, be this [life] the truth or a dream / what matters is to do good [works] / If true, for the sake of good; / if not, to win friends / for the day we awaken).
>
> SEGISMUNDO, in *La vida es sueño,* verses 2423–27

The European medieval romance of Barlaam and Josaphat centers on the life of the South Asian prince Iodasaph (transliterated into Greek as Ioasaph and Latin as Josaphat: for the sake of consistency, I will use Josaphat throughout), who, according to a seer, is destined to attain otherworldly glory by becoming a religious (presumably Christian) guide.[2] His pagan father, King Abenes, attempts to drive all Christians out of his kingdom. He also builds a city for his son, complete with a tutor and many slaves to attend to his every wish, but with the proviso that "no man, nor any sick person, should on any account be shown to the boy, nor should death ever be mentioned to him; for he wished him to be brought up ... without encountering any form of affliction in the shape of either old age or infirmity or death" (Lang, *The Balavariani* 66). Josaphat's eventual awareness of his imprisonment leads him to demand his liberty from his father. Although the father continues to attempt to prevent his son's exposure to the three aforementioned maladies (sickness, old age, death), Josaphat chances upon a deformed man, a blind man and later, an old man. These experiences lead him to an awareness of time and the universality of death. With this recognition, he renounces his father King Abenes's pagan worship of idols, converts to Christianity under the spiritual pastorship and tutelage of the hermit Barlaam ("Balahvar" in transliterated Georgian), and Josaphat eventually quits his kingdom in order to be reunited with Barlaam in the desert, where both die as holy men.

According to religious scholar Philip Almond, while never formally canonized by the Church, Josaphat and his spiritual advisor Barlaam "enjoyed a popularity attained by perhaps no other legend [in the Christian West]. It spread into nearly all the countries of Christendom and is extant in over sixty versions in the main languages of Europe, the Christian East and Africa" (Almond 391). Yet Almond's assessment neglects the particular interest among monks and missionaries in spreading the exemplum of saints Barlaam and Josaphat in the sixteenth and seventeenth centuries, not to mention the adoption of its premise by Golden Age playwrights Lope de Vega (*Barlán y Josafá* [1614]) and Pedro Calderón de la Barca (*La vida es sueño* [1635]). Following the full retranslation and circulation of the Barlaam and Josaphat romance to Latin, French, and Spanish in the sixteenth century, missionaries translated and published the romance into Japanese (1591), Mandarin (1602), and the Filipino languages of Ilocano (seventeenth century) and Tagalog (1712) (Dehergne, et al. 434). The Tagalog version was itself a translation from a Spanish translation (by Baltasar de la Cruz OP) of the *Latin* version, published in Manila in 1692. Finally, the Barlaam and Josaphat romance inspired a number of plays written by Jesuits, which were presumably performed in and for the colleges they administered (Cañizares 270).

But of course, the spread of the Barlaam and Josaphat story from the Mediterranean to the Pacific is in fact only *half* of the story. For the nineteenth-century investigation into the story's origins and transmission would reveal that the inspiration behind the invention of Christian saint Iodasaph/Josaphat was the life of Prince Siddhartha or Sakyamuni Gautama, who became the "enlightened one" or Buddha several centuries before the birth of Christianity (Almond 395–96; López and McCracken 188–215). In recent years, the quest of scholars of Christianity and the anthropology of religion to understand how the life of the Buddha became transmitted or perhaps "transculturated" into the life of Saint Josaphat has converged with the larger preoccupation with telling, retelling, or dismantling conflictive (and conflicted) narratives of globalization: the "who-started-this-before-it-became-that?" But until the recent rediscovery and subsequent publication of the colonial Tagalog translation of the Barlaam and Josaphat romance (originally published in 1712), an essential chapter of the story's transmission has remained fuzzy (see Borja). That chapter, of which this essay is but a sketch, would concern the importance of Barlaam and Josaphat to the political theology of the Counter-Reformation and Catholic missionaries (particularly the Jesuits) in the Philippines and Asia during the period of Iberian expansion (in the sixteenth and seventeenth centuries).

By studying this importance, my intention is to link the European missionary enterprise overseas (i.e., in the Americas and Asia) with the otherwise abstract theological debates and controversies to emerge in the wake of the Counter-Reformation (1515–1545). At stake in both developments, I argue, is the attempt to redefine the concept of divine will or grace as a permanent destabilizing element in the emergence of modern, secular politics, insofar as it expressed itself in and through the exercise of human freedom. In Calderón de la Barca's famous play *La vida es sueño* (1635), the Josaphatine figure of Segismundo invents a spiritual exercise that dramatizes and resolves the contradiction between human freedom and absolute (monarchial) authority. By contrast, Fray Antonio de Borja (S.J.)'s early eighteenth-century translation of Barlaam and Josaphat (in 1712) reinforces the pastoral power of missionary prudence throughout the overseas missions in the Philippines *over* that of the regal or viceregal authority.[3] These two examples show the way the Barlaam and Josaphat romance was employed to illustrate and explain the nature of Counter-Reformation and colonial Christianity in Asia. For at the heart of its retelling, the Barlaam and Josaphat romance expresses how the only political resolution to the dichotomy between monarchial authority and human freedom cannot be secured within the realm of politics, but rather through an "economy of grace" that it was the task of the Church to administer. That this economy was eclipsed by the political economy of European colonialism in the Americas and Southeast Asia, however, should not lead us to conclude that it ceased to exist. On the contrary, for neophytes in areas like the Tagalog region of the Philippines, the dusk of global Christendom in Europe coincided with the dawn of global Christendom on Europe's frontier.

Globalizing Emancipation As Ascetic Ideal: The Buddha becomes Josaphat

The transculturation of the Buddha story suggests the important similarities and differences in the way early medieval Christian writers imagined the correspondence between human freedom and the nature of the universe, with the way this correspondence would appear in the life of the Buddha. Scholars of the Barlaam and Josaphat romance have generally followed David Marshall Lang's landmark studies of the Georgian texts, from which Euthymius would write the Greek version, which later made its way into the Latin West during the medieval period. According to Lang, "[Barlaam and Josaphat] is a composite, synthetic work, built up stage by stage on the basis of genuine Buddhist tradition, but modified and expanded under the impact of external sources during the story's migration from India to the West" (Lang, *The Wisdom of Balahvar* 23). These "external sources" include any number of Mediterranean and Asian cultures exchanging stories, philosophies, and religious beliefs across both land and maritime routes of the Silk Road [Fig 11.1] throughout the second half of the first millennium, with the likelihood of both Manichean and perhaps even Islamic monotheistic beliefs facilitating the romance's transmission and circulation.[4]

It is no surprise, however, that the first parallel between religious traditions that Lang observes is the impermanence of the world and Josaphat's confrontation with this impermanence (Lang, *The Wisdom of Balahvar* 17–18). In early Buddhist texts, beginning with the Pāli Canon's second discourse of the Buddha ("Anatta-lakkhana Sutta," On the No-Self [anatta] Characteristic discourse), the state of impermanence (*anicca* or *anitya*) constitutes one of the three universal characteristics shared by all living beings (the other two being suffering or stress (*dukkha*) and non-essentiality (*anatta* or *anatman*). The following passage from the Greek version by Euthymius, spoken by Josaphat to his unrepentant father, anticipates both Jesuit spirituality and the baroque sensibility of Calderón in the sixteenth and seventeenth centuries: "And forasmuch as everything here is fleeting and subject to decay, and passeth and vanisheth as a dream, and as a shadow and vision of sleep . . . what simplicity, nay, what folly and madness it is to choose the corruptible and perishable, the weak things of no worth, rather than the incorruptible and everlasting" (St. John Damascene, *Barlaam and Ioasaph*, trans. Rev. G. R. Woodward and H. Mattingly 363).

From this disenchantment with reality arises the ascetic ideal that Buddhism and medieval Christianity would share.[5] At the same time, however, the transculturation of this message between the Buddhist and Christian traditions, as evidenced in the modulation of Prince Siddhartha Gautama/Sakyamuni to Boddhisattva and then to Josaphat, belies other changes in the Old Georgian text—and later, the Greek—that strip Josaphat from his association with Buddhism, not to mention the Manichean and Persian traces from which the Christian(ized) Barlaam and Josaphat is derived (Nozari 325–28). These changes paved the way for the Greek translator of the Barlaam and Josaphat romance, Euthymius, to "fill in" the text, if not entirely saturate it, with references to the Old and New Testaments, as well as the Church Fathers and (more occasionally) Greek philosophers.[6] Chief among these insertions are extensive paraphrases of the work of St. John of Damascus, whose discussions of free will, images, and

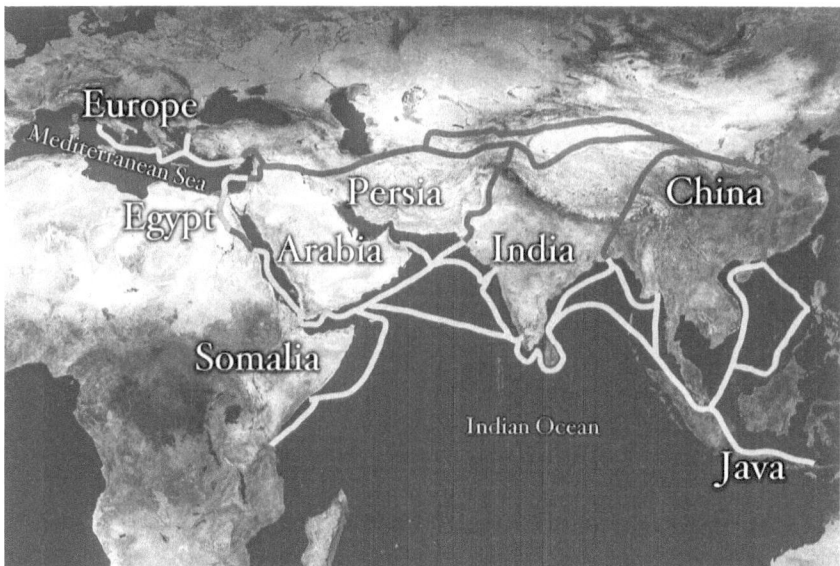

FIGURE 11.1. The overland and maritime silk routes, second century BCE to fifteenth century CE. NASA/Goddard Space Flight Center. Copyright: public domain (2010).

relics become part of Church orthodoxy; as well as the complete reproduction of a hitherto lost treatise by Aristides, a second-century Athenian philosopher and Christian apologist, on the error and idolatry of pagan religions as against Christianity.[7] With these changes, the "Buddhist" Buddha becomes the receptacle and transmitter of Christian doctrine.

This Christianization changes the thrust of the narrative in at least three ways, which served as the polemical basis of Catholic spirituality during the Counter-Reformation. The first concerns the act of conversion as a liberation or emancipation from the false appearance(s) of the world and worldly attachment to those appearances. In the Barlaam and Josaphat romance, the Buddhist theme of emancipation by (self-) enlightenment (as we see in the case of Barlaam) shrinks in importance in relation to the theme of emancipation as brought about by the revelation and explanation of the Christian mysteries.[8] A hymn to Josaphat, written no later than 1065, states this difference plainly: "Most exalted, blessed one," it reads, "wisdom was granted to you *from heaven, and you were made worthy* of apostolic grace (italics added)."[9] This inversion of the enlightenment theme corresponds with the increased role that Josaphat's tutor, Barlaam, must play in Josaphat's conversion and resistance to temptation and apostasy (Forster 182). In response to Barlaam's role in enlightening

Josaphat, the latter at one point exclaims, "Grudge not . . . to shew me other such like figures, that I may know for certain what the manner of our life is, and what it hath in store for its friends" (St. John of Damascene, *Barlaam and Iosaph*, 191).[10] Needless to say, such a tendency goes against most accounts of the Buddha's awakening or enlightenment, which stress the ultimate failure or insufficiency of received doctrines to explain or illustrate the nature of human existence.

With this emphasis comes the necessity for Josaphat to not only listen to Barlaam's instruction, but to heed it unquestioningly, even when Josaphat cannot comprehend or accept those mysteries. In the Greek version of Euthymius, Barlaam tells Josaphat: "This therefore be thy belief; *but seek not to understand the manner of the generation or procession, for it is incomprehensible. . . . And do thou receive these things without question, never seeking to know the manner*" (*Barlaam and Ioasaph* 275–77, emphasis added).[11] Paradoxically, then, we see the emancipatory theme of Christianity here as predicated on the acceptance of, and obedience to, a faith that remains, at its heart, a mystery of grace; and a dependence on the spiritual leadership of a pastor who is identified, not necessarily by a deeper *knowledge* of these mysteries, but rather a deeper conviction, perhaps even resignation, that the truth lay behind the mysteries of the faith. The emergence of what Foucault has called Christian "pastoral power" thus not only binds a pastor to his flock (and vice-versa), but also characterizes the institution of the Church as the orthodox administration of the sacraments necessary for living a Christian life (Foucault, *Security, Territory, Population* 175–81). Not surprisingly, the romance ends with Josaphat abandoning the kingdom he has inherited from his father (who at the end of his life abjures his pagan gods and embraces Christianity), and going off in search of his pastor, Barlaam, in the desert. After two years of wandering, the two are reunited, and Josaphat "dwell[s] with him as with a father and tutor, in all obedience and lowliness, exercising himself in every kind of virtue" (*Barlaam and Ioasaph* 581).

The third aspect of Christianization involves a new relationship between desire and freedom. This entails not simply the freedom *from* desire, as it appears in Buddhists texts like the *Lalita-Vistara*, but rather the *intensification* and *augmentation* of desire to confess the Christian faith, as the highest expression and achievement of (Christian) freedom. When asked about how Barlaam became a devoted monk, the latter answers: "I trained my heart day by day, until it was converted to love Christ and yearn for virtue" (Lang, *The Balavariani* 85). At first sight, this expression of (Christian) emancipation appears self-contradictory, inasmuch as Barlaam here adopts an ascetic practice of training in mind and body not in order to suppress or demystify the nature of desire—as one does, for example, through the Mahayana Buddhist understanding of emptiness (*sunyata*) and non-self (*anatta*)—but rather intensify and focus it. In the Greek version (wrongly) attributed to John of Damascus, Josaphat undergoes the same process: "And he kept his ardor unquenched from beginning to end, ever ascending in his heart and going from strength to strength, and continually adding desire to desire, and zeal to zeal, until he arrived at the long-desired bliss (he sought)" (*Barlaam and Ioasaph* 582–83: translation modified).

What explains this seemingly excessive focus on the desiring subject? Josaphat's education and preparation to religious conversion includes an explanation of the relationship of desire to free will: much of it is a paraphrase from the writings of John of Damascus (see St. John of Damascene, *Barlaam and Ioasaph* trans. Rev. G. R. Woodward and H. Mattingly 222–23). The passage in question immediately follows Barlaam's Manichean-inspired parable regarding a city that represents "the vain and deceitful world [in which] the citizens are the principalities and powers of the devils, the rulers of the darkness of this world, who entice us by the soft bait of pleasure" (*Barlaam and Ioasaph* 203). When pressed by Josaphat to explain why desire has gone awry, leading some to "willingly choose darkness," Barlaam introduces the concept of free will as "the Sovran motion of an intelligent soul," which enables free choice and the recognition of one's desires through choice: choice as "desire accompanied by deliberation, or deliberation accompanied by desire for things that lie in our power" (*Barlaam and Ioasaph* 223). Barlaam further explains:

> Virtuous activities are in our power, therefore in our power are virtues also; for we are absolute masters over all our souls' affairs and all our deliberations. Since then it is of free will that men deliberate, and of free will that men choose, a man partaketh of the light divine, and advanceth in the practice of this philosophy in exact measure of his choice (225).[12]

The exercise of free will toward virtuous activities, and to Christianity more broadly, signifies participation in "the light divine," i.e., as human agency in the realization of divine Providence. Through these activities, characterized as good works, or works of charity [from the word *kharis*, also grace and gift], the complementary expressions of human freedom and that of divine favor converge.[13] To sum up, while the centrality of disenchantment runs throughout Buddhist and Christian approaches to the Indian prince-turned-ascetic, the medieval Christian portrait of Saint Josaphat absorbs the Buddha's askesis in order to reorient the Buddha's awakening toward a Christian dialectic of God's grace and the human freedom *to be subject* in the unfolding of a divine and providential Plan.

Josaphat and Counter-Reformation Spirituality

The preceding analysis, however schematic, highlights three facets of the Buddha's Christianization that would become the subject of controversy and investigation to writers and theologians of the Reformation and Counter-Reformation: 1) the revealed nature of divine truth, or God's act of grace in the salvation of humankind; 2) the necessary institution of pastoral agency in administering the meaning and implications of this message; 3) (Christian) freedom as the prerequisite of human participation in the divine plan. The Reformation expressed, among other things, a systematic revaluation of the meaning and consequences of Christianity as revealed truth; a radical critique of pastoral agency; and a corresponding critique of human freedom (based in part on the new, more immediate condition of popular access to works like the Bible in printed vernacular editions). Moreover, the economic transition from feudalism to capitalism in Western Europe corresponded with the emergence of sovereign states and princes, whose authority did not depend on the Church. In the case of Machiavelli's *The Prince*, the Church represented an outright obstacle to stable and prudent political rule: "a wise lord cannot, nor ought he to, keep [religious] faith when such observance may be turned against him, and when the reasons that caused him to pledge it exist no longer" (Machiavelli, *The Prince*, chapter 18 ["Concerning the way in which Princes should keep the faith"], web; see also Höpfl 164–85). Finally, beyond the theater of continental Europe, the expansion of the Catholic kings (Spain and Portugal) overseas following the discovery and conquest of the Americas placed Church, Crown, and conquistador into close collaboration, which oftentimes failed, erupting into the open hostility of friars against conquistadors, and either (or both) against vice-regal or monarchial authority.

Against this backdrop of the European Reformation, the rise of secular sovereignty, and the role of missionaries in Western expansion, the romance of Barlaam and Josaphat was re-translated into Latin from the Greek by the Benedictine monk Jacques de Billy (around 1577), as well as French (1574) and Spanish (in 1608 and 1692). These translations, in turn, inspired Jesuit missionaries to translate one or more versions of Barlaam and Josaphat into Japanese (1591),

Mandarin (1602), and the Filipino languages of Ilocano (seventeenth century) and Tagalog (1712) (Dehergne, et al. 434).[14] Beyond the romance's translation, the Jesuits were also responsible for adapting the story to the stage in at least seven versions in Spain (see Cañizares 270). One of these versions, titled *Comedia Tanisdorus* (n.d.: probably written in the 1590s), contains narrative elements to be found also in Calderón's 1635 play *La vida es sueño*, and has led scholars to believe that Calderón may have been inspired by the play (see Marcos Villanueva 30–35; and González Gutiérrez 182). Finally, Lope de Vega wrote a dramatic representation of Barlaam and Josaphat in 1611, based on his reading of the 1608 Spanish translation of Barlaam and Josaphat by Juan de Arce Solórzano. Both Lope de Vega and Calderón, it should be noted, were educated in Jesuit colleges; and included many Jesuit-inspired themes in their works (see Marcos Villanueva 17–21). In fact, virtually all of the debates concerning the relationship of Christianity to law and political authority in this period pass through Jesuit political thought in one way or another (Höpfl).

Some of the immediate reasons for the story's popularity throughout the latter half of the sixteenth and seventeenth centuries are easy to guess. The story provided a perfect exemplum for missionaries in Asia, insofar as most cultures throughout present-day East and Southeast Asia had engaged in commercial and political relations with one or more of the Indian kingdoms for centuries (see Coedès). Given, too, that ascetic practices associated with Buddhism and various forms of Hinduism had spread East as well as West, missionaries must have found the story to be particularly useful in communicating the act of Christian conversion to pagan peoples in a hauntingly familiar way. The Buddhist theme of impermanence makes its way into the Jesuit play *Comedia Tanisdorus* as the baroque theme of *mudanza* (movement, change); which, together with the experience of transience [*fugacidad*] constituted for cultural historian José Antonio Maravall the two characteristics of a baroque epistemology (Maravall 362, 380). Compare, for example, the words of anchorite Apolonius (the Barlaam character) from the Jesuit play *Tanisdorus*, with the Euthymius quote in the first section of this essay:

> Todo pasa, todo se acaba; al fin todo pereçe; todo el bien de acá abaxo está suieto a perpetua mudança. Si no, dime: ¿no ves trocarse el tiempo? Di, ¿no aduiertes que se pasa el verano y le sucede el seco estío, a este el frío inuierno? ¿no ves aquestas flores que al aurora se abren con el sol y en vn momento las marchita el calor y al fin pereçen? . . . ¿ qué es de aquellos criados que tenías? ¿Por qué, si piensas, se pusieron otros? Porque no conocieses la mudança que por ellos venía, siendo viejos. (Anonymous 338–39)

> *Everything passes, everything comes to an end; in the end all things perish; every good thing from here on earth is subject to perpetual modification / transformation [mudança]. If it were not, then tell me: do you not see things changing in time? Tell me, do you not take note of how early summer passes and late summer follows, and after that the cold winter? Do you not see those flowers that open with the sun's dawning and [yet] soon wither with the heat and finally perish? ... What happened to the stewards that once took care of you? Why, in your mind, were they replaced by others? Because you could not have known the transformation [mudança] that befell them, having become old.*

The transformation(s) of which Apolonius speaks refers back to the Buddha's (and later, Josaphat's) initial rude awakening or realization (in the Spanish *desengaño*) that the world in which he had grown up is an illusion, fostered by a well-intentioned but pagan father and king who remains "captive" to his beliefs and convictions. And yet, given the historical context of the European Reformation, Counter-Reformation, and Jesuit spirituality in this period, the theme of *desengaño* immediately evokes the decline of Spain in Europe, as well as the diminution or "desacralization" of the Church in temporal (i.e., political) affairs. Beginning with the Reformation, the publication of Erasmus's re-translation of the New Testament from the original Greek to Latin allowed Luther and others to indict centuries of the Catholic Church tradition as the product of misunderstanding and misinterpretation, all for the benefit of a corrupt and hypocritical system. On a larger level, there was considerable dismay and confusion over the idea that, with the revolt of the Netherlands, war and peace no longer fit the frame of a religious or moral crusade, and the relationship of Catholic kings to heretical ones no longer entailed the crusade or conquest of the latter by the former. Between the 1555 Peace of Augsburg (guided by the principle: "*cuius regio, eius religio*" [whose realm, their religion]) and the Treaty of Westphalia at the conclusion of the Thirty Years War (1618–1648), the very structure of international law would undergo seismic changes, rendering religion and religious identity and difference as illegitimate criteria for the recognition or exclusion of political authority or the status of contracts (Gross 20–41).

From these points of reference, the retranslation and reintroduction of the Barlaam and Josaphat romance can be read in at least two ways, both of which are reflected in the narrative as well as various introductions to the text. As an example of Counter-Reformation literature, much of the Barlaam and Josaphat story contributes immediately to a restatement, justification, and explanation of Church *tradition* as the second pillar (besides written Scripture) of the "one" holy and apostolic faith. Of particular interest are the novel's extensive citations from

FIGURE 11.2. Frans Hogenberg, "Beeldenstorm" [Statue Storm or Riot] (1585), depicting the 1566 destruction of Our Lady of Antwerp by iconoclastic followers.

the writings of St. John of Damascus, which (as we have seen) led translators like Jacques de Billy to attribute (mistakenly) the romance to St. John of Damascene (see Billy, in St. John of Damascene, *Historia de vitis et rebus gestis B. Barlaam et Josaphat, Indiae regis, Jacobo Billio Prunaeo interprete*, "Praefatio" [n.p.]). The most prominent example of the authority of Church tradition in John's works comes from his *Apologetic Treatises Against Those Decrying Holy Images* and *An Exact Exposition of the Orthodox Faith*, which were written in the heat of the Byzantine iconoclastic controversy (eighth to ninth centuries). This controversy, which disputed the veneration of Christian holy images as a form of idolatry, reemerged with a vengeance in the wake of Reformation struggles, in which followers of Calvin and Zwingli went as far as the destruction and looting of churches as protest against the perceived worship of images (Eire 105–65, 279–81; see also Fig. 11.2). Needless to say, these debates would resonate strongly with the "iconophilic" soldiers and missionaries traveling to the New World under the banner of the Catholic kings in Spain and Portugal, and who used holy images to stimulate and encourage Christian worship (Gruzinski 184–200).

Yet another reason suggests itself in the preface to the French version (1600) of Barlaam and Josaphat (from the Latin translation of the Greek text by Euthymius). Incidentally, the translator of the French version was Carthusian monk Jean de Billy, the brother of the Latin translator Jacques de Billy: and while Jean de Billy's French version appeared several years before the Latin version of his brother, there is little doubt that Jean's text was translated from Jacques's rather than another (see Anonymous, *Le roman de Barlaam et Josaphat* [Jean Sonet edition], Vol. 1, 100).[15] Here, the author's preface orients the reader to the intended effect of the translated text:

> Tous ceux qui sont poussent de l'esprit de Dieu, sont enfants de Dieu, comme dit l'Apôtre [Paul]. Or être inspiré du saint Esprit, et être faits enfants de Dieu, c'est une chose que *l'on doit souverainement desire*. . . . Et est certain, que tous les Saints qui ont été depuis le commencement du monde, *sont parvenue a ce comble de tous désiré*, par opération et exercice de toute vertu, tant ceux qui ont souffert martyre . . . que les autres qui ont bataillé contre les diables par les monastères et deserts . . . *martyrs de désir et volonté* (St. John of Damascene, *Histoire de Barlaam et de Iosaphat* 3, emphasis added).

> *All who are possessed by the Holy Spirit, are children of God, as the Apostle [Paul] says. As we are all children of God, whether or not one is inspired by the Holy Spirit is something that one must sovereignly desire.* . . . *And it is certain, that all the Saints that have existed since the beginning of the world,* have reached this fulfillment of every desire, *through the performance and exercise of every truth, whether it be those that suffer as martyrs . . . or be it those others who do battle against demons throughout the monasteries and the deserts . . .* martyrs by desire and will.

We have already seen an example of this agency of desire and free will in the early medieval Christianization of the Buddha's life. Closer to Jean de Billy's time, the passage also touches on a later development of European medieval theology, one not captured or stressed in the Scholastic synthesis but running alongside it: Billy's Carthusian predecessor Nicholas Kempf (after Jean Gerson) called it *theologia affectus*, the theology of feeling or desire (also called mystical theology) opposed to *theologia intellectus*, theology of the intellect or understanding.[16] Here, desire (*affectus*) in its relation to divine wisdom refers less to an immediate impulse and more to the end point or achievement of a process: a form of training or exercise, which transforms the will and allows for its infinite application.

From even a cursory description of this approach to theology, one can already sense the pulse of this Carthusian mysticism that will shape Jesuit spirituality in the sixteenth century.[17] Jumping from Jean de Billy's gloss of Barlaam and

Josaphat to the anonymous Jesuit's dramatic adaptation of the Barlaam and Josaphat story, *Comedia Tanisdorus*, during the late sixteenth century, one finds that Tanisdorus's journey to spiritual awakening resembles that of the Jesuit retreatant undergoing spiritual instruction. In both cases, desire and its fulfillment become at once the consequence of free will and the condition of freedom from attachment to the world.

In the anonymous Jesuit's play, written sometime in the late sixteenth century, Tanisdorus makes his appearance as a prince prone to spending hours looking at the sky from within the castle, where he has been sequestered all his life, longing for a freedom he does not understand. While Ringibertus, his custodian, assures him that as a prince and the "único y solo / legítimo heredero del Oriente, / a quien mil reynos rinden vasallaje" (Anonymous 293–94) (the "only / legitimate heir of the Orient / to whom a thousand kingdoms render vassalage"), Tanisdorus replies that his wealth and privilege are useless to him without the one "precious jewel" that he is missing: freedom (*libertad*). When the Christian hermit, Apolonius (the Barlaam figure), comes disguised as a hermit, he claims to be selling the very jewel of "freedom" Tanisdorus longs to see. After revealing to Tanisdorus the mysteries of the Christian faith, he exhorts the latter to think about it as the satisfaction of his deepest desire: "piensa en ello; *esto es lo que tu alma deseaba sino que carecía de la lumbre del cielo y no atinaba a dar en ello*" (347, italics added) (think on it; *this is what your soul desired, but it was lacking in the enlightenment of heaven and did not succeed in reaching it*). Christianity, under Apolonius's tutelage, "liberates" Tanisdorus by disenchanting him of his (and later, his father's) belief in pagan gods and their prophecies; and with this knowledge, Tanisdorus leaves the castle and kingdom, with the desire to adopt the life of a hermit.

On the surface, the plots of both the medieval Barlaam and Josaphat and its Jesuit adaptation are the same. Yet the play refocuses the basic narrative away from an emphasis on the renunciation of worldly desires and toward what one might anachronistically call the "sentimental education" of Christian ascetic desire—the desire to know and freely pursue desire's *true* object. When Tanisdorus expresses his desire to follow Apolonius and lead a hermit's life, his servant, Sabirus, says: "a Thanisdoro es cumplido / lo que ha tanto que apeteçe; / ya tiene quien su deseo le cumpla y pueda enseñar este Dios que anda a buscar" (354) (Tanisdorus finally possesses / what he has longed for so much; / he has the one who completes his desire, and who can teach [him about] this God that he has been searching for). Later, when Tanisdorus is caught in a deception that leads to his temptation, he imagines the allegorical figure of Faith [Fides] coming to guide and encourage him, with the words: "El çielo augmente / en ti ese zello ardiente, mas no quiera / que Thanisdoro muera hasta que vea,/ lo que tanto desea, que este estado / sea desengañado" (401) (May heaven augment / in you this burning desire, and may it not seek / Tanisdorus's death until he sees / what he so desires, the demystification / of this state of affairs). Even up to Tanisdorus's parting letter to his subjects, the anonymous playwright reminds us that our hero's renunciation of the world does not come about because of his disenchantment and renunciation of the world, but rather his longing to live a liberated existence *within* it: "el deseo que en mí ardía y la palabra y fe que tengo dada de seguir la vida heremítica" (443) (the desire that burns in me and the oath and faith I have given to follow the life of a hermit). Freedom *from* desire for the world (as in the theme of worldly renunciation) has become freedom *to* desire the highest freedom in the world: that is, as desiring subjects trained in recognizing the divine will as desire's true object.[18]

Taken together, these two interpretations of Barlaam and Josaphat's importance to the Jesuits (the doctrine of images and the arousal of "sovereign desire") reflect a key Jesuit strategy in the European Counter-Reformation and the missionary endeavor overseas: the emancipation and stimulation of the imagination in the service of political theology and Catholic piety. On one level, the reorientation of ascetic spirituality in this period emphasized Church authority by tradition (as in the doctrine of holy images), "sovereign desire," and the human freedom that it presupposes, as a way of refuting Reformation aspersions against Church orthodoxy. On another level, however, this pivot away from the extremes of Reformation iconoclasm and the Manichean implications of predestination was foregrounding something else—the concept of God and divine providence that remained perfectly compatible with a world produced and governed by the exercise of human freedom and the incitement of the passions.[19] In Jesuit scholar Luis de Molina's controversial treatise on free will, *La Concordia liberi arbitrii cum gratiae donis, divina prascientia, providentia, praedestinatione et reprobatione* (The Concordance of Free Will with the Bestowed Graces of Divine Pre-Knowledge, Providence, Predestination and Reprobation) [1588], the author uses the term "contributing and grace" (*gracia adyuvante y cooperación*) to conceptualize this concordance:

> Es fácil de entender que una y la misma gracia, *en la medida en que excita, atrae e invita a nuestro arbitrio a realizar los actos de creer, de tener esperanzas, de amar o de arrepentirse*, se denomina "gracia previniente y excitante"—por esta razón, previene a nuestro arbitrio en relación a estos actos —, pero en la medida en que—una vez que nuestro arbitrio ya ha consentido y coopera en los actos hacia los cuales *esta gracia invita y atrae*—también coopera en estos actos con una acción e influjo nuevos, se denomina "gracia adyuvante y cooperación." (Molina 327 [Disputa XL: 6], italics added)

> It is easy to understand why one and the same grace (to the degree that it excites, attracts, and invites our free will to achieve those acts of belief, of having hopes, of loving or regretting) *would be called "prevenient and solicitous grace"—for the reason that it anticipates* [previene] *our will in relation to these acts. But to the degree that [this grace] also co-operates in these acts—once our will has consented and cooperates in those acts toward which this grace invites and attracts us—with a new action and influence, we call that "contributing and cooperative grace."*

This language of desire, from Ignatius de Loyola's *Spiritual Exercises* to the adaptation of the Barlaam and Josaphat romance to the theater of Lope de Vega and Calderón de la Barca, here appears under the category of "cooperative grace."[20] By spurring ("exciting, attracting, inviting") the will toward the desire for virtuous acts, without (and this is the key condition) predetermining them, this "mode" of divine grace animates the faculty of human freedom and also fulfills it. By heightening one's desire to participate in the becoming of divine providence, cooperative grace simultaneously provides freedom's condition of possibility and directs the Christian subject to its furthest realization. Rather than abandon the ever-widening gulf between the mystery of divine grace and the profane, all-too suspicious ends of human freedom and passion, the promoters of Barlaam and Josaphat insisted on maintaining each as the conduit of the other.

Grace and Freewill at the Absolute End of the Earth

The doctrine of cooperative grace, which became one of the controversial issues (along with the missions in China and Japan) that set the religious orders within the Church against each other throughout the seventeenth century, would appear too elegant and even glib in the eyes of writers like Pascal and Voltaire during the eighteenth. But the disappearance of such doctrines in Europe neglects their spread in the colonies, in which religious missionaries were engaged in an amorphous laboratory of conversion and apostasy or "backsliding" (*reincidencia, volverse atrás*) with peoples and cultures that neither needed nor welcomed Christianity prior to the arrival of the Iberians.[21] A final example of the spread of Barlaam and Josaphat demonstrates the difficulty of reconciling the omnipotence of God's authority and the autonomy of human freedom not only in the context of the rise of the concept of absolute authority or sovereignty in Europe, but also in the context of overseas Christian evangelization.

At the end of the seventeenth century, Fr. Antonio de Borja [SJ] was instructed by his superiors to translate the Barlaam and Josaphat romance into Tagalog. The

Latin version had already been translated into Spanish by Dominican professor, historian, and high-ranking colonial official of the Philippines, Fr. Baltasar de Santa Cruz [OP], in 1692. Following in Calderón's footsteps, Santa Cruz dedicates the Spanish translation of Barlaam and Josaphat to the governor General D. Fausto Cruzat y Góngora, enjoining the latter to bear in mind the mutually reinforcing nature of the spiritual and temporal powers. Employing the terms familiar to the political philosophy of the Spanish monarchy, Santa Cruz restates the necessity of understanding the inseparability of Christian prudence from reason of state, human agency from holy providence.

When Borja publishes his Tagalog version in 1712, however, he addresses a very different audience: he dedicates the work "Sa mga kapatid kong Tagalog, na dating masunurin sa mga amang nag-aandukha sa kaluluwa nila" (Borja 14) (to my Tagalog brothers and sisters, who for some time have remained obedient to the (religious) fathers who care for their souls). Here, Borja specifies by omission that significant part of the population still living outside the towns and villages, which implied either the active or the passive resistance of these communities to adopt fixed urban settlement patterns, pay tribute, and accept the obligation of compulsory labor in exchange for baptism and the administration of Christian sacraments. Opposed to these were the native Tagalog converts who had accepted Christianity, and thereby entered into a new community under the Church as well as colonial authority.

The dedication provides Borja an opportunity to share his reflections with his Tagalog neophytes, in a narrative that anticipates and parallels that of Barlaam and Josaphat:

> [A]ng lahat ng yao'y noong naroon pa kami sa bayan namin sa Castilla, para-para na naming tinalikda't winalang-bahala, tuloy pinanawa't iniwan, at naparito kami sa Filipinas at kapuluan ng Maynila. Kaya sa ganitong pagninilay-nilay, tapat na sa inyo ko rin ipalagay itong aking pinagkabagaba't pinagkapagalan, yayang ang inyo ring kamay ang talagang uuwia't kapaparoonan (Borja 14)

> *All that we had, when we were still in our homes in Castile, we turned our backs on and ceased to care for, then settled our debts and left, and had ourselves brought here to the Philippines and the islands around Manila. Following this reflection, I also entrust to you my labor and good work [pinagkapagalan], since my future home and destination are in your hands.*

The narrative contrasts dramatically with the tales of conquest and crusade brought by Spaniards to the Philippines (represented in the dramatic tradition of the *moro-moro* [dramatization of Spanish romances pertaining to the Spanish Reconquest] and later, the Tagalog poetry *awit* [12-syllable verse] and *korido* [8-syllable verse]); or even the self-fulfilling rhetoric of biblical prophecy in works like Gaspar de San Agustín's *Conquistas de las Islas Filipinas*, published in 1698. Borja bemoans the fact that for someone who has invested so much time and effort in missionary work, he seems to have accomplished so little (Borja 15). Comparing missionaries to the Barlaam figure, he writes: "iniwan [nila] ang kani-kanilang bayan, sampu ng kayamana't bahay, mga magulang at kamag-anakan, at nangagsadyang tumawid dito sa kawakas-wakasang lupa" (16) (they leave their respective countries, along with their possessions and homes, parents and relatives, and willfully cross over to the absolute end of the earth). These and other examples betray a certain petulance that pervades the text, in which Borja mentions several times how difficult the work of translation has been; that he was ordered to undertake the translation by his superiors (and he probably would not have undertaken it otherwise), and that Tagalog neophytes should consider themselves fortunate to have so many pastors, as opposed to the Indian kingdom that only had one (Barlaam)!

Borja's self-pity borders on caricature; yet we should not hastily overlook an original moment in the history of Tagalog literature taking place. For the first time, outside the place of the pulpit and the rhetoric of the sermon, a pastor is addressing his converts—in public, and *in their language*—about how he has come to see himself as caught between the orders of his superiors, the short-comings of his flock, the presumed nobility of his intentions, and the meager accomplishments that belie the time he has spent "at the absolute end of the earth" (ibid.). In the scenario in which he now sees himself, he has come to depend on the very colonial and Christian subjects that he has been sent to instruct and guide. Borja's dedication thus ends with a cheeky half-apology and half-exhortation:

> At tungkol sa kagarilan ng pangungusap o pagsasaysay kayang kulang na masusum-pungan ninyo't matutuklasan dito'y kayo na ang bahalang magpuno't magtuwid ng magandang loob, yaya siya kong nakaya palibhasa'y di ko sariling wika at hiram ko lamang sa inyo. At nang di nga kayo magpatisod-tisod na lubha ... sa pagbasa ninyo nito ay tikis akong nakikimukha sa mga batang eskuwela sa pagpapatuwid ko nitong gawang pinagkapagalan ko sa mga maginoong Tagalog (Borja 17)

> *And regarding the errors of speech and expression that may irk you, finding it wanting, and realizing that it is up to you (*kayo na ang bahala*) to fill and correct [the grammar and syntax] of this sincere intention, I invite you to make the effort and do so, seeing as it is not my language and I only borrowed it from you. And when you no longer have to*

hazard stumbling through your reading [of this book], I will gladly face you in the new schools in order to make the corrections to this labor/work [gawang pinagkapagalan] of mine, on behalf of the Tagalog nobles.[22]

The author's dedicatory preface not only serves to introduce the Barlaam and Josaphat tale; it also provides a commentary on the limits of the main text's ability to convey the particular experience of Philippine missionaries to themselves and their converted flock. Even as Borja casts missionaries in the role of Barlaam, he also sees the fate of his message in the hands of the colonial subjects upon whom he has come to depend. As he chastises them for failing to internalize what remained a foreign message of salvation, he also resorts to a number of metaphors and Tagalog proverbs as a way to win their fraternal sympathy. Far from demonstrating his mastery of Tagalog—and its corollary implication, which is the reification of the Tagalog language as an instrument or technique for the transmission of instruction and command—Borja confesses the effective limits of his labor, or good work, which he translates into Tagalog as *gawang pinagkapagalan ko* (deed resulting from my effort) (Borja 17).

In short, the same thematic elements we saw in the European Counter-Reformation promotion of the Barlaam and Josaphat tale—the mediatory role of the Church, the agency of free will (which is translated in the text as *sariling kalooban*) and desire as the vehicle of cooperative grace, the solicitation of sympathy and the fraternal bond between pastor and flock, good works as the expression of human participation in a Divine Plan—remain, but are here oriented to an entirely different audience. If a text like Calderón's *La vida es sueño* serves as a new exemplum for the Counter-Reformation prince, Borja's *Barlaam at Josaphat* labors—in a style that highlights, even performs, its belabored effort—to imagine the terms and conditions under which Tagalog neophytes would desire Christianity *freely*.

Not surprisingly, one of these ways would involve portraying Christianity as a form of liberation or emancipation from pre-Hispanic social stratification. In one of several passages in which Barlaam or Josaphat convey this, Borja departs from a direct translation of the Spanish version of the text and elaborates on his own: "Ako nama'y," says Josaphat, "inilayo Niya at *tinimawa* sa malupit na panunuyo sa mga anitong puno ng dilang mga kamalian at doon sa kaugaliang walang kabu-kabuluhan. . . . Kinuha kayo't inalis doon sa laong *kaalipinang pinaghihirapan*" (Borja 357) (God set me apart and emancipated [*tinimawa*] me from the cruel subjection of the ancestral gods and spirits, whose tongues told nothing but lies, mired in meaningless old customs [*kaugalian*]. . . . You were gotten and removed from the ancient slavery/enslavement you suffered). Both of the words for emancipation (*timawa*) and slavery (*alipin*) refer to pre-Hispanic social categories, each of which denoted various privileges and obligations that Spaniards would associate with "free men" and "slavery." Emancipation, however, would involve not solely an external agent, but the "free will" (Tagalog: *sariling kalooban*) of the neophyte:

> Ang pagtutulot sa sariling kalooban ay isang kapangyarihang bigay sa kaluluwang may bait at pagninilay na di isa man sasawatain sa balang maibig gawin, masama man kaya't magaling, sa pagkakabanalan man o sa masama kayang kagagawan. Ipinalagay ng Diyos sa kaluluwa ng tao ang buong pahintulot at pagkamahadlika ng pagtanggap at pag-ayaw sa anumang bagay na maisipan niya. Gayundin namang sukat nating wikain na itong pagpapabahalang ito sa tao, ay isang kamahadlikaan ng kaluluwa na sukat bilingi't baliktarin sa masama't magaling na ibig niyang sundin (Borja 163)

> *The sanction of free will [sariling kalooban] is a power given to a good and reflective soul, one that goes unchecked toward whatever it wants to do, good or bad, for the sake of holiness or to promote evil. God was so disposed to give human souls complete sanction and freedom [pagkamahadlika, fr. mahadlika or maharlika, free vassal] of accepting [or] rejecting anything before his [or her] consideration. This is the same as saying that a person's disposition or inclination to something is a freedom [kamahadlikaan] of every soul that can equally turn or reverse toward a good or bad end to a desired path.*

With this declaration, the Jesuit priest who has arrived at "the absolute end of the earth" also arrives at the absolute frontier of his theology: did native converts come to Christianity of their free will? Would a negative answer call into question the entire missionary enterprise? The Jesuit initiative to admit members of the Tagalog nobility into seminaries and, eventually, the priesthood offers the beginning of an answer.

Conclusions

I conclude with two observations: one pertaining to the implications of Counter-Reformation spirituality and another on the truncated legacy of the Counter-Reformation modernity in the Philippines. Regarding the first, Mexican sociologist Bolívar Echeverría has pointed out at least two implications of the Catholic theology that underwrites Barlaam and Josaphat, as well as its avatars. On one level, this theology "plantea una idea de Dios como un Dios haciéndose, es decir, como un Dios creándose a sí mismo, como Dios en proceso de ser Dios, y no como un Dios que ya lo es" (Echeverría 79–80) (asserts an idea of God as a God in the process of becoming, that is, a God in the process of creating Himself, God in the process of being God, and not a God that already exists). On another level, it implies that:

> Al haciéndose, Dios depende en alguna medida de su propia creación, depende del ser humano. Esta peculiar inserción del ser humano y su libre albedrío como una entidad necesitada por Dios para que su creación funcione efectivamente, este intento de conciliar o hacer que concuerden la omnipotencia de Dios y la dignidad humana, es el punto donde, efectivamente, la doctrina teológica de los jesuitas parece dirigida a revolucionar toda la teología tradicional" (Echeverría 80)

> *God depends in some way on His own creation, on human beings. This peculiar insertion of human beings and their free will as an entity needed by God in order for his creation to function effectively, this attempt to reconcile or correlate God's omnipotence with human dignity, is the point where, in effect, the theological doctrine of the Jesuits seems destined to revolutionize all traditional theology.*

These two conclusions remain controversial even today, as the Catholic Church effectively prohibited their debate from continuing after the seventeenth century. As Borja's translation of Barlaam and Josaphat shows, however, such "concordances" find their limit and frontier at the moment that the missionary's freedom and desire solicits and acknowledges that of the native convert. The Age of the World Crusade was over. It was the Jesuits' self-assigned task to communicate something of that age in another: one in which neither the strength of Spanish arms nor the promise of Christendom they carried meant much to absolute sovereigns, royal companies, and pirates of the high seas, much less natives subjected to every form of servitude and enslavement.

This last point means to highlight the contradictory legacy of Catholic Christianity in the Philippines, today the third largest Catholic nation in the world. On the one hand, it would be fair to say that missionaries had in a sense accomplished or contributed to the success of what they had imagined their task to be: the "emancipation" of indigenous peoples, in the Philippines and elsewhere, from the cultures and practices that had once anchored their place in the universe according to their own frames of reference. And those aspects of native society that remained were wholly transfigured, converted into new opportunities for exploitation (as in the case of indentured servitude), corruption (as in the case of native offices), and superstition (as in the case of the cults of saints). Yet they also (wittingly or unwittingly) made available an idea that would nurture the uprisings and revolutions of the eighteenth and nineteenth centuries: what might this Christian freedom mean, once it has been translated into native languages and made available for public conversation and reflection? What might it mean to know that missionaries—perhaps even other vice-regal officials and *encomenderos* (royal grantees)—depended on the desire and will of the neophyte?

Perhaps not surprisingly, the nineteenth-century Tagalog poem that would inspire a generation of revolutionaries to overthrow Spanish rule, *Florante at Laura* [Florante and Laura] (1838), begins with a trapped prince, expressing his longing and desire for freedom (Balagtas). Unfortunately for Spain, perhaps, the protagonist's desire places him on the road not toward Christian orthodoxy, but rather friendship and solidarity with a Muslim prince.

NOTES

1. I would like to thank Claudia Vizcarra, Parimal Patel, Luis Gómez, Satoko Kakihara, and the editors for their invaluable support and comments on earlier drafts of this essay. All translations are my own, unless otherwise noted.
2. The legend chronicling the lives of Barlaam and Josaphat as Christian saints was translated from Georgian to Greek and Latin in the 11th century (around 1048), although its translation from Latin to Spanish first occurs around 1470, and again in 1608. See David Lang's "Introduction" in St. John of Damascene, *Barlaam and Ioasaph* xxvi–xxxii; and Keller and Linker, xxii–xxix.
3. See Borja. The Tagalog version appears to be, for the most part, a translation of Dominican priest Balthasar de Santa Cruz's Spanish version, itself a translation of the Latin version by Jacques de Billy: see St. John of Damascene, *Historia de vitis et rebus gestis B. Barlaam et Josaphat, Indiae regis, Jacobo Billio Prunaeo interprete*. As we will see, Borja's version differs from that of both Santa Cruz and Billy in certain significant respects.
4. See Lang, *The Balivariani* 11–64; Almond 404–6; and Gimaret 61.
5. As Barlaam relates to Josaphat regarding his conversion to Christianity: "I trained my heart day by day, until it was converted to love Christ and yearn for virtue. Then I began to wean my desires and appetites away from their accustomed habits, and get them under my own control . . . thus did I govern my own nature" (Lang, *The Balavariani* 85; also cited in Almond 399).
6. Lang, following the work of K. S. Kekelidze, suggests the possibility that, between the death of Euthymius in 1028 and the publication of the romance in Greek around 1048, there was "ample opportunity for the copy to fall into the workshop of Simeon Metaphrastes and his disciples," who would have embellished and elaborated on the text with biblical and scholarly references. See Lang, "Introduction," in St. John of Damascene, *Barlaam and Ioasaph* xxxii.

7. See St. John of Damascene, *Barlaam and Iosaph* (trans. G. R. Woodward and H. Mattingly: on free will, 222–25; on images, 280–83; on relics, 334–35; and for the complete reproduction of a hitherto lost treatise by Aristides, 397–425.
8. For an interesting discussion on the concept of free will between Buddhism and Christian traditions, see Gier and Kjellberg.
9. See Lang, *The Balavariani* 43. As Graeme MacQueen writes elsewhere: "Enlightenment [in the Buddhist tradition] is now [Christian] revelation. . . . The [Buddha or Boddhisattva's] enlightenment, while still important, is being reduced in stature and content, and God is beginning to replace [Gautama] as protagonist of the narrative and hence as actor in the story of cosmic liberation" (5).
10. The Tagalog version heightens the obsequiousness of Josaphat's plea: see Borja 143.
11. One cannot help but observe here that the Christianization of the bodhisattva to Josaphat conforms to and coincides with two suggestive theses advanced by Foucault. The first concerns Christian practices of penance in the early medieval period, in which he observes the growing importance of *exagoreusis*—"an analytical and continual verbalization of thoughts carried on in the relation of complete obedience to someone else"—over that of *exomologesis*—"a dramatic expression of the situation of the penitent as sinner which makes manifest his status as sinner" (see "Technologies of the Self"). The second concerns his theory of "pastoral power" characteristic of the Church, which is based (in part) on the permanent obedience of the neophyte to a spiritual pastor (see *Security, Territory, Population* 175–81).
12. Compare Barlaam's statement, for instance, to the following passage from John of Damascus's *Exact Exposition of the Orthodox Faith* (Book II, chapter 30): "We ought to understand that while God knows all things beforehand, yet He does not predetermine all things. . . . So that predetermination is the work of divine command based [only] on fore-knowledge" (John of Damascus, "Concerning Free Will and Predestination").
13. This accords with Pelikan's characterization of Christianity in the Eastern Orthodox tradition, which "characteristically substituted a complementarity for this antithesis [between God's grace and human freedom]. . . . They interpreted grace simultaneously as a totally unearned divine gift and as an affirmation of continuity with nature and creation—and therefore with freedom" (Pelikan, *Mary Through the Centuries* 89).
14. Dehergne notes that the first translation of Barlaam and Josaphat into Japanese appears in the Jesuit correspondence with Rome in 1577.
15. For an incisive study of Jean de Billy's life and work, particularly his experience with Protestant iconoclasm, see Oddo 191–210.
16. See Martin 71–85. In *De recto fine* [1447], Kempf writes: ". . . Secunda, scilicet mistica, [theologia] acquiritur per affectus solo Deo illustrante inmediate intellectum humanum ex affectu seu amore intenso previo in voluntate" [The second theology, namely mystical, is acquired through feeling, with God alone conveying it to the human intellect immediately, from feelings or an intense love transformed into will] (quoted in Martin 309, my translation).

17. This influence has been noted in all the biographies of Ignatius de Loyola. See Foss 68.
18. A more detailed analysis would have to include this rhetoric of desire in the *Spiritual Exercises*. Suffice it to say, for now, that most of the meditations begin with a narrative, an accompanying visualization or composition of a scene or image, followed by the prompt for the retreatant to "solicit what I want" [*demandar lo que quiero*]. This instruction to demand, in turn, is followed by a specification of *what* exactly it is that the retreatant wants. As we later see, the perpetual transformation of the object of desire leads to an emptying of the retreatant's investment in desire: a surrender to the divine will or Other, which renders him indifferent to desires (see St. Ignatius Loyola, *Ejercicios espirituales*, "Principio y Fundamento," [par. 23], web). For an excellent essay on this aspect of Loyola's text, see Certeau, "The Space of Desire."
19. The Manichean implications of predestination were summed up by Hans Blumenberg: "The escape into transcendence, as the possibility that is held out to man and has only to be grasped, has lost its human relevance precisely on account of the absolutism of the decisions of divine grace, that is, on account of the dependence of the individual's salvation on a faith that he can no longer [even] choose to have" (137, 488–89).
20. For an incisive study of the *Spiritual Exercises* as a language of desire that unfolds through the expansion and contraction of the imagination, see Barthes 38–75.
21. For an essay on the influence of Molinism in Latin America, see Kuri Camacho 91–122.
22. Borja's mention of the "new schools" probably refers to King Philip V's 1702 decree to found seminaries for *Indios* in Manila. It would make sense that the students who would qualify for this form of higher education would come from the families of the Tagalog nobility. According to religious historian John Schumacher, S.J., it seems that the policy did not really become implemented until after 1720, eight years following the publication of Borja's *Barlaam at Josaphat*. See Schumacher 197–202.

WORKS CITED

Almond, Philip. "The Buddha of Christendom: A review of 'The Legend of Barlaam and Josaphat.'" *Religious Studies* 23 (1987): 391–406.

Anonymous. *Le roman de Barlaam et Josaphat* (4 volumes). Edition by Jean Sonet. Namur (Paris): Bibliothèque de la Faculté de Philosophie et Lettres and J. Vrin, 1949–1950.

Anonymous. *Comedia Tanisdorus*. *Comedia de Santa Catalina/Comedia Tanisdorus: Teatro clásico del siglo XVI*. Ed. Cayo González Gutiérrez. Guijón, 2003. 265–448. www.yumpu.com/es/document/view/4324394/cayo-gonzalez-gutiarrez-comedia-de-santa-telecable. Web. October 28, 2015.

Balagtas, Francisco. *Florante at Laura*. EBook #15845, Project Gutenberg: 2005. www.gutenberg.org/files/15845/15845-h/15845-h.htm. September 22, 2015. Web.

Barthes, Roland. *Sade, Fourier, Loyola*. Trans. Richard Miller. Berkeley: University of California Press, 1989.

Blumenberg, Hans. *The Legitimacy of the Modern Age*. Trans. Robert M. Wallace. Cambridge, Mass: MIT Press, 1983.

Borja Antonio de. *Barlaan at Josaphat: Modernisadong Edisyon ng salin ni Fray Antonio de Borja*. Edited by Virgilio Almario. Quezon City: Ateneo de Manila University Press, 2003.

Calderón de la Barca, Pedro. *La vida es sueño. Con cuadros cronológicos, introducción, bibliografía, notas y llamadas de atención, documentos y orientaciones para el estudio a cargo de José María García Martín*. Madrid: Editorial Castalia, 1984.

Cañizares, Patricia. "La Historia de los dos soldados de Cristo, Barlaam y Josafat traducida por Juan de Arce Solorenzo (Madrid 1608)." *Cuadro Filiológico Clásico (Estudios Latinos)* 19 (2000): 259–72.

Certeau, Michel de, S.J. "The Space of Desire." *Arte y Espiritualidad Jesuitas: Principio y fundamento. Artes de México* (Revista libro) 70: 2004. 93–97.

Coedès, George. *The Indianized States of Southeast Asia*. Honolulu: University of Hawai'i Press, 1968.

Cruz Palma, Oscar de la, editor. *Barlaam et Iosaphat: Version vulgata latina*. Barcelona: Editorial CSIC, 2001.

Dehergne, Joseph, S.J. and Roman Malek. "Catéchismes et Catéchèse des Jésuites de Chine de 1584 à 1800." *Monumenta Serica* 47 (1999): 397–478.

Eire, C. N. M. *The War Against the Idols: The Reformation of Images from Erasmus to Calvin*. New York: Cambridge University Press, 1986.

Echeverría, Bolívar. *La modernidad de lo barroco*. Mexico: Ediciones Era, S.A. de C.V., 1998.

Foss, Michael. *The Founding of the Jesuits, 1540*. London: Hamilton, 1969.

Foucault, Michel. *Security, Territory, Population: Lectures at the Collège de France 1977–1978*. Ed. Michel Senellart. New York: Picador, 2009.

———. "Technologies of the Self." Edited by Luther H. Martin, Huck Gutman and Patrick H. Hutton. Cambridge: University of Massachusetts Press, 1988. 16–49. Online version: Michel Foucault Info. foucault.info/doc/documents/foucault-technologiesof-self-en-html. Web. July 1, 2017.

Gier, Nicholas F., and Paul Kjellberg. "Buddhism and the Freedom of the Will: Pali and Mahayanist Responses." *Freedom and Determinism: Topics in Contemporary Philosohy*. Eds. J. K. Campbell, D. Shier, M. O' Rourke. Cambridge, Mass: MIT Press, 2004. 277-304. www.webpages.uidaho.edu/ngier/budfree.htm#_ednref8. Web. June 21, 2017.

Gimaret, Daniel. *Le Livre de Bilawhar et Būdāsf selon la version arabe ismaélienne*. Geneva and Paris: LIbraire Droz, 1971.

González Gutiérrez, Cayo. *El teatro escolar de los Jesuitas (1555–1640) y edición de la Tragedia de San Hermenegildo*. Oviedo: Servicio de Publicaciones de la Universidad de Oviedo, 1997.

Gross, Leo. "The Peace of Westphalia, 1648–1948." *American Journal of International Law* 42:1 (1948): 20–41.
Gruzinski, Serge. *The Conquest of Mexico: The Incorporation of Indigenous Societies into the Western World, 16th–18th Centuries.* Trans. Eileen Corrigan. Malden: Polity Press, 1993.
Haan, F. de. "Barlaam and Joasaph in Spain." *Modern Language Notes* X:1 (1895): 11–17.
Höpfl, Harro. *Jesuit Political Thought: The Society of Jesus and the State, c. 1540–1630 (Ideas in Context).* Cambridge, UK: Cambridge University Press, 2008.
John of Damascus. "Concerning Free Will and Predestination." *Orthodox Christian Information Center.* orthodoxinfo.com/inquirers/exact_freewill.aspx. Web. June 21, 2017.
Kantorowicz, Ernest. *The King's Two Bodies: A Study of Medieval Political Theology.* Princeton: Princeton University Press, 1998.
Keller, John E., and Robert W. Linker, editors. *Barlaam e Josafat.* Madrid: Consejo Superior de Investigaciones Científicas, 1979.
Kuri Camacho, Ramón. "*Libertad Divina y Humana* en algunos jesuitas novohispanos: Pedro de Abarca, Miguel de Castilla y Antonio de Figueroa Valdés." *Estudios de Historia Novohispana (EHN)* 37 (July–December 2007): 91–122.
Lang, David M. *The Wisdom of Balahvar: A Christian Legend of the Buddha.* London: George Allen and Unwin Ltd., 1957.
———. *The Balavariani (Barlaam and Josaphat): A Tale from the Christian East Translated from the Old Georgian.* Berkeley: University of California Press, 1966.
López, Donald, and Peggy McCracken. *In Search of the Christian Buddha: How an Asian Sage Became a Medieval Saint.* New York: W. W. Norton and Co., Inc., 2014.
Machiavelli, Niccolò. *The Prince.* Translated by W. K. Marriott. The Project Gutenberg EBook of The Prince, by Nicolo Machiavelli. www.gutenberg.org/files/1232/1232-h/1232-h.htm. Web. July 1, 2017.
MacQueen, Graeme. "Rejecting Enlightenment?: The Medieval Christian Transformation of the Buddha-legend in Jacobus de Voragine's *Barlaam and Josaphat*." *Studies in Religion/Sciences Religieuses* 30:2 (2001): 151–65.
Maravall, José Antonio. *Culture of the Baroque: Analysis of a Historical Structure.* Trans. Terry Cochran. Theory and History of Literature, Volume 25. Minneapolis: University of Minnesota Press, 1986.
Marcos Villanueva, Balbino. *La ascética de los jesuitas en los autos sacramentales de Calderón.* Bilbao: Universidad de Deusto, 1973.
Martin, Dennis D. *Fifteenth-Century Carthusian Reform: The World of Nicholas Kempf.* Leiden: E. J. Brill, 1992.
Meinecke, Friedrich. *Machiavellism: The Doctrine of Raison d'État and its Place in Modern History.* Trans. Douglas Scott. New Haven: Yale University Press, 1957.
Molina, Luis de. *Concordia del libre arbitrio con los dones de la gracia y con la presciencia, providencia, predestinación y reprobación divina.* Translated from Latin into Spanish, with introduction and notes, by Juan Antonio Hevia Echevarría. Oviedo: Biblioteca Filosofía en español, 2007.

Mondzain, Marie-José. *Image, Icon, Economy: The Byzantine Origins of the Contemporary Imaginary*. Series: Cultural Memory in the Present. Stanford: Stanford University Press, 2004.

Nozari, Jalil. "The Role of the Shi'a in Preserving and Disseminating the Story of Barlaam and Ioasaph." *Journal of Shi'a Islamic Studies* III:3 (Summer 2010): 313–30.

Oddo, Nancy. "Hagiographie et Politique." *Discours politique et genres littéraires: XVIe-XVIIe siècles*. Eds. Sabine Gruffat and Oliver LePlate. Geneva: Librarie Droz, SA, 2008. 191–210.

"On the No-Self Characteristic: The Anatta-lakkhana Sutta." Translated, with an introduction by N. K. G. Mendis. *Access to Insight (Legacy Edition)*, 24 November 2013. www.accesstoinsight.org/lib/authors/mendis/wheel268.html. Web. June 21, 2017.

Pelikan, Jaroslav. *The Christian Tradition: A History of the Development of Doctrine*. Volume 3: The Growth of Medieval Theology (600–1300). Chicago: University of Chicago Press, 1978.

———. *The Christian Tradition: A History of the Development of Doctrine*. Volume 4: Reformation of Church and Dogma (1300–1700). Chicago: University of Chicago Press, 1984.

———. *Mary Through the Centuries: Her Place in the History of Culture*. New Haven: Yale University Press, 1998.

The Play in Full [Lalitavistara]. Trans. Dharmachakra Translation Committee. Version 2.22. 84000, 2013. read.84000.co/browser/released/UT22084/046/UT22084-046-001.pdf. Web. September 18, 2014.

San Agustín, Gaspar de. *Conquistas de las Islas Filipinas (1565–1615)*. Madrid: Consejo Superior de Investigaciones Científicas, Instituto Enrique Florez, 1975. Biblioteca Missionalis Hispánica, v. 18. Originally published in 1698.

St. Ignatius Loyola. *Ejercicios espirituales. Texto autógrafo de San Ignacio de Loyola*. www.jesuitas.org.co/documentos/3.pdf. Web. July 1, 2017.

St. John of Damascene. *Barlaam and Ioasaph*. Trans. Rev. G. R. Woodward and H. Mattingly. Introduction by D. M. Lang. Cambridge, Mass: Harvard University Press, 1983.

———. *Histoire de Barlaam et de Iosaphat, roy des Indes*. Trans. F. Jean de Billy, 1600. archive.org/details/histoiredebarlaoounkngoog. Web. June 21, 2017.

———. *Historia de vitis et rebus gestis B. Barlaam et Josaphat, Indiae regis, Jacobo Billio Prunaeo interprete*. Coloniae Agrippinae: Kalcoven, 1643. digital.onb.ac.at/OnbViewer/viewer.faces?doc=ABO_%2BZ179096009. Web. June 21, 2017.

Santa Cruz, Fr. Balthasar. *Verdad nada amarga hermosa bondad: Honestta, vtil, y deleitable, grata, y moral historia de la rara vida de los famosos y singvlares Sanctos Barlaan y Iosaphat, segvn la escrivió en sv idioma griego el gloriosso doctor, y Padre de la Iglefia S. Iuan Damafceno: y la paſſo al Latino del Docttiſſimo Iacobo Biblio: de donde la expones en lengua Caſtellana a ſus Regnicolas el minimo de los Predicadores de la Prouincia del Sancto Roſario de las Iſlas Philippinas . . . Manila en el Colegio de*

Sancto Thomas de Aquino Por el Capitan D. Gafpar de los Reyes Impreffor de la Vniuerfidad Año de MDCXCII (1692).

Schumacher, John, S.J. *Readings in Philippine Church History*. Quezon City: Loyola School of Theology, Ateneo de Manila University, 1987.

◆ AFTERWORD

Reimagining Colonial Latin America from a Global Perspective

*Raúl Marrero-Fente and
Nicholas Spadaccini*

The present volume of Hispanic Issues proposes a new paradigm in the study of colonialism and globalization that takes into account economic, cultural, moral, religious, and legal questions, among others, keeping in mind both local and global factors. Such an approach is especially fruitful given the far reaches of the Iberian empires across the Atlantic, Pacific, and Indian Oceans; the interrelatedness of some of their colonizing practices; and the impact of global exchanges in the economic and cultural spheres.

Thus, for example, Spain's opening of a trade post in Manila (1571) and the galleons' regular voyages between Manila and Acapulco were to have profound implications for the extensive silver trade with China, in which the metal served as a means of tax payment and exchange following the Ming dynasty's (1368–1644) abandonment of paper currency and the reform of their tax code (1580), which replaced rice with silver as a method of payment. That decision also seems to have had implications on a global scale, as Spain came to rely on silver exports to help finance its European wars (at least until demand from China subsided as a result of an overabundance of supply coming from the Spanish colonies and Japan), while native peoples who supplied labor for the extraction of the metal were subject to harsh working conditions in the silver mines of Potosí (first discovered in 1545) in present-day Bolivia and later in those of Zacatecas in present-day Mexico. In Potosí's case, there was a significant displacement of communities to an area (at over 15,000 feet above sea level) that had been sparsely habited until then, and which in a relatively short period of time became of key importance to the local, trans-local, and global economies.

The complex webs of trade also involved Brazil, which "was oriented toward the export of bulk commodities" (Lockhart and Schwartz 249), Portugal, and other European powers, among them the Dutch, who ultimately contested Portuguese regal supremacy over territory, people, and trade in Northeastern Brazil (especially in the period 1620–1654) by capturing the sugar captaincy of Pernambuco and eventually seizing "African slave ports, recognizing that a constant supply of slaves was essential to success" (Lockhart and Schwartz 251). Thus, a case can be made that an understanding of the impact of globalization on the Iberian empires offers broader and more nuanced insights into economic, geopolitical, cultural, religious, and social exchanges as they are contextualized through global and trans-local perspectives.

In a recent essay, the historian J. H. Elliott reminds us of the long-term resilience and survival of the *monarquía hispánica* as "a pluralist, composite state" that included "all, or part of, the Netherlands, Spain's Italian possessions, and, for sixty years, Portugal," with various kingdoms and territories connected to the royal government in Madrid "by numerous official and unofficial ties," with "events in one part of this extended *monarquía* [that] could all too easily have repercussions in others" (370–71). Moreover, its reach extended well beyond the Atlantic "to embrace the world" (371; see also Fernández-Armesto), with Spanish and Portuguese navigators being prominent in the expansion of global commerce, as seen in the movement of commodities and the slave trade (as indicated above). Elliott further reminds us that those transfers went beyond the economic realm to include "culture and beliefs," with a centerpiece being the spread of the Gospel (371).

As we know, such a global undertaking was carried out through various disciplinary means and intentions by a number of different religious orders, among them the Jesuits, who boasted a global reach and a direct line to Rome and took a pragmatic approach to adjusting to both local exigencies and geopolitical realities. The far-reaching impact of this order in the colonizing process figures prominently in some of the contributions to this volume (see especially More, Corsi, Villaseñor Black, Wilde, and Blanco).

The volume is organized according to geographical areas, with a focus on both the structures of globalization and its various agents, while the issues analyzed are approached for the most part through cultural analysis, which with some exceptions is inspired largely by postcolonial theory. The "Introduction" makes it clear that an understanding of the structures of early modern Iberian globalization hinges on "interdisciplinary interpretations of local details" (5) that can provide valuable insights into the process's hidden "mechanics" (30), and argues that Iberian colonialism can be assessed more accurately if Iberian empires are viewed as being multi-centered, with shifting political, economic, cultural, and social circumstances and realities.

The essays draw on both well-known materials and more recent work in support of their scholarly aims. Thus, engaging the work of Dennis O. Flynn and Arturo Giraldes on the importance of Latin American silver in the early globalization of world trade, which they view as being "centered on China and its tributary system" (144), Bernd Hausberger (in this volume) argues for a new global-trans-local analysis that challenges the world systems model, which is said to have marginalized Latin America from these discussions.

Hausberger's point is an important one that nevertheless complements the following notion expressed by Flynn and Giraldes: "[T]he fact that Spain's empire owed its financial foundation to distant Ming China is a forceful reminder that much of what passes for local history in the early modern period can only be understood in terms of world history" (156). On his part, Hausberger contends that "it was the Spanish-American demand for European and Asian products that unleashed and, above all, maintained these flows, and not necessarily the monarchs nor Chinese demand" (17), pointing to an emerging American elite and its impact on the transformation of the Americas through the amassing of "wealth" and the preservation of their interests in "consumption, status, and power" (12). He further highlights the importance of different types of networks of relations—namely, those that connected "Asian manufacturing systems, miners in the Americas, and European merchants... just as different Spanish American agricultural and manufacturing production zones were connected with mining centers and urban centers" (24).

It is becoming increasingly clear that a more holistic approach to colonial Latin American cultural production offers a broader and more nuanced perspective on a range of relevant questions, including the changing face of colonialism over time as it adjusted to local beliefs and practices. We also notice the difficulty of drawing sweeping conclusions when multiple points of view are expressed on given issues from various loci of enunciation. Let us now examine these and other issues discussed in the present volume and briefly engage some of the key arguments.

Relying on cultural analysis, Ivonne del Valle (in this volume) examines Vasco de Quiroga's "Información en derecho" (1535; Report of law), a theological, legal, and political project that exposes the tensions between the religious idea of a globalized humanity under natural law and a secular tendency to enslave indigenous populations in New Spain. Del Valle's analysis points to the complexity of a Spanish empire that subjected indigenous peoples to brutality and violence while proclaiming a civilizing project through a "hospital-republic," thus espousing "a civilizing order that was at the same time a form of exploitation, though one preferable to the model of slavery" (17).

Interestingly, this report by Vasco de Quiroga, bishop of Michoacán, is also cited by Mendieta, another famous Franciscan, in a letter to the King of Spain that identifies Quiroga as a partisan of legal formalism as opposed to Mendieta's own espousal of a "derecho libre" (natural right) ("Informe al Rey [1586]," in *Cartas de religiosos* 148, qtd. in Maravall 94–95). Moreover, Mendieta goes even further by aligning his own views with those of Motolinía, an earlier missionary to New Spain, and argues for the restoration of a primitive Church and a pristine Christianity that provided both religious as well as sociopolitical guidance to indigenous peoples while keeping them protected from the greed of the powerful, which also included the so-called "obispos de renta" (Maravall 93). Mendieta also "likens his image of terrestrial paradise to the seven cities of Antillia of the Ancients... [making] the New World the geographical location of the millennial kingdom of the Apocalypse" (Jara and Spadaccini 14).

The respective readings of Del Valle and Mendieta regarding Quiroga's "Información" offer a cautionary tale about the complexities of those discussions: after all, colonial laws are both a set of rules put forward by the institutions and the people who represent them and discursive practices that are vital to imperial domination based on a genealogy of ideas. In other words, "if laws are not reducible to a set of abstract principles in their application, it is because legal discourse is itself a social construction founded in the hierarchical nature of empire" (Marrero-Fente 248–49), which, in any case, is also subject to interpretation.

In a different context, María Elena Martínez (in this volume) compares the policies of accommodation among cosmopolitan Iberian empires in India, the Americas, and Africa with actual practice, thus highlighting the fact that while the political and religious fictions of empire favored inclusion, colonial policies and practices tended to promote hierarchies and exclusion. Through an examination of the discourse of *limpieza de sangre* (blood purity), Martínez argues that both in Asia and in the Atlantic world, the European infantilization of colonial populations was normally rooted in claims about inadequate rational capacities. Moreover, her analysis of the languages of religion and race allows her to demonstrate a shared orientalizing discourse. Similarly, Bruno Feitler (in this volume) examines practices of discrimination, particularly as they extended to the Inquisition in the various centers of empire. Feitler finds that it differentiated among local peoples of the Americas, Atlantic Africa, and South Asia based not only on their adherence to Christianity but also on their perceived racial locations.

Among institutions with a global reach, one must also include the Society of Jesus, founded by Ignatius of Loyola to reinvigorate the Catholic Church within the framework of the Counterreformation. Anna More (in this volume) investigates the development of a global consciousness within Jesuit networks and finds that while the Society of Jesus was involved in the slave trade, it remained silent on the ethics of enslavement, thus making Sandoval's treatise regarding African histories and testimonies from the slave trade into Cartagena all the more remarkable. She also shows how the Jesuits' established policies were subject to autonomous interpretations, as they were often applied on a case-by-case basis, a practice that was common in other sectors of colonial society, as seen in a wide range of colonial discourses that were legitimated by Spanish laws as well as the Church's doctrine of salvation. Interestingly, "the discourse produced by this intra-imperial dialogue significantly altered the influence of the evangelization project and divine right embedded in the texts that legalized the Spanish conquest" (Arias and Marrero-Fente ix).

One could argue that the complexities of many of the issues discussed in this volume can be seen especially in connection with the Jesuits, whose global reach exposed them to a variety of cultural and political realities that were not always propitious to Christian evangelization. Such seems to have been the case in China, where their policy of accommodation was not always successful, as seen in their neutering of the original content of Christian images and the reception of the same by the lettered Chinese, who saw them "as exotic and 'curious' vestiges, suitable for the enjoyment of the lettered and the collector" (Corsi 27). Corsi examines how the Jesuits were compelled to change their strategies and mind-sets to access seventeenth-century Chinese society and how they adapted images of Christianity to respond to Confucian understandings of the sacred. And while those adaptations suggested a strong desire on their part to communicate with Chinese intellectuals, apparently their altered images of Christian religious figures no longer performed the function of increasing what Gadamer calls "the picturability of being" and thus no longer possessed "an exemplary significance" (Gadamer 143, qtd. in Corsi 9).

The wide-ranging impact of the Jesuits along religious, political, and social lines is more readily seen in the founding of the thirty "reducciones" established with the *guaraníes,* where they turned the missions into profitable undertakings while being sensitive to the abuses committed against the native communities and even creating a native army to guard against their enemies, especially Portuguese slave traders, known as *bandeirantes.* In the end, there is also substantial evidence to show that they "were champions of assimilation; [that] with them sacrifice became sacrament, and fertility rites were changed into processions, masquerades, and religious plays" (Jara and Spadaccini 85). Those practices were adopted in other areas as well, as recorded by El Inca Garcilaso, who was to comment on the staging of religious plays in the cities of Cuzco and Potosí, with the participation of indigenous children (*Comentarios reales de los Incas* 95–97). In the specific case of the *guaraníes*, while it is indeed the case that the Jesuits proposed a disciplinary model that implied regulations, and sought to bring them into the Catholic fold, they also instituted a system of communal and individual rights and obligations that aspired to self-sufficiency (Ordóñez 207–10), a utopian project, which even in its failure was to have political ramifications far into the future in the Río de la Plata region and "its republican history" (209).

The complexities presented by colonial tests are also evident in the essays by Rachel Sarah O'Toole and María Eugenia Chaves (in this volume). O'Toole examines how enslaved people negotiated the purchase of their freedom and how both freed slaves and those who remained enslaved imagined it outside the context of legal precedents in reference to slavery and manumission. The essay also highlights their resistance through the creative uses of documentation, which helped shift the battle over freedom into public realms. Chaves, for her part, argues that in Spanish America the idea of natural freedom was conditioned by doubts regarding the legitimacy of enslavement, citing a 1681 text by Francisco José de Jaca, a Capuchin missionary who understood freedom both as a divine, natural right and as a secular one in reference to property, commerce, and territorial exploration. Moreover, Jaca's radical opposition to slavery is said to have extended to his "just war" ideas, thus offering a legal basis for Africans and their descendants to be integrated into the Christian Spanish empire.

We know that discussions regarding "freedom," "natural rights," and "just war" are part of the history of colonization, which also includes the production of dissenting texts, of which Jaca's is an important exponent for its position on slavery. Yet it can also be argued that those texts do not alter the weight of the "conjuncture between religion, the law, and coloniality . . . [which has] a long and tortuous history that begins with the Iberian *reconquista* and reaches back in space and time to the distant Philippines and Marianas and the anticolonial wars of the nineteenth century" (Arias and Marrero-Fente xiv).

The appropriation and repositioning of Jesuit doctrinal texts by the indigenous peoples of Paraguay is the subject of study by Guillermo Wilde (in this volume), who examines their local production and circulation in Paraguay and the Río de la Plata region from the beginning of the eighteenth century. Wilde finds that while those texts were altered to integrate local content into the global practices of conversion, the changes were nevertheless in line with Jesuit standards and even exhibited an early form of literate globalization.

It is fair to say that in the colonies, art often becomes "an instrument of transformation in that it converts history into myth and symbol" (Gisbert 668, qtd. in Jara and Spadaccini). This is seen in drama as a transmitter of ideology and in festivals, dances, processions, painting, and other arts, and it often goes to the issue of "resistance" as a way of preserving pre-Columbian cultures through syncretism (Gisbert 668). The extent of this phenomenon in artistic manifestations from other centers of empire is less clear and would benefit from additional scholarly work in this area.

Charlene Villaseñor-Black (in this volume) examines *enconchados* (a technique involving the inlaying of mother-of-pearl into an oil painting depicting a religious subject) and points to links between the materiality of these works and Catholic theology. Moreover, through an examination of trade routes, she establishes a relationship between *enconchados* and other artworks, explaining that artists employ iridescent nacre fragments and the strategic use of shimmering shell to invoke religious meaning. Her essay also deals with feather works and *tornasol* fabrics produced throughout the Americas and Europe.

Finally, John Blanco (in this volume) offers a close reading of the Barlaam and Josaphat exemplum through its simultaneous revivals in Spanish baroque theater and examines how translations of the exemplum were used for proselytizing purposes in areas of missionary activity such as the Philippines, thus revealing the theological and political stakes behind the imagining of Spain's world empire in the seventeenth century. Blanco demonstrates how the rhetoric of *desengaño* (disenchantment), so dominant in the Spanish baroque, serves as a technique for the constitution of a global society under the universal Spanish monarchy through re-enchantment via Christian revelation.

We have seen how the present volume explores multiple facets of early modern Iberian globalization and its impact on colonizing practices in the various centers of empire, among them those of the Pacific, which brought Iberian colonialism into conflict with societies more diverse and complex than the American ones (Camino). In this sense, it is hoped that future studies will continue to reassess the importance of the Philippines as a model of long-term colonialism from the sixteenth to the nineteenth century so as to complement what has already been done in the area of economic history, with a focus on commercial relations with Mexico and Spain (the Galleon of Manila) and the Philippines's membership in global commercial circuits.

It is also the case that while studies on the Portuguese empire in Asia have an extensive bibliography (Brockey), those focusing on the Spanish empire in Asia are concentrated largely on the Pacific, with a recent book that analyzes Spanish texts dealing with China, Cambodia, Thailand, and other countries in the region (Ellis). New studies dealing with the expansion of Christianity through the missionary presence in the Philippines, China, and Japan would expand the scope of the project undertaken in this volume and perhaps provide additional insights about the range of global exchanges implicating Iberian empires in the early modern period.

As previously argued, the essays in this volume fall largely within the area of interdisciplinary analysis of the theories and practices of globalization in Iberian empires while articulating a number of key points—among them, the importance of contributions from different cultural areas as well as perspectives that bring to bear scholarly disciplines such as economics, history, literature, law, religion, and politics, among others. Of equal note is the weight of postcolonial theory in both its conceptualization and its contributions, which emphasize cross-cultural relations, colonialism, subaltern agents, borderlands, otherness, and identity.

As suggested in the "Introduction," the connection between colonialism and imperialism and the structure of early modern globalization can be seen in the manner in which "economic forces and social hierarchies as well as . . . textual and visual discourses influenced political intentions and administrative policies" (5). Yet the "Introduction" also makes it clear that "even when globalization brought about radical transformations, it did not homogenize the world, but . . . created heterogeneity within a connected and complex system" (10). The latter is an important point, for such a system also brought about *mestizaje* as a new form of human and cultural creativity (Gruzinski, *Les quatre parties*) that was to change the social and political landscape in some of the centers of those empires, something that did not escape major writers of the period, among them El Inca Garcilaso and Miguel de Cervantes, whose literary representations were to deal with issues of hybridity and *mestizaje*, respectively, in *Comentarios reales de los Incas* and *Los trabajos de Persiles y Sigismunda* (Suárez). As Gruzinski explains, from a historical perspective, "right from the Renaissance, Western expansion has continuously spawned hybrids all over the globe, along with reactions of rejection (the most spectacular of which was the closing of Japan in the early seventeenth century). The planetwide mestizo phenomena thus seem closely linked to the harbingers of economic globalization that began in the second half of the sixteenth, a century which, whether viewed from Europe, America, or Asia, was the Iberian century *par excellence*, just as our own has become the American century" (*Mestizo Mind* 4).

One of the major points emerging from this volume is that, given the cultural and material production and practices of the Iberian empires on several continents, colonial Latin America cannot be fully understood in isolation from other geographical regions or from the trans-oceanic and global exchange from which it emerged. Similarly, one could argue that by focusing on the study of the reciprocal influences among Africa, the Americas, Asia, and Europe, scholars can move beyond the more limited confines of the Iberian empires.

Interestingly, the process of contemporary globalization has resulted in the emergence of a New Global history, which in turn is also changing the way we do "History" (Hopkins; Mazlish). Thus, it has also been argued that a new history of colonialism should be "decolonized" from the intellectual prejudices that privilege certain geo-cultural areas to the detriment of others (Mignolo), while granting that a broader understanding of European imperialism and colonialism could play a useful role in filling the prevailing historical vacuum and incomplete analysis of Iberian imperialism that has long prevailed in the field of colonial Latin American studies (see Blackmore; Hart; and Mignolo).

The present volume advances the critical scholarship at the nexus of colonialism, imperialism, and globalization, while its overarching contribution is manifested in several ways, including its acknowledgement of the need for an interdisciplinary and cross-cultural understanding of Iberian imperialisms and their global legacy; its exploration of the links between the experience of colonialism in Latin America and other histories and forms of domination in Africa and Asia; its examination of the salient aspects of colonialism and imperialism and their representations in Africa, the Americas, and Asia from a postcolonial perspective that takes into account the situated nature of these discourses; the manner in which it expands the cultural, legal, literary, and historical study of Iberian imperialism as a ruling discourse that also encompassed a plurality of nonofficial discourses that were often enunciated in opposition to hegemony; and, finally, its valuable contribution to the growing scholarship in global colonial studies with analyses of both canonical and less well-known individuals, institutions, and programs that played key roles in the conflictive history of the imperial project.

Iberian Empires and the Roots of Globalization fits within the scope of the Hispanic Issues series by taking a fresh look at a topic concerning the global history of colonialism and imperialism and the place of the Hispanic and Lusophone worlds within it. The volume's cross-cultural and interdisciplinary approach is evident both in the themes that it deals with and in the diversity of authors from several disciplines who consider issues and methods raised by scholars within and outside their fields.

It is hoped that future research in colonial Latin American studies will expand on the literature of African colonial studies as it intersects with anthropology, cultural studies, gender studies, history, political theory, and the history of science. Such an expansion could take into account geographies of knowledge production, utilizing a postcolonial theoretical inflection that allows for consideration of the spaces of knowledge production as well as the politics of representation and the practices that transformed the world in the early modern period.

WORKS CITED

Arias, Santa, and Raúl Marrero-Fente, eds. *Coloniality, Religion and the Law in the Early Iberian World*. Hispanic Issues, vol. 40. Nashville: Vanderbilt University Press, 2014.

Blackmore, Josiah. *Moorings: Portuguese Expansion and the Writing of Africa*. Minneapolis: University of Minnesota Press, 2009.

Brockey, Liam M. *Journey to the East: The Jesuit Mission to China, 1579–1724*. Cambridge, MA: Belknap Press of Harvard University Press, 2007.

Camino, Mercedes Maroto. *Exploring the Explorers: Spaniards in Oceania, 1519–1794*. Manchester, UK: Manchester University Press, 2008.

Elliott, J. H. "The History of Early Modern Spain in Retrospect." *The Early Modern Hispanic World*. Ed. Kimberly Lynn and Erin Kathleen Rowe. New York: Cambridge University Press, 2017.

Ellis, Robert Richmond. *They Need Nothing: Hispanic-Asian Encounters of the Colonial Period*. Toronto: University of Toronto Press, 2012.

Fernández-Armesto, Felipe. *Pathfinders: A Global History of Exploration*. New York: W. W. Norton, 2007.

Flynn, Dennis O., and Arturo Giraldes. "Latin American Silver and the Early Globalization of World Trade." *National Identities and Sociopolitical Changes in Latin America*. Hispanic Issues, vol. 23. New York: Routledge, 2001. 140–159.

Garcilaso de la Vega, El Inca. *Comentarios reales de los Incas*. Ed. José de la Riva Agüero. Mexico City: Editorial Porrúa, 1984.

Gisbert, Teresa. "Art and Resistance in the Andean World." *Amerindian Images and the Legacy of Columbus*. Ed. René Jara and Nicholas Spadaccini. Hispanic Issues, vol. 9. Minneapolis: University of Minnesota Press, 1992. 629–77.

Gruzinski, Serge. *The Mestizo Mind: The Intellectual Dynamics of Colonization and Globalization*. Trans. Deke Dusinberre. New York: Routledge: 2002.

———. *Les quatre parties du monde. Histoire d'une mondialisation*. Paris: La Martinière, 2004.

Hart, Jonathan L. *Comparing Empires: European Colonialism from Portuguese Expansion to the Spanish-American War*. Houndmills, Basingstoke, Hampshire, England: Palgrave Macmillan, 2003.

Hopkins, A. G., ed. *Globalization in World History*. New York: Norton, 2002.

Jara, René, and Nicholas Spadaccini. "Introduction." *Amerindian Images and the Legacy of Columbus.* Ed. René Jara and Nicholas Spadaccini. Hispanic Issues, vol. 9. Minneapolis: University of Minnesota Press, 1992. 1–95.

Lockhart, James, and Stuart B. Schwartz. *Early Latin America: A History of Colonial Spanish America and Brazil.* Cambridge: Cambridge University Press, 1983.

Maravall, José Antonio. *Utopía y reformismo en la España de los Austrias.* Madrid: Siglo XX, 1982.

Marrero-Fente, Raúl. "Human Rights and Academic Discourse: Teaching the Las Casas–Sepúlveda Debate at the Time of the Iraq War." *Human Rights and Latin American Cultural Studies.* Ed. Ana Forcinito and Fernando Ordóñez. Hispanic Issues Online, 2009. 247–57. Web.

Mazlish, Bruce. *The New Global History.* New York: Routledge, 2006.

Mignolo, Walter. *Local Histories/Global Designs: Coloniality, Subaltern Knowledges, and Border Thinking.* Princeton: Princeton University Press, 2012.

Ordóñez, Fernando. *Las reducciones jesuitas del Paraguay y la cuestión de los derechos fundamentales.* Diss. University of Minnesota, 2007.

Suárez, Silvia. "Perspectives on *Mestizaje* in the Early Baroque." *Hispanic Baroques: Reading Cultures in Context.* Ed. Nicholas Spadaccini and Luis Martín-Estudillo. Hispanic Issues, vol. 31. Nashville: Vanderbilt University Press, 2005. 184–204.

◆ CONTRIBUTORS

JODY BLANCO is associate professor at the University of California, San Diego, specializing in colonial and postcolonial literature and culture (Philippines, Latin America, and the US). He is the author of *Frontier Constitutions: Christianity and Colonial Empire in the Philippines During the Nineteenth Century*, as well as numerous articles on Spanish colonialism in a trans-Pacific context. His current project focuses on the pastoral care of anarchy in the Philippines during the seventeenth century.

MARÍA EUGENIA CHAVES is professor of history at the Universidad Nacional de Colombia, Sede Medellín, specializing in subaltern history. Her work has focused particularly on the history of Africans and their descendants in the colonial and republican periods, especially on women slaves in the late colonial period, and the concepts of race and freedom from the sixteenth to nineteenth centuries in Spanish America. She is the author of numerous articles on these subjects as well as the editor of *Genealogías de la diferencia: Tecnologías de la salvación y representación de los africanos esclavizados en Iberoamérica colonial* (2009). She is also the author of *Honor y libertad: Discursos y recursos en la estrategia de libertad de una mujer esclava* (2001). Her current project focuses on the concept of freedom from the Spanish Renaissance to the Creole Republic.

ELISABETTA CORSI is professor and chair of sinology at Sapienza, State University of Rome, specializing in the study of the intellectual encounters between China and Europe during the early modern period, mainly in the field of "mixed mathematics," optics, and linear perspective. She is author of *La fábrica de las ilusiones: Los jesuitas y la difusión de la perspectiva lineal en China* (2004). An expanded edition in English is in preparation under the title of *Fabricating Illusions: The Jesuits and the Dissemination of Linear Perspective in China (1698–1766)*. She is editor of *Órdenes religiosas entre América y Asia: Ideas para una historia misionera de los espacios coloniales* (2008). Her current project focuses on the dissemination of Galileo Galilei's *Le operazioni del compasso geometrico e militare* (The operations of the geometric and military compass) in early modern China.

IVONNE DEL VALLE is associate professor at the University of California, Berkeley, where she specializes in Mexico, colonial Latin America, and the connections between the colonial period and the present. She is the author of *Escribiendo desde los márgenes: Colonialismo y jesuitas en el siglo XVIII* (2009) and co-editor of *Cardenismo: Auge y caída de un legado político y social* (2017) and the special journal issues: *Radical Politics and/or the Rule of Law in Mexico* (2015) and *Carl Schmitt and the Early Modern World* (2014). Her current project focuses on how indigenous peoples, the Spanish colonial state, and the Mexican government established contrasting social pacts through their differing understandings of land and water.

BRUNO FEITLER is professor of early modern history at the Universidade Federal de São Paulo (Brazil) and researcher at the Conselho Nacional de Desenvolvimento Científico e Tecnológico (CNPq—Brazil), specializing in the history of the Portuguese Inquisition, the secular church in colonial Brazil, and Portuguese Jews. He is the author of numerous texts related to those subjects, especially two books *Nas Malhas da Consciência: Igreja e Inquisição no Brasil* (2008) and *The Imaginary Synagogue: Anti-Jewish Literature in the Portuguese Early Modern World (16th–18th Centuries)* (2015). Currently, he is completing a book on the legal history of the Portuguese Inquisition.

BERND HAUSBERGER is professor of history at El Colegio de México in Mexico City. He holds a doctorate from the University of Vienna. His research interests include colonial history of Latin America, Jesuit missions, silver mining, ethnic networks of Basque migrants, global history, and film history. He has published numerous articles and chapters in each of these fields, and he is the author or editor of several books, including *La Nueva España y sus metales preciosos* (1997),

La industria minera colonial a través de los "libros de cargo y data" de la Real Hacienda, 1761–1767 (1997), *El peso de la sangre: Limpios, mestizos y nobles en el mundo hispánico* (2011), with Nikolaus Böttcher and Max Hering Torres, and *Miradas a la misión jesuita en la Nueva España: Antología* (2015). His current project focuses on the representation of the Mexican Revolution in movies and their global reception (1930–1975).

RAÚL MARRERO-FENTE is professor of Spanish and law at the University of Minnesota. Among his most recent books are *Poesía épica colonial del siglo XVI: Historia, teoría y práctica* (2017) and the co-edited volumes *Gender and the Politics of Literature: Gertrudis Gómez de Avellaneda* (2017) and *Coloniality, Religion and the Law in the Early Iberian World* (2014). He is also the author of *Trayectorias globales: Estudios coloniales en el mundo hispánico* (2013), *Bodies, Texts, and Ghosts: Writing on Literature and Law in Colonial Latin America* (2010), *Epic, Empire and Community in the Atlantic World: Silvestre de Balboa's Espejo de Paciencia* (2008), *Playas del árbol: Una visión trasatlántica de las literaturas hispánicas* (2002), *La poética de la ley en las Capitulaciones de Santa Fe* (2000), and *Al margen de la tradición: Relaciones entre la literatura colonial y peninsular de los siglos XV, XVI, y XVII* (1999).

MARÍA ELENA MARTÍNEZ was associate professor of colonial Latin American history at the University of Southern California, where she specialized in the history of race in colonial Mexico, early modern Iberian legal theory, and queer history. She authored *Genealogical Fictions: Limpieza de Sangre, Religion, and Gender in Colonial Mexico* (2008), which received the American Historical Association's 2009 James A. Rawley Prize in Atlantic History and the American Historical Association's Conference on Latin American History's prize for the best book on Mexican history. At the time of her passing in 2014, she was working on her new book, *The Enlightened Creole Science of Race and Sex: Naturalizing the Body in the Eighteenth-Century Spanish Atlantic World*.

ANNA MORE is professor of Hispanic literatures at the Universidade de Brasília. She is the author of *Baroque Sovereignty: Carlos de Sigüenza y Góngora and the Creole Archive of Colonial Mexico* (2013), which was awarded honorable mention for the best humanities book by the Mexico Section of the Latin American Studies Association (LASA). She is the editor of *Sor Juana Inés de la Cruz: Selected Works*, a Norton Critical Edition (2016), as well as articles on baroque literature and Iberian colonization in the Americas and Africa. She is currently working on two projects. The first is a study of the writing of the Iberian slave trade in

Africa and the Americas, and the second explores the concept of freedom in the late Iberian Baroque.

RACHEL SARAH O'TOOLE is associate professor of colonial Latin American history at the University of California, Irvine, specializing in the Andes and the African Diaspora. She is the author of *Bound Lives: Africans, Indians, and the Making of Race in Colonial Peru*, the co-editor with Sherwin Bryant and Ben Vinson III of *Africans to Spanish America: Expanding the Diaspora*, and articles on gender and race construction in colonial Latin America. Her current project focuses on how Peru's African Diaspora defined freedom as kinship claims in the colonial era.

NICHOLAS SPADACCINI is professor of Hispanic studies and comparative literature at the University of Minnesota. He has published books, critical editions, articles and collective volumes on the literature and cultures of Spain's early modern period and has co-edited two volumes of literary/cultural criticism on Colonial Latin America. His most recent published volumes (co-edited) are *New Spain, New Literatures* (2010), *Hispanic Literatures and the Question of a Liberal Education* (2011), *(Re)reading Gracián in a Self-Made World* (2012), *Memory and Its Discontents* (2012), and *Writing Monsters: Essays on Latin American and Iberian Cultures* (2014). He is editor-in-chief of Hispanic Issues and Hispanic Issues On Line (HIOL).

CHARLENE VILLASEÑOR BLACK is professor of art history and Chicana/o studies at the University of California, Los Angeles, specializing in art of the early modern Iberian world and contemporary Chicana/o art. She is author of *Creating the Cult of St. Joseph* (2006) and numerous articles on gender and representation, art and materiality, and Chicana/o art. Her current project focuses on early modern art, global trade, and materiality.

GUILLERMO WILDE is a researcher at the Argentinian National Scientific Council and professor at Universidad Nacional de San Martín, specializing in indigenous history of the Americas, colonial art and music, and Jesuit mission history from a comparative perspective. He is the author of *Religión y poder en las misiones guaraníes* (2009), awarded the Latin American Studies Iberoamerican Award (2010), and numerous articles related to religious conversion in colonial times. He edited the collection *Saberes de la Conversión: Jesuitas, indígenas e imperios coloniales en las fronteras de la cristiandad* (2012). His current project focuses on early modern Catholic global missions and cultural accommodation in Latin America and Asia.

INDEX

Page numbers in **bold** indicate a figure.

abolitionism, 185–86, 191, 193, 195, 197.
  See also Africans: enslavement of;
  Jaca, Francisco José de; Las Casas,
  Bartolomé de; slavery
Abu-Lughod, Janet, 26, 40n19
acheiropoietai/acheiropoietic images, 278,
  280, 285–86, 296n12, 296n18
Acosta, José de, 1, **2**, 68n3, 109, 118, 133–34,
  137, 144–45, 147, 225n16; *De procuranda
  indorum salute*, 133, 137, 144–45; *Historia
  natural y moral de las Indias* (*Natural
  and Moral History of the Indies*), 1, 17n1,
  134, 137, 225n16, 273; on idolatry, 273–74,
  278; influence on Sandoval, 154n8;
  racial classification of, 211–12, 225n13
Africa, 10, 26, 134; Atlantic, 8, 335;
  Christianization in, 91–92, 137;
  commerce and, 32; correspondence
  from Jesuits in, 140, 147–49, 154n11
  (*see also* Brandão, Luis de; Sandoval,
  Alonso de); Iberian empires and, 90–91,
  93; 94n3, 334, 339; Latin America and,
  91; legend of *Barlaam and Josaphat*
  and, 304; native clergy in, 85, 113 (*see
  also* Africans: ordination of); North,
  25, 32, 67–68n2, 107, 115; Portuguese
  colonialism and, 76–77, 79–8, 94n11,
  97n32, 107, 111–12, 115, 124n10, 190
  (*see also* Brandão, Luis de; Jesuit
  missionaries; Las Casas, Bartolomé
  de; Portuguese Inquisition; Sandoval,
  Alonso de); slavery and, 14, 133, 135, 138,
  151; southwest, 54; Spanish empire and,
  81, 88, 90; third-gender categories in
  Central, 95n13; West Central, 153
African diaspora, 7, 176–77
Africans, 7, 111, 148–50, 162–63; baptism of,
  112, 133, 137, 146, 174–75, 192, 194, 196; as
  clergy, 114, 118; enslavement of, 111, 132–
  37, 141–42, 145–47, 150–52, 153n5, 159–60,
  162, 170, 176, 185–92, 194, 198n9 (*see
  also* abolitionism; Jaca, Francisco José

347

de; Las Casas, Bartolomé de; slavery); evangelization of, 133, 163, 199n25; forced migration of, 37, 132; Iberian conceptions of, 111; inquisitorial jurisdiction over, 106, 108, 110, 112; North, 107; ordination of, 86; political reparations for, 193; Portuguese wars against, 199n21; West, 154n17
agency, 309, 314, 318, 320; of enslaved humans, 159, 168; indigenous, 208, 222, 261; of Latin America, 24; pastoral, 310
Alencastro, Luiz Felipe de, 131, 142–43
Amati, Scipione, 273–74, 295n6
Angola, 12; black clergy in, 118–19; inquisitorial activity in, 112; Jesuits in, 143, 154n12; slavery and, 136–37, 140–41, 153n5, 199n21
animism, 4, 112
Annual Letters (published Jesuit correspondence), 143, 224n10, 274
archive, 6, 13, 16–17, 19n13; of early globalization, 15; Jesuit, 224n8
Arendt, Hannah, 16, 65–67, 71n23. *See also* human rights
Aristotle, 188–89, 198–99n20, 199n28
Assadourian, Carlos Sempat, 36–37
Augustine, 63, 259
autonomy, 224n8, 317; Habsburg, 177; of hospital republics (Quiroga), 64–65; indigenous, 210, 215–16, 220, 222; manumission and, 172; of the Spanish Crown, 31
Aztecs, 33, 212; shellwork and, 245, 247
Balbuena, Bernardo de, 247–48, 253, 259, 264n23. *See also* enconchados/ enconchado art; mother-of-pearl
barbarism, 47, 54–56, 58–59, 65–67, 151, 199n20
Barlaam and Josaphat (romance/legend of), 303–7, 310–18, 320–22, 323n2, 324n14, 337. *See also* Billy, Jean de; Buddha; Calderón de la Barca, Pedro; *Comedia Tansidorus*; Saint John Damascene

(Saint John of Damascus); Vega, Lope de
baroque, the, 247, 249, 253, 261–62, 265n33, 306, 311; Spanish, 337
Barreto Xavier, Ángela, 89, 95–96nn22–23
Bartoli, Daniello, 274–76, 280–81, 292–93, 295n9
Bayly, Christopher A., 24–25, 39n4, 40n12
Benveniste, Émile, 61–62
bigamy, 79, 120, 122
Billy, Jean de, 310, 313–14, 323n3, 324n15. *See also Barlaam and Josaphat* (romance/ legend of)
Blanco, Jody, 14, 332, 337
blood purity. *See limpieza de sangre*
Borja, Antonio de, 305, 317–22, 323n3, 325n22
Borja González, Galaxis, 224nn9–10, 226n22
Boxer, Charles R., 96n28, 109, 111, 113
Brahmans, 113–14, 116, 118
Brandão, Luis de, 140–43, 145, 147, 152. *See also* Jesuits: correspondence of; Molina, Luis de; *Naturaleza, policia sagrada y profana, costumbres, ritos, disciplina y catecismo, de todos etiopes* (Sandoval); Sandoval, Alonso de
Brazil, 5, 332; black priests in, 111, 118–19; blood purity in, 97n31; *casta* in, 82, 85; indigenous peoples in, 118–20, 123; the Inquisition in, 79, 94–95n11, 105–6, 112, 117, 119; *mestizos/mestiços* in, 110; Portuguese colonization of, 32, 76, 105; slavery in, 95n13, 136
Buddha, 14, 304–8, 310, 312, 314, 324n9; history of, 12; images of, 9; statues of, 298n29
Buddhism, 272, 275, 284, 288, 293, 296n20, 298n29, 306–11, 324nn8–9, 335
Burton, Jonathan, 80, 98n45
Butler, Judith, 131–32, 146, 152–53n2, 153n6
caciques, 36, 212, 220
Calderón de la Barca, Pedro, 14, 304–5, 317; *La vida es sueño*, 14, 303, 305, 311, 320
Camaño, Joaquín, 214, 225n19

Cañizares-Esguerra, Jorge, 18n6, 19n12, 98n43
Cape Verde (Cabo Verde), 85, 112, 114, 139, 141
capitalism, 28, 37–38, 131–32, 153n4, 310; imperial, 152; proto-, 57, 70n14. *See also* finance capital; labor
Cardinal Henrique. *See* Henrique I of Portugal
Cartagena de Indias, 9, 197n6; Holy Office tribunals in, 77, 105, 173; as slave-trading port, 133–39, 142–43, 145–46, 148–51, 186, 199n25, 335
Cascardi, Anthony J., 249, 261–62, 264n18, 265n33
casta/caste, 75, 82–84, 87–89, 92–93, 95n19, 96n24, 165
castiços, 83, 87, 96n28. *See also criollos*/creoles
Catholic Church, 162, 176, 312, 322. *See also* ecclesiastical authorities; evangelization; Holy Office; Holy Office inquisitional tribunals; Inquisition; Jesuit missionaries; Portuguese Inquisition; Spanish Inquisition
Catholicism, 109–10, 115–17, 121, 123, 297n29
Cerro Rico, 3, 34. *See also* Potosí; precious metals; silver mining
China, 8, 26–32, 291–93, 297n29, 298n34, 338; Jesuit missionaries in, 15, 86, 90, 96n10, 271–72, 274–75, 286, 288, 290–91, 294n2, 297n26, 317, 335; Latin American silver trade and, 331, 333; mother-of-pearl inlay and, 235, 263n8; Qing, 9. *See also* Guan Yin; Ming Dynasty
Christianity, 11, 92, 114, 211, 294n5, 295n8, 334–35; Africa and, 147; asceticism of medieval, 306; in Asia, 288; *Barlaam and Josaphat* (romance/legend of) and, 304–5, 308–9, 315, 317, 320, 323n5; in China, 271, 275, 293; early, 192; Eastern Orthodox, 324n13; Ethiopian, 124n7; expansion of, 48, 338; as global institution, 4–5; Hindu converts to, 80, 82, 84; hospitals (Quiroga) and, 63; idolatry and, 307; indigenous leaders' loyalty to, 86–87; Jesuit political thought and, 311; labor and, 5; *limpieza de sangre* (blood purity) and, 85; mysteries of, 119, 123, 287–89, 307–8, 315; native clergy, 85, 87, 111, 113; native forms of, 224n11; in the Philippines, 322; religious images and, 278; as revealed truth, 310; Rome as the center of, 291, 298n34; slavery and, 151–52, 188; Tagalog converts to, 318; West African, 18n11. *See also* indigenous peoples: Christian conversion of; *moriscos*; New Christians/*conversos*
cimarrones (runaway slaves), 186, 197n6
civilization, 23, 47–49, 55, 118; Chinese, 291, 295n8; Christian-Western, 48, 54–55, 63; discourse on, 109; European ideals of, 121; hospitals (Quiroga) and, 57, 61–62; Iberian empires and mandate to spread, 76; indigenous, 54, 56, 58, 69–70n11; labor and, 59; police and, 68n6; rights and, 66. *See also* barbarism
Cobo, Bernabé, 225n16, 264n12
colonial economy, 36–37, 39, 172
colonialism, 49, 91, 95n12, 96n24, 338–39; early modern, 75; European, 305; Iberian, 3–4, 333, 337; inquisitorial, 107, 124n3; Spanish, 144; study of, 331
colonial studies, 13, 339
colonial subjects, 86–87, 320
colonization, 9, 77, 144, 212, 336; conquest and, 4, 7, 56, 183, 197n4; European, 96n23; hospitality and, 67; Iberian, 3, 90, 92; opposition to, 261; Portuguese, 124; Spanish, 27, 47–49, 69n6
Columbus, Christopher, 26, 32–34, 40n18
Comedia Tansidorus, 311, 315–16. *See also Barlaam and Josaphat* (romance/legend of)
Confucianism, 7, 9, 271–72, 275, 292–93, 294n4, 295n8
Confucius, 272, 292, 295n8
conquistadors, 31–33, 51, 95n16, 274, 310

conversos. See New Christians/*conversos*
Corsi, Elisabetta, 14–15, 335
Council of Trent, 273, 280, 295n7. See also Counter-Reformation; Tridentine reforms
Counter-Reformation, 296n12, 305, 307, 310, 312, 316, 320–21. See also Council of Trent; Tridentine reforms
criollos/creoles, 83–84, 96n24, 160, 263n3; elite, 68n4, 184, 193, 197, 233, 257
Crown, the. See Spanish Crown
debt, 3, 318; slavery and, 161–66, 171
Deleuze, Gilles, 262–62
del Valle, Ivonne, 5, 16, 144–45, 223n5, 224n10, 264n18, 333–34
desengaño (disenchantment), 312, 337
Dom Henrique. See Henrique I of Portugal
Dominican order, 77, 81, 169, 189
Dutch colonialism, 25, 120, 136, 332
early modern studies, 13, 18n10
ecclesiastical authorities, 78, 80, 86–88, 97n4, 159, 173–74, 208
economic determinism, 58, 62, 70n14
economic history, 15, 23, 337
El Greco, 249, **251**
Elliot, J. H., 6, 18n4, 332
empire, 6–7, 93, 108, 177, 191, 223n5; administration of, 10; centers of, 337; colonial, 197; European model of, 18n5; fictions of, 92, 334; law and, 12. See also Ming dynasty; Portuguese empire; Spanish empire
enconchados/*enconchado* art, 12–13, 233–49, 253, 257–59, 261–62, 263n3, 265n28, 337. See also feather artwork/featherwork; iridescence; mother-of-pearl; Nanban art; textiles; Virgin of Guadalupe
enslavement of Africans, 134, 184–85, 191, 194–96
Estado da Índia (Portuguese territories in Asia), 77, 81, 83, 86, 89, 105, 115–16. See also Goa; Portuguese empire
evangelization, 12, 86, 92, 145, 183, 191, 317, 335; in China, 274; of enslaved Africans, 133–34, 137, 147, 150, 162, 163, 191n25; images and, 280, 287; of indigenous populations, 3, 54, 209; Jesuit, 207–8, 211, 217, 222, 223n2, 224n11, 272
exploitation, 4, 31, 35, 47, 67; economic, 3; Freud on, 55, 70n12; of indigenous peoples, 49–50, 58, 69n7
export economy, 31, 35, 37
feather artwork/featherwork, 33, 234, 239, 245, 247, 254–57, 259, 264n25, 337. See also *enconchados*/*enconchado* art; iridescence; textiles
Feitler, Bruno, 15, 334
finance capital, 4, 131–32. See also capitalism
Flynn, Dennis O., 25, 39n3, 333
Foucault, Michel, 97n37, 153n4, 308, 324n11
Franciscan Order, 69n7, 77, 80–81, 86, 97n34, 113, 272; missionaries in Japan, 298n32; Virgin of Guadalupe and, 258
Frank, André Gunder, 26, 30
Freud, Sigmund, 47, 49, 55, 70n12
Friedrich, Markus, 144, 210, 224n8
Gadamer, Hans-Georg, 277–78, 293, 295n10, 335
García Sáiz, María Concepción, 257, 263n3, 265n28
geography, 11, 96n25, 145, 150; of Africa, 134; of blackness, 135, 137, 148–49, 154n11; of the global South, 138, 226n30; of Iberian empires, 151
global history, 23, 30, 98n43, 339; Iberian, 9. See also world history
globalization: early, 15, 24, 28, 30, 49, 132, 333; early modern, 5–6, 8, 13–15, 18n10, 261, 338; effects of, 131–32; historicity of, 25, 39; structures of, 332
global South, 138, 149, 151–52
Goa, 8, 12, 84–85, 113, 117, 140; blood purity in, 97n36; Christianity in, 80–81, 92; Holy Office tribunal in, 77–79, 105, 114–16, 123, 124n3, 125n12 (see also Portuguese Inquisition); Jesuit missionaries in, 77, 96n22; racial

classification in, 85–87, 89, 96n23, 97n41. *See also* Estado da Índia
gold, 15, 26–28, 31–34, 194, 245, 253, 256, 264n15, 289; mines, 8. *See also* precious metals; silver mining
Gómez, Fernando, 49, 57, 65, 69n7, 70n14
González, Juan, 233, 236, 242, **244**, 245
González, Manuel, 233, 236, **240**, **241**, 242–45
Gruzinski, Serge, 25, 107, 124n4, 278, 338
Guan Yin, 281, **282**, 284–85, 293, 296n20, 297n25. *See also* Virgin of Guadalupe
Guaraní, 14, 227n33, 336; language, 212, 217–18, 220, 226n26, 227n31; scribes in Jesuit missions, 7, 10
Guaraní missions (*reducciones*), 14, 213–14, 227n31, 335
Guzmán, Nuño de, 52–53, 69n8
Hamilton, Earl J., 24, 40n15, 40n23
Harris, Steven J., 143–44, 215, 224nn9–10
Hausberger, Bernd, 15, 224n10, 333
heliotropism, 253, 256–57, 259
Henrique I of Portugal (Dom Henrique; Cardinal Henrique), 106, 115, 119, 123
heresy, 79, 95n14, 106, 109–10, 115, 121; Jewish, 105
hierarchies, 11, 86, 92, 109, 334; *casta*, 87, 89; cultural, 123; local, 113; private, 161; racial, 75, 89; social, 5, 17, 110, 338
Hinduism, 117, 311
Hindus, 82, 86, 96n23, 114–17; converts to Christianity, 79–80, 84, 113
historiography, 9, 11, 208, 274; globalization and, 26; Iberian imperial, 6, 12, 95n16; Indo-Portuguese, 96n23; Portuguese Inquisition and, 107; traditional, 30; trans-Atlantic slave trade and, 133
Holy Office, 77–80, 110, 112, 116, 119, 122–24, 289; Portuguese, 105 (*see also* Portuguese Inquisition)
Holy Office inquisitorial tribunals, 77, 94n5, 106, 112, 123, 124n1; in Aragón, 79; in Cartagena de Indias, 77, 105, 173; in Goa, 77–79, 105, 114–16, 123, 124n3, 125n12 (*see also* Portuguese Inquisition);

in Lima, 77–78, 105; in Lisbon, 94n11; in Mexico City, 77–78; in Portugal, 108
hospitality, 56, 62, 67
hospital republics, 56–58, 60, 65, 334
hospitals (Quiroga), 12, 14, 16, 48–50, 56–58, 60–62, 64–66, 67n1, 68n4, 70n12, 70n14, 71nn17–18, 81, 96n22. *See also* macehuales; *Ordenanzas*; poor, the
human rights, 65–66, 187
iconoclasm, 273, 277, 313, 316, 324n15
idolatry, 48, 80, 91, 95n12, 95n16, 106, 273–76, 278, 281, 295n9, 307, 313; eradication of, 64, 77, 79, 81, 92–93, 94n4
Ignatius of Loyola (Ignacio de Loyola), 143, **252**, 253, 272, 288, 325nn17–18, 335; *Spiritual Exercises*, 146, 272, 317, 325n18, 325n20. *See also* Jesuits
Incas, 33, 35, 89, 212
Indian Ocean, 10, 26, 32, 331
indigenous languages, 51, 208, 219
indigenous peoples: Christian conversion of, 76, 88, 96n22, 208–9; enslavement of, 34, 47, 50–53, 56–57, 68n2, 69n8, 70n11, 185, 189; evangelization of, 209; exploitation of, 49; the Inquisition and, 120–23
Información en derecho [Report of law] (Quiroga), 47–50, 57–58, 62, 68n2, 68n4, 333–34
Inquisition, 7, 12, 77–78, 95n14, 98n47, 109–10, 124n2, 125n14, 334–35. *See also* Portuguese Inquisition; Spanish Inquisition
inquisitorial jurisdiction, 106–7, 109, 115, 118, 123
iridescence, 259, 261, 337. *See also* enconchados/enconchado art; feather artwork/featherwork; heliotropism; mother-of-pearl; pearls; textiles
Islam, 79–80, 95n14, 108, 112, 117, 294n5, 306; Christian converts to, 115; influence on *enconchados*, 261
ius gentium, 183–85, 187–92, 194–97, 198n11. *See also* slavery: justification of

Jaca, Francisco José de, 185–88, 191–97, 197n7, 198n11, 199n22, 199n25, 200n28, 200n30, 336. *See also* abolitionism; Las Casas, Bartolomé de

Japan, 295n6, 332; immigration to Mexico from, 237–38; Jesuits in, 86, 90, 96n27, 224n8, 288, 317, 338; lacquerware in, 236; Latin American mining and, 28; world system and, 26

Jesuit missionaries, 9, 15, 80, 119, 224n10, 226n30, 310; in China, 15, 86, 90, 96n10, 271–72, 274–75, 286, 288, 290–91, 294n2, 297n26, 317, 335

Jesuits: correspondence of, 80–81, 115, 135, 140, 143–44, 147, 152, 208, 211–12, 215–16, 224n8, 224n10, 226n22, 226n30, 324n14 (*see also* Annual Letters; Brandão, Luis de; Sandoval, Alonso de); expulsion of, 118, 207, 213–15, 222; Guaraní missions of, 14; plays written by, 304–5, 311, 315; print production and, 14, 80, 208–9, 211, 213, 215–17, 223n4, 224n9, 226n23, 226n26, 297n26; textual production and, 208–11, 213, 215, 219, 221, 224n9; Third Council of Lima, 211, 224n10; "way of proceeding," 210, 218, 223n6. *See also* Acosta, José de; Bartoli, Daniello; Brandão, Luis de; Camaño, Joaquín; Cobo, Bernabé; Ignatius of Loyola (Ignacio de Loyola); Molina, Luis de; Nieremberg, Eusebio; Peramás, José; Restivo, Paulo; Sandoval, Alonso de; Valignano, Alessandro

Johnson, Carina, 109, 124n7

Judaism, 78–79, 95n14, 108; crypto-, 112

justice, 67, 139, 142, 144–45, 160, 190; of enslavement, 138–39, 141–42, 145, 151, 199n24

just war, 47, 51, 134–35, 138, 150–51, 187, 189, 194, 336

kinship, 3, 89–90, 167, 221

Klein, Herbert S., 27, 39n5

Krippner-Martínez, James, 65, 71n22

labor, 3, 10, 35–38, 48–51, 59, 135, 320; affective, 177; Christianity and, 5; compulsory, 318; debt arrangements, 171; division of, 28, 49; enslaved, 38, 47, 136, 162, 167; forced, 35, 37, 117, 132, 152 (*see also* slavery); globalized, 134; indigenous, 1, 7–8, 35, 332; laws, 88; manumission and, 164–65, 168, 172–73; pedagogical, 92; precarization of, 133, 147, 153n4; regulation of, 65; wage, 3, 38, 153n4. *See also* capitalism; *mita*

Lang, David Marshall, 305–6, 323n6

Las Casas, Bartolomé de, 34, 40n18, 109, 144, 190–91, 256; debate with Sepúlveda, 68n2, 71n21. *See also* Jaca, Francisco José de; Sepúlveda, Ginés de

Latour, Bruno, 143–44

law, 18n5, 56, 63, 161, 189, 212, 336, 338; canon, 67n2, 115; Christianity and, 311; colonial, 159–60, 177, 334; divine, 62–64, 191; of free communication, 199n20; of "free womb," 185, 195–96; Iberian, 160, 162, 170; international, 11, 312; Judaic, 79; labor, 88; manumission and, 163; Mosaic, 63–64; of nations (*see ius gentium*); positive, 48, 183–84; Roman, 61, 192, 195–96; Spanish Crown, 7; Spanish Indian, 70n14. *See also* natural law

Lima, 37, 135, 137; archbishopric court in, 169; Holy Office tribunal in, 77–78, 105; legal category of "minor" in, 161; manumission in, 164; Third Council of, 211, 224n10 (*see also* Jesuits)

limpieza de sangre (*limpeza de sangue*, blood purity), 75–76, 85, 87–89, 92–93, 97n31, 97n34, 97n36, 111, 334

local, the, 8, 14, 93, 160, 223n4

Longobardi, Niccolò, 286–87, 289, 297nn24–25

Loomba, Ania, 80, 98n45

López de Velasco, Juan, 83–84, 87

Lorey, Isabell, 153n2, 153n4

Luanda, 9, 135, 137, 139–41, 147, 154n12. *See also* Angola

macehuales, 58–60, 62, 64
Manila, 304, 318, 325n22; trade route between Acapulco and, 33, 235, 331, 337. *See also* Philippines
manumission, 176, 178n3, 195, 336; agreements, 160, 163, 165–66, 168–72, 175; conditional, 167–68; gradual, 185, 197; legal, 160–64, 166, 168, 172, 177, 178n2; notarized, 169, 174–75; testamentary, 163–64, 166, 169, 173–74
Marcocci, Giuseppe, 106–7, 109, 111, 115, 124n3, 124n7
marriage, 117, 174; blood purity and, 89–90; Christian, 162; double, 79 (*see also* bigamy); of enslaved people, 159; prohibitions, 83
Martínez, María Elena, 16–17, 68n3, 109, 334
materiality, 12, 234, 258, 263n4, 273, 288, 291, 337; of *enconchados*, 235, 239, 261; of shells, 247
Mercado, Tomás de, 151, 189–90
mercantilism, 29, 32, 37, 135–36. *See also* slavery: mercantile
mercury, 28–29
mestizos/mestiços, 8, 18n11, 83, 87, 97n28, 97n34, 109–10, 338; elite, 68n4, 118; the Inquisition and, 119, 122
Mexico, 5, 78, 332, 337; central, 48; Christian conversion in, 77, 80–81, 95n16, 95–96n22, 213; colonial mining in, 34; *enconchado* art in, 233–34, 236, 238–39, 246, 259, 261, 263n12, 264n2; forced labor in, 35; indigenous artists in, 256; indigenous practices in, 89, 97n40; indigenous slavery in, 47, 50–53, 56–57, 69n8, 70n11 (*see also* Guzmán, Nuño de; hospitals (Quiroga)); Japanese immigrants to, 237–38; *limpieza de sangre* (blood purity) in, 89, 97n34; manumission in, 164, 173; Nanban art in, 235–38; pre-Columbian shellwork in, 247–48; Second Audiencia of, 47; slave trade and, 29
Mexico City, 37, 52, 94n7; Holy Office tribunals in, 77–78; Jesuits in, 292; National Archives in, 289; Profesa Jesuit School in, 288; Virgin of Guadalupe and, 242, 257–58
Michoacán, 52, 68n2, 71n22; hospitals (Quiroga) in, 16, 48–49, 68n4, 69n7; indigenous inhabitants of, 7, 14, 55, 69n8, 70n11. *See also* Quiroga, Vasco de
middle passage, 134, 137, 147, 190. *See also* slavery; slave trade
Mignolo, Walter, 9, 19n12
Ming Dynasty, 25, 29, 275, 291, 294n4, 331, 333
mining, 27–28, 34–39, 39n5; industry, 31, 35; Latin American, 27, 30. *See also* Cerro Rico; gold; mercury; Potosí; silver mining
mita, 3–5, 8, 11, 14, 35
mitayos, 4, 38
Molina, Luis de, 135, 138–39, 142, 189–90, 193, 198n19, 199nn21–22, 316. *See also* Brandão, Luis de; Sandoval, Alonso de
monotheism, 48, 63, 76, 306. *See also* polythcism
More, Anna, 5, 15, 265n31, 332, 335
More, Thomas, 12, 48, 64, 70n14, 96n22
moriscos (Muslim converts to Christianity), 79–80, 95n17, 116, 123
Moses, 49, 56, 63–65
mother-of-pearl, 233–35, **237**, 237–38, **240**, **241**, **243**, **244**, 245–47, 258, 264n12, 337. *See also* Balbuena, Bernardo de; *enconchados/enconchado* art; iridescence; pearls
mulatos, 83, 165
Muriel, Josefina, 61, 69n18
Muslims, 79–80, 90, 106, 110, 113–18, 162, 323. *See also* Islam; *moriscos*
Nadal, Jerónimo (Jerome), 143, 218, 287, 292–93, 297n26
Nahuas, 56, 58–59, 89–90
Nanban art, 235–36, 238–39, 245, 261. *See also* *enconchados/enconchado* art
"native Christians," 114–16

Naturaleza, policia sagrada y profana, costumbres, ritos, disciplina y catecismo, de todos etiopes (Sandoval), 133–35, 137, 142, 144–52, 153n8, 154nn10–11, 154n13, 335

natural law, 48, 54–55, 62, 71n23, 150, 184–92, 194–96, 198n11, 198nn19–20, 334; divine, 200n31; in imperial Rome, 197n2; police and, 68n6. *See also* law

New Christians/*conversos* (Jewish converts), 78–80, 85, 94nn7–8, 97n36, 106, 114–15, 286. *See also moriscos*; Old Christians/*cristianos viejos*

New Granada (Viceroyalty), 136, 185, 193

New Spain (Viceroyalty), 9, 40n17, 78, 80, 92, 94n10, 96n26, 98n46; caste in, 85; conversion campaigns in, 77, 81; education in, 118; *enconchados/enconchado* art in, 233, 235, 257–58, 261–62, 263n3; feather artwork in, 256; history of, 265n28; hospitals (Quiroga) in, 12, 49–50, 61, 67, 67–68n2; indigenous peoples in, 86–87, 89, 98n47, 334; the Inquisition in, 107; Japanese immigrants to, 236, 238; Jesuits in, 144, 224n10; *limpieza de sangre* in, 97n34; missionaries in, 272, 274, 334; religious images in, 285, 288–91, 297n23; religious institutions of, 16; shellwork in, 247–48; silver mining and, 24, 33–36; textiles of, 253; transpacific trade networks of, 13, 18n10, 33

Nieremberg, Eusebio, 217, 219

Old Christians/*cristianos viejos*, 79–80, 84–85, 87, 114. *See also* New Christians/*conversos*

Ordenanzas [Ordinances] (Quiroga), 48–49, 56–58, 61–62, 64–65, 68n4

O'Toole, Rachel Sarah, 5, 14–15, 82, 153n6, 336

Pagden, Anthony, 6, 18n5, 60, 62, 65, 124n5

Paleotti, Gabriele, 273–74, 278, 295n7

pearls, 246–48, 257–59, 264nn12–13, 264n15, 265n29

Peramás, José, 212–13, 221

Peru (Viceroyalty), 208, 210. *See also* Acosta, José de; African diaspora; Africans; Incas; Lima; manumission; Potosí; silver mining; slavery; Trujillo (Peru)

Philippines, 8, 12, 77, 149, 336; Catholicism in, 322; Counter-Reformation in, 321; missionaries in, 305, 337–38; New Christians and Jews in, 94n8; silver flows and, 34; Spanish colonialism in, 318, 337. *See also* Tagalog language

Phipps, Elena, 249, 264n20

Pino, Agustín del, 233, **252**, 253

police (sixteenth-century notion of), 54–55, 59, 68–69n6, 70n15

polygamy, 79–80, 91. *See also* bigamy

polytheism, 48, 54, 63–64. *See also* monotheism

Poma de Ayala, Felipe Guamán, 4–5, 69n10, 89, 97n40

poor, the, 49, 58, 61–62, 65. *See also* hospitals (Quiroga); *macehuales*; poverty

Portuguese empire, 13, 17, 18n10, 75, 81, 87, 90, 92, 124, 337. *See also* Africa: Portuguese colonialism and; Brazil; *Estado da Índia*; Spanish empire

Portuguese Inquisition, 16, 75, 79–80, 92, 94n11, 105–8, 112, 114–24, 124n3, 153n6. *See also* Africa: Portuguese colonialism and; Inquisition; inquisitorial jurisdiction; Spanish Inquisition

Potosí, 1, 3–5, 10, 34–35, 37, 40n17, 332, 336. *See also* silver mining

poverty, 58, 60, 62, 64, 67, 69n7, 121

precarity, 131, 132–33, 147, 150, 152–53n2, 153n4

precious metals, 26–28, 32, 34, 39; circulation of, 31; export of, 30, 40n15, 40n23; flows of, 24, 26–27, 30; logic of, 15. *See also* Cerro Rico; gold; mining; Potosí; silver mining

P'urhépechas, 14, 49, 53, 59–60

Quiroga, Vasco de, 47–52, 54–62, 64–65, 67, 67–68nn1–2, 68nn4–5, 69n7, 69n11,

70nn14–16, 71nn21–22, 154n16, 334; *Información en derecho* [Report of law], 47–50, 57–58, 62, 68n2, 68n4, 333–34; *Ordenanzas* [Ordinances], 48–49, 56–58, 61–62, 64–65, 68n4. *See also* hospitals (Quiroga)

race, 6, 11, 68n3, 75–76, 87–88, 89–93, 95n20, 334. *See also casta*/caste; *castiços*; *criollos*/creoles; *mestizos*/*mestiços*; *mulatos*; *reinól*; *zambos*

reconquista, 60, 90, 336

reducciones, 81, 185, 287, 355

reinól (European-born Portuguese), 83, 87, 97n28

Restivo, Paulo, 216–17, 220, 226–26

Restrepo, Eduardo, 149, 154n18

Restrepo, Félix de, 185, 194–97, 200n30

Ricci, Mateo, 275, 280, 284–86, 288, 290–93, 294n1, 297n25, 298n34

Río de la Plata, 194, 207, 213, 336

Russo, Alessandra, 234–35, 238, 261

Sahagún, Bernardino de, 56–57

Said, Edward W., 81, 91, 95n20

Saint Augustine, 63, 259

Saint John Damascene (Saint John of Damascus), 306, 308–9, 313–14, 324n12

Sandoval, Alonso de, 133–35, 137–52, 154n17, 199n25; Acosta's influence on, 144, 154n8; *Naturaleza, policia sagrada y profana, costumbres, ritos, disciplina y catecismo, de todos etiopes*, 133–35, 137, 142, 144–52, 153n8, 154nn10–11, 154n13, 335. *See also* Alencastro, Luiz Felipe de; Brandão, Luis de; Jesuits: correspondence of; Molina, Luis de; Vila Vilar, Enriqueta

São Tomé, 85, 111–12, 118–19, 139–41

scholasticism/scholastics, 138, 148, 184, 189, 314; neo-, 200n31

School of Salamanca, 184, 189, 196. *See also* Vitoria, Francisco de

Sepúlveda, Ginés de, 48, 54, 60, 62–63, 65, 68n2, 71n21, 71n23, 198n20. *See also* Quiroga, Vasco de; Vitoria, Francisco de

Siete Partidas, 162–63, 172–73, 178n3

silver mining, 3, 8, 34–35, 40n9, 332. *See also* Potosí

slavery: among indigenous groups, 50–51, *carta de libertad* (freedom letter), 163, 165–66, 168; as commodification of humans, 132–34, 146, 151, 153n5 (*see also* slave trade); domestic relations and, 160–62, 164, 166, 168–69, 173, 176–77, 197; justification of, 51, 135, 138–39, 147, 150, 187–89, 191 (*see also ius gentium*); mercantile, 136, 154n12; natural, 60, 189. *See also* abolitionism; *cimarrones* (runaway slaves); indigenous peoples: enslavement of; middle passage; social death

slave trade: defense of, 133, 142–43, 150–51; Portuguese, 137–38, 153n5, 335; transatlantic, 15, 132–35, 138, 151–52, 153n5, 176. *See also* middle passage

social death, 50, 132, 146

Society of Jesus. *See* Jesuit missionaries; Jesuits

Soto, Domingo de, 189, 198n19

sovereignty, 66–67, 184, 310, 317; Spanish, 14

Spanish Crown, 7–9, 27–28, 30–31, 33–34, 38, 63, 68n2, 79, 88, 310; enslavement of Africans and, 136; enslavement of indigenous people and, 7, 134; manumission and, 160–63, 177; union with Portuguese Crown, 91, 94n7

Spanish empire, 13, 17, 18n10, 34, 62, 75, 81–82, 87, 90, 92, 135, 160–61, 177, 257, 334, 336–37. *See also* Portuguese empire

Spanish Inquisition, 48, 75, 78–80, 92, 173, 289. *See also* Inquisition; Portuguese Inquisition

Subrahmanyam, Sanjay, 18n10, 94n2

suffering, 63, 147, 306

Tagalog language, 7, 304–5, 311, 317–21, 323, 323n3, 324n10

TePaske, John J., 27, 34

textiles, 36, 239, 247, 249, 253, 259, 264n23;
    metaphor of, 291. *See also enconchados/
    enconchado* art; feather artwork/
    featherwork; iridescence
Toledo, Francisco de, 3, 60
Tridentine reforms, 108–10, 122. *See also*
    Council of Trent; Counter-Reformation
Trujillo (Peru), 25, 160–61, 163, 165–70, 172,
    174, 177
Valignano, Alessandro, 83–84, 87–88, 96n27,
    289–91
Vega, Lope de, 304, 311, 317. *See also Barlaam
    and Josaphat* (romance/legend of)
Velázquez, Diego, 259, 262
Vila Vilar, Enriqueta, 153n8, 154n13
Villaseñor Black, Charlene, 13, 332, 337
Virgin of Guadalupe, 240–45, **240**, **241**, **243**,
    257–59, 285–86, 288, 297n23. *See also
    enconchados/enconchado* art; Guan Yin
Vitoria, Francisco de, 48, 65, 68n5, 71n23,
    144, 184, 189, 191, 197n1, 198–99nn20–21,
    199–200n28. *See also* Quiroga, Vasco
    de; School of Salamanca; Sepúlveda,
    Ginés de
Wallerstein, Immanuel, 26, 49. *See also*
    world systems
Wilde, Guillermo, 14, 223n5, 332, 336
world history, 6, 13, 39, 333. *See also* global
    history
world systems, 6–7, 9, 12, 26, 49, 333
Zacatecas, 34, 37
zambos, 83, 149

VOLUMES IN THE HISPANIC ISSUES SERIES

44 *Iberian Empires and the Roots of Globalization,*
   edited by Ivonne del Valle, Anna More, and Rachel Sarah O'Toole
43 *Cartographies of Madrid,*
   edited by Silvia Bermúdez and Anthony L. Geist
42 *Ethics of Life: Contemporary Iberian Debates,*
   edited by Katarzyna Beilin and William Viestenz
41 *In and Of the Mediterranean: Medieval and Early Modern Iberian Studies,*
   edited by Michelle M. Hamilton and Núria Silleras-Fernández
40 *Coloniality, Religion, and the Law in the Early Iberian World,*
   edited by Santa Arias and Raúl Marrero-Fente
39 *Poiesis and Modernity in the Old and New Worlds,*
   edited by Anthony J. Cascardi and Leah Middlebrook
38 *Spectacle and Topophilia: Reading Early (and Post-) Modern Hispanic Cultures,*
   edited by David R. Castillo and Bradley J. Nelson
37 *New Spain, New Literatures,*
   edited by Luis Martín-Estudillo and Nicholas Spadaccini
36 *Latin American Jewish Cultural Production,*
   edited by David William Foster
35 *Post-Authoritarian Cultures: Spain and Latin America's Southern Cone,*
   edited by Luis Martín-Estudillo and Roberto Ampuero
34 *Spanish and Empire,* edited by Nelsy Echávez-Solano
   and Kenya C. Dworkin y Méndez
33 *Generation X Rocks: Contemporary Peninsular Fiction, Film, and Rock
   Culture,* edited by Christine Henseler and Randolph D. Pope
32 *Reason and Its Others: Italy, Spain, and the New World,*
   edited by David Castillo and Massimo Lollini
31 *Hispanic Baroques: Reading Cultures in Context,*
   edited by Nicholas Spadaccini and Luis Martín-Estudillo
30 *Ideologies of Hispanism,* edited by Mabel Moraña
29 *The State of Latino Theater in the United States: Hybridity,
   Transculturation, and Identity,* edited by Luis A. Ramos-García
28 *Latin America Writes Back: Postmodernity in the Periphery
   (An Interdisciplinary Perspective),* edited by Emil Volek
27 *Women's Narrative and Film in Twentieth-Century Spain:
   A World of Difference(s),* edited by Ofelia Ferrán and Kathleen M. Glenn
26 *Marriage and Sexuality in Medieval and Early Modern Iberia,*
   edited by Eukene Lacarra Lanz
25 *Pablo Neruda and the U.S. Culture Industry,* edited by Teresa Longo
24 *Iberian Cities,* edited by Joan Ramon Resina
23 *National Identities and Sociopolitical Changes in Latin America,*
   edited by Mercedes F. Durán-Cogan and Antonio Gómez-Moriana

www.ingramcontent.com/pod-product-compliance
Lightning Source LLC
Chambersburg PA
CBHW030519230426
43665CB00010B/675